DATE DUE

D1271352

DIGITAL SYSTEM

IMPLEMENTATION

Prentice-Hall
Series in Automatic Computation

MARTIN, *Systems Analysis for Data Transmission*

MARTIN, *Telecommunications and the Computer*

MARTIN, *Teleprocessing Network Organization*

MARTIN AND NORMAN, *The Computerized Society*

MCKEEMAN, et al., *A Compiler Generator*

MEYERS, *Time-Sharing Computation in the Social Sciences*

MINSKY, *Computation: Finite and Infinite Machines*

NIEVERGELT, et al., *Computer Approaches to Mathematical Problems*

PLANE AND MCMILLAN, *Discrete Optimization: Integer Programming and Network Analysis for Management Decisions*

POLIVKA AND PAKIN, *APL: The Language and Its Usage*

PRITSKER AND KIVIAT, *Simulation with GASP II: A FORTRAN-based Simulation Language*

PYLYSHYN, ed., *Perspectives on the Computer Revolution*

RICH, *Internal Sorting Methods Illustrated with PL/1 Programs*

RUDD, *Assembly Language Programming and the IBM 360 and 370 Computers*

SACKMAN AND CITRENBAUM, eds., *On-Line Planning: Towards Creative Problem-Solving*

SALTON, ed., *The SMART Retrieval System: Experiments in Automatic Document Processing*

SAMMET, *Programming Languages: History and Fundamentals*

SCHAEFER, *A Mathematical Theory of Global Program Optimization*

SCHULTZ, *Spline Analysis*

SCHWARZ, et al., *Numerical Analysis of Symmetric Matrices*

SHAH, *Engineering Simulation Using Small Scientific Computers*

SHAW, *The Logical Design of Operating Systems*

SHERMAN, *Techniques in Computer Programming*

SIMON AND SIKLOSSY, eds. *Representation and Meaning: Experiments with Information Processing Systems*

STERBENZ, *Floating-Point Computation*

STOUTEMYER, *PL/1 Programming for Engineering and Science*

STRANG AND FIX, *An Analysis of the Finite Element Method*

STROUD, *Approximate Calculation of Multiple Integrals*

TANENBAUM, *Structured Computer Organization*

TAVISS, ed., *The Computer Impact*

UHR, *Pattern Recognition, Learning, and Thought: Computer-Programmed Models of Higher Mental Processes*

VAN TASSEL, *Computer Security Management*

VARGA, *Matrix Iterative Analysis*

WAITE, *Implementing Software for Non-Numeric Application*

WILKINSON, *Rounding Errors in Algebraic Processes*

WIRTH, *Algorithms + Data Structures = Programs*

WIRTH, *Systematic Programming: An Introduction*

YEH, ed., *Applied Computation Theory: Analysis, Design, Modeling*

DIGITAL SYSTEM IMPLEMENTATION

GERRIT A. BLAAUW

Technische Hogeschool Twente
Enschede, Netherlands

PRENTICE-HALL, INC.

ENGLEWOOD CLIFFS, NEW JERSEY

Library of Congress Cataloging in Publication Data

BLAAUW, G. A.
  Digital system implementation.

  Includes bibliographies and index.
  1. Electronic digital computers. 2. APL
(Computer program language) I. Title.
QA76.5.B532   001.6′4′044   75–30841
ISBN 0–13–212241–3

© 1976 by Prentice-Hall, Inc.
Englewood Cliffs, N. J.

All rights reserved. No part of this book
may be reproduced in any form or by any means
without permission in writing from the publisher.

10 9 8 7 6 5 4 3 2 1

Printed in the United States of America

JOINT UNIVERSITY LIBRARIES
SCIENCE
LIBRARY
NASHVILLE, TENNESSEE

PRENTICE-HALL INTERNATIONAL, INC., *London*
PRENTICE-HALL OF AUSTRALIA PTY. LIMITED, *Sydney*
PRENTICE-HALL OF CANADA, LTD., *Toronto*
PRENTICE-HALL OF INDIA PRIVATE LIMITED, *New Delhi*
PRENTICE-HALL OF JAPAN, INC., *Tokyo*
PRENTICE-HALL OF SOUTH-EAST ASIA PRIVATE LIMITED, *Singapore*

To Paula

CONTENTS

4   DIVISION   103

4 DIVISION

6 INTERNAL CONTROL

PREFACE

The design of digital systems can be viewed from three levels. The highest level concerns the architecture, which specifies the functional behavior of a system. The lowest level concerns the realization, and deals with the components from which a system may be constructed. The middle level of systems design concerns the implementation, or the logic structure that embodies the architecture and utilizes the logic of the components of the realization.

Within the implementation, two main areas can be distinguished. Close to the realization level lies the engineering discipline of the theory of switching circuits. It uses logical components as individual entities. The other implementation area is closer to the architecture. It deals with the organization of functional units, or system components, built from individual components. It is the subject of this text. Since this area is usually intended when the term implementation is used, the title 'digital system implementation' has been chosen.

The design of an implementation can be viewed as a translation process. The description of the architecture, which tells what functions are performed by the system, leads to an implementation description, which shows how the system can be built. The use of formal languages, which permit an exact description at each of these levels, makes it possible to ensure that the implementation really implements the given architecture. It is the aim of this text to present this controlled design process. The text further aims to present a representative set of system components, such as adders, decoders and stores. Therefore, the design process is applied to the major areas of a digital structure: processing, control, storage, and communication. Thus, it is hoped that the reader will feel reasonably at home in a digital system, knowing both its tools and its materials.

Summary of Chapter Contents

Since an architecture is the point of departure for an implementation, the architecture of a digital system is briefly reviewed in Chapter 1. The prime example of a digital system is the computer. It is prominent and widespread. Also, it clearly presents the major areas of digital system design. As a particular example the IBM System/360 architecture will be taken. This system and its successors are widely used. The author is moreover particularly familiar with this system, since he participated in its design.

Chapter 1 is introductory and can be skipped. The main theme of the book starts in Chapter 2. Chapter 2 introduces the transition from an architectural definition to an implementation. The chapter also introduces the language APL, which is used in this process. APL is particularly suited to this purpose, since it allows expression at the high architectural level, at the lowest implementation level, and at all levels between. Only a subset of APL is used and most of its elements are introduced in the course of this chapter. If desired, the brief introduction to APL in Appendix A can be studied beforehand. Chapter 2 uses machine addition to illustrate the design of simple and complex combinational system components.

Chapter 3 deals with multiplication. This operation is usually performed sequentially and illustrates the design of sequential system components. Since multiplication uses repeated addition, an intermediate design step is introduced which produces a high order implementation, using adders as system components. At this level various alternatives in trading equipment against time are considered.

In Chapter 4 division is discussed. Division is also typically a sequential process. Hence, the issues of Chapter 3 reappear. Since division is one order more complex than multiplication, being result-dependent, rather than operand-dependent, the relation between the various implementation solutions is particularly important here for a proper understanding and a careful verification. A controlled design process requires the designer to know what he is doing and to know that his solution is correct. Therefore, understanding and verification recur throughout the chapters of this text.

From the high-level implementation algorithms a description in terms of equipment present in space, the dataflow, or datapath, and the use of this equipment in time, the control, can be derived. Chapter 5 discusses the various datapaths, leaving the control of these paths still at a conveniently high level. The alternatives between parallel and series processing are particularly discussed in this chapter.

In Chapter 6 the transformation of the algorithm for the control of the dataflow into a microcode or a 'hard-wired' control is described. The alternatives here are those of encoding and specialization.

The control of a datapath, particularly when using microcoding, has much in common with the control section of a digital system. Therefore, this subject is treated next in Chapter 7. The fetching and storing of information by the datapath and control program of an instruction unit is described. The system components used in the implementation of a control section, mainly encoders and decoders, are mentioned at this point.

With discussion of the datapath and its control, the description of the design process is completed. In each of these areas, however, the use of storage and communication between system components has been encountered. These subjects are treated in Chapters 8 and 9. They encompass the important system concepts of modularity, hierarchy, access, and internal communication. Since the design procedure is by now established it is not reiterated at length in these chapters. Rather, Chapter 8 discusses subjects like storage access via a cache or pipeline, using a high level implementation description.

Chapter 9 concentrates on communication via an interface. The problems relating to the conversation between concurrently operating system components are considered at this point. Their solution consists in reducing the problem to that of a plurality of independent system components, each with an architecture which includes the interface definition. Thus the design procedure of the previous chapters again applies.

How to Use This Text

In using the text I have found it useful to treat Chapters 5 and 6 immediately following Chapter 3. Thus the student can follow the high-level implementation of a multiplier through to its datapath and control. Chapters 5 and 6 have been written with this approach in mind. The first two sections of Chapter 5 and the first section of Chapter 6 are particularly intended for this first pass. In a second round Chapter 4 can be taken up, followed by the remaining sections of Chapters 5 and 6. This spiral approach eliminates the danger that the design goal is forgotten in the process of contemplating the algorithmic alternatives. For the same reason the last sections of Chapters 2, 3, and 4 may be skipped on a first reading. Remarks to this effect are included in the text.

APL is a key tool both for the student and the teacher. I have found no need for the 'live' use of the terminal in teaching, other than in a laboratory session on terminal use. It is of great value, however, to have all algorithms mentioned in the text available to the student in an APL terminal system. Thus, he can get first-hand experience on their operation. Also, the exercises assume that existing algorithms can be used in arriving at a problem solution.

APL makes it possible to describe what really occurs in a complex system. This is crucial to our purpose, since mastering complexity is the essence of systems design. Without it, the examples and exercises would all be on a plane different from the real problems we try to attack.

The terminal is of course, also, a great help in checking the solutions of assignments and encourages the student to think through his verification methods.

The advantage of APL over specialized hardware description languages is its general applicability. Thus the investment in learning the language pays of in- and outside the field of computer design.

The text aims at the senior and master levels in a computer science or electrical engineering department. Since the methods that are described are increasingly used in industrial development laboratories, the text should also be of interest to those professionals who would like to upgrade their technical skill.

The reader is assumed to be familiar with college algebra and a course on switching circuits. In the appendix the main methods of number representation and circuit minimization are summarized as a review.

This text was developed from a one semester course on digital system implementation given since 1967 at the Technische Hogeschool Twente (Twente Institute of Technology) in the Netherlands. The early lectures used the older APL version and lacked the terminal implementation. Nevertheless the advantage of a formal language was clear.

It was fortunate, though not entirely unpredictable, that the terminal implementation APL\360 became available at the end of the sixties. The preparation of an English text has become possible by presenting this material in the Computer Science department of the University of North Carolina during the spring of 1974. Whereas the academic tradition of continental Europe stresses self-study, that of America stresses close contact between teacher and student. It is hoped that this text is usable in both environments.

Acknowledgments

I owe much to the reviewers of this text. In particular the thoughful and thorough criticism of Dr. Frederick P. Brooks has been invaluable. Dr. Raymond P. Polivka and Dr. J. Craig Mudge have been very helpful in securing machine examples of design details.

The members of the sub-department of Digitale Techniek at the T. H. T. have been a great support in this undertaking. Much of the material of Chapter 9 has been provided by Ir. C. A. Vissers. Several algorithms have been improved by J. Al. Valuable comments on the Dutch text were given by Ir. Th. R. C. Bonnema, Ir. B. van den Dolder, Ir. A. van der Knaap and Ir. J. Wilmink.

J. G. Raatgerinks effective THTEXT editing system and Dr. Jim Sneeringer's excellent and simple OCCAM system have been key tools in preparing the manuscript. The patient, accurate and cheerful typing of Mrs. Susan Bennett and Mrs. Alice Hoogvliet has been a much needed and much appreciated contribution to this book.

I thank God, that He enabled me to do this work, imperfect as it may be.

G.A.B.

DIGITAL SYSTEM
IMPLEMENTATION

1 INTRODUCTION

The topic of this text is the implementation of digital systems.

Digital Technique

The term 'digital' is used here in contrast to analog. The *digital technique* assigns discrete values to physical quantities, whereas the *analog technique* assigns continuous values to these quantities. Thus, the lights of a car are digitally controlled to be either bright, dim, parking, or out. The dashboard light, on the other hand, may, in analog fashion, assume any brightness from fully on to entirely out.

Since physical entities appear to the human senses to have a magnitude that changes in a continuous manner, the analog technique is seemingly more suited to record, modify, and represent reality than the digital technique. Set against the low accuracy of the digital technique, however, is its great reliability. It is much easier to recognize and reproduce a discrete number of physical states than the theoretically unlimited number of states required for continuous behavior. Furthermore, when the number of discrete states is limited to two, as in *binary representation*, the ease of recognition, and hence the reliability, is even more pronounced.

Digital Systems. By using a multitude of physical entities, digitally interpreted, the digital technique can obtain any desired accuracy with great reliability. This principle is used in counting on our fingers. Rather than using the distance between, say, the tips of the thumb and the index finger, in analog fashion, the presence or absence of each of the 10 fingers is used to signify the numbers 0 to 10.

The digital technique thus inherently leads to the use of a multitude of components. A purposeful interconnection of such a multitude of components forms a

1

system. The purpose of this text is to discuss the implementation of these digital systems.

System Implementation. The concept of implementation is used here in contrast to the concept of architecture. While the *architecture* describes what a system performs, the *implementation* decides how this is to be done. This text, therefore, takes the specification of the system functions given by the architecture as a starting point. It discusses how these functions can be logically performed in time and space.

Time is expressed here as a function of the delay times of the physical components that realize the desired elementary logical function. *Space* refers to the number of physical components employed. Taken in this sense, time and space reflect the cost and performance of the implementation.

The implementation of a digital system is composed of a number of *system components* that can be identified with a certain subfunction of the system and therefore may be called *functional units*. The arithmetic organ of a computer is an example of such a functional unit. These functional units can, in turn, be constituted from more elementary system components, such as adders or counters. This text will center around the design of these functional units and their combination into a larger system. We shall not dwell on the lowest level of implementation, the minimization of logical circuits. The reader is assumed to be familiar with the design of elementary switching circuits, as summarized in Appendix D.

System Realization. The implementation assumes the availability of physical circuits made from components, such as relays, diodes, and transistors, that can perform the elementary logical functions such as 'and', 'or,' and 'not.' The design of physical components, involving their electronic actions, their operation times, and their space requirements, is the realm of system *realization*. In contrast to the '*what*' of the architecture and the '*how*' of the implementation, the realization deals with the '*which*,' '*when*,' and '*where*' of component type, speed, and location. It is assumed that the reader has a general knowledge of this subject.

Organization of the Chapter

The nature and application of digital systems differs widely. Besides general-purpose systems, specialized digital systems are used in applications such as elevators, traffic lights, telephone exchanges, process control, and the navigation of ships, airplanes, and spacecraft. The characteristics of these special-purpose systems can be recognized, although in different proportions, in the general-purpose computer.

Since the general-purpose computer is widely used, it is, in particular, the subject of this text. In Section 1-1, a discussion of the nature of computers is given, and in Section 1-2, a sketch of its historical development. In Section 1-3, the architecture of the computer is summarized as a background for the discussion of implementation in subsequent chapters. Finally, Section 1-4 briefly surveys the literature of digital system implementation.

1-1 NATURE OF COMPUTERS

A *computer* can be defined as a digital system that can perform an automatic changeable succession of arithmetic and logical operations. To compute means 'to determine by calculation' and is derived from the Latin *computare*, which literally means 'to think along'.

The sequence of operations to be performed by a computer depends in general on the results of previous operations. Although these results are not known beforehand, the procedure to be followed is known. Thus, the thinking functions of the computer can always be represented by algorithms.

The requirement that a succession of processes must be performed differentiates the computer from office machines, cash registers, and calculators, such as those of Pascal in 1645 and Leibniz in 1673, where each operation requires a separate manipulation.

In general, a digital system contains functional units for the processing, controlling, storing, obtaining, and representing of information. The cooperation of these system components is sketched in Figure 1-1. The functional units are particularly apparent in the computer, where they are named execution unit; instruction unit; storage, consisting of main and auxiliary storage; and input and output. The input and output devices and the auxiliary storage are together called the *peripheral units*. They may be the most extensive and most expensive part of a computer installation.

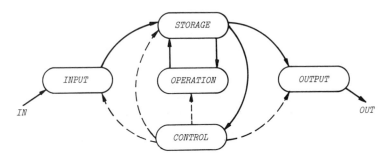

Figure 1-1 Structure of a digital system.

The various chapters of this book reflect the system organization of Figure 1-1. Chapters 2 through 4 discuss some of the operations of the system and introduce the design method used. Chapters 5 and 6 concern the execution unit; Chapter 7, control; Chapter 8, storage; and Chapter 9, communication with input and output.

1-2 HISTORY OF COMPUTERS

Man cannot calculate very well without aids. At a minimum, he uses his fingers—in Latin *digiti*, from which the term 'digital' as derived. The abacus was in use as early as 1000 B.C. In Western culture, written calculation came into use at the end of the Middle Ages.

Pascal hoped to ease the work of his father, a customs official, with his adding machine. Leibniz declared that "it is unworthy for excellent men to lose hours like slaves in the labor of calculation which could safely be relegated to anyone else if machines were used" (Bowden, 1953). Thus, the need of an apparatus that can eliminate the routine work and the frequent errors in repetitive calculations was felt increasingly.

The first important attempt at the construction of a computer was undertaken by the nineteenth-century mathematician Charles Babbage (Morrison and Morrison, 1961), Babbage was motivated by the need for accurate and reliable astronomical tables to be used in navigation. In his design can be found many principles of the modern computer. Babbage was assisted in the implementation of his computer by Joseph Clement. They could, however, not bring his ambitious designs to completion in a mechanical realization. A more modest version of his design was completed by George and Eduard Scheutz and used in the preparation of astronomical and actuarial tables (Randell, 1973). Babbage's work has not directly influenced the twentieth-century development of the computer.

During the time of World War II, the need of ballistic tables gave rise to two developments in the United States. In 1944, the Automatic Sequence Controlled Calculator, Mark I, was completed, as designed by Howard Aiken of Harvard and implemented by C. D. Lake, F. E. Hamilton, and B. M. Durfee of IBM (Aiken and Hopper, 1946; Staff of the Computation Laboratory, 1946), Mark I made use of electromechanical parts designed for IBM bookkeeping machines.

In 1946, the Electronic Numerical Integrator and Computer, ENIAC, was completed by J. P. Eckert and J. W. Mauchly of the Moore School of Engineering at Philadelphia (Goldstine and Goldstine, 1946). Although more primitive in design than the Mark I, the ENIAC was a considerable step ahead in its realization by its use of the electron tube as switching element. Approximately 18,000 tubes were used, which gave the ENIAC an add time of 200 microseconds and a multiply time of 2300 microseconds. The electronic realization made the ENIAC 1000 times faster than the Mark I—but still 1000 times slower than computers that are now routinely produced.

Development of the Realization

In the years following the development of the ENIAC, cheaper, faster, smaller, and more trustworthy parts have become available for the realization of computers.

Storage Elements.   Babbage had made plans for a mechanical store with a capacity of 1000 numbers of 50 digits each. In the storage locations the data for and the results of the operation could be placed. Mark I had room in its electromechanical storage for merely 60 numbers of 24 digits and ENIAC in its electronic storage for 20 numbers of 10 digits. The invention of core storage in 1951 by J. W. Forrester of M.I.T. and J. A. Rajchman of R.C.A. (Forrester, 1951; Rajchman, 1953) allowed, as early as 1957, internal stores for 32K numbers, that is, 32×1024 numbers. Stores with a capacity 100 times larger again are now commercially available.

Switching Elements.   The electron tube was abandoned as a switching element for the transistor around 1955. In the following years, more and more thought was given to the *packaging* of switching elements. Packaging is very prominent in the realization of *integrated circuits*, in which ever larger numbers of transistors are built together as a single electronic component. Packaging also includes the mounting of components on cards, which in turn are placed on boards, the use of printed wiring and exchangeable parts, and the necessary provisions for cooling and maintenance.

Development of the Architecture

Simultaneously with the development of the realization during the past 30 years, a development has taken place in the architecture of the computer.

Instruction Sequence.   Babbage specified the sequence of operations by means of cards, being inspired by the automatic weaving loom that Jacquard had developed in 1801. Holes punched in the card determined which operations must take place and where the data associated with this operation could be found in storage. This information is called an *instruction*. The code that relates the holes in the card to the operation to be performed and the data to be used is called the *machine code* and is part of the *machine language*. A sequence of instructions is called a *procedure*. In Babbage's machines, the procedure was contained in a pack of cards. A *program* consists of one or more procedures and their related data.

For the Mark I, the instructions were punched into a wide paper tape. Each instruction occupied a row of holes in the tape. A *loop* was created by attaching the far ends of the tape together. Thus, the same procedure could be executed repeatedly. Since the reading of paper tape was too slow for the ENIAC, its instruction sequence was specified by wire connections on a *plug board*, a mechanism borrowed from tabulating machines.

The mathematician John von Neumann proposed in 1945 to use the same internal storage for instructions and data (Burks et al., 1946). This principle was first applied by Maurice Wilkes in the EDSAC, which was completed in Cambridge in 1949. Using this principle, instructions can be manipulated as data. The available storage capacity is allocated to instructions and data as required by the program to be executed.

Addressing.   The stored-program principle also allows instructions to be changed by computation. In particular, the data location specified in the instructions can be altered. Thus, elements of an array can be addressed successively by the same procedure. In the Manchester University Computer of 1949, Kilburn considerably improved this address computation by introducing an index register whose content could be added to the instruction address.

Development of Software

After it was demonstrated around 1950 that workable and fast computers could be realized, an attempt was made to enlarge the utility of the computer. It became clear that along with higher speed, lower cost, and greater reliability, particular thought should be given to the programmability of the computer.

Since it is impractical to specify the instructions of a computer in their binary form, an alphanumeric form was developed for use in the first machines, the *assembly language*. Each instruction was represented by one word from the assembly language. The assembly language was translated to the machine language by an *assembler*. The Harvard Mark III and IV computers employed an auxiliary machine for this purpose. It soon became clear, however, that a computer could assemble its own programs. The assemblers allowed symbolic addressing as well.

In 1957 FORTRAN was introduced as one of the first languages to allow algebraic problem formulation. In these *compilers*, one expression corresponds to a set of instructions. Through these languages, one can direct oneself to the computer more easily.

About 1960, the *operating systems* were introduced for a more efficient manipulation of programs. Operating systems that allow simultaneous interaction of different users with the machine by means of terminals are called *time-sharing systems*. The first of these originated about 1962. Computer equipment is called *hardware;* in contrast, the language translators and operating systems are collectively called *software*.

Further details about the history of the computer are given by Randell (1973), Bell and Newell (1971), Rosen (1969) and Richards (1966); Sammet (1969 and 1972) has written about the development of software.

As computer design has become a mature art, the languages used to describe the architecture, implementation, and realization have received more attention. In this text, the general-purpose language APL is used for the architecture and implementation. A summary of hardware description languages has been given by Su (1974).

1-3 COMPUTER ARCHITECTURE

The architecture of a system can be defined as the functional appearance of the system to the user. (Blaauw, 1972). The architecture of a computer is composed of the machine language and the usage directions, which are important for the programmer. This information is used in the first place in the design of the hardware and the accompanying software. The final user normally knows the computer only through its software.

The *central processing unit*, or *CPU*, of a computer is composed of the *execution unit* and the *instruction unit*. The execution unit performs the operations specified by an instruction; the instruction unit, or the *system control*, decides in what order the instructions will be executed. The system control also assigns instructions, which refer to input and output, to units that take care of the traffic between the peripheral units and storage, often called *channels*.

Operations

Operations involve:

(a) The *data* that participate in the operation, such as the *operands*, and the *result*.
(b) The *operators*, such as the arithmetical and logical operators.

These two parts are discussed in turn, using as an example the IBM System/360 (Blaauw and Brooks, 1964; Amdahl et al., 1964). This computer and its successor, the System/370, are used as a major example in this text.

Formats. The nature of the operations that a computer can perform is for a large part determined by the *formats* of the instructions and data. These formats give the purpose of the groups of *bits*, the binary information units that represent the data and instructions. Since the result of an operation may be used as an operand in a succeeding operation, these formats must be largely uniform. Even for a versatile computer, such as System/360, the number of formats is limited.

Data

In the System/360, the types of data that participate in an operation are descriptive data, logical data, and numerical data, or numbers. Figure 1-2 provides a visual representation of the data formats.

Descriptive Data. *Descriptive data* are represented by 1 to 256 groups of 8 bits each. Such a group of 8 bits is called a *byte*. Normally each byte represents a character. The format of descriptive data therefore varies in length, with a minimum of 8 bits and a maximum of 2048 bits.

Logical Data. The variable-length format used for descriptive data can also be used for *logical data*. Thus, the number of bits is a multiple of 8, although the subdivision in bytes has less meaning here. Some logical data have a format with a fixed length of 32 bits. Such a group of 32 bits is called a *word*. The word format is also used for numbers.

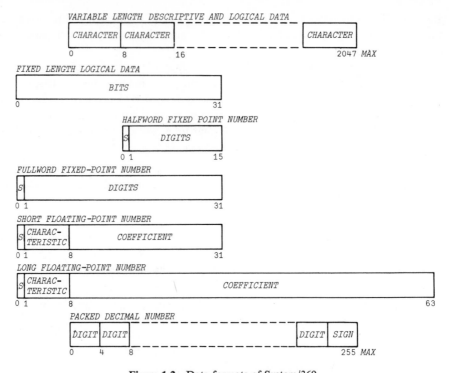

Figure 1-2   Data formats of System/360.

Numbers.   The space available in storage for each operand or result is always limited. Therefore, attention must be given to both the precision and the range of *numbers*. Numbers are often represented in *binary* notation to give maximum precision. The range of numbers can be increased for a given set of bits through the use of *floating-point* notation. This notation is especially important for calculations of a technical or scientific nature.

System/360 uses:

(a) Binary fixed-point numbers with fixed length.
(b) Decimal fixed-point numbers with variable length.
(c) Base 16, or *hexadecimal*, floating-point numbers with fixed length.

Binary numbers have two formats: the *word format* of 32 bits, and the *half-word format* of 16 bits. Numbers are interpreted as integers with 2's-complement notation. The leftmost bit, bit 0 of the format, represents the sign.

The length of the decimal format may vary from 1 to 16 bytes. Each byte contains two digits, except for the rightmost byte, which contains one digit and one sign. Decimal numbers are interpreted as integers represented by signed-magnitude notation. The maximum number of digits is 31, the minimum 1.

Floating-point formats occupy one or two words. The latter is called a *double-word format*. In both cases, the leftmost bit, bit 0, represents the sign of the number.

Bits 1 through 7 are the *characteristic*, which represents the *exponent* of the notation. The remaining bits represent the *coefficient* of the notation. The base of the floating-point notation is 16. This number is raised to the power specified by the exponent and multiplied with the coefficient. The sign is then attached to this value to obtain the proper interpretation of the floating-point representation.

Although mentioned here for the sake of completeness, decimal and floating-point arithmetic are not treated in this book.

Operators

Operators can be subdivided into data handling, logical, and arithmetic operators. Usually the name of the operator is attached to the class of operations in which it is used.

Data Handling.   *Data-handling operations* generally concern only one variable. They can change the location of this variable or the code in which the data are represented. Data handling is the most frequently executed class of operations. Only large technical or scientific calculations make more frequent use of the arithmetic operations.

Logic.   The *logical operations* include the elementary logical relations of two variables, such as the 'and' and 'or.' Logical operations are used mainly in the preparation of the decisions required by the program.

Arithmetic.   In System/360, as in most general-purpose computers, only the elementary *arithmetic operations*—Add, Subtract, Multiply, and Divide—can be performed. In some computers, division and even multiplication are missing. These are then obtained from the remaining operations by means of a *subroutine*, that is, a program section that can be used at various points in the main program.

Instructions

The instruction formats give the *syntax* of the machine language that is specified by the architecture. The main parts of the instruction format are the operation code and the addresses. The *operation code* indicates what operation must be performed. The *addresses* locate the data with which this operation must be performed. Thus, the operation code and the architecture of the corresponding operations together give the *semantics* of the machine language.

Operation Code.   Each data manipulation, logical, arithmetic, input, output, and control operation of the computer has its own code. There are approximately 20 fundamentally different operations, but because of the alternatives in the handling of sign, precision, number base, data format, and location, the total code list can have a length of 50 to 200 items. The length of the instruction set is, however, not an accurate gauge for the capabilities of a computer, because many important functions of the computer are not specified by an operation code.

Addresses. The address part of an instruction contains one or more addresses. For a typical operation, the location of two operands and one result must be given, and the location of the following instruction must be known. If these locations are each explicitly given by an address, then four addresses are required. Storage space can be used more efficiently, however, by implying some addresses. Thus, instructions are usually executed in numerical order, which eliminates the need for an explicit instruction address.

The location of the result is often the same as that of one of the operands, so that in essence one operand is replaced by the result. In this way the *two-address* instruction arises, which is especially effective for administrative applications. Most widely used, however, is the *one-address* instruction. This instruction assumes the presence of an auxiliary register, often called an *accumulator*, which can be used without further reference.

The one-address instruction specified some elementary operations by a series of instructions. Thus, $C \leftarrow A + B$ requires the following instruction series:

(a) Place the contents of the location of A in storage, as given by the address part of the instruction in the accumulator.
(b) Add B, from its storage location, to the contents of the accumulator.
(c) Place the contents of the accumulator in the storage location allocated to C.

The one-address instruction is at its best when the result, $A + B$, must be used in further calculations. In that case, the third instruction can be omitted and $A + B$ is directly available for further operations.

The efficiency of the one-address instruction can be improved by providing several auxiliary registers. Thus, System/360 uses 16 registers, which serve as intermediate result location and as index location, and therefore are called *general-purpose registers*. The registers are addressed by a 4-bit address field. Formally, the instruction now contains two addresses. In practice, however, it is still called a one-address instruction.

Instruction Format. In System/360 the operation code always occupies the first 8 bits of the instruction. The first 2 bits of the code determine the instruction type, including the length of the instruction.

The address part of the instruction can point to a register or to a main storage location. Depending on this choice, it occupies 4, 16, or 20 bits. Since for each of the two operand locations the choice can be made between a register and main storage, there are three instruction lengths. These three lengths and several other variations result in the five instruction formats shown in Figure 1-3. The first two instruction formats are most frequently used and will be considered further in this text.

Figure 1-3 shows that the storage addresses are composed of several parts. The instruction fields X and B refer to general-purpose registers whose content, the *index* and *base address*, is added to the D, or *displacement*, field of the instruction. The resulting sum, the *effective address*, is used to address main storage.

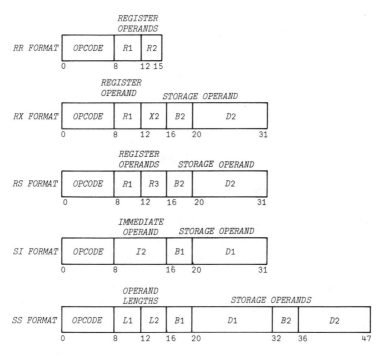

Figure 1-3   Instruction formats of System/360.

Instruction Sequence

The sequence in which instructions are executed is either uniquely determined or dependent upon a decision.

Branch.   If at a certain point the numerical order of the instruction addresses is not satisfactory, a *branch* can be used. This instruction contains an address that points to the place where the next series of instructions begins.

Decisions.   Decisions can be made in a program either by a decision instruction or by an interruption. The usual decision instruction is the conditional branch.

Conditional Branch.   A *conditional branch* is executed only when specific conditions are satisfied. For example, the sum $A + B$ could be used as a divisor in a subsequent division. To avoid division by 0, the addition of *A* and *B* can be followed by a conditional branch instruction which tests the condition 'last result was zero.' When the condition is not satisfied, the following instruction, here Divide, is executed. When the sum is 0, however, the series of instructions specified by the branch is executed. This simple procedure is shown in Program 1-4.

INSTRUCTION ADDRESS	OPERATION CODE	REGISTER ADDRESS STORAGE ADDRESS INDEX BASE DISPLACEMENT			MEANING OF INSTRUCTION
712	01011000 58	0101 5	0000	0000 000001110000 112	FETCH FROM LOCATION 112 TO GPR 5
713	01011010 5A	0101 5	0000	0000 000001110011 115	ADD FROM LOCATION 115 TO GPR 5
714	01010000 50	0101 5	0000	0000 000010000001 129	STORE FROM GPR 5 IN LOCATION 129
715	01000111 47	1000 MASK	0000	0000 001100011000 792	BRANCH IF RESULT 0 TO LOCATION 792

Program 1-4   Machine language program.

Interruption.   Some conditions are seldom satisfied or are satisfied at an unknown time. Thus, it is difficult to determine ahead of time the moment at which a peripheral unit makes new data available. In such a case an interruption may be desirable.

The *interruption* stops a procedure when a specified event occurs. A new series of instructions starts subsequently at a predetermined location. The state of the computer at the moment of interruption is saved such that the interrupted series of instructions can be resumed as if no interruption had occurred.

The interruption avoids the repeated use of a conditional branch instruction. It requires a more involved program, however, and is thus mainly used where the computer must react quickly to outside influences or exceptional circumstances.

1-4 LITERATURE

The development of the implementation of digital systems is recorded in magazine articles that have appeared over the last 25 years. Most prominent among these are the *Transactions on Electronic Computers* (from 1951) of the Institute of Radio Engineers (IRE), changed in 1962 to *Transactions on Computers of the Institute of Electrical and Electronic Engineers* (IEEE). Also of importance are the *IBM Systems Journal* (from 1961) and the *Computing Surveys of the Association for Computing Machinery* (from 1969). The following chapters will make reference to articles in these and other journals.

There are relatively few comprehensive books on digital system implementation. Richards's 1955 book has long been a standard reference on computer arithmetic. Other books restricted to machine arithmetic are by Flores (1960) and by

Stein and Munro (1971). Bell and Newell have compiled several classical articles and have described a number of computer designs, which also include implementation details. Buchholz (1962), Thornton (1970), and Organick (1973) have devoted books to the IBM 7030, the CDC 6600, and the Burroughs B5700, respectively. Of these, Thornton gives the most implementation details, while Organick's book almost entirely concerns architecture and software. Discussions that concur with the algorithmic approach followed in this text are given by Hill and Peterson (1973) and by Hellerman (1972).

REFERENCES

AIKEN, H. H., and G. M. HOPPER: "The Automatic Sequence Controlled Calculator." *Electrical Engineering*, vol. 65, pp. 384–391, 449–454, 522–528 (1946). Reprinted in Randell, pp. 199–218 (*see below*).

AMDAHL, G. M., G. A. BLAAUW, and F. P. BROOKS, JR.: "Architecture of the IBM System/360." *IBM Journal of Research and Development*, vol. 8, no. 2, pp. 87–101 (April, 1964).

BELL, C. G., and A. NEWELL: *Computer Structures: Readings and Examples*. McGraw-Hill, New York, 1971.

BLAAUW, G. A.: "Computer Architecture." *Electronische Rechenanlagen*, vol. 14, no. 4, pp. 154–150, (1972). Reprinted in Spruth, W. G., and H. Hasselmeier, *Rechnerstrukturen*. Oldenbourg, Munich (1974).

BLAAUW, G. A., and F. P. BROOKS, JR.: "The Structure of System/360, Part I: Outline of Logical Structure." *IBM Systems Journal*, vol. 3, no. 2, pp. 119–135 (1964). Reprinted in Bell and Newell, pp. 588–601.

BOWDEN, B. V.: *Faster Than Thought*. Pitman, New York, 1953.

BUCHHOLZ, W.: *Planning a Computer System, Project Stretch*. McGraw-Hill, New York, 1962.

BURKS, A. W., H. H. GOLDSTINE, and J. VON NEUMANN: *Preliminary Discussion of the Logical Design of an Electronic Computing Instrument*. Institute for Advanced Study, Princeton, June, 1946. Reprinted in Bell and Newell, pp. 92–119.

FLORES, I.: *The Logic of Computer Arithmetic*. Prentice-Hall, Englewood Cliffs, N.J., 1963.

FORRESTER, J. W.: "Digital Information Storage in Three Dimensions Using Magnetic Cores." *Journal of Applied Physics*, vol. 22, pp. 44–48 (1951).

GOLDSTINE, H. H., and A. GOLDSTINE: "The Electronic Numerical Integrator and Computer (ENIAC)." *Mathematical Tables and Aids to Computation*, vol. 2, no. 15, pp. 97–110 (1946). Reprinted in Randell, pp. 333–347 (*see below*).

HELLERMAN, H.: *Digital Computer Systems Principles*. McGraw-Hill, New York, 2nd ed., 1972.

HILL, R. J., and G. R. PETERSON: *Digital Systems: Hardware Organization and Design*. Wiley, New York, 1973.

MORRISON, P., and E. MORRISON, eds.: *Charles Babbage and His Calculating Engines: Selected Writings by Babbage and Others.* Dover Publications, New York, 1961.

ORGANICK, E. I.: *Computer System Organization. The B5700/B6700 Series.* Academic Press, New York, 1973.

RAJCHMAN, J. A.: "A Myriabit Magnetic-Core Matrix Storage." *Proceedings of the IRE,* vol. 41, pp. 1407–1421 (October, 1953).

RANDELL, B., ed.: *The Origins of Digital Computers. Selected Papers.* Springer-Verlag, Berlin, 1973.

RICHARDS, R. K.: *Arithmetic Operations in Digital Computers.* Van Nostrand Reinhold, New York, 1955.

RICHARDS, R. K.: *Electronic Digital Systems.* Wiley, New York, 1966.

ROSEN, S.: "Electronic Computers: A Historical Survey." *Computing Surveys,* vol. 1, no. 1, pp. 7–36 (March, 1969).

SAMMET, J. E.: *Programming Languages: History and Fundamentals.* Prentice-Hall, Englewood Cliffs, N.J., 1969.

SAMMET, J. E.: "Programming Languages: History and Future." *Communications of the ACM,* vol. 15, no. 7, pp. 601–610 (July, 1972).

STAFF OF THE COMPUTATION LABORATORY: *A Manual of Operation for the Automatic Sequence Controlled Calculator.* Harvard University Press, Cambridge, Mass., 1946.

STEIN, M. L., and W. O. MUNRO: *Introduction to Machine Arithmetic.* Addison-Wesley, Reading, Mass., 1971.

SU, S. Y. H.: "A Survey of Computer Hardware Description Languages in the U.S.A." *Computer,* vol. 7, no. 12, pp. 45–51 (December, 1974).

THORNTON, J. E.: *Design of a Computer, the Control Data 6600.* Scott, Foresman, Glenview, Ill., 1970.

2   ADDITION

The adder is the most frequently used arithmetic element in the implementation of digital systems. It is also a systems component whose implementations are quite diverse. Several of these implementations will be used to illustrate a number of design principles.

The discussion will be confined to binary adders. Negative numbers are assumed to be represented by the 2's complement. By complementing the subtrahend, the adder can be used for subtraction. The binary adder can be changed into a counter or a decimal adder by eliminating or incorporating appropriate circuits.

Organization of the Chapter

As a first step toward an implementation, the designer should assure himself of a proper architectural specification. Hence, Section 2-1 discusses the architecture of an adder, and Section 2-2 presents a formal description of this architecture.

Most arithmetic algorithms are derived from the algorithms of manual calculation, which are based upon the positional representation. In Section 2-3, therefore, the basic addition process for one bit position within an adder is considered. This bit adder can be used repeatedly in time as described in Section 2-4, or in space, as described in Sections 2-5 and 2-6. Sections 2-7 through 2-13 describe various means of increasing the adder speed.

The carry-predict adder, described in Sections 2-8 and 2-9, is the most prominent parallel adder type. Hence, for a first pass through this chapter the reader may wish to skip the other adder types and their evaluation in Section 2-14 and proceed with Section 2-15, which discusses the verification of an implementation.

2-1 ARCHITECTURE OF THE ADDER IN WORDS

The operands of an addition are the addend and augend. The *addend* is added to the *augend* to form a *sum*. Often the augmented operand, the augend, is replaced by the sum, whereas the addend retains its original value.

In the arithmetic system of Figure 2-1, for example, the addend is fetched from storage and possibly complemented for subtraction, whereas the augend is obtained from the sum register and is replaced by the sum. The sum is derived from the addend and augend in the combinational add circuit. This add circuit is the main subject of this chapter. For brevity the addend and augend will be denoted as the *operands A* and *B*.

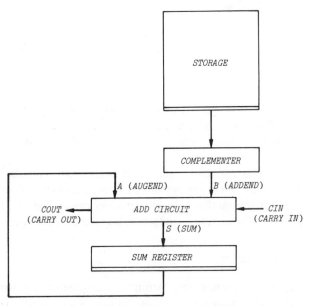

Figure 2-1 Adder organization.

Figure 2-1 shows that besides the operands *A* and *B*, the *carry-in CIN* participates in the addition. The carry-in is required when the adder is used for subtraction. In that case the complementer produces the 1's complement of the number to be subtracted, which a carry-in of 1 will change into the 2's complement.

The result of the addition is the *sum S* and the *carry-out COUT*. The carry-out can be used to determine whether the sum has become too large or too small.

The presence of *CIN* and *COUT* makes the definition of the adder more elaborate. Thus one could state: "The adder forms the sum *S* from the operands *A* and *B* and the carry-in *CIN*, and gives an overflow indication *COUT*." This definition, however, omits the concept of representation and thus is imprecise in details such as the range of the sum.

Representation. Machine arithmetic always operates upon the representation of numbers. The operands A and B as well as the sum S are not numbers. They are a set of signals, or, if interpreted as switching variables, a set of 0s and 1s.

Therefore, the architecture of the adder should be stated as: "The adder forms the signals S, which represent the low-order N digits of the binary sum of the binary integers represented by the N signals A, the N signals B, and the signal CIN. The adder also forms the signal $COUT$, which is 1 when the sum is not fully represented by the signals S."

The architectural description in words has become quite lengthy in the process of including the necessary detail. Yet it still assumes many conventions, which, if spelled out, would make the description even longer. Thus, the arithmetic concepts of sum and integer are assumed to be known. Also, the ordering of the signals and the association of the digits with these signals are not mentioned. Yet the description of the architecture should be specific. Otherwise, the implementer or user may misinterpret the intention of the designer. This problem can be alleviated by the use of a formal language, as will be described in the next section and is illustrated throughout this book.

2-2 ARCHITECTURE OF THE ADDER IN APL

The requirement that an architecture be carefully formulated to be of practical use poses a dilemma. On the one hand, there is the danger that the description is ambiguous. On the other hand, the description soon becomes abundant in words and stylized in expression, using terms in carefully defined senses. Thus, it comes to resemble the carefully crafted wording of guarantee certificates, contracts, policies, and laws.

Because of these difficulties, an exact, concise, and unambiguous formulation, as used in mathematics, is desirable. Such a formal description has its own drawbacks, such as the unfamiliarity of the symbols and the catastrophic effect of each error. It is therefore attractive to use both methods side by side. Possible misconceptions in the text can be eliminated by the algorithmic expressions, while the expressions, in turn, are explained by the text. Each description, however, should be complete in itself. One description should be designated as *definitive*, and the other as *derived*, so that priority is clear in the case of inadvertent conflicts between the two. In this text, the formal description is definitive.

APL

In this text the exact formulation is given in the language *APL* (A Programming Language) developed by Iverson (1962). In particular, the terminal language APL\360 (Falkoff and Iverson, 1968; Pakin, 1972) and its successor APLSV (Lathwell, 1973) will be used. Only part of these languages will be used, such that only a limited amount of symbolism and conventions needs to be introduced.

A virtue of the terminal implementation of APL is its ability to execute algorithms. Thus, the error problem is reduced considerably, since the implementation detects errors by verifying the description for syntactical correctness. Furthermore, the implementation avoids errors by reducing the number of transcription errors, by its filing system and editing functions. The use of the terminal also helps in getting acquainted with the symbolism.

The concepts of APL will be introduced gradually in this text. A summary of APL is given in Appendix A.

General-Purpose Character of APL.   Iverson has designed APL as a general-purpose language. As such it is well established and widely implemented. Thus, the designer learning this language acquires a tool that is not limited to his immediate goal of description and simulation, but also allows him to develop tests, acquire statistics, process text, schedule his work, and prepare his income tax. He furthermore can profit from interaction with many others using this language. These advantages are well worth the disadvantage of having to live with the inevitable shortcomings of a language that is established and is not limited to one purpose.

Arrays.   In APL, the variables normally are arrays. This makes the language especially attractive as a programming language, since the effort invested in the writing of a program is more readily justified when the program applies to arrays rather than simple variables.

An *array* consists of one or more elements. An *element* can be:

(a) A *symbol*, such as a character;
(b) A *logical value*, which is 1 for true and 0 for false; or
(c) A *number*.

The elements of an array are considered in groups. This grouping is called the lowest *dimension* of the array. The number of elements in the group is the value of this dimension. The groups, in turn, can be taken together, forming the following dimension. This process can be continued as desired. The number of dimensions is called the *rank* of the array. A simple spatial representation of the array is possible up to and including three dimensions, or rank 3, but this is no formal limitation. A *matrix* is an array of two dimensions, a *vector* an array of one dimension, and a *scalar* an array without dimensions. Examples of these are given in Table 2-2.

Dimension.   The *dimension vector* of an array is the vector whose elements, from left to right, are the values of the dimensions, from high to low, of the array. Obtaining the dimension vector for a given array is an operation. The operator that performs this operation is represented by the Greek letter rho ρ and is called the *size*. For instance, in Table 2-2 *MATRIXI* is a matrix of 15 elements grouped in 3 rows of 5 elements each, and $\rho MATRIXI$ is the vector 3 5. The rank of the matrix, $\rho\rho MATTRIXI$, is 2.

For the adder, the operands A and B are logical vectors with dimension ρA

```
       SCALAR                          VECTOR                              ARRAY3
7                            3    5    11    10    13    6              0    1    2
                                                                       3    4    5
       ρSCALAR                         ρVECTOR                         6    7    8
                             6                                         9   10   11

       MATRIXI                         MATRIXII                       12   13   14
      7   18   17   3   4      1    2    3    1    2                   15   16   17
     10    8   15  16  13      3    1    2    3    1                   18   19   20
      1    2    9   6   5      2    3    1    2    3                   21   22   23

       ρMATRIXI                        ρMATRIXII                          ρARRAY3
3   5                         3    5                           2    4    3

       ρρMATRIXI                       ρρMATRIXII                         ρρARRAY3
2                                 2                            3
```

Table 2-2 Examples of arrays.

and ρB. The signal *CIN* can be considered as a vector with dimension 1 or as a scalar.

Scalar. A scalar is a number without dimension. The differences between a scalar and a one-element array appear in particular when the dimension of an operand is changed. These differences will only be discussed as far as the purpose of this text requires.

Monadic and Dyadic Operators. The operator ρ is used here monadically. The term *monadic* indicates that the operator has one operand. The operator ρ can also be used with two operands in the form $X\rho Y$, hence *dyadic*. This is analogous to the monadic and dyadic use of the minus sign in algebra, as in $-X$ and $X-Y$. These two modes of use are possible for most operators in APL.

Reshape. The dyadic use of ρ has the meaning *reshape*, or restructure. $X\rho Y$ gives the form specified by X to the elements of Y. The dimension vector of the result is thus X. The elements of Y are taken in sequence from low to high dimension. If there are not enough elements, then the elements of Y are used repeatedly. Thus, the result of $5\rho 2$ is the vector 2 2 2 2 2.

Decode. The architecture requires that a representation be interpreted as a number. The operator *decode*, or base value, $\perp$, performs this operation. The operation $X \perp Y$ determines the number that is represented by the vector Y when interpreted according to the base X. The vector X gives the correct base for each digit position. Thus, 1 24 60 60 $\perp$ 1 2 3 4 can be used to find the number of seconds equal to 1 day, 2 hours, 3 minutes, and 4 seconds. The result of this decode operation is $(24 \times 60 \times 60 \times 1) + (60 \times 60 \times 2) + (60 \times 3) + 4$, which is the scalar 93784. Note that the leftmost element of X is not used.

Extension to an Array. The decode operator permits a mixed-number system. In most applications, however, a single base will be used and all elements of X

are the same. Thus, the interpretation of a 5-bit augend A as a 5-bit binary number would be specified as $2\ 2\ 2\ 2\ 2 \perp A$.

When the vector X consists of identical elements, it may be replaced by a scalar or a one-element array. Thus, $2 \perp 1\ 0\ 1$ results in the number 5. The scalar 2 is thought to be extended first to a vector of dimension 3, with each element equal to 2 and then used in the decode operation. Similarly, the interpretation of A may be written as $2 \perp A$ for any dimention of the logical vector A. This extension of one element to a vector or an array, with each element equal to the given element, is a general feature of APL.

Encode. The opposite of the decode operator $\perp$ is the *encode*, or representation operator $\top$. $X \top Y$ is the representation of the scalar Y as a vector, in the number system specified by X. The elements of this vector are, from right to left, the digits, from low to high, in this representation. The vector X contains the coefficients for the series development of the positional representation. For example, the representation of a number Y by five binary digits requires for X the value $2\ 2\ 2\ 2\ 2$. When Y is greater than 31, only the lowest five digits are given. In other words, the number is represented modulo 32. When Y is negative, the complement is represented. For binary representation this is the 2's complement. Thus, the result of $2\ 2\ 2\ 2\ 2 \top -7$ is $1\ 1\ 0\ 0\ 1$.

Extension of the left operand of the encode operator from a scalar to an array is not defined in APL, since in this case the right operand gives no indications of the desired dimension.

Encoding and Decoding of Arrays. When encode is applied to an array, the rank of the array is increased by 1. Similarly, the right operand of decode may be an array. In that case, decode reduces the rank by 1. Encode extends the array with a high dimension, and decode eliminates the highest dimension. It appears that extension and reduction of an array with a low dimension would have been a more appropriate definition. This text, however, uses encode and decode mainly to convert vectors to scalars, and vice versa.

The operators described so far are especially meaningful for arrays. They have no direct equivalent in classical algebra, since the application of this algebra emphasized scalars rather than arrays.

Arithmetic Operators. The well-known arithmetic operators $+$, $-$, $\times$, and $\div$ are part of APL. Exponentiation is represented by $*$, so $2 * 5$ is equal to 32. The logarithm is expressed by $X \circledast Y$, with X the base of the logarithm and Y the number of which the logarithm is to be determined. Hence $2 \circledast 32$ is equal to 5.

The use of these operators with arrays does not follow, however, the somewhat specialized definitions of traditional vector and matrix multiplication. Those composite operations have their own operators in APL as described in Chapter 7. Rather, the arithmetic operators are simply applied to the corresponding elements of both arrays. The arrays should have the same dimensions, which will be the dimensions of the result as well.

```
           3 5 9+1 2 3                           7 8 9÷2
    4    7  12                           3.5    4   4.5

           VECTOR-1 2 3 4 5 6                   VECTOR×2
    2    3  8   6  8  0            6    10   22   20   26   12

           MATRIXI+MATRIXII                  MATRIXI+SCALAR
    8   20  20   4   6            14   25   24   10   11
   13    9  17  19  14            17   15   22   23   20
    3    5  10   8   8             8    9   16   13   12

           MATRIXI×MATRIXII                  MATRIXI>SCALAR
    7   36  51   3   8           0  1  1  0  0
   30    8  30  48  13           1  1  1  1  1
    2    6   9  12  15           0  0  1  0  0

           MATRIXI>MATRIXII                  MATRIXI<SCALAR
 1  1  1  1  1                   0  0  0  1  1
 1  1  1  1  1                   0  0  0  0  0
 0  0  1  1  1                   1  1  0  1  1
```

Table 2-3 Array arithmetic.

Table 2-3 gives several examples of array arithmetic, using the arrays from Table 2-2. The figure shows that for these operations also a scalar is extended when necessary to an array with the dimensions of the other operand.

The sum of the interpretation of the operands A and B can now be expressed as $(2 \perp A) + (2 \perp B)$. To this sum the value of the carry-in can further be added by stating $(2 \perp A) + (2 \perp B) + CIN$. Since a scalar added to a vector yields a vector, this sum would be a vector when CIN is a one-element vector. To make sure that the sum is a scalar the expression is rewritten as $(2 \perp A) + (2 \perp B) + (2 \perp CIN)$.

Relations.   The relations *greater than*, $>$; *equal to*, $=$; and *less than*, $<$; and their negations, *less than or equal*, $\leq$; *unequal*, $\neq$; and *greater than or equal*, $\geq$, are also APL operators. A relational expression has the value 1 if true and 0 if false. Hence, the expression $7 = 7$ has the value 1, and $7 \neq 7$ has the the value 0.

Specification.   The equal symbol is used only as a relational operator in APL. The use of this symbol with the imperative meaning 'is made equal to' is replaced by the *specification*, or assignment, symbol, the arrow pointing left, $\leftarrow$. The expression SUM $\leftarrow (2 \perp A) + (2 \perp B) + (2 \perp CIN)$ assigns to the variable SUM the value of the sum of the interpretations of A, B, and CIN.

Evaluation of Expressions.   The architecture of an adder is given by Program 2-4. The expressions of such a program are evaluated in sequence from top to bottom. Within an expression, the operations are performed from right to left. The conventional priority of operations, such as that of multiplication over addition, is not followed. Parentheses must be used to deviate from the right to left scan.

```
SUM←(2⊥A)+(2⊥B)+2⊥CIN
S←((ρA)ρ2)⊤SUM
COUT←SUM≥2*ρA
```

Program 2-4 Expressions of adder architecture.

This convention avoids the complexities of extending priorities to new operators such as encode and reshape.

The execution from right to left harmonizes with the reading of expressions from left to right, in the sense that each operator is applied to the entire expression to the right. It can been argued, on the other hand, that an execution from left to right would be even more in harmony with the direction of reading in Western culture. In that case, the operator would apply to all that has been read rather than all that has not yet been read. The current definition of APL, however, has proved to be highly workable; the alternate definition has troubles all its own. Hence, it is not useful at this time to propose a change in direction.

Parentheses.   The use of *parentheses*, ( ), is conventional. The expression within the parentheses is evaluated before the remaining operations are applied to it.

Program for Adder Architecture

In Program 2-4, it is assumed that A, B, and CIN are given as vectors of logical values, *logical vectors*, of a specified dimension. The algorithm uses these dimensions, whatever they are; they need not be explicitly declared. The auxiliary variable SUM is determined as the sum of their interpretations as base 2 integers. SUM, in turn, is represented by S. S receives the same dimension as A, the augend. The carry-out $COUT$ is made 1 when SUM is larger than or equal to the smallest number that can no longer be represented by S. If B has significant digits beyond the length of A, then $COUT$ has the meaning of overflow rather than carry-out.

Function.   The expressions of Program 2-4, when entered at a terminal, are executed once. To repeat the program, the expressions would have to be entered again. This impractical procedure can be avoided by making the expressions part of a function.

A *function* has a name and remains in storage. It can be executed repeatedly from storage by calling upon its name. In Program 2-5, the function $ARCHADD$ is defined, which contains the expressions of Program 2-4.

```
      ∇ ARCHADD;SUM
[1]     SUM←(2⊥A)+(2⊥B)+2⊥CIN
[2]     S←((ρA)ρ2)⊤SUM
[3]     COUT←SUM≥2*ρA
      ∇
```

Program 2-5   Function for adder architecture.

A function is defined by preceding it with the symbol ∇ (del). The end of the function definition is also given by a del. The line numbering is done by the APL system. For the use of this numbering in the writing and correcting of programs, the reader is referred to the bibliography (Pakin, 1972; Falkoff and Iverson, 1968).

Scope of Variables.   The architecture specifies that the variables A, B, and CIN are inputs of the adder, while S and $COUT$ are outputs. In specifying the relation between inputs and outputs, it proved convenient to define the auxiliary variable *SUM*. It is not the intention of the architect, however, to specify *SUM* as an output. Therefore, *SUM* is declared to be a local variable. The implementer or user need not concern himself with *SUM* other than in understanding the architectural specification.

Local and Global Variables. A variable that exists only within the function in which it is defined is called *local*. In contrast, a variable is *global* with respect to a given function when it is valid inside as well as outside that function. A variable is identified as local by placing its name after the function name, separated from the function name by a semicolon. Thus, in *ARCHADD*, *SUM* is declared to be local while all other variables are global. A reference to *SUM* outside *ARCHADD* produces an error report or the value of a different variable with the same name.

Header. The information immediately following the del of a function and preceding its first line is called the *header* of the function. The header thus contains the function name and the names of the local variables.

Further Specification of the Adder Architecture. *ARCHADD* is independent of the length of the operands *A* and *B*. Therefore, it can specify adders of various lengths, as indeed will be the case in the various chapters of this book. For each application, of course, the proper adder length must be stated. Usually, this length follows from the known length of *A*.

ARCHADD also allows different lengths for *A* and *B*. In most applications *A* and *B* have the same length, however. Again, the adder can be so restricted by specifying the lengths of the operands.

Application of Adder Architecture. *ARCHADD* describes the function of the add circuit within the adder organization of Figure 2-1. This adder organization, when properly controlled, permits the addition and subtraction of numbers in the 2's complement representation.

The operands and the sum are treated as integers in *ARCHADD*. *A*, *B*, and *S*, however, can also be considered as negative numbers or as fractions. These alternative interpretations need not be mentioned in *ARCHADD*, since they do not influence the working of the add circuit. The architecture should be complete with regard to what happens; it need not tell how it can be used.

The organization of Figure 2-1 can also be used for addition and subtraction of 1's complement numbers. In that case, *COUT* should be connected as the *end-around carry* to *CIN*, as explained in Appendix C.

For signed-magnitude representation, a complementer is required between the sum register and the *A* input of the adder, to allow recomplementation. Furthermore, the sign bit of this representation should be treated separately from the magnitude bits. The organization of Figure 2-1, therefore, should be modified accordingly. The add circuit of that organization, however, still has the architecture of *ARCHADD*.

In subsequent chapters, the use of *ARCHADD* in subsystems both similar and dissimilar to Figure 2-1 will be discussed. The remainder of this chapter, however, aims at finding suitable implementations of *ARCHADD*.

2-3 BIT ADDER

An architecture can be implemented in many different ways. This diversity is particularly noticeable for the adder, since it has received much—sometimes too much—attention in the literature.

Basic Addition Algorithm. All adder implementations are based upon the algorithm that is suggested by the positional representation and which also is used in manual calculation. In this algorithm the corresponding digits of the operands are added pair by pair, starting at the low order. To this sum a possible carry from the next-lower digit position is added; in turn, a resulting carry is passed to the next higher position.

In binary arithmetic the digits, or bits, are either 0 or 1. For each digit position, called *bit position*, two operand bits and a carry bit should be added. The equipment required for this addition is called a bit adder. Figure 2-6 shows the positions of a bit adder within an adder. Since all adder implementations are derived from the bit adder, it will be discussed here first.

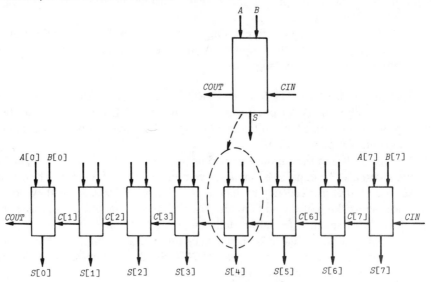

Figure 2-6   Bit adder within an adder.

Architecture of the Bit Adder

A *bit adder* can be considered as an adder whose operands and sum are vectors with a single element, hence with dimension 1. The architecture of *ARCHADD* is therefore applicable, but can also be simplified, as in *ARCHBITADD*, Program 2-7.

```
        ∇ ARCHBITADD;SUM
    [1]    SUM←A+B+CIN
    [2]    S←2⊤SUM
    [3]    COUT←SUM≥2
        ∇
```

Program 2-7   Bit adder architecture.

Implementation of the Bit Adder

The bit adder is a circuit with three inputs and two outputs. It can be designed as an entity using the known minimization methods of switching theory, as discussed in Appendix D. A minimum circuit for the bit adder, however, does not guarantee a minimum circuit for the entire adder. It is desirable, therefore, to recognize the functional components of the adder. These are shown in the circuit of Figure 2-8 and in *IMPBITADD*, Program 2-9.

Half Adders.   Figure 2-6 shows how for each bit adder the operands A and B belong to the numbers to be added and are available at the start of the operation. In contrast, the carry-in CIN of a bit adder arises as the carry-out of the adjacent bit adder and is normally available later than A and B. This time difference suggests splitting the bit adder into two parts, named *half-adders*. A and B are added in the first half-adder and CIN is added to their sum in the second half-adder. In contrast to the term 'half-adder,' the whole bit adder is called *full adder*.

Transmission.   The sum of bits A and B is again a single bit. Hence, this sum is determined modulo 2 and is equivalent to the exclusive-or of A and B. This sum is called the *partial sum*, or *transmission T*.

Carry Generation.   The first half-adder also determines if A and B give rise to a carry. This signal is called the *generated carry*, or for short the *generation, G*. A carry can only be generated if both A and B are 1. Hence, the circuit for the carry generation is equivalent to an 'and.' Sometimes the 'and' is part of the exclusive-or circuit for the transmission.

Carry Assimilation.   In the second half-adder the partial sum is added to the carry-in, the *carry assimilation*. The result is the ultimate sum S.

Carry Propagation.   The second half-adder also determines if the carry-in, together with the partial sum, gives rise to a carry-out of the bit adder, the *propagated carry P*. Thus, the carry-in is transmitted through the circuit if T is 1, hence the name transmission.

Carry-out.   Since T and G cannot be 1 simultaneously, the generated and propagated carry never appear at the same time. Therefore, the carry-out $COUT$

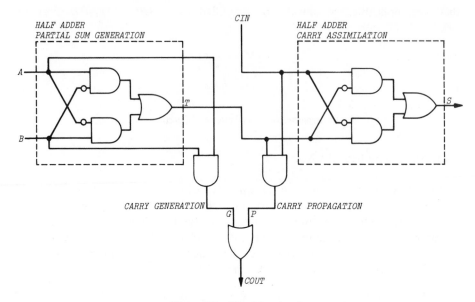

Figure 2-8   Bit adder circuit.

```
      ∇ IMPBITADD
[1]      ⍝ TRANSMISSION AND GENERATION
[2]      T←A≠B
[3]      G←A∧B
[4]      ⍝ CARRY PROPAGATION
[5]      P←T∧CIN
[6]      ⍝ CARRY ASSIMILATION
[7]      S←T≠CIN
[8]      COUT←G∨P
      ∇
```

Program 2-9   Bit adder implementation.

need not be determined as the sum of G and P but can simply be the 'or' of G and P. For the same reason, the carry-in can be transmitted by the 'or' of A and B rather than by the exclusive-or T. Since T is required in the carry assimilation, however, it usually is used in carry propagation as well.

Circuit for the Bit Adder.   Figure 2-8 shows a circuit for the bit adder, which is constructed from 'and,' 'or,' and 'not' components. The two exclusive-ors are also constructed from these elements, although they are sometimes available as a single switching element.

Logical Operators.   Program 2-9 shows the APL expressions for the bit adder *IMPBITADD: IMPBITADD* uses the logical symbol ∧ for *and* and ∨ for *or*; for *exclusive-or*, the relation 'unequal' ≠ is used.

Comment.   The various parts of the circuit, which have been encountered above, are identified in *IMPBITADD* by the comments of lines 1, 4, and 6. These lines are preceded by the symbol A. This symbol indicates that the text is a *comment*. The purpose of the comment is to explain the program. The comment line is not executed.

APL Description of a Circuit. *IMPBITADD* has a one-to-one correspondence to the circuit elements of Figure 2-8, assuming that the exclusive-or is available as a unit. When the exclusive-or is to be constructed from 'and,' or,' and inverter elements, lines 2 and 7 should be changed accordingly.

When the entire bit adder is available as a single component, such as the Texas Instrument (TI) SN7480, the functional behavior of this component is best given by *ARCHBITADD*, since the user of the component is not directly concerned with its internal construction.

Bit Adder Built from Nands. The bit adder can also be constructed from nands, as shown in Figure 2-10, and *NANDADD*, Program 2-11. APL uses for the nand a symbol that is obtained by overstriking the symbols for 'and' and 'not.'

NANDADD shows directly that nine nands are necessary. *NG* and *NP*, the

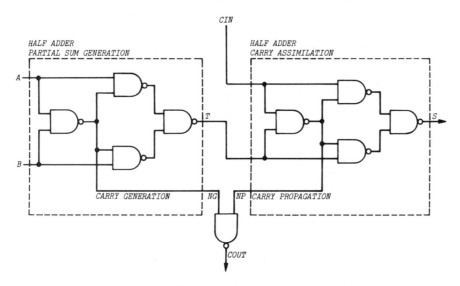

Figure 2-10 Nand circuit for a bit adder.

```
    ∇ NANDADD
[1]   A TRANSMISSION AND GENERATION
[2]   NG←A⍲B
[3]   T←(A⍲NG)⍲B⍲NG
[4]   A CARRY PROPAGATION
[5]   NP←T⍲CIN
[6]   A CARRY ASSIMILATION
[7]   S←(T⍲NP)⍲CIN⍲NP
[8]   COUT←NG⍲NP
    ∇
```

Program 2-11 Bit adder using nands.

inverses of the carry signals G and P, are obtained as part of the exclusive-or circuit. A single nand derives $COUT$ from NG and NP.

Figures 2-8 and 2-10 are only two of many circuits that can be used for a bit adder. Liu et al. (1974) have listed 43 circuits, each of which is minimal with respect to a set of circuit constraints. Figures 2-8 and 2-10, however, have been chosen since they clearly illustrate the functional elements of the bit adder.

$ARCHADD$, $IMPBITADD$, and $NANDADD$ illustrate how APL can be used both for a high-level specification and for a detailed circuit description. This breadth of expression makes the language particularly suitable for the design of a system implementation.

Circuit Realization.   Once the individual circuit components are identified by an APL function, the circuit can be realized. This realization still involves many decisions, such as the selection of the component type, the location of the component within a module or on a chip, and the routing of the connecting wires (Breuer, 1972). These decisions are much influenced by electrical and physical considerations, such as voltage distribution, grounding and cooling. This part of the design is not discussed in this text. The implementation functions that will be derived constitute the logical specification of the realization design.

Number of Circuit Levels.   The maximum number of circuit elements that must be passed in a circuit to reflect a change of the inputs fully in the outputs is called the number of *levels* of the circuit. This number can serve as a rough estimate of the speed of the implementation. The estimate is independent of the realization since the delay time of the circuit elements does not enter into it.

When a bit adder is constructed from 'and,' 'or,' and 'not' components, as in Figure 2-8, six levels must be passed to obtain the output signal S from the input signals A, B, and CIN. Each half-adder contributes three levels to this total. Similarly, the nand circuit of Figure 2-10 requires three levels per half-adder.

When both polarities of the signals A and B are available, for instance as register outputs, the inverters in the first half-adder are not required and only two levels are passed in that half-adder. Also, components are available which produce the exclusive-or in the equivalent of two levels. Therefore, a certain ambiguity exists whether a half-adder requires two or three circuit levels.

In subsequent level counts, the number of circuit levels for a half-adder, an exclusive-or, or an and-or circuit will systematically be taken as two. In actuality, more levels may be required. The ultimate evaluation of the speed of a design, however, always requires a detailed knowledge of the delays of the circuits involved, usually counted in nanoseconds rather than levels. Therefore, the level counts given can only be a first approximation. The standard use of two levels for a half-adder is consistent with the precision of this approximation.

Extension of the Bit Adder to an Adder.   The extension of the bit adder to an adder for numbers can take place in time or in space. As stated in Chapter 1, the term 'time' refers here to the number of circuits to be passed by the signals to complete the operation. The term 'space' refers to the number of circuits used in the implementation.

The use of the bit adder can be extended in time by passing the bit positions of the numbers to be added successively through the same bit adder: the *series adder*.

In the spatial sense the extension occurs by placing a multiplicity of bit adders side by side and servicing each bit position by a separate bit adder: the *parallel adder*.

The parallel adder gains speed at the expense of equipment. This exchange of time for space can be extended further by applying extra hardware, usually resulting in a more complex adder. Also, time may be gained by taking the nature of the operands into account. These implementation possibilities will be discussed in the following sections.

2-4 SERIES ADDER

For an elementary series adder just one bit adder is necessary. The operand bits are selected from right to left and the sum bits are stored accordingly. The carry-out of a given bit position is used as the carry into the following position by storing it temporarily in a storage element, the *carry buffer CB*, as shown in Figure 2-12.

Selection.   In most applications of the series adder the selection of operand and result bits is performed in a storage unit that delivers and receives the bits in series. Thus, the selection, initiation, and terminination are not designed as part of the series adder.

At the beginning of the addition the carry-in is assumed to be in the carry buffer *CB*, while at the end the carry-out remains in this buffer. As a consequence of these assumptions, the hardware and the program for the series adder can be extremely simple.

APL Description.   *SERADD*, Program 2-13, which describes the series adder, uses the previously defined function *ARCHBITADD*. The bit adder is expressed in terms of its architecture to indicate that there is still a choice with respect to its implementation. By calling *ARCHBITADD* in line 2, the signals *A* and *B*, obtained from the bit selection, and the carry-in *CIN*, obtained from *CB* in line 1, are used to form the signals *S* and *COUT*. Subsequently, in line 3, *CB* is given a new content, namely *COUT*, the carry-out of the bit adder. One pair of bits is added in this manner. The function *SERADD*, therefore, will have to be called as often as there are bits to be processed. This repeated use of an adder to perform an entire addition will be discussed further in Chapter 5.

Block Diagram.   Figure 2-12 shows the block diagram of the series adder. Since the carry buffer is a sequential circuit, it is represented by a block with a

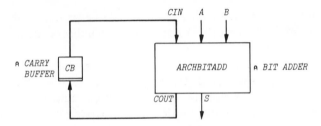

Figure 2-12   Series adder.

```
    ∇ SERADD
[1]   CIN←CB
[2]   ARCHBITADD
[3]   CB←COUT
    ∇

    ⋀ REFERENCE:
    ⋀ ARCHBITADD    BIT ADDER ARCHITECTURE
```

Program 2-13   Series adder.

double line underneath. The circuit for *ARCHBITADD*, on the other hand, is combinational and has a single line underneath. The properties of buffers and storage elements will be discussed in Chapters 5 and 8.

   Adder Application.   The series adder is only justified when the storage containing its operands is also organized in series. In that case, the bit selection is free and the adder speed is governed by the storage speed. Most storages, however, transmit at least a few bits in parallel. When such storages are used with a series adder, selection circuits for the operand and result bits must be supplied. The equipment required by these selection circuits is usually better invested in a more parallel adder.

2-5   SERIES–PARALLEL ADDER

   For small digital systems, such as pocket calculators, a series–parallel organization is attractive. Here a number is subdivided in several groups, called *bytes*, or *characters*, typically comprising 4, 6, or 8 bits. The bits of a byte are processed in parallel, while the bytes of a number are processed in series. The adder required by this type of organization is the series–parallel adder.

   The *series–parallel adder* is actually a short parallel adder with provisions for the buffering of the carry between bytes, similar to the carry buffer of the serial adder. Hence, Figure 2-12 and Program 2-13 describe the series–parallel adder when *ARCHBITADD* is replaced by *ARCHADD*. The ripple adder, table-look-up adder, and carry-predict adder, described in Sections 2-6, 2-7, and 2-8, are particularly suited to serve in a series–parallel organization.

2-6 RIPPLE ADDER

A parallel adder can be obtained by placing a sufficient number of bit adders side by side. Figure 2-14 shows the block diagram for this adder; Programs 2-15 and 2-17 give an APL description.

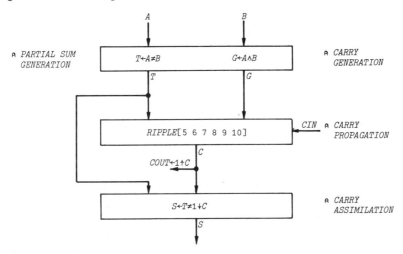

Figure 2-14   Ripple adder.

Block Diagram.   The block diagram shows that the transmission T and the generated carry G can be made in parallel. Likewise, the sum S can be determined in parallel from the transmission T and the carry C. Hence, the upper and lower blocks of the diagram consist of N independent half-adders each, where N is the number of bits of the operands, or $N \leftarrow \rho A$.

For both sets of half-adders, two logical levels are required. The center block of the diagram, which takes care of the carry propagation, is, on the other hand, a circuit of $2 \times N$ levels. Since the carry ripples, so to speak, through this circuit, the adder is called a *ripple adder*.

The block diagram matches the APL description of Program 2-17. In the upper and lower blocks the corresponding APL expressions are shown. The center block, however, has not enough space to show all expressions. Therefore reference is made to the lines of the function that contain these expressions—a practice that will also be followed in other diagrams.

Four-Bit Ripple Adder

*RIPPLE*4, Program 2-15, describes a ripple adder of 4 bits. Lines 2 and 3 show the circuits for the generated carry and the transmission. These two lines are identical to the first two lines of the bit adder *IMPBITADD*, except that the

```
      ∇ RIPPLE4
[1]     ⍝ TRANSMISSION AND GENERATION
[2]     T←A≠B
[3]     G←A∧B
[4]     ⍝ CARRY PROPAGATION
[5]     C←5⍴0
[6]     C[4]←CIN
[7]     C[3]←G[3]∨T[3]∧C[4]
[8]     C[2]←G[2]∨T[2]∧C[3]
[9]     C[1]←G[1]∨T[1]∧C[2]
[10]    C[0]←G[0]∨T[0]∧C[1]
[11]    ⍝ CARRY ASSIMILATION
[12]    S←T≠1↓C
[13]    COUT←1↑C
      ∇
```

Program 2-15 4-Bit ripple adder.

operands are now vectors of four elements each. The carry is a vector of five elements. The rightmost element is the carry-in *CIN*, and the leftmost is the carry-out *COUT*. Individual elements of the vector are indicated with the help of an index, identified by square brackets, [ ].

Index. Indexing is generally defined in APL. The value of the *index* is placed between square brackets and identifies the elements of the array. The elements are identified by giving their coordinates in each dimension. A semicolon separates the specification for the different dimensions. The coordinates are identified by numbering. The *direction* of numbering is from left to right and the *origin* of numbering used in this text is 0.

Table 2-16 gives several examples of indexing, using the arrays of Table 2-2.

```
      VECTOR                    MATRIXI                   ARRAY3
3  5  11  10  13  6          7  18  17   3   4         0   1   2
                            10   8  15  16  13         3   4   5
                             1   2   9   6   5         6   7   8
                                                       9  10  11

                                                      12  13  14
                                                      15  16  17
                                                      18  19  20
                                                      21  22  23

      VECTOR[1]                 MATRIXI[1 2;2 3]          ARRAY3[0;3;2]
5                           15  16                    11
                             9   6

      VECTOR[3 2 0]             MATRIXI[1 2;3 2]          ARRAY3[0;;2]
10  11  3                   16  15                    2  5  8  11
                             6   9

      VECTOR[4 4 4 4]           MATRIXI[2 1;3 2]          ARRAY3[;3;]
13  13  13  13               6   9                     9  10  11
                            16  15                    21  22  23
```

Table 2-16 Indexing examples.

Index Direction. The numbering of the elements in APL is from left to right. This direction corresponds with the convention followed for reading and writing in Western culture.

In the ripple adder the carry is propagated from right to left. As a consequence the value of the index of C in lines 6 through 10 of $RIPPLE4$ progresses from high to low. The direction of the carry propagation follows the increase in weight of the digits of the number representation, which is from right to left. This direction places the most important part of a number to the left. Thus, it is said first and written first. Interpreting and pronouncing 432 as "four-and-thirty-and-two hundred" has too large an element of surprise. This preference in writing numbers is also clear in the representation by Roman numerals.

As a result, there is an inherent conflict between the direction of writing and the direction in which the weight of the digits increases. Therefore, in the literature concerning arithmetic implementations, one often finds an index direction from right to left. Arithmetic, however, is only a part of data processing. The APL index convention properly follows the writing direction.

Index Origin.   The numbering of the elements starts in APL either with 0, the *zero origin*, or with 1, the *one origin*. Both origins are often applied. The zero origin more closely matches identification, the one origin, counting. Thus, the X digits belonging to a number system with base X are identified by the symbols for zero through $X - 1$. In the binary number system, these are the two symbols 0 and 1.

Since in the descriptions of implementations indexing is used primarily for identification, zero origin will be used throughout this book. Thus, an easy connection can be made between an index and the logical values, the binary digits, and, more generally, the binary codes.

Declaration of Dimension.   The five elements of vector C are made 0 in line 5. In lines 6 through 10, however, these 0s are again replaced by logical values. For the description of the ripple adder, line 5 might as well be omitted. To execute the program, however, it is desirable that the dimensions of an array are known before separate elements are defined. Thus, $RIPPLE4$ can only be simulated on a terminal if the dimensions of C are known. Line 5 serves as a *declaration* of the dimension of C such that in lines 6 through 10, values can be assigned to the elements of C. The elements of C are, in line 5, set to 0 as a matter of convention and ease. Any other combination of 0 and 1 is just as acceptable.

Drop and Take. $RIPPLE4$, line 12, demonstrates the operator *drop*, $\downarrow$. Drop eliminates the first elements of the vector upon which it operates. The value to the left of the operator determines the number of elements to be eliminated. In expression 12, this value is 1; thus, the leftmost element of C, $C[0]$, does not take part in the exclusive-or operation.

Besides the drop operator, there is the operator *take*, $\uparrow$, which selects the first elements of a vector. In $RIPPLE4$, line 13, take is used to select the leftmost element of C as the carry-out $COUT$.

When the value to the left of the drop or take operator is negative, the last elements of the vector are indicated. When drop and take are applied to arrays, the left operand must be a vector that has an element for each dimension of the array.

General Ripple Adder

When the operands of the adder have a large number of bits, or a yet-undetermined number of bits, the notation of *RIPPLE*4 is either impractical or impossible. In such a case, *RIPPLE*, Program 2-17, which is independent of the operand lengths, can be used.

```
     ∇ RIPPLE;J
[1]    ⍝ TRANSMISSION AND GENERATION
[2]    T←A≠B
[3]    G←A∧B
[4]    ⍝ CARRY PROPAGATION
[5]    J←ρT
[6]    C←(J+1)ρ0
[7]    C[J]←CIN
[8]  CONT:J←J-1
[9]    C[J]←G[J]∨T[J]∧C[J+1]
[10]   →(J≠0)/CONT
[11]   ⍝ CARRY ASSIMILATION
[12]   S←T≠1↓C
[13]   COUT←1↑C
     ∇
```

Program 2-17   Ripple adder.

Branch.   *RIPPLE* contains a simple loop that is controlled by a branch in line 10. The arrow pointing to the right, →, indicates that a *branch* must be made. The expression left of the slash, /, in line 10 is the *branch condition*. When the condition is satisfied, the branch is made to the line indicated to the right of the slash, the *branch target*. When the condition is not satisfied, no branch is executed. In the example of *RIPPLE*, line 10, the branch to line 8 will succeed if J is not zero.

Label.   The branch in line 10 does not refer directly to the target, line 8, but uses the label *CONT*. A *label* is a name used to identify an expression. The label is separated from the associated expression by a colon. The value of the label is the number of the line on which it appears, here 8. A label is always a local variable; hence, different programs may use the same name for a label.

The use of a label instead of a line number has the advantage that the label is not affected by program modification. Besides, a label can have mnemonic value, as appears from the use of *CONT* for 'continuation.'

The use of the slash in the branch expression corresponds to the more general use of the operator /. The type of expression used in line 10 will be used for most branches throughout this text. Any expression, however, which produces a line number to the right of the right-pointing arrow may be used as a branch in APL.

Index Variable.   The variable J is used as a running index variable. For each value of J a carry-propagation circuit as specified by line 9 is obtained. J is a scalar used in describing the circuit but is not a part of the circuit. Therefore, J is specified as a local variable, as indicated in the header of *RIPPLE*.

Realizable Expressions. The expressions of the previous implementation programs usually represent one circuit each. Depending on the available switching components, such an expression can be translated more or less directly to a circuit. Lines 5, 8, and 10 of *RIPPLE*, however, do not correspond to circuits. Therefore, *RIPPLE* must be transformed to a form that corresponds to *RIPPLE*4 when the dimensions of the operands are known. This transformation eliminates the index variable *J*. As a result, the loop disappears: the program is 'unrolled.' This process can be programmed if desired.

Expressions such as lines 7 and 13, which change a name, and line 6, which declares a dimension, are not realized directly because they result in trivial circuits. They do not cause any misinterpretation, however, and therefore can be retained in the circuit description.

Adder Speed. The number of levels required in the ripple adder for the transmission and generation is assumed to be 2. Once the transmission is known, the carry can be propagated. In the extreme case, a carry-in ripples through the entire adder length, requiring two levels per bit position. The carry-out is obtained simultaneously with the leftmost sum bit $S[0]$. Therefore, the maximum add time is the equivalent of $2 + 2 \times N$ levels to be passed.

Critical Path. The succession of switching elements that determine the speed of a circuit is called the *critical path* of the circuit. The preceding discussion, as illustrated in Figure 2-18, gives the critical path of the ripple adder. The critical path shows which parts of a design determine its speed. There may be more than one critical path through a circuit. In that case they all have the same length.

Critical Case. The operand combinations that require the use of the critical path will be called *critical cases*. In the ripple adder, the critical path requires that the carry-in and each bit of the transmission be 1. In terms of the operands there are many critical cases; in terms of the transmission, however, there is only one critical case.

When a designer wants to improve the speed of an implementation, he must make the critical path faster. He may do so by concentrating on the circuits of this path, and keeping the critical cases the same. The remaining adder types in this section are based on this approach. The designer can, however, also modify his design such that more parts of the design are involved in the critical path. Thus the critical path is made wider and the number of critical cases increases. Later sections will show that this approach is more effective than just speeding up the critical path.

Adder Application. An example of the use of a straight ripple adder is the 16-bit adder of the DEC PDP11/20. The emphasis in this design was on low cost and minimal space requirements. The ripple adder is available in various building blocks, such as the 4-bit TI SN7483, which is equivalent to *RIPPLE*4 (Morris and Miller, 1971).

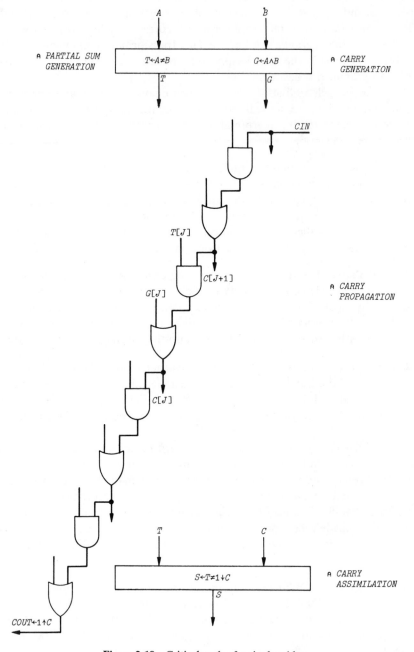

Figure 2-18 Critical path of a ripple adder.

Accelerated Ripple Adder

The critical path of the ripple adder shows that the hardware is not used optimally. The speed is almost entirely dependent upon the carry propagation, while the circuits for T, G, and S are almost completely outside the critical path. Thus, only about two of the nine nands per bit position are used in the critical path.

The critical path shows that a local speed-up, which accelerates the bit adder from four to two levels, is not a solution; it merely reduces the add time from $2 + 2 \times N$ to $2 \times N$ level times. It is worthwhile, therefore, to give special attention to the carry-propagation circuit.

The carry propagation time can be halved by using one rather than two components in the critical propagation path (Quatse and Keir, 1967). Figure 2-19 and *RIPONE*4, Program 2-20, describe such an adder. Since the basic structure of the ripple adder is preserved, the circuit is called an *accelerated ripple adder*.

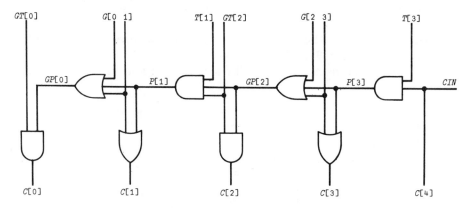

Figure 2-19   Accelerated ripple propagation.

```
          ∇ RIPONE4
    [1]     ⋀ TRANSMISSION AND GENERATION
    [2]     T←A≠B
    [3]     G←A∧B
    [4]     ⋀ CARRY PROPAGATION
    [5]     C←5ρ0
    [6]     P←4ρ0
    [7]     GP←4ρ0
    [8]     GT←4ρ0
    [9]     C[4]←CIN
    [10]    P[3]←T[3]∧CIN
    [11]    C[3]←G[3]∨P[3]
    [12]    GP[2]←G[2]∨G[3]∨P[3]
    [13]    GT[2]←G[2]∨T[2]
    [14]    C[2]←GT[2]∧GP[2]
    [15]    P[1]←T[1]∧GT[2]∧GP[2]
    [16]    C[1]←G[1]∨P[1]
    [17]    GP[0]←G[0]∨G[1]∨P[1]
    [18]    GT[0]←G[0]∨T[0]
    [19]    C[0]←GT[0]∧GP[0]
    [20]    ⋀ CARRY ASSIMILATION
    [21]    S←T≠1↓C
    [22]    COUT←1↑C
          ∇
```

Program 2-20   4-Bit accelerated ripple adder.

Redundant Encoding.   In *RIPONE*4 the carry is encoded as two signals. Out of the odd bit positions, these signals are the generated carry *G* and the propagated carry *P*. Out of the even bit positions, the carry is represented by the signals *GT* and *GP*. *GT* is the 'or' of generation and transmission and *GP* the 'or' of generation and propagated carry. The actual carry is obtained for the odd bit positions by taking the 'or' of *G* and *P*, as usual, as shown in lines 11 and 16. For the even bit positions, the 'and' of *GT* and *GP* is taken, as shown in lines 14 and 19. These 'or' and 'and' circuits are not in the critical path, however, as illustrated in Figure 2-19.

The representation of one signal, such as *C*, by two or more signals, such as *G* and *P*, or *GT* and *GP*, is called a *redundant encoding*. The term 'redundant' emphasizes the fact that more signals are used than are strictly necessary.

Adder Speed and Cost.   Since the critical path for the carry propagation has been reduced to one level per bit position, the maximum add time amounts to $4 + N$ level times. The number of nands is increased from 9 to 10 per bit position.

Adder Application.   The accelerated ripple adder has been used in the Electrologica X1 computer (1957). The redundant encoding of the carry, demonstrated here for the ripple adder, can also be applied to the adders described in Sections 2-10 and 2-13.

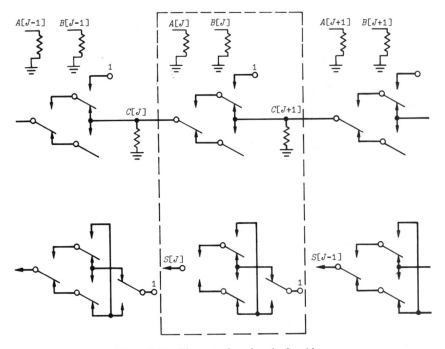

Figure 2-21   Element of a relay ripple adder.

Kilburn Adder

The ripple adder can also be accelerated by the use of fast components for the carry propagation. Kilburn et al. (1959) proposed to use saturated transistors with very fast switching times in the carry progagation circuit (see also Salter, 1960).

Relay Ripple Adder

The Kilburn adder can be illustrated by a relay circuit. In a relay, the current passes very rapidly through the contacts, in contrast to the speed with which the relay coil becomes energized or deenergized. Figure 2-21 shows part of a ripple adder built with relays. The carry passes through the circuit from right to left and is, in fact, determined at the moment the relays for A and B are energized.

The relay adder of Figure 2-21 uses three relay coils and seven sets of relay contacts per bit position. The speed of this adder is determined by the time required for the energizing of the relays for A and B, followed by the energizing of the carry relays C. The carry relays are effectively energized, or deenergized, in parallel.

The parallel determination of the carry was also a design feature of Babbage's mechanical adder in his Analytical Engine of 1867 (Randell, 1973, p. 29).

2-7 TABLE-LOOK-UP ADDER

When only a small number of bits is added in parallel, it is attractive to eliminate the adder completely, as is done in the table-look-up adder. The *table-look-up adder* uses a table in storage which contains the sum and carry-out for each value of the operands and the carry-in. Figure 2-22 and *TLUADD*, Program 2-23, illustrate this type adder.

The two operands and the carry-in are joined to form the argument of the table. The location in storage of the addition table is given by the vector *ADDTAB*. *ADDTAB*, concatenated with the argument, is interpreted and used as a storage address in reading the sum and carry-out. A part of the storage contents is illustrated in Table 2-24.

Catenation. The joining of *ADDTAB*, A, B, and *CIN* in line 1 of *TLUADD* is expressed by commas. The comma is used in APL as the *catenation* operator. This dyadic operator unites its operands in one result. Thus, if *ADDTAB*, A, B, and *CIN* are vectors with 6, 4, 4, and 1 element, respectively, the result of the catenation is a vector of 15 elements.

Adder Speed and Cost. The speed of the table-look-up adder is determined by the storage that contains the table. This store can also contain other data, thus reducing the cost per bit. For instance, the results of other operations can be placed

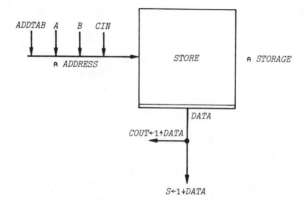

Figure 2-22 Table-look-up adder.

```
     ∇ TLUADD
[1]    DATA←STORE[2⊥ADDTAB,A,B,CIN;]
[2]    S←1↓DATA
[3]    COUT←1↑DATA
     ∇
```

Program 2-23 Table-look-up adder.

ADDRESS									STORE				
A	A	A	A	B	B	B	B	CIN	COUT	S	S	S	S
0	0	0	1	1	1	0	0	0	0	1	1	0	1
0	0	0	1	1	1	0	0	1	0	1	1	1	0
0	0	0	1	1	1	0	1	0	0	1	1	1	0
0	0	0	1	1	1	0	1	1	0	1	1	1	1
0	0	0	1	1	1	1	0	0	0	1	1	1	1
0	0	0	1	1	1	1	0	1	1	0	0	0	0
0	0	0	1	1	1	1	1	0	1	0	0	0	0
0	0	0	1	1	1	1	1	1	1	0	0	0	1
0	0	1	0	0	0	0	0	0	0	0	0	1	0
0	0	1	0	0	0	0	0	1	0	0	0	1	1
0	0	1	0	0	0	0	1	0	0	0	0	1	1
0	0	1	0	0	0	0	1	1	0	0	1	0	0

Table 2-24 Partial storage content for table-look-up adder.

in storage besides the sum and carry-out. Since the contents of the store remain unchanged, a read-only technology can be used.

The disadvantage of the table-look-up adder is the extent of the table. For an adder of N bits, $2 * 1 + 2 \times N$ (APL notation) locations of $N + 1$ bits each are required. Because of this, the cost of the adder, even in an inexpensive storage realization, quickly becomes larger than that of a logical circuit. For N equal to 4, a total of 512×5, or 2560, storage bits are needed. A simple parallel adder requires 4×9, or 36, nands. A nand may thus be 70 times as expensive as a storage bit and only needs to be 10 times faster than a storage cycle. A read-only store is still competitive here; as N increases this no longer is possible.

Adder Application.   The table-look-up adder is much used in pocket calculators, which tend to have a 4-bit-wide series–parallel organization for decimal arithmetic. An example of a large computer using the table-look-up approach is the decimal adder of the System/370 Model 168.

Replacing Logic with Storage. The use of storage instead of logical circuits, as illustrated by the table-look-up adder, is an important implementation technique. As storage becomes less expensive in relation to logical circuits, it finds more and more application.

2-8 CARRY-PREDICT ADDER

The optimum in speed is the adder that is built entirely in two levels. Since the number of components of an adder with N bit positions increases by at least $2 * N + 2$, this is only acceptable for N equal to 1, 2, or 3. Moreover, as soon as the *fan-in* or *fan-out* of the switching elements (Apprendix D-5) is exceeded for large N, the number of levels becomes larger than two, anyway.

For a proper evaluation of the efficiency of a parallel adder, the number of components should be weighed against the maximum number of successive levels for a given fan-in and fan-out of the components. The carry-predict, carry-look-ahead, or simultaneous-carry, adder (Weinberger, 1956) is an example of such a fast adder, as are the adders to be discussed in Sections 2-9, 2-10, and 2-11.

As the name suggests, the *carry-predict adder* tries to accelerate the source of the parallel adder's slowness: the carry propagation. Only the carry-propagation part is reduced to two levels, instead of attempting this for the entire adder.

Four-Bit Carry-Predict Adder

Figure 2-25 gives the block diagram for a 4-bit carry-predict adder. A comparison with the ripple adder of Figure 2-14 shows that only the carry propagation is different.

In the expression for $C[2]$ of *RIPPLE*4, Program 2-15, the expression for $C[3]$, shown in line 7, can be substituted. Also, it may be noted that $C[4]$ is the carry-in *CIN*. Thus, line 5 of the carry-predict function *PRED*5, Program 2-26, is obtained. The new expression for $C[2]$, in turn, can be substituted in the expression for $C[1]$, and this process can be continued for $C[0]$. The carry vector C is thus obtained as a two-level function *PRED*5 of the generated carry G, the transmission T, and the carry-in *CIN*. *PREDICT*4, Program 2-26, shows the application of *PRED*5 in a 4-bit adder of six levels.

Forms of Functions. The function *PRED*5 is defined in Program 2-26 as a function of the variables G and T. In the functions introduced to this point, there were no variables explicitly mentioned in the function header.

In APL it is possible to mention zero, one, or two arguments and zero or one result in the function definition. This makes it possible to use a function as

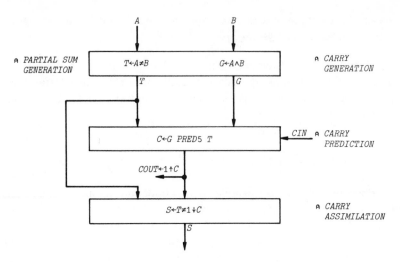

Figure 2-25   Carry-predict adder.

a monadic or dyadic operator. Thus, the monadic forms *FUNCTION X* and *Z←FUNCTION X* and the dyadic forms *X FUNCTION Y* and *Z←X FUNCTION Y* are possible. The last form is used for *PRED5*.

In principle, functions of three or more variables could also be defined. The present version of APL, however, limits itself to the function forms that correspond to the forms of the APL operators. Besides the local variables mentioned in the function header, global variables can, of course, be used in the function, such as the carry-in *CIN* in the function *PRED5*.

Defined and Primitive Functions.   The term 'function' has been used for the functions that are introduced by the programmer. Such a function, however, is not basically different from the monadic or dyadic operators that are implemented in APL. Hence, the term 'function' is applied to these operators as well. The functions introduced by the programmer are then called *defined functions*, while the functions available as operators are called *primitive functions*. For convenience of expression, the terms 'operator' and 'function' will be used in this text, however.

Passing By Value and By Name.   A calling function such as *PREDICT4* passes the value of its operands—not the names of its operands—to a subfunction, such as *PRED5*. Similarly, the value of the result is passed to the calling function. Passing *by value* exclusively and not *by name* is a restriction of the current APL\360 definition, which will be observed here, although later extensions eliminate it.

The header of *PRED5* has the same appearance as line 5 of *PREDICT4*. This is not a requirement. The expression could also have been $Z \leftarrow X PRED5 Y$, with *X*, *Y*, and *Z* correspondingly used in lines 2 through 7 of *PRED5*. The letters *C*, *G*, and *T* were chosen, however, to allow easy recognition of the carry, generation, and transmission.

```
       ∇ PREDICT4
[1]    ⍝ TRANSMISSION AND GENERATION
[2]    T←A≠B
[3]    G←A∧B
[4]    ⍝ CARRY PREDICTION
[5]    C←G PRED5 T
[6]    ⍝ CARRY ASSIMILATION
[7]    S←T≠1↓C
[8]    COUT←1↑C
       ∇
```

```
       ∇ C←G PRED5 T
[1]    ⍝ 5-BIT CARRY PREDICTION
[2]    C←5⍴0
[3]    C[4]←CIN
[4]    C[3]←G[3]∨T[3]∧CIN
[5]    C[2]←G[2]∨(T[2]∧G[3])∨T[2]∧T[3]∧CIN
[6]    C[1]←G[1]∨(T[1]∧G[2])∨(T[1]∧T[2]∧G[3])∨T[1]∧T[2]∧T[3]∧CIN
[7]    C[0]←G[0]∨(T[0]∧G[1])∨(T[0]∧T[1]∧G[2])∨(T[0]∧T[1]∧T[2]∧G[3])∨T[0]∧T[1]∧T[2]∧T[3]∧CIN
       ∇
```

Program 2-26   4-Bit carry-predict adder.

Adder Speed and Cost.   The carry-predict adder of Figure 2-25 requires 46 nands, which is 28% more nands than for a 4-bit ripple adder. The time gain amounts to 40%.

2-9 GROUPED CARRY PREDICTION

For an adder with a width of a few score bits, a single carry prediction is no longer realistic. It is possible, however, to apply the prediction principle to groups of operand bits. For this purpose, the operands are divided into groups, which can be considered as digits in a higher number system. The transmission and generation are now determined for each group, and from these a group carry can be found. The group carry, in turn, is used to find the individual carries.

100-Bit Carry-Predict Adder

The adder *PREDICT*100, Figure 2-27 and Program 2-28, is an example of a 100-bit carry-predict adder divided into 20 groups of five bits, which in turn are combined into four groups of 25 bits (MacSorley, 1961).

Group Transmission.   In the expressions 2 and 3 of *PREDICT*100, the individual transmission and generation for each of the 100 bit positions are again formed. They are, however, considered as 20 groups of five signals, thus, 20 digits in the base 32 number system.

A *group transmission* is 1 when a carry entering the group also leaves the group. This is the case if the transmission is 1 for each element of the group. Therefore, in line 5 of *PREDICT*100, the elements of a row are combined with an 'and' condition to a single element. This is expressed by the 'and' operator followed by the reduction operator, /.

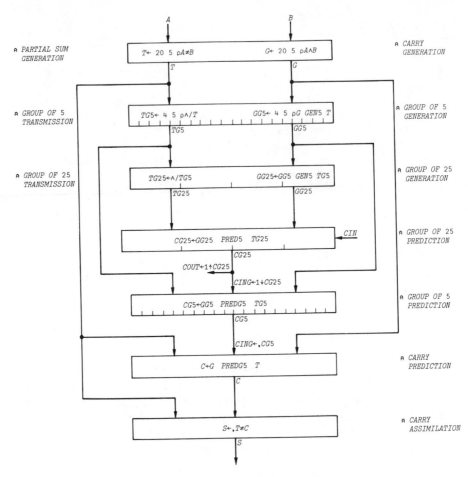

Figure 2-27 Carry-predict adder using groups of five.

Reduction.   The slash, /, is used here for the first time as the reduction operator. In general, the *reduction* operator has to its left a dyadic operator, here ∧. The effect of this combination of operators is the same as if the dyadic operator were placed between all the elements in the row of the matrix. The operation subsequently takes place, from right to left, as usual.

Reduction is a generalization of the well-known repeated addition and multiplication represented by the symbols Σ and Π. It yields a notation that is almost as compact as these symbols but is not limited to addition and multiplication.

In expression 5 of *PREDICT*100, the 'and' is applied to each of the 20 rows of five signals. This yields 20 signals grouped as a vector with dimension 20. In the same expression, this vector is again converted into an array with four rows of five elements each

```
     ∇ PREDICT100
[1]    ⍝ TRANSMISSION AND GENERATION
[2]    T← 20 5 ρA≠B
[3]    G← 20 5 ρA∧B
[4]    ⍝ TRANSMISSION AND GENERATION FOR GROUPS OF 5
[5]    TG5← 4 5 ρ∧/T
[6]    GG5← 4 5 ρG GEN5 T
[7]    ⍝ TRANSMISSION AND GENERATION FOR GROUPS OF 25
[8]    TG25←∧/TG5
[9]    GG25←GG5 GEN5 TG5
[10]   ⍝ CARRY PREDICTION FOR GROUPS OF 25
[11]   CG25←GG25 PRED5 TG25
[12]   COUT←1↑CG25
[13]   ⍝ CARRY PREDICTION FOR GROUPS OF 5
[14]   CING5←1↓CG25
[15]   CG5←GG5 PREDG5 TG5
[16]   ⍝ CARRY PREDICTION
[17]   CING5←,CG5
[18]   C←G PREDG5 T
[19]   ⍝ CARRY ASSIMILATION
[20]   S←,T≠C
     ∇


     ∇ GG5←G GEN5 T
[1]    ⍝ GENERATED CARRY FOR GROUPS OF 5
[2]    GG5←G[;0]∨(T[;0]∧G[;1])∨(∧/T[; 0 1],G[;2])∨(∧/T[; 0 1 2],G[;3])∨∧/T[; 0 1 2 3],G[;4]
     ∇


     ∇ C←G PRED5 T
[1]    ⍝ 5-BIT CARRY PREDICTION
[2]    C←5ρ0
[3]    C[4]←CIN
[4]    C[3]←G[3]∨T[3]∧CIN
[5]    C[2]←G[2]∨(T[2]∧G[3])∨T[2]∧T[3]∧CIN
[6]    C[1]←G[1]∨(T[1]∧G[2])∨(T[1]∧T[2]∧G[3])∨T[1]∧T[2]∧T[3]∧CIN
[7]    C[0]←G[0]∨(T[0]∧G[1])∨(T[0]∧T[1]∧G[2])∨(T[0]∧T[1]∧T[2]∧G[3])∨T[0]∧T[1]∧T[2]∧T[3]∧CIN
     ∇

     ⍝ REFERENCE:                                PROGRAM:
     ⍝ PRED5      5-BIT CARRY PREDICTION             2-26
```

Program 2-28   Carry-predict adder using groups of five.

Group Generation. A *group generation* is 1 when a carry is generated within a group, which leaves the group as a carry-out. In expression 6 of *PREDICT*100, the group generation for the 20 groups of five bit positions is determined by the function *GEN5*.

The indexing used by *GEN5* specifies only one dimension of an array with two dimensions. The location of the semicolon indicates that the lowest dimension is indexed while the higher dimension is complete. $G[$; 0$]$ is thus a vector with dimension 20, which contains the leftmost element from each row of the original array. In line 6 the vector that results from the function *GEN5* is again converted into an array with dimension 4 5 by the reshape operator ρ.

Figure 2-27 shows that the reduction of the transmission and generation signals from 100 to 20 is followed by a reduction from 20 to 4 by means of the same type of circuits. In *PREDICT*100 this is indicated in lines 8 and 9.

Group Carry. A carry prediction circuit is used to determine *CG*25, the carry-out of each group of 25 bits, from the group transmission and generation. The carry-out of a given group is, of course, the carry-in of the following group. Line 11 of *PREDICT*100 indicates that the function *PRED*5 of Program 2-26 is used for this purpose.

Carry-out.   The carry-out *COUT* is determined in line 12 of *PREDICT*100 as part of the output of the prediction circuit. Since the carry is used in some applications to control the action of the arithmetic unit, it may be attractive to have it available well before the end of the addition. If it is not necessary to have the carry available so early, *CG*25[0] can be made from *CG*25[1] and hence becomes available at lower cost two levels later.

Carry and Sum.   Figure 2-27 and *PREDICT*100, line 15, show that the next two levels determine the carry, *CG*5, which passes between groups of five. The following circuit, line 18, determines the carry *C* for each bit position. Finally, the sum is obtained in line 20 from this carry. Each of these circuits again requires two levels.

Ravel.   As a dyadic operator, the comma performs the function of catenation. The functions *GEN*5 and *PREDG*5 show that this operator can also be applied to matrices. In lines 17 and 20 of *PREDICT*100, the comma is used monadically, however. This operator indicates that the array to which it refers is *raveled* to a vector. The elements of the array are, from low to high, used as the elements of a vector, from left to right. For line 20 this means that the matrix determined by $T \neq C$ is converted to a vector of 100 elements.

Demonstration of Adder Action.   An example of the action of *PREDICT*100 is given in Table 2-29. Table 2-29 uses the function *PRINT* to obtain a compact representation of the vectors and matrices. The normal presentation of an array has spaces between the elements to identify each separately. The compact representation is more attractive when each element is known to be either 0 or 1. The function *PRINT* will be explained in Section 2-15.

Adder Speed and Cost.   *PREDICT*100 uses a total of 14 levels instead of the 202 of the ripple adder. The number of switching elements, however, has increased from 900 to 1318 nands. When the adder is reorganized, so that grouping becomes 5 5 4 instead of 4 5 5, this count can be reduced somewhat. The original organization, however, uses the same circuits in all levels, which in itself may represent a cost reduction.

Adder Application.   The grouped carry-prediction adder is widely used when large numbers of bits must be added. Thus, the CDC 6600 uses this principle for its 60-bit integer adder, with a grouping high to low of 5 4 3, and for its floating-point adder, with a grouping 6 3 3 2 (Thornton, 1970).

Other examples of carry prediction are the 60-bit floating-point adder of the DEC PDP11/45, which uses a grouping of 4 4 4, and the 32-bit integer adder of the System/370 Model 158, with a grouping of 2 4 4.

```
    PRINT A
010100010100001101100011100000011010001100110001110011111010110111111011010101001101111011001001111
    PRINT B
110110011011110010011100011111001011100110011100011000001010010000001000011110000010110011110001011
    CIN
0
    PREDICT100

    PRINT S
001010110000000000000000000000000000000000000000000000000000000000000000000001111001101000011000101011001000010110010
```

PRINT G	PRINT T	PRINT GG5	PRINT CG5	PRINT C
01010	10001	10000	01111	10100
00100	00011	00000	11111	01111
00000	11111	00010	11101	11111
00000	11111	10110	01100	11111
00000	11111			11111
00000	11111	PRINT TG5		11111
00000	11111	00111		11111
00000	11111	11111		11111
00000	11111	11100		11111
00000	11111	00000		11111
00000	11111			11111
00000	11111	PRINT GG25		11111
00000	11111	1011		11111
00001	11110			11110
00001	01100	PRINT TG25		00011
01000	10110	0100		10000
00000	01111			11111
11000	00111	PRINT CG25	COUT	11111
11000	00101	11110	1	10000
00011	01100			11110

Table 2-29   Example of carry-predict addition.

The carry prediction circuit is available as a circuit component, such as the TI SN74182. This component is intended for groups of 4 bits and includes a group generation and transmission circuit, to be used for multiple levels of prediction.

Verification of the Adder Design. The next sections will describe several alternatives and refinements of the adder types described so far. For a first pass, the reader may, however, wish to skip these and proceed directly to Section 2-15, on circuit verification.

2-10 CARRY-SKIP ADDER

The time gain of the carry-predict adder over the ripple adder is notable. Yet in the example of Section 2-9 the carry prediction requires an extra investment in circuits of nearly 50%. It is meaningful, therefore, to determine which of these circuits contributes most to the time gain; perhaps a more modest investment still yields an efficient design.

The three main functions used in the grouped carry-predict adder are the group transmission, $\wedge /$; the group generation, $GEN5$; and the carry prediction, $PRED5$ and $PREDG5$. Of these, the group transmission is the least expensive. When only this function is used, the *carry-skip adder*, illustrated in Figure 2-30 and $SKIP100$, Program 2-31, results.

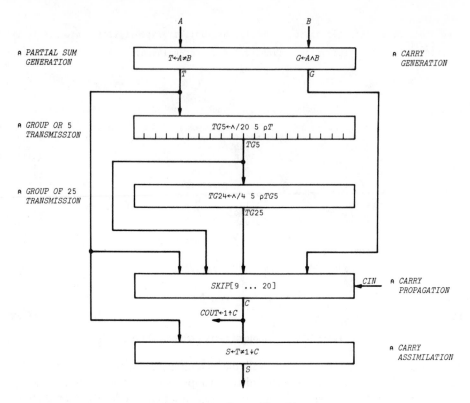

Figure 2-30 Carry-skip adder.

```
      ∇ SKIP100;J
[1]    ⍝ TRANSMISSION AND GENERATION
[2]    T←A≠B
[3]    G←A∧B
[4]    ⍝ TRANSMISSION FOR GROUPS OF 5
[5]    TG5←∧/ 20 5 ⍴T
[6]    ⍝ TRANSMISSION FOR GROUPS OF 25
[7]    TG25←∧/ 4 5 ⍴TG5
[8]    ⍝ CARRY PROPAGATION
[9]    J←⍴T
[10]   C←(J+1)⍴0
[11]   C[J]←CIN
[12] CONT:J←J-1
[13]   →(0=5|J)/GROUP5
[14]   C[J]←G[J]∨T[J]∧C[J+1]
[15]   →CONT
[16] GROUP5:→(0=25|J)/GROUP25
[17]   C[J]←G[J]∨(T[J]∧C[J+1])∨TG5[J÷5]∧C[J+5]
[18]   →CONT
[19] GROUP25:C[J]←G[J]∨(T[J]∧C[J+1])∨(TG5[J÷5]∧C[J+5])∨TG25[J÷25]∧C[J+25]
[20]   →(J≠0)/CONT
[21]   ⍝ CARRY ASSIMILATION
[22]   S←T≠1↓C
[23]   COUT←1↑C
      ∇
```

Program 2-31 Carry-skip adder.

100-Bit Carry-Skip Adder

*SKIP*100 is an extension of *RIPPLE*, Program 2-17. A group transmission is superimposed on the ripple propagation of the carry. The group transmission causes the carry to skip quickly over long propagation series. The group transmission does not replace the normal carry propagation, as in *PREDICT*100, but makes the result of the propagation, per group, known earlier. The group propagation and the ripple propagation are combined by an 'or' and so form the carry-in for the following group.

Residue.   Line 13 of *SKIP*100 checks to see if the end of a group of 5 is reached. This line uses the *residue* operator to find the residue modulo 5 of J. The result is thus equal to the positive remainder of J divided by 5. Similarly, in line 16, the end of a group of 25 is found. Lines 17 and 19 illustrate once again that an index value can be determined by an expression.

Critical Path.   The critical path of the carry-skip adder is formed by the carry generation of the rightmost bit, followed by the carry propagation into the leftmost bit. Therefore, for a critical case $G[99]$ is 1 and $T[1]$ through $T[98]$ are 1. This case is illustrated in Table 2-32.

```
      PRINT A
0010110110101111000001011001111010100000100011010110011101110101000110100001001010011001001011011
      PRINT B
0101001001010000111110100110000010101111011100101000110001000101011100101111011010110001101101 00101
      CIN
0
      SKIP100

      PRINT G
0000000000000000000000000000000000000000000000000000000000000000000000000000000000000000000000001
      PRINT T
0111111111111111111111111111111111111111111111111111111111111111111111111111111111111111111111110
      PRINT TG5
0111111111111111111110
      PRINT TG25
0110
      PRINT C
0111111111111111111111111111111111111111111111111111111111111111111111111111111111111111111111110
      PRINT S
1000000000000000000000000000000000000000000000000000000000000000000000000000000000000000000000000000
      COUT
0
```

Table 2-32   Example of carry-skip addition.

Adder Speed.   For the critical case, the generated carry of the low-order bit must pass eight levels before it emerges from the rightmost group of 5 bits as a group carry. Subsequently, it is transmitted over four groups of 5 bits to come out of the first group of 25 bits, which once again involves eight levels. Next, it passes two groups of 25 bits and four groups of 5, involving four and eight levels, respectively, to enter the leftmost group of 5. Finally, it passes through four bit positions in this last group, which involves another eight levels. If one includes the four levels for the original generation and the ultimate sum, a total of 40 levels is passed.

Adder Cost.   The number of switching elements used in *SKIP*100 is 972 nands. Therefore, 8% in cost makes the carry-skip adder five times faster than the ripple adder. On the other hand, the carry-predict adder is yet again three times faster, but it requires considerably higher costs.

Skip Length

In the given example, the length, in bits, of the carry skips is constrained by a maximum fan-in of 5. Moreover, skips over skips are used. Lehman has determined the best skip length for an adder of N bits with only one level of skips (Lehman and Burla, 1961). If the adder uses K groups of L bits each, the critical path has $4 + 2 \times ((K - 2) + 2 \times (L - 1))$ levels. Since N is $K \times L$, a minimum is reached for K equal to $(2 \times N) * 0.5$. A 100-bit adder, thus, would use 14 skips of about 7 bits each. The critical path for such an adder has 52 levels.

A shorter critical path can be obtained by using groups of different lengths. Lehman proposes to decrease the group size by 1 bit starting at the middle of the adder and proceeding toward the leftmost and rightmost ends. Thus, the distribution 5 6 7 8 9 10 10 9 8 7 6 5 gives a critical path of 42 levels. The carry strings that begin in bit position 64, 73, 81, 88, 94, or 99 and end in bit position 0, 5, 11, 18, 26, or 35 all pass through 42 levels. Therefore, the number of critical cases has increased markedly and the critical path has widened. As stated before, such a wide path is an indication of a more balanced design. The variable skip length, however, gives a less orderly adder structure and is not used much, therefore.

2-11 CARRY-SELECT ADDER

Upon inspection of a critical path the designer may note that some signals arrive earlier at a given point in the path than others. The early signals must wait, so to speak, for the later ones. Having noted this, the designer may attempt to adjust the design.

(a) The late signals may be made earlier by trading equipment against time. This has been the main approach described so far.
(b) The early signals may be made more in series, using a smaller number of components, thus trading the available time against equipment.
(c) The early signals may be put to use more profitably, often at the expense of added equipment, so that the number of remaining levels is reduced.

The first and second approaches optimize the existing critical path. The third approach often revamps the entire path.

Less-Expensive Prediction.   An inspection of *PREDICT*100, Program 2-28, shows that all inputs to the circuits up to and including level 8, line 12, are recent. The only exception, the carry-in *CIN*, does not seem very promising. In line 15, levels 9 and 10, however, the group carry $CG5$ is made by $PREDG5$ on the basis of the recent carry $CG25$ combined with the generation $GG5$ and transmission $TG5$, which are available as early as level 4. Method (b) mentioned above now results in the more economical function $PREDS5$ shown in Program 2-34.

$PREDS5$ uses the available time to propagate the generated carries in series. This modification gains 12 nands over $PREDG5$. When applied systematically in $PREDICT100$, the number of components reduces from 1318 to 1236.

100-Bit Carry-Select Adder

For levels 11 and 12 of $PREDICT100$, the same observation can be made as for levels 9 and 10. Here, the transmission T and generation G are already available on level 2. In $SELECT100$, Program 2-34 and Figure 2-33, however, the third of the methods mentioned above is applied by making use of the carry select, or conditional sum, principle (Sklansky, 1960).

In the *carry-select adder*, two sums are developed during the carry prediction. One sum assumes that the carry into the group is 0, the other that this carry is 1. Subsequently, the predicted group carry is used to choose between these two sums. Figure 2-33 and $SELECT100$, Program 2-34, illustrate the carry-select adder and the reduced prediction circuit $PREDS5$ (Bedrij, 1962).

Advance Preparation of Sums. For each group of 5 operand bits, the sum is formed with the carry-in equal to 1 in the function $SUMYES$ and with the carry-in equal to 0 in the function $SUMNO$. Since the group carry-in, $CG5$, which selects between $SUMYES$ and $SUMNO$ is known only at level 10, these adders can be built in 10 levels. Two of these levels are needed for carry generation and transmission and again two for carry assimilation, so that six levels remain for the carry propagation. With the carry-in known as 0 or as 1, the first carry circuit can be simplified, as indicated in line 3 of both functions. For the remaining bit positions a ripple propagation is used, as shown in lines 4, 5, and 6.

Selection of the Sum. In levels 11 and 12 of $SELECT100$, a choice is now made between the two sums SY and SN, based on the group carry $CG5$. Line 20 shows this selection. Each of the 20 elements of $CG5$ must be used five times directly and five times inverted. For this purpose, in line 20, the vector $CG5$ is first extended to an array $CG5$ with five identical rows. Thereafter, the rows and columns are interchanged by means of the transpose operator. Similarly the inverse of $CG5$ is extended to a 20 by 5 matrix.

Transpose. The *transpose* operator $\lozenge$ interchanges the last two coordinates of an array. As a result, the array not only takes on another form, as with the dyadic operator ρ, but the elements of the array also get a different sequence. Thus, a matrix is reflected with respect to the main diagonal. A more general dyadic use of the transpose operator is described in the APL literature (Pakin, 1972).

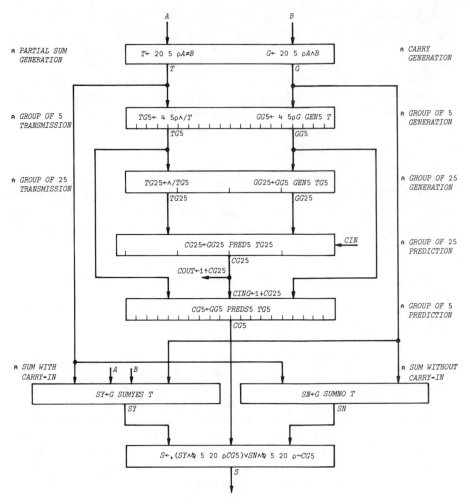

Figure 2-33 Carry-select adder.

    The extended matrix $CG5$ is combined with the sum matrix SY in line 20 by an 'and' operator. Correspondingly, the sum matrix SN is combined with not-$CG5$, after which the 'or' of both results is finally raveled to a vector of 100 elements.

    An example of a carry-select addition is shown in Table 2-35.

    Adder Speed and Cost.   The 12 levels of the carry-select adder require 1986 nands. Compared with the carry-predict adder, the number of levels is reduced by two at the expense of 50% more components. The adder is a good illustration of the law of diminishing returns.

    Adder Application.   The principle of carry selection can also be combined with other adder types. Thus, the System/370 Model 168 uses in its decimal arithmetic

```
      ∇ SELECT100
[1]   ⍝ TRANSMISSION AND GENERATION
[2]   T← 20 5 ρA≠B
[3]   G← 20 5 ρA∧B
[4]   ⍝ TRANSMISSION AND GENERATION FOR GROUPS OF 5
[5]   TG5← 4 5 ρ∧/T
[6]   GG5← 4 5 ρG GEN5 T
[7]   ⍝ TRANSMISSION AND GENERATION FOR GROUPS OF 25
[8]   TG25←∧/TG5
[9]   GG25←GG5 GEN5 TG5
[10]  ⍝ CARRY PREDICTION FOR GROUPS OF 25
[11]  CG25←GG25 PRED5 TG25
[12]  COUT←1↑CG25
[13]  ⍝ CARRY PREDICTION FOR GROUPS OF 5
[14]  CING5←1↓CG25
[15]  CG5←GG5 PREDS5 TG5
[16]  ⍝ SUM FOR CARRY-IN OF 1 AND 0
[17]  SY←G SUMYES T
[18]  SN←G SUMNO T
[19]  ⍝ SUM SELECTION
[20]  S←,(SY∧⍉ 5 20 ρCG5)∨SN∧⍉ 5 20 ρ~CG5
      ∇
```

```
      ∇ S←G SUMYES T                                   ∇ S←G SUMNO T
[1]   ⍝ 1-CARRY PROPAGATION FOR GROUPS OF 5     [1]   ⍝ 0-CARRY PROPAGATION FOR GROUPS OF 5
[2]   CY← 20 5 ρ1                                [2]   CN← 20 5 ρ0
[3]   CY[;3]←(20 5 ρA)[;4]∨(20 5 ρB)[;4]         [3]   CN[;3]←G[;4]
[4]   CY[;2]←G[;3]∨T[;3]∧CY[;3]                  [4]   CN[;2]←G[;3]∨T[;3]∧CN[;3]
[5]   CY[;1]←G[;2]∨T[;2]∧CY[;2]                  [5]   CN[;1]←G[;2]∨T[;2]∧CN[;2]
[6]   CY[;0]←G[;1]∨T[;1]∧CY[;1]                  [6]   CN[;0]←G[;1]∨T[;1]∧CN[;1]
[7]   ⍝ CARRY ASSIMILATION FOR GROUPS OF 5       [7]   ⍝ CARRY ASSIMILATION FOR GROUPS OF 5
[8]   S←T≠CY                                     [8]   S←T≠CN
      ∇                                                ∇
```

```
      ∇ C←G PREDS5 T
[1]   ⍝ SLOW CARRY PREDICTION FOR GROUPS OF 5
[2]   C←(ρT)ρ0
[3]   C[;4]←CING5
[4]   C[;3]←G[;4]∨T[;4]∧CING5
[5]   C[;2]←G[;3]∨(T[;3]∧G[;4])∨∧/T[; 3 4],CING5
[6]   C[;1]←G[;2]∨(T[;2]∧C[;2])∨∧/T[; 2 3 4],CING5
[7]   C[;0]←G[;1]∨(T[;1]∧C[;1])∨∧/T[; 1 2 3 4],CING5
      ∇
```

```
      ⍝ REFERENCE:                                         PROGRAM:
      ⍝ GEN5      GENERATED CARRY FOR GROUPS OF 5          2-28
      ⍝ PRED5     5-BIT CARRY PREDICTION                   2-26
```

Program 2-34 Carry-select adder.

```
      PRINT A
010100010100001101100011100000011010001100110001110011111010110111111101101010100110111111011001001 1 1
      PRINT B
110110110111110010011100011111100101110011001110001100000101001000000100001111000001011001111000010 1 1
      CIN
1
      SELECT100

      PRINT S
0010101100000000000000000000000000000000000000000000000000000000000000000001111001101000011000101011001 1
```

PRINT G	PRINT T	PRINT GG5	PRINT CG5	PRINT SY	PRINT SN
01010	10001	10000	01111	00110	00101
00100	00011	00000	11111	01100	01011
00000	11111	00010	11101	00000	11111
00000	11111	10110	01101	00000	11111
00000	11111			00000	11111
00000	11111	PRINT TG5		00000	11111
00000	11111	00111		00000	11111
00000	11111	11111		00000	11111
00000	11111	11100		00000	11111
00000	11111	00000		00000	11111
00000	11111			00000	11111
00000	11111	PRINT GG25		00000	11111
00000	11111	1011		00000	11111
00001	11110			00001	00000
00001	01100	PRINT TG25		01111	01100
01000	10110	0100		00111	00110
00000	01111			10000	01111
11000	00111	PRINT CG25	COUT	11000	10111
11000	00101	11111	1	10110	10101
00011	01100			10011	10010

Table 2-35 Example of carry-select addition.

the carry-select principle with a table-look-up sum determination. The alternative sums are obtained simultaneously from small read-only stores and the carry is used to select the proper result.

2-12 CARRY-SAVE ADDER

The *carry-save adder* has been known for quite some time. It was mentioned by Babbage in 1837 (Randell, 1973, p. 29) and in 1947 by von Neumann (Burks et al., 1946) and used in 1950 in the Whirlwind computer at M.I.T. The carry-save adder avoids the source of the delay, the carry propagation, by simply not adding the carry to the partial sum. Thus, the result of the addition is the transmission T and the generated carry G. Since the sum consequently requires twice as many bits as needed, one can consider this a representation in a *redundant number system*. The carry-save principle can be applied to two types of adders. The first type adds three operands, the second type only two operands.

Three-Input Carry-Save Adder

The three-input carry-save adder has its main application in multipliers, as will be discussed in Chapter 3. It assumes that a long series of numbers must be added and that the intermediate sum can be remembered without objection in the redundant number system as if it were two numbers. The adder is able to add a third number to these two and to represent the sum as a transmission T and a generation G.

Carry-Save Architecture.   The architecture of the carry-save adder differs from *ARCHADD* because a different number of operands and results take part in the operation. This architecture is given in *ARCHSAVE*, Program 2-36. Where *SUM* is a scalar in *ARCHADD*, it is a vector in *ARCHSAVE*. The modulo 2 sum and carry are determined from this vector. *ARCHSAVE* corresponds to a series of independent bit adders, each with architecture *ARCHBITADD*.

```
     ∇ ARCHSAVE;SUM
[1]    SUM←K+L+M
[2]    T←2⊤SUM
[3]    G←SUM≥2
     ∇
```

Program 2-36   Carry-save adder architecture.

Carry-Save Accumulator.   The application of the carry-save principle to an accumulator is shown in Figure 2-37 and *SAVEACC*, Program 2-38. The figure shows an implementation form consisting of two sets of half-adders. The operands of the addition are the addend A, the previous transmission T, and the previous generation G. The generation is shifted 1 bit. Its leftmost bit becomes the carry-out *COUT*, while a carry-in *CIN* is inserted as the rightmost bit.

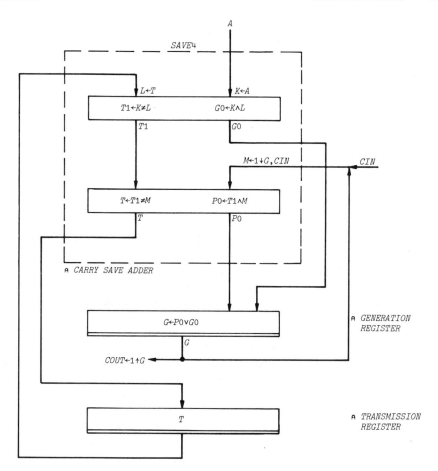

Figure 2-37   Carry-save accumulator.

```
      ∇ SAVEACC
 [1]    K←A
 [2]    L←T
 [3]    M←1↓G,CIN
 [4]    COUT←1↑G
 [5]    ARCHSAVE
      ∇

      ⍝ REFERENCE:
      ⍝ ARCHSAVE        CARRY-SAVE ADDER ARCHITECTURE
```

Program 2-38   Carry-save accumulator.

Carry-Save Implementation.   The carry-save accumulator *SAVEACC* specifies the carry-save adder in terms of its architecture. In Figure 2-37 a four-level implementation *SAVE*4, Program 2-39, is used for the carry-save adder. *SAVE*4 corresponds to the two uppermost blocks of Figure 2-37 and the 'or' condition with which the signals *P*0 and *G*0 enter the register *G*. The setting of the registers will be discussed later.

```
      ∇ SAVE2
[1]     ⍝ TRANSMISSION AND GENERATION
[2]     T←K≠L≠M
[3]     G←(K∧L)∨(L∧M)∨M∧K
      ∇
        ⍝ TWO LEVEL CIRCUIT


      ∇ SAVE4
[1]     ⍝ TRANSMISSION AND GENERATION
[2]     T1←K≠L
[3]     G0←K∧L
[4]     P0←T1∧M
[5]     T←T1≠M
[6]     G←P0∨G0
      ∇
        ⍝ FOUR LEVEL CIRCUIT
```

Program 2-39   Two and four level carry-save adders.

As an alternative to the four-level implementation of $SAVE4$, the two-level implementation $SAVE2$ is also shown in Program 2-39.

The carry-save adder can also be implemented by table-look-up methods. In that case a few bits from each operand are concatenated to form the address and a corresponding number of bits of the transmission and generation is obtained from the table.

Adder Speed and Cost.   The combinatoric part of the accumulator incorporates the same hardware as a ripple adder. The number of levels passed, however, is only four and is independent of the length of the operands. The adder can be reduced to two levels as shown in $SAVE2$, Program 2-39. The logical elements in $SAVE2$ can be converted further, as desired, to nands or other circuits. Expressed in nands, $SAVE2$ and $SAVE4$ each use nine components. $SAVE2$, however, uses 25 inputs, whereas $SAVE4$ has only 18 inputs.

The TI SN74H183 is an example of a 2-bit carry-save adder using the two-level approach of $SAVE2$.

Partial Carry-Save Adder.   When it proves to be too expensive to save all carries, the addition can be completed for every other bit position, while the partial sum and carry are saved for the bits in between. The number of carries that must be saved is thus halved.

$HALFSAVE$, Program 2-40, shows the architecture for a half carry-save adder. The operands K and L have the full length and are each shaped as an array with two rows. The operand M, which represents the generated carry of a previous operation, has half the number of elements and has the form of a vector. Correspondingly, the resulting transmission T has two rows and the generated carry G is a vector.

```
      ∇ HALFSAVE;SUM
[1]     SUM←(2⊥K)+(2⊥L)+M
[2]     T← 2 2 ⊤SUM
[3]     G←SUM≥4
      ∇
```

Program 2-40   Half carry-save adder architecture.

Two-Input Carry-Save Adder

The two-input carry-save adder requires half the hardware of the three-input carry-save adder. The number of variables before and after the operation is two and thus is not reduced. The results are repeatedly passed through the adder, however, such that the carry eventually becomes entirely zero. The transmission then represents the sum. The number of cycles necessary to obtain the zero carry depends upon the operands. Therefore, the addition requires a variable amount of time. Figure 2-41 shows a block diagram of this adder, and *SAVEADD*, Program 2-42, describes the operation.

At the beginning of the addition, the operands are placed in registers T and G. At the end of the first cycle, they are replaced by S and P. P is placed one position

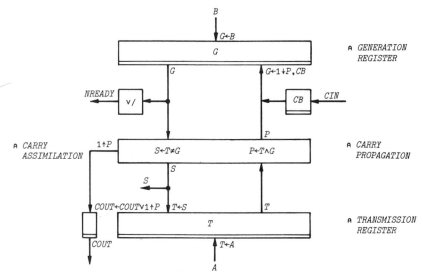

Figure 2-41   Carry-save adder.

```
       ∇ SAVEADD
[1]      ⋀ PROLOGUE
[2]     CB←CIN
[3]     COUT←0
[4]      ⋀ TRANSMISSION AND GENERATION
[5]     T←A
[6]     G←B
[7]      ⋀ CARRY PROPAGATION AND ASSIMILATION
[8]     CONT:P←T∧G
[9]     S←T≠G
[10]    COUT←COUT∨1↑P
[11]    T←S
[12]    G←1↓P,CB
[13]    CB←0
[14]     ⋀ TEST FOR ZERO GENERATION
[15]    NREADY←∨/G
[16]    →NREADY/CONT
       ∇
```

Program 2-42   Carry-save addition.

to the left in register G. The carry-in, CIN, comes into the lowest position of the register. The operation is now repeated, except that CIN is now 0. When no more carries are generated, that is, G is entirely 0, the partial sum T has become the ultimate sum S. The operation is now completed. The carry-out may appear during any cycle as the high-order bit of P. To preserve this carry, $P[0]$ is 'or'-ed in the register $COUT$ during the operation.

Number of Cycles.   Table 2-43 shows the successive results of a two-input carry-save addition. The process requires at most N cycles for operands of N bits. Von Neumann proved that the average longest carry series is approximately $2 \circledast N$, the 2-logarithm of N (Burks et al., 1946). Briley (1973) refined this to $(2 \circledast N) - 0.5$. Thus, for a 100-bit adder, an average of six cycles is necessary; for a 40-bit adder, five cycles.

```
      PRINT A
0110111111011011111010111011110011010101100011111100110000010001011000100000000011101110001010100000
      PRINT B
0100110000000010111111110100101000101100110110100001101011100010000000010000010101110110110000111110 0
      CIN
1
      SAVEADD

T 0110111111011011111010111011110011010101100011111100110000010001011000100000000011101110001010100000
G 0100110000000010111111110100101000101100110110100001101011100010000000010000010101110110110000111110 0

T 0010001111011110000101010100010100011001101110011110100111100110010110011000010101001101010010010110 0
G 1001100000000011110101010010100010010001000010000100100000000000000000000000001100101000001010000 1

T 1011101111011101111000000011000101010001001111011100110111100110010110011000010100101000010011000110 1
G 0000000000000100010010101000010000001000100000000100000000000000000000000000010001010000000100000 0

T 1011101111011100111101010011100101000000001111011000110111100110010110011000010110100001001001110011 01
G 0000000000000100000000000000000000100010000000010000000000000000000000000000001000000000000000000 0

T 1011101111011000111101010011100101100010001111010000110111100110010110011000010110110010010011100110 1
G 0000000000000100000000000000000000000010000000000100000000000000000000000000000000000000000000000 0

T 1011101111000001111010100111001011000100011110000011011110011001011001100001011011001001001110011 01
G 0000000000010000000000000000000000010000000000000000000000000000000000000000000000000000000000000 0

      PRINT S
1011101111110000111101010011100101100010001111100000110111100110010110011000010110110010010011100110 1
```

Table 2-43   Example of carry-save addition.

Adder Speed and Cost.   The attractiveness of this adder is the small amount of equipment. The speed, however, is disappointing. The combinatoric part is fast enough, requiring only two levels. For a 100-bit adder, an average of $6 \times 2 = 12$ levels must be passed. If the setting of the registers and their control is taken into consideration, however, easily six times as much time is necessary. Therefore, the method is not often applied.

2-13   ASYNCHRONOUS ADDER

For the two-input carry-save adder, the addition time is variable, since the number of cycles is dependent upon the value of the operands. In contrast, the preceding adders have a fixed addition time. Their addition time is determined by the time required by the critical cases to pass the critical path. All other cases used less than the allotted time. For the adders to be handled hereafter, the addition time is variable, not because the number of cycles varies, the *synchronous* solution, but because the cycle length is adjusted to the requirements of the operands and the circuits, the *asynchronous* solution.

The asynchronous adder was developed by Gilchrist, Pomerene, and Wong (1955). For the *asynchronous*, or carry-completion, *adder*, the time of the cycle is determined by the propagation of the carry. The addition stops when the propagation is completed. This moment is determined by forming for each bit position not only the carry C but also the not-carry NOC, and by waiting until one of these is present. Figure 2-44 shows the circuit required for one bit, as contrasted to the circuit of Figure 2-8. For a complete adder, the signals $COUT$ and $NOCOUT$ form the vectors C and NOC.

At the beginning of the addition, both polarities of each operand and of the carry-in are made 0. As a result, both $COUT$ and $NOCOUT$ are 0. Next, the adder inputs are made normal again, representing correctly the operands and the carry-in, as well as their inverse. This information now flows through the circuit and makes one of the outputs $COUT$ or $NOCOUT$ 1. This event is recognized by an 'or' circuit. When the 'or's for all bit positions are 1, an 'and' circuit gives the signal *READY*.

RIPASYNC, Program 2-45, gives the algorithm for the asynchronous adder. *RIPASYNC* differs from *RIPPLE* by using both polarites of the various signals. Again a branch is introduced to be able to use the algorithm for simulation as well as description. The termination of the loop depends upon the signal *READY*, however, and not upon a count.

Carry Length.   The speed of *RIPASYNC* is determined by the average maximum length of both the carry $COUT$ and the not-carry $NOCOUT$. This is illustrated in the example of Table 2-46.

Where the average longest carry might be compared to the life expectancy of a single person, the average longest carry and not-carry would resemble the life expectancy of the survivor of a couple. The calculation of von Neumann mentioned for the carry-save adder is therefore not applicable.

A good approximation of the average longest carry or not-carry is $2 \oplus 1.25 \times N$. Gilchrist et al. have experimentally determined this carry time for a 40-bit adder. They found an average length of 5.6 bits, which approximates $2 \oplus 1.25 \times 40$. The carry length was statistically determined as 5.69 by Reitwiesner (1960) and exhaustively determined as 5.64 by Hendrickson (1960).

These numbers show that the proposed question can be answered in various ways. They assume an average distribution of 0s and 1s, however, which does not match the numbers encountered in fixed- or floating-point arithmetic. Thus, integers normally have strings of 0s or 1s as their leftmost bits. As a result, the

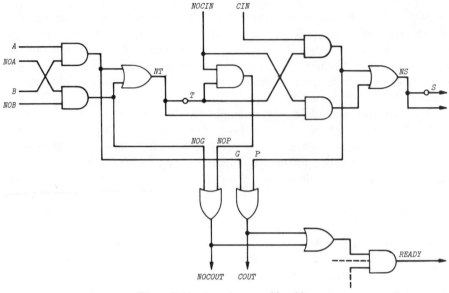

Figure 2-44   Asynchronous bit adder.

```
      ∇ RIPASYNC
[1]      ⍕ PROLOGUE                    [13] CONT:P←T∧1↓C
[2]      NOA←~A                        [14] NOP←T∧1↓NOC
[3]      NOB←~B                        [15] NOC←(NOG∨NOP),NOCIN
[4]      NOCIN←~CIN                    [16] C←(G∨P),CIN
[5]      ⍕ TRANSMISSION AND GENERATION [17] READY←∧/C∨NOC
[6]      G←A∧B                         [18] →(~READY)/CONT
[7]      NOG←NOA∧NOB                   [19] ⍕ CARRY ASSIMILATION
[8]      NT←G∨NOG                      [20] NS←P∨NT∧1↓NOC
[9]      T←~NT                         [21] S←~NS
[10]     ⍕ CARRY PROPAGATION          [22] NOCOUT←1↑NOC
[11]     NOC←((ρA)ρ0),NOCIN           [23] COUT←1↑C
[12]     C←((ρA)ρ0),CIN                  ∇
[13]
```

Program 2-45   Asynchronous ripple adder.

average maximum carry length is increased when numbers of opposite sign are added, whereas it is reduced marginally when numbers of like sign are added.

Adder Speed and Cost.   For a 100-bit adder, the average maximum carry or not-carry length is theoretically about 7. When the time for the verification of completion is also taken into consideration, about 18 levels of actual switching time are required as opposed to the 14 formal levels of the carry-predict adder. The double logic of carry and not-carry and the verification logic for *READY* require 1250 nands against the 900 from the ripple adder.

The asynchronous approach is not limited to the ripple adder. For instance, a skip or prediction could be used for the carry as well as the not-carry. Since the large carry propagations no longer affect the speed significantly and the skip and prediction were intended exactly for this purpose, their extra cost is normally not justified.

```
      PRINT A
011011111101101111101011110111100110101011000111111001100000100010110001000000000111011100010101 0000
      PRINT B
010011000000001011111111101001010001011001101101000011010111000100000000010000010101110110110000 1111100
1     CIN
1
      RIPASYNC

T    001000111110111100001010101001010001100110111001111010011110011001011001100001010100110101001 00101100
G    010011000000000011110101010010100010010001000010000100100000000000000000000000000001100101000 0010100 00
NOG  100100000010000000000000001000011000010000001000000010000011001101001100111101010000000011010 000 00011

C    010011000000000111101010100101000010010001000010000100100000000000000000000000000001100101000 0010100 001
NOC  100100000010000000000000001000011000010000001000000010000011001101001100111101010000000011010 0000 0110

C    010011000C0000011111111111100111000101100110000100011001000000000000000000000000001110111100 00011100001
NOC  101100000110000000000000011000111000010000011000000110000111011111011101111111110000000011111 00001110

C    010011000000001111111111111001110001110110110000100110010000000000000000000000001111111100000 11100001
NOC  101100001100000000000000011000111000010000111000000011000111111111111111111111111000000011111 00011110

C    010011000000011111111111111001110001110110110000101110010000000000000000000000001111111100000 11100001
NOC  101100011110000000000000011000111000010001110000000110011111111111111111111111111000000001111 100011110

C    010011000001111111111111111001110001110110110000111110010000000000000000000000001111111100000 11100001
NOC  101100111110000000000000011000111000010001110000000110111111111111111111111111111000000001111 100011110

      PRINT S
101110111110000111101010011100101100010001111100000101111001100101100110000101101100100100111001 101
```

Table 2-46 Example of asynchronous addition.

Asynchronous Logic

The asynchronous adder has all the advantages and disadvantages of *asynchronous logic* (Maley and Earle, 1963, p. 182). Speed is the main advantage. Not only can one assume an average carry instead of the longest possible carry, but also, the actual circuit time is used instead of the nominal time, which includes tolerances for the slowest, or *worst case*, and the aged, or *end-of-life*, circuit elements.

A secondary advantage of asynchronous logic may be that many types of defects cause the operation to stop. Thus, errors can be detected by noticing that the operation lasts extravagantly long. Also, finding a fault is easier when the circuit 'stays stuck' in the fault situation. Finally, intermittend faults cause a time delay, not an erroneous result.

Set against these advantages are several disadvantages. If the circuit waits for the completion of the operation, this moment must be recognizable. This recognition costs time and equipment, and causes a part of the abovementioned speed gain to be lost again. Only in a limited number of cases is it possible to find an elegant completion criterion, as with this adder.

A second disadvantage is that the circuit must be made with extra care to prevent erroneous completion indications. Thus, the circuit of Figure 2-44 assumes that the assimilation of the carry in the sum is faster than the verification by the 'or' and 'and' circuits. In general, this may be the case, but the assumption makes the circuit less self-verifying. To eliminate this risk, more components must be used.

To guarantee proper operation extra actions may also be required, such as making both polarities of the operands 0. These actions also cost time and equipment. Thus, the hardware for an asynchronous solution may well turn out to be double that of a synchronous solution.

As a result of these disadvantages, the asynchronous approach is not much used. Although it is possible to make a design partially synchronous and asynchronous, in most cases a uniform synchronous solution is preferable.

2-14 EVALUATION

Table 2-47 provides a summary of the adder types mentioned in this chapter. A choice from these adders, as well as their alternatives, requires a careful evaluation in which the surroundings of the adder and the available realizations

Table 2-47   RELATION OF ADDER TYPES.

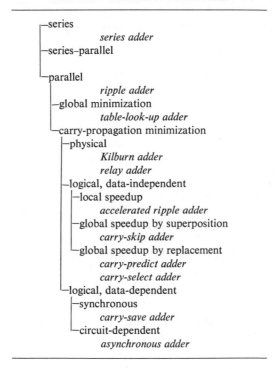

Table 2-48   SUMMARY OF ADDER COST PERFORMANCE.

100-Bit Adder	Nands	Levels
Ripple	900	202
Accelerated ripple	1000	104
Carry skip	972	40
Asynchronous	1250	'18'
Carry predict	1318	14
Carry select	1968	12

play a major role (Lehman, 1962). The number of levels to be passed and nands to be used can deviate considerably from what was mentioned here as a first approximation and is summarized in Table 2-48. This deviation is all the more to be expected since these adders can be further refined. Further refinement, however, involves designing against clearly defined constraints, such as the fan-in, fan-out, cost, speed, and availability of individual components. This level of detail is outside the scope of this text.

2-15 VERIFICATION

Implementation as Input to Realization. Each implementation program described in this chapter can be taken as the starting point for the realization of an adder. Having determined the correctness of the program, it can be expanded so that, apart from declarations, each logical component is described separately. Subsequently, the logical components can be identified with physical components and placed upon carriers, such as chips or cards, and connected with wires, either deposited or discrete. In so doing a lot of information is accumulated.

It is outside the scope of this text to consider the realization in detail. The information processing for the realization can be performed, in principle, with *automation of design*, be it batched or interactive in nature. This makes it all the more necessary that the starting point, the implemention program, is correct.

Verification Methods

Since the architecture is the specification of the design, the *verification* must establish equivalence between the implementation and the architecture. The various verification methods can be divided into the static and dynamic methods (Weber, 1974).

Static Verification. *Static verification* is performed independent of the operands of the system. This verification may be obtained by automatic translation from the problem statement to its solution, or by algebraic verification.

Automatic Generation of the Implementation. With an automatic generation of the implementation, the burden of proof is shifted from the correctness of the solution to the correctness of the translation program. This method is satisfactory between implementation levels, for instance, in transforming a general implementation description, such as *RIPPLE*, into a specific one, such as *RIPPLE*4. Since the transition from an architecture to an implementation usually requires invention, an automatic translation between these two design levels is not possible, as a rule.

Algebraic Verification. APL permits classical algebraic manipulations. Iverson has pointed out several useful additional transformations (Iverson, 1972). Therefore, algebraic verification of the equivalence of some expressions is possible in principle. Algebraic verification has the advantage that usually the equivalence is established via another route than was used in the original design. In practice, however, the designer may be inclined to distrust his algebraic manipulations as much as he distrusts his design. This objection also holds for the verification of the equivalence of programs by such methods as the assertion method of Floyd (1967).

Dynamic Verification.   *Dynamic verification* uses the operands of the system. It usually simulates the design for a set of test cases. Where static verification, when applicable, is complete, dynamic verification normally is not.

Simulation.   An algorithmic implementation description is a major help in verifying the correctness of a design. Thus, simulation via a terminal quickly discloses many design faults. For small parts of a design, it may even be possible to check the circuit exhaustively for all possible input values. For larger parts of a design, the exhaustive test, as a rule, is too time-consuming. Several well-chosen test cases, may, however, provide much assurance, if not absolute certainty.

Exhaustive Verification

TESTADD, Program 2-49, is an example of a test program for adders. The program compares the results of a given architecture with the results from an implementation.

```
     ∇ TESTADD;X;VX;COMPARAND                         ∇ PRINTADD
[1]    ⍝ N←DIMENSION OF OPERANDS                 [1]    '    A  ';PRINT A
[2]    ⍝ STARTVALUE X HAS ALL OPERAND BITS 1     [2]    '    B  ';PRINT B
[3]    X←(2*N×2)-1                               [3]    '  CIN ';(ρA)ρ' ';CIN
[4]    CIN←0                                     [4]    'COUT,S ';PRINT COUT,S
[5]    ⍝ CONSTRUCTION OF OPERANDS                       ∇
[6]  CONT:VX←((2×N)ρ2)⊤X
[7]    A←N↑VX                                           ∇ CHAR←PRINT X
[8]    B←N↓VX                                    [1]    CHAR←'01'[X]
[9]    ⍝ COMPARISON ALGORITHM                           ∇
[10] CONT1:ARCHADD
[11]   ⍝ SAVE RESULT
[12]   COMPARAND←COUT,S
[13]   ⍝ ALGORITHM TO BE TESTED
[14]   RIPONE4
[15]   ⍝ COMPARE RESULTS
[16]   →(∧/COMPARAND=COUT,S)/END
[17]   ⍝ PRINT
[18]   PRINTADD
[19]   ' RIGHT ';PRINT COMPARAND
[20]   ' '
[21]   ⍝ CHANGE CIN
[22] END:CIN←~CIN
[23]   →CIN/CONT1
[24]   ⍝ NEXT X
[25]   X←X-(1+2*N)
[26]   ⍝ END TEST
[27]   →((2⊥VX)≠2*(2×N)-1)/CONT
[28]   'READY'
     ∇

     ⍝ REFERENCE:                                    PROGRAM:
     ⍝ ARCHADD       ADDER ARCHITECTURE                2-5
```

Program 2-49   Exhaustive adder test.

Exhaustion. *TESTADD* supposes that the dimension N of the operands is sufficiently small to test the adder exhaustively for all combinations of A and B and the two values of *CIN*.

The number of required tests, $2 * 1 + N \times 2$, can be almost halved, when the design to be tested is symmetric with respect to A and B, i.e., when A and B can be interchanged in any expression without change in action. The value that reduces the running value of X in line 25 has been so chosen that only one of a pair of symmetric cases occurs.

Quote. The *quote*, ', which appears in lines 19, 20, and 28 of *TESTADD*, indicates the start of a series of characters. The series is closed off by a second quote. Such a character series is considered as a vector, with each character an individual element. As such, the vector is available for further use. In this example it is printed. In line 3 of *PRINTADD*, a vector of space characters is obtained by the use of the reshape operator. The use of quotes distinguishes a sequence of characters from a sequence representing a number or name.

Print Out. The result of an expression that is not used for the definition of a variable is printed directly on the terminal. In *TESTADD* this case occurs in lines 19, 20, and 28. In each of these lines a character series is printed. A number of expressions can be printed next to each other by placing them side by side on a line, separated by a semicolon, as on line 19 of *TESTADD*.

Indexing of Characters. In *TESTADD* and *PRINTADD*, logical vectors are printed compactly. In a normal printing of vectors, the elements are separated by one or more spaces to facilitate their recognition as distinct units. For logical vectors this spacing is not necessary and a compact printing is possible. *PRINT* is used to obtain this compact printing.

In line 1 of *PRINT*, the input X is used as an index of the character series 01, which is enclosed by the quotes. The result of the indexing is again a character series, but now with a length equal to the number of elements of X. If an element of X is 0, then a 0 is printed; if it is 1, then 1 is printed. Since a series of characters is printed without intervening spaces, the desired compact representation is obtained. The use of the function *PRINT* is shown in the examples of adder actions, such as Table 2-29.

Selective Verification

For the testing of adders with a large width, such as the 100-bit adders, *TESTADD* is not suitable, since an exhaustive treatment would last too long. To test a number of cases, *QUIZADD*, Program 2-50, can be used.

As indicated in the comments, two algorithms are compared to each other in *QUIZADD*. *ARCHADD* cannot always be used here as a comparison, since APL\360 records very large numbers in floating point and does not preserve all bits exactly.

```
        ∇ QUIZADD X;COMPARAND
[1]     ⍝ X←MATRIX CONTAINING OPERANDS TO BE TESTED
[2]     ⍝ CONSTRUCTION OF OPERANDS
[3]     CIN←0
[4]     CONT:A←X[0;]
[5]     B←X[1;]
[6]     ⍝ COMPARISON ALGORITHM
[7]     PREDICT100
[8]     ⍝ SAVE RESULT
[9]     COMPARAND←COUT,S
[10]    ⍝ ALGORITHM TO BE TESTED
[11]    SELECT100
[12]    ⍝ COMPARE RESULTS
[13]    →(∧/COMPARAND=COUT,S)/END
[14]    ⍝ PRINT
[15]    PRINTADD
[16]    ' RIGHT ';PRINT COMPARAND
[17]    ' '
[18]    ⍝ CHANGE CIN
[19]    END:CIN←~CIN
[20]    →CIN/CONT
[21]    ⍝ NEXT A AND B
[22]    X← 2 0 ↓X
[23]    ⍝ END TEST
[24]    →(0≠1↑⍴X)/CONT
[25]    'READY'
        ∇
```

```
        ⍝ REFERENCE:                                      PROGRAM:
        ⍝ PRINT        COMPACT LOGICAL PRINTOUT            2-49
        ⍝ PRINTADD     ADDER DATA DISPLAY                  2-49
```

Program 2-50   Selective adder test.

The operand X of $QUIZADD$ is a matrix containing in its rows the adder operands A and B. The first two matrix rows are selected in lines 4 and 5 and used with both CIN 0 and 1. Subsequently, the first two rows are eliminated in line 22, and the process is repeated until the matrix becomes empty.

Selection of Test Cases.   The designer can prepare several test series by constructing the corresponding matrices. It is worthwhile to develop a proper set of tests, since these tests may also be used in later stages of the design, even in the physical test of a first model.

Candidates for inclusion in a test set are:

(a) Extreme cases, such as all 0 and all 1 operands.
(b) Critical cases, which test the critical path.
(c) Branch cases, which test both sides of a branch condition.
(d) Boundary cases, which test both sides of the boundary of the operating domain, such as between overflow and no overflow.
(e) Circuit cases, which test the functioning of individual components, assuming that their environment is faultless.
(f) Diagnostic cases, which give easily recognizable intermediate and final results, thus helping in finding the cause of a malfunction.

Several criteria can often be combined in one case. The order of the tests should be such that some diagnostic cases are used first and a rough overall verification is quickly established.

REFERENCES

BEDRIJ, O. J.: "Carry-Select Adder." *IRE Transactions on Electronic Computers* vol. 11, no. 2, pp. 340–346 (June, 1962).

BREUER, M. A., ed.: *Design Automation of Digital Systems*, volume one, *Theory and Techniques*. Prentice-Hall, Englewood Cliffs, N. J. (1972).

BRILEY, B. E.: "Some New Results on Average Worst Case Carry." *IEEE Transactions on Computers*, vol. C-22, no. 5, pp. 459–463 (May, 1973).

BURKS, A. W., H. H. GOLDSTINE, and J. VON NEUMANN: *Preliminary Discussion of the Logical Design of an Electronic Computing Instrument*. Institute for Advanced Study, Princeton, June, 1946. Reprinted in C. G. Bell and A. Newell: *Computer Structures: Readings and Examples*, pp. 92–119. McGraw-Hill, New York, 1971.

FALKOFF, A. D., and K. E. IVERSON: *APL\360 User's Manual*. IBM Corporation, Yorktown Heights, N.Y., 1968.

FALKOFF, A. D., AND K. E. IVERSON: "The Design of APL." *IBM Journal of Research and Development*, vol. 17, no. 4, pp. 324–334 (July, 1973).

FLOYD, R. W.: "Assigning Meanings to Programs." Proceedings of a Symposium in Applied Mathematics, vol. 19. In J. T. SCHWARTZ, ed.: *Mathematical Aspects of Computer Science*, pp. 19–32. American Mathematical Society, Providence, R.I., 1967.

GILCHRIST, B., J. H. POMERENE, and S. Y. WONG: "Fast Carry Logic for Digital Computers." *IRE Transactions on Electronic Computers*, vol. EC-4, no. 4, pp. 133–136 (December, 1955).

HENDRICKSON, H. C.: "Fast High-Accuracy Binary Parallel Addition." *IRE Transactions on Electronic Computers*, vol. EC-9, no. 4, pp. 465–469 (December, 1960).

IVERSON, K. E.: *A Programming Language*. Wiley, New York, 1962.

IVERSON, K. E.: *Algebra: An Algorithmic Treatment*. Addison-Wesley, Reading, Mass., 1972.

KILBURN, T., D. B. G. EDWARDS, and D. ASPINALL: "Parallel Addition in Digital Computers: A New Fast Carry Circuit." *Proceedings IEE*, vol. 106, pt. 8, pp. 464–466 (1959).

LATHWELL, R. H.: "System Formulation and APL Shared Variables." *IBM Journal of Research and Development*, vol. 17, no. 4, pp. 353–359 (July, 1973).

LEHMAN, M.: *A Comparative Study of Propagation Speed-up Circuits in Binary Arithmetic Units*. International Federation of Information Processing Societies, 1962. North-Holland, Amsterdam, Netherlands (1963).

LEHMAN, M., and N. BURLA: "Skip Techniques for High-Speed Carry-Propagation in Binary Arithmetic Units." *IRE Transactions on Electronic Computers*, vol. EC-10, no. 4, pp. 691–698 (December, 1961).

LIU, T. K., K. R. HOHULIN, L. E. SHIAU, and S. MUROGA: "Optimal One-Bit Full Adders with Different Types of Gates." *IEEE Transactions on Computers*, vol. C-23, no. 1, pp. 63–70 (January, 1974).

MacSorley, O. L.: "High-Speed Arithmetic in Binary Computers." *Proceedings of the IRE*, vol. 49, no. 1, pp. 67–91 (January, 1961).

Maley, G. A., and J. Earle: *The Logic Design of Transistor Digital Computers*. Prentice-Hall, Englewood Cliffs, N.J., 1963.

Morris, R. L., and J. R. Miller: *Designing with TTL Integrated Circuits*. McGraw-Hill, New York, 1971.

Pakin, S.: *APL/360 Reference Manual*. Science Research Associates, Chicago, 2nd ed., 1972.

Quatse, J. T., and R. A. Keir: "A Parallel Accumulator for a General-Purpose Computer." *IEEE Transactions on Electronic Computers*, vol. EC-16, no. 2, pp. 165–171 (April, 1967).

Randell, B., ed.: *The Origins of Digital Computers. Selected Papers*. Springer-Verlag, Berlin, 1973.

Reitwiesner, G. W.: "The Determination of Carry Propagation Length for Binary Addition." *IRE Transactions on Electronic Computers*, vol. EC-9, no. 1, pp. 35–38 (March, 1960).

Salter, F.: "High-Speed Transistorized Adder for a Digital Computer." *IRE Transactions on Electronic Computers*, vol. EC-9, no. 4, pp. 461–464 (December, 1960).

Sklansky, J.: "Conditional Sum Addition Logic." *IRE Transactions on Electronic Computers*, vol. EC-9, no. 2, pp. 226–231 (June, 1960).

Thornton, J. E.: *Design of a Computer, the Control Data 6600*. Scott, Foresman, Glenview, Ill., 1970.

Weber, H.: "Ein Programmiersystem zur Unterstutzung der Rechnerentwicklung." In H. Hasselmeier and W. G. Spruth: *Rechnerstrukturen*, pp. 372–394. Oldenbourg, Munich, 1974.

Weinberger, A., and J. R. Smith: "A One-Microsecond Adder Using One-Megacycle Circuitry." *IRE Transactions on Electronic Computers*, vol. EC-5, no. 2, pp. 65–73 (June, 1956).

EXERCISES

All functions presented in this text may be used in the exercises. It is often advisable to start with an existing function and modify it as required.

2-1   Design the function $YES \leftarrow OFADD$, which makes YES 1 when the sum produced by $ARCHADD$, Program 2-5, exceeds the 2's-complement-representation range. The inputs and outputs of $ARCHADD$ are available as operands.

2-2   Give the interpretation functions for:
   (a)   Signed-magnitude representation, with the leftmost bit used for the sign: $N \leftarrow SMAG\ R$.

(b)   One's-complement representation, $N \leftarrow ONEC\ R$.

In each case R is the logical representation vector and N the number represented.

2-3   Give the implementation function $T \leftarrow A\ XOR\ B$ for the exclusive-or function $T \leftarrow A \neq B$, using only 'and,' 'or,' and 'not' components. Show how you would test this function.

2-4 $ARCHUP$, Program 2-51, gives the architecture of a counter which, when called, adds 1 to the operand A. Start from the ripple adder and determine the implementation $RIPUP$ of this counter.

```
      ∇ ARCHUP;SUM
[1]     SUM←(2⊥A)+1
[2]     S←((ρA)ρ2)⊤SUM
[3]     COUT←SUM=2*ρA
      ∇
```

Program 2-51   Incrementing counter architecture.

2-5 $ARCHDOWN$, Program 2-52, gives the architecture of a counter which, when called, subtracts 1 from the operand A. Start from the ripple adder and determine the implementation $RIPDOWN$ of this counter.

```
      ∇ ARCHDOWN;SUM
[1]     SUM←(2⊥A)-1
[2]     S←((ρA)ρ2)⊤SUM
[3]     COUT←SUM=-1
      ∇
```

Program 2-52   Decrementing counter architecture.

2-6 $ARCHTRIPLE$, Program 2-53, gives the architecture of a tripling circuit, the output representing three times the value of the input. Start from the ripple adder function $RIPPLE$, Program 2-17, and develop $RIPTRIPLE$, the implementation of $ARCHTRIPLE$. Why is it necessary to extend the sign of IN in line 1 of $ARCHTRIPLE$?

```
      ∇ OUT←ARCHTRIPLE IN
[1]     OUT←((2+ρIN)ρ2)⊤3×2⊥IN[0 0],IN
      ∇
```

Program 2-53   Architecture of tripling circuit.

2-7   Write a program $MAKETLU$ that generates the contents of $STORE$ for the table-look-up adder $TLUADD$, Program 2-23. Assume the dimensions of A and B to be 4 bits each.

2-8   Give a description of the accelerated ripple adder of Figure 2-19 with the function $RIPONE$, which is valid for all operand lengths.

2-9   Determine the cost advantage of an adder grouping of 5 5 4 over 4 5 5, as used in $PREDICT100$, Program 2-28.

2-10   Design *PREDICT*16, a 16-bit carry-predict adder as used in the DEC PDP11/45, which makes use of four groups of 4 bits. Also determine the auxiliary functions, *GEN*4 and *PREDG*4.

2-11   Design *PREDICT*60, a 60-bit carry-predict adder as used in the CDC 6600, which uses the high-to-low grouping 5 4 3. Also determine the necessary auxiliary functions. Why would you not take the grouping 3 4 5?

2-12   Determine an optimum grouping of one level of skips for a carry-skip adder of 32 bits.

2-13   Determine experimentally the average longest carry length for an *N*-bit adder, by writing an auxiliary program for this purpose. Use the APL random operator ?, as described in Appendix A, to generate *N*-bit operands with a random 0 and 1 distribution.

2-14   Refine the experiment of Exercise 2-13 by generating operands that look more like integers encountered in actual practive. Assume that the average operand length is one half the adder length of *N*.

2-15   Repeat the experiments of Exercises 2-13 and 2-14 for the average longest carry and not-carry as required for the asynchronous adder.

2-16   Design an implementation for *HALFSAVE*, Program 2-40.

2-17   Design a carry-save adder that reduces seven operands to one partial sum and two generated carries. Determine first the architecture *ARCH2SAVE* and thereafter an implementation *IMP2SAVE*; start from circuits such as *ARCHSAVE*.

2-18   Determine the architecture *DECADD* of a decimal adder that uses a 4-bit 8421 code and records negative numbers with 10's-complement.

2-19   Write a program *MAKETLU*10 which gives the content of the store for a decimal adder, as used in the System/370 Model 168. The addition follows *DECADD*, as specified in Exercise 2-18. The operand length is 4 bits. The carry-out and three high-order sum bits are found in storage. The low-order sum bit is obtained with an exclusive-or. Give the function *TLUADD*10, which uses the store and an exclusive-or for decimal addition.

2-20   Design a 16-bit parallel implementation *IMPDEC* for the decimal adder *DECADD*, specified in Exercise 2-18.

2-21   *ARCHONE*64, Program 2-54, gives the architecture for an *all-ones count* as found in the IBM 7030 and similar to the *population count* of the CDC 6600. The output of *ARCHONE*64 is a binary representation of the number of 1s that occur in the 64 input signals. Give an implementation *IMPONE*64; use

```
         ∇  OUT←ARCHONE64 IN
    [1]      OUT←(7ρ2)⊤+/IN
         ∇
```

Program 2-54   All-ones count architecture.

carry-save adders combined with other adders. Try to keep the number of levels low.

2-22   Rewrite the ripple adder as given by Program 2-17, as a purely descriptive algorithm *RIPPLED*, eliminating the count J; and as a simulatable algorithm *RIPPLEQ*, that tests for the quiescence of the carry C, similar to *RIPASYNC*, Program 2-45.

3 MULTIPLICATION

In arithmetic, *multiplication* is defined as repeated addition. The number to be added is the *multiplicand*, the number of times this number is to be added is indicated by the *multiplier*, and the result is the *product*. As long as the series of additions is not yet completed, the intermediate sum is called the *partial product*. The series of additions may start with an *initial value*, in which case the multiplication is called *cumulative*. When there is no initial value, the series of additions begins with zero and is called, in contrast, a *clear multiplication*.

Commutativity. Since multiplication is commutative, the multiplicand and multiplier are not distinguished in the architecture of the multiplication. Therefore, they could be called more generally operands, as was the case with the augend and addend. In the implementation, however, the multiplicand and multiplier are handled differently. Therefore, the separate names will be used.

Organization of the Chapter

In this chapter, the architecture of the function to be implemented, the multiplication, is again discussed in the first section. Next, in Section 3-2, the basic multiplication algorithm is considered. This basic algorithm assumes positive operands. Therefore, in Section 3-3 the algorithm is expanded to allow both positive and negative operands. The following sections, Sections 3-4 through 3-6, describe the speed improvement that can be obtained by processing more than one multiplier bit at once. The chapter is concluded by a brief evaluation in Section 3-7.

The algorithm that uses two multiplier bits per cycle, as discussed in Section 3-4, will be further developed in Chapters 5 and 6. Hence, the reader may, on a first pass through the text, wish to proceed directly from Section 3-5 to Chapter 5.

3-1 ARCHITECTURE OF THE MULTIPLIER

In multiplication the operands usually contain the same number of bits, as was the case in addition. The length of the product, however, depends on the interpretation of the operand bits. When the operands are interpreted as integers, the product usually has twice the length of the operands to preserve the information content. When, on the other hand, the operands are considered as fractions, the precision of the product is about that of the operands, and a single-length product is satisfactory. In that case, a form of rounding of the product may be desired. The interpretation as fractions is especially prominent in floating-point arithmetic. Provisions for increased precision, however, may again make a double length desirable. The interpretation as integer is normal in fixed-point arithmetic. Both interpretations occur frequently.

Architecture in Words

In this text, the operands are treated as integers represented with 2's-complement notation. A double-length product and a single-length initial value are assumed.

The multiplier can now be specified as the equipment that obtains PD as the sum of the initial value VL and the product of the multiplier MR and multiplicand MD. The operands and the result are represented in 2's complement. The length of VL equals that of MD and the length of PD is the sum of the lengths of MD and MR.

Architecture in APL

The architecture of the multiplication is given by $ARCHMPY$, Program 3-1. This program makes use of the traditional multiplication operator $\times$, which is one of the arithmetic operators of APL. The function $TWOC$ interprets the logical vectors according to the 2's-complement notation. $TWOC$ shows that in this interpretation the leftmost bit, the sign bit, should be taken negative. The algebraic operations with the interpreted operands yield the scalar $PRODUCT$, which is a local variable of the architecture. In line 2, $PRODUCT$ is again represented in 2's complement. Here no special representation function is introduced, since in APL negative numbers are represented with complement notation.

```
      ARCHMPY;PRODUCT
[1]   PRODUCT←(TWOC VL)+(TWOC MR)×TWOC MD
[2]   PD←((ρMR,MD)ρ2)⊤PRODUCT
   ∇

   ∇ N←TWOC R
[1]   N←2⊥(-1↑R),R
   ∇
```

Program 3-1 Multiplier architecture.

Alternative Architectures. *ARCHMPY* can be modified to represent a clear multiplication by omitting the term *TWOC VL*. In that case, the operands may be interpreted either as integers or as fractions. By 'taking' part of the product representation, a single-length product can be specified.

Since *ARCHMPY* is the most ambitious architectural alternative, it will be used in this chapter for the various implementations to be discussed. First, however, a different form of this architecture will be considered.

Effect of 2's-Complement Notation. The architecture of the adder *ARCHADD* was valid for operands represented as unsigned binary as well as in 2's-complement. As a consequence, the implementations could treat the sign bit the same as the other operand bits. *ARCHMPY*, however, assumes only 2's-complement representation, as is apparent from the use of the function *TWOC*. Consequently, the implementations cannot assume that the sign may be treated as an operand bit.

For multiplication, therefore, the signed-magnitude representation appears to be more attractive. In that representation the multiply algorithm needs to be worked out only for positive numbers, and the sign of the result is determined independently.

The signed-magnitude representation, however, is less efficient for addition and subtraction, owing to the extra recomplementation cycles. Therefore, some machines that use complement notation convert to and from signed-magnitude notation at the start and end of the multiplication. Examples are the PDP11/40 and the System/370 Model 158 integer multipliers.

The extra complementing cycles required by conversion to and from signed magnitude take time, however, and add to the complexity of the machine. It is therefore attractive to determine if the architecture cannot be restated in terms of a positive interpretation of the operands.

Positive Interpretation of Operands

In 1951 Booth showed that the extra complementing cycles used in 2's-complement multiplication are superfluous. The key to Booth's method is to make the modulus of the operands the same as the modulus of the product, therefore using $2 * 2 \times N$ instead of $2 * N$ as modulus. This is equivalent to representing the operands with $2 \times N$ bits and not N bits. Hence, the operands must be extended with N high-order bits, which are equal to the sign bit. This extension of course implies a larger number of bits to be added and a larger number of additions. The implementation, however, need not take all these actions, as will be shown.

Algebraic Justification. An extended negative operand is noted in 2's-complement notation as $(2 * 2 \times N) - A$, with A equal to the absolute value of this operand. When the representation of this number is interpreted as a positive integer and is multiplied as such with a positive operand B, the product becomes

```
 PD     VL   MR   MD                                   PD     VL   MR   MD
0000 ← 00 + 00 × 00      0 ←  0 +  0 ×  0            1110 ← 10 + 00 × 00      ¯2 ← ¯2 +  0 ×  0
0000 ← 00 + 00 × 01      0 ←  0 +  0 ×  1            1110 ← 10 + 00 × 01      ¯2 ← ¯2 +  0 ×  1
0000 ← 00 + 00 × 10      0 ←  0 +  0 × ¯2            1110 ← 10 + 00 × 10      ¯2 ← ¯2 +  0 × ¯2
0000 ← 00 + 00 × 11      0 ←  0 +  0 × ¯1            1110 ← 10 + 00 × 11      ¯2 ← ¯2 +  0 × ¯1
0000 ← 00 + 01 × 00      0 ←  0 +  1 ×  0            1110 ← 10 + 01 × 00      ¯2 ← ¯2 +  1 ×  0
0001 ← 00 + 01 × 01      1 ←  0 +  1 ×  1            1111 ← 10 + 01 × 01      ¯1 ← ¯2 +  1 ×  1
1110 ← 00 + 01 × 10     ¯2 ←  0 +  1 × ¯2            1100 ← 10 + 01 × 10      ¯4 ← ¯2 +  1 × ¯2
1111 ← 00 + 01 × 11     ¯1 ←  0 +  1 × ¯1            1101 ← 10 + 01 × 11      ¯3 ← ¯2 +  1 × ¯1
0000 ← 00 + 10 × 00      0 ←  0 + ¯2 ×  0            1110 ← 10 + 10 × 00      ¯2 ← ¯2 + ¯2 ×  0
1110 ← 00 + 10 × 01     ¯2 ←  0 + ¯2 ×  1            1100 ← 10 + 10 × 01      ¯4 ← ¯2 + ¯2 ×  1
0100 ← 00 + 10 × 10      4 ←  0 + ¯2 × ¯2            0010 ← 10 + 10 × 10       2 ← ¯2 + ¯2 × ¯2
0010 ← 00 + 10 × 11      2 ←  0 + ¯2 × ¯1            0000 ← 10 + 10 × 11       0 ← ¯2 + ¯2 × ¯1
0000 ← 00 + 11 × 00      0 ←  0 + ¯1 ×  0            1110 ← 10 + 11 × 00      ¯2 ← ¯2 + ¯1 ×  0
1111 ← 00 + 11 × 01     ¯1 ←  0 + ¯1 ×  1            1101 ← 10 + 11 × 01      ¯3 ← ¯2 + ¯1 ×  1
0010 ← 00 + 11 × 10      2 ←  0 + ¯1 × ¯2            0000 ← 10 + 11 × 10       0 ← ¯2 + ¯1 × ¯2
0001 ← 00 + 11 × 11      1 ←  0 + ¯1 × ¯1            1111 ← 10 + 11 × 11      ¯1 ← ¯2 + ¯1 × ¯1
0001 ← 01 + 00 × 00      1 ←  1 +  0 ×  0            1111 ← 11 + 00 × 00      ¯1 ← ¯1 +  0 ×  0
0001 ← 01 + 00 × 01      1 ←  1 +  0 ×  1            1111 ← 11 + 00 × 01      ¯1 ← ¯1 +  0 ×  1
0001 ← 01 + 00 × 10      1 ←  1 +  0 × ¯2            1111 ← 11 + 00 × 10      ¯1 ← ¯1 +  0 × ¯2
0001 ← 01 + 00 × 11      1 ←  1 +  0 × ¯1            1111 ← 11 + 00 × 11      ¯1 ← ¯1 +  0 × ¯1
0001 ← 01 + 01 × 00      1 ←  1 +  1 ×  0            1111 ← 11 + 01 × 00      ¯1 ← ¯1 +  1 ×  0
0010 ← 01 + 01 × 01      2 ←  1 +  1 ×  1            0000 ← 11 + 01 × 01       0 ← ¯1 +  1 ×  1
1111 ← 01 + 01 × 10     ¯1 ←  1 +  1 × ¯2            1101 ← 11 + 01 × 10      ¯3 ← ¯1 +  1 × ¯2
0000 ← 01 + 01 × 11      0 ←  1 +  1 × ¯1            1110 ← 11 + 01 × 11      ¯2 ← ¯1 +  1 × ¯1
0001 ← 01 + 10 × 00      1 ←  1 + ¯2 ×  0            1111 ← 11 + 10 × 00      ¯1 ← ¯1 + ¯2 ×  0
1111 ← 01 + 10 × 01     ¯1 ←  1 + ¯2 ×  1            1101 ← 11 + 10 × 01      ¯3 ← ¯1 + ¯2 ×  1
0101 ← 01 + 10 × 10      5 ←  1 + ¯2 × ¯2            0011 ← 11 + 10 × 10       3 ← ¯1 + ¯2 × ¯2
0011 ← 01 + 10 × 11      3 ←  1 + ¯2 × ¯1            0001 ← 11 + 10 × 11       1 ← ¯1 + ¯2 × ¯1
0001 ← 01 + 11 × 00      1 ←  1 + ¯1 ×  0            1111 ← 11 + 11 × 00      ¯1 ← ¯1 + ¯1 ×  0
0000 ← 01 + 11 × 01      0 ←  1 + ¯1 ×  1            1110 ← 11 + 11 × 01      ¯2 ← ¯1 + ¯1 ×  1
0011 ← 01 + 11 × 10      3 ←  1 + ¯1 × ¯2            0001 ← 11 + 11 × 10       1 ← ¯1 + ¯1 × ¯2
0010 ← 01 + 11 × 11      2 ←  1 + ¯1 × ¯1            0000 ← 11 + 11 × 11       0 ← ¯1 + ¯1 × ¯1
```

Table 3-2 All multiplications with 2-bit operands.

$(B \times 2 * 2 \times N) - A \times B$. For modulus $2 * 2 \times N$, this expression is equivalent to $(2 * 2 \times N) - A \times B$, which is the 2's-complement notation of the product. When both operands are negative, with absolute values A and B, the product becomes $(2 * 4 \times N) + (-(A + B) \times 2 * 2 \times N) + A \times B$, which is equal to $A \times B$, since the first two terms fall outside the range of representation.

Architecture with Positive Interpretation of the Operands.   The architecture of the multiplier may thus consider the operands as positive, provided that they are satisfactorily extended, prior to the multiplication. This architecture is given by *ARCHMPYX*, Program 3-3. *ARCHMPYX* uses the function *EXTEND* for the

```
       ∇ ARCHMPYX;VLX;MRX;MDX;PRODUCT
  [1]     ⍝ OPERAND EXTENSION
  [2]     VLX←(ρMR) EXTEND VL
  [3]     MRX←(ρMD) EXTEND MR
  [4]     MDX←(ρMR) EXTEND MD
  [5]     ⍝ MULTIPLICATION
  [6]     PRODUCT←(2⊥VLX)+(2⊥MRX)×2⊥MDX
  [7]     PD←((ρMRX)ρ2)⊤PRODUCT
       ∇

       ∇ RX←N EXTEND R
  [1]     RX←R[Nρ0],R
       ∇
```

Program 3-3 Multiplier architecture with extended operands.

operand extension. This function extends the operand to the left with the required number of sign bits. The extended operands VLX, MRX, and MDX are local variables, since they are not results of the operation.

Restating the Architecture. $ARCHMPYX$ is equivalent to the architecture $ARCHMPY$ given early in this chapter. The purpose of $ARCHMPYX$ is to state the architecture in a form that is more attractive to the implementer. The development of such an alternative architecture is a typical task for the implementer. Before building is begun, the implementer tries to state the specification in the form that is clearest from his point of view and which may already indicate how he intends to solve the problem. The architect, in contrast, should refrain from suggesting solutions, lest they be interpreted as part of the specification. $ARCHMPY$, therefore, best represents the basic architecture.

Operand Length. When an algorithm is verified by exhaustive execution, it is desirable to use short operands. Table 3-2 shows a complete multiplication table for 2-bit operands. Further verification may be obtained by keeping one operand short and giving the other a more normal value. For this purpose the lengths of MR and MD are kept variable in the multiplication algorithms. The length of VL is assumed to be equal to that of MD. One may readily see how the expressions are simplified when VL, MR, and MD all have length N.

3-2 BASIC MULTIPLIER ALGORITHM

The repeated addition which is suggested by the arithmetic definition is so slow that it is always replaced by an algorithm that makes use of the positional number representation. In these algorithms, the multiplicand is shifted as it is added to the partial product. All prominent multiplication algorithms, as well as the manual calculation of Table 3-4, make use of this principle. These algorithms differ only in the number of shifts and the nature of the addition after each shift.

The elementary application of the basic multiplication algorithm for binary base and positive operands is shown in the block diagram of Figure 3-5 and in $POSMPY$, Program 3-6. This algorithm is the machine version of the manual calculation.

In the basic algorithm, the multiplicand and partial product are added during each multiplication cycle in which the active multiplier bit is 1; no addition takes place when this bit is 0. Subsequently, the multiplicand and partial product are shifted with respect to each other by 1 bit.

Series versus Parallel Multiplication. The addition of multiplicand and partial product is specified in line 11 of $POSMPY$, by referring to $ARCHADD$. Hence, any implementation may be used that satisfies this adder architecture.

For the adder, a series, series–parallel, or parallel implementation is possible. In the case of a series adder, the multiplicand is processed in series, and the shifting

```
        BINARY                    DECIMAL EQUIVALENT

        100101    MD                   37
       1100111  × MR                  103 ×
       -------                        ---
          1001    VL                    9
        100101                         37  ←   1×37
        100101.                        74  ←   2×37
        100101..                      148  ←   4×37
    100101.....                      1184  ←  32×37
    100101......                     2368  ←  64×37
    -----------                      ----
    111011101100   PD                3820
```

Table 3-4   Manual multiplication.

of the partial product is executed in time instead of space. A series–parallel execution will be considered in Chapter 5. In this chapter, a parallel adder, which can process the multiplicand in one cycle, will be assumed.

The multiplier *MR* is used in series in the basic algorithm. The aim of the algorithms to be discussed in Sections 3-4 through 3-6 is to treat the multiplier more and more in parallel.

Prologue and Epilogue.   Lines 2 and 3 of *POSMPY* show that at the start of the operation, the initial value *VL* and the multiplier *MR* are in registers *P* and *Q*; line 18 shows that ultimately the product *PD* occupies that place. The initial value *VL* can thus be interpreted as the initial partial product and the product *PD* as the final partial product. The multiplicand *MD* is in *R* at the start of the multiplication, as shown in line 4, and remains there unchanged.

The registers *P*, *Q*, and *R* are the work registers of the arithmetic organ. The initial and final steps which place the operands in and take the result out of these registers are identified in the program as separate from the actual multiplication by the comments *PROLOGUE* and *EPILOGUE*. These initial and final steps do not change the data. They have the character of declarations.

Registers.   During the operation, new information is placed in registers *P* and *Q*, as indicated in lines 12 and 13. The purpose of the designer is sufficiently stated here with the simple assignment. The details of the read-in signals and the internal working of the registers need not be considered at this point.

Shift Direction and Shift Relation.   In the manual multiplication, the multiplicand is shifted to the left with respect to the partial product. Instead, in *POSMPY*, the partial product and multiplier are so placed in *P* and *Q*, that they are effectively shifted to the right, and the multiplicand is not shifted.

Right Shift of Multiplier.   Shifting multiplier and partial product to the right results in a simple implementation because:

(a) The multiplier bit that determines whether or not the multiplicand is added is always in the rightmost position of *Q*.

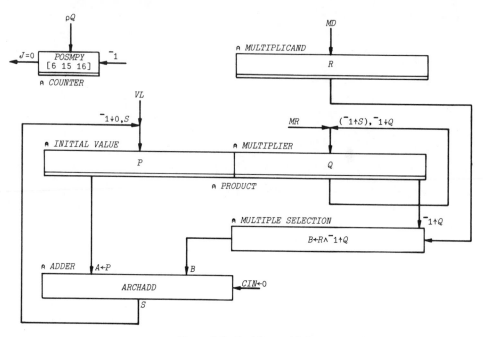

Figure 3-5   Positive multiplier.

(b) The partial product bits to which the multiplicand is added always go to and from the adder from the same positions in register P.

(c) The total number of active bits remains constant, since in each cycle the multiplier becomes 1 bit shorter and the partial product 1 bit longer.

Left Shift of Multiplier.   An algorithm that uses the multiplier bits from left to right and shifts the partial product to the left relative to the multiplicand is also possible. The left shift has the advantage that it matches the shift direction used in division. For left to right operation, however, the adder must be extended to a width of $2 \times N$ to accommodate possible carries.

The IBM 650 (1957) used the multiplier bits from left to right. The addition was performed in series. The full length of the sum register had to be passed through the adder anyway, because the contents of its capacitive elements needed refreshing.

The System/370 Model 158 integer multiplier also processes the multiplier left to right. A full 64-bit product is passed through a 32-bit adder in two cycles. The first cycle performs an addition, and the second cycle propagates a possible carry.

Fixed Multiplier.   One could also propose an implementation in which the multiplier does not shift during the operation. The active multiplier bit must then be selected from successive register positions. In APL, such a selection can be simply formulated as $X \leftarrow Y[J]$; in hardware, however, this requires an 'and' circuit

```
      ∇ POSMPY
[1]   ⍝ PROLOGUE
[2]   P←VL
[3]   Q←MR
[4]   R←MD
[5]   ⍝ MULTIPLICATION
[6]   J←⍴Q
[7]   ⍝ ADDITION
[8]   CONT:A←P
[9]   B←R∧¯1↑Q
[10]  CIN←0
[11]  ARCHADD
[12]  P←¯1↓0,S
[13]  Q←(¯1↑S),¯1↓Q
[14]  ⍝ COUNT
[15]  J←J-1
[16]  →(J≠0)/CONT
[17]  ⍝ EPILOGUE
[18]  PD←P,Q
      ∇
```

```
      ⍝ REFERENCE:                                    PROGRAM:
      ⍝ ARCHADD         ADDER ARCHITECTURE            2-5
```

Program 3-6   Positive multiplier.

for each bit position with associated selection controls and therefore is an expensive solution.

Minus Sign.   In lines 9, 12, and 13 of *POSMPY*, the minus sign is used. APL distinguishes the monadic *negation* operator and the dyadic *subtraction* operator, as in line 15, from the *minus sign*, which is a part of the number representation, as in line 9. The sign is placed higher than the operator to make the distinction apparent. In line 9 the number minus 1 is used to select the right bit of Q. If the negation operator were used in line 9, the left bit of Q would be taken negatively.

Counter.   The count in *POSMPY*, lines 6 and 15, is part of the implementation. Hence, it differs from the counting in the previous implementation programs, as in *RIPPLE*, Program 2-17, where the count is an aid in the description. The counter of *POSMPY* must be built as part of the hardware, as is indicated in the upper left corner of Figure 3-5. Similarly, the branch in line 16 is part of the hardware. The condition for this branch requires the circuit $J = 0$, which is a portion of the counter. The hardware for the branch itself is not shown in Figure 3-5.

Completeness of Block Diagram.   These considerations show that the block diagram of Figure 3-5 does not represent the complete multiplier. The figure shows the available components and connections, but not the equipment that determines when the connections must be used. The circuit of the block diagram must yet be controlled, as will be discussed in Chapter 6.

Initial Algorithm.   The algorithm *POSMPY* must be worked out further to be entirely realizable, as appears from the treatment of the adder, the registers, and the count. In contrast to the block diagram, however, the APL description is complete. Although on a high level, this type of description constitutes a proper first step in the design of the implementation and will be used as such in this chapter and Chapter 4. These *initial algorithms* give a first conversion from operators such as multiply and divide, for which a functional unit is not assumed to be available, to operators such as add, for which an implementation as a functional unit is available. The description in terms of circuits, which are realizable in detail, will be discussed in Chapter 5.

3-3 MULTIPLIER FOR POSITIVE AND NEGATIVE OPERANDS

ARCHMPYX has shown that negative numbers can be multiplied as positive numbers, provided they are sufficiently extended. The extension of the multiplicand and the partial product yields few problems. During the addition the sign bit of the operands need only be extended by one or two positions to know the sign of the sum. Thus, a single-length adder can still be used. The extension of the multiplier, however, might double the duration of the operation. For a negative multiplier the extension of the sign bit causes a series of 1s, each requiring an add cycle. Table 3-7A shows how the extended operands contribute to the product.

```
----EXTENSION OF MD AND MR        DECIMAL       ----EXTENSION OF MD
11111001    MD                      ⁻7           11111001    MD
11111010 × MR                       ⁻6 ×            1010 × MR
--------                            --            ----
1111001.                            42           1111001. ← 2×MD
11001...                                          00111... ←⁻8×MD
1001....  |                                       --------
001.....  |                                       00101010    PD
01......  |
1.......  |EXTRA CYCLES FOR EXTENDED MR
--------
00101010    PD

A.                                              B.
```

Table 3-7   Effect of extended operands.

Coding of the Multiplier with 1, 0, and ⁻1

The extra multiplication cycles for a negative multiplier can be eliminated by using ⁻1, as well as 1 and 0, for multiplier digits. In other words, the multiplicand is not only added but also subtracted. This coding assumes that the arithmetic unit can perform subtraction as easily as addition. This is normally the case since the arithmetic unit must be able to perform both operations efficiently. As mentioned in Chapter 2, subtraction requires only a complementing unit at one of the adder inputs.

The recoding of the multiplier replaces a string of K 1s by 1, followed by $K - 1$ times 0, and then ⁻1. For instance, 31, represented binarily as $0\ 0\ 1\ 1\ 1\ 1\ 1$, can also be represented as $0\ 1\ 0\ 0\ 0\ 0\ ^-1$, that is, as $32 - 1$.

Recoding of the Sign Extension.   The string of 1s that results from the extension of a negative multiplier sign can now be replaced by $^-1$ at the original sign position, with a string of 0s to its left and a 1 bit completely to the left. For the digits 0 no multiply cycle is necessary, whereas the 1 bit to the left falls outside the number range and thus does not require a multiply cycle either. Therefore, the multiplier no longer needs to be extended. This solution is demonstrated in Table 3-7B.

General Recoding.   The recoding of the sign extension of the multiplier with 1, 0, and $^-1$ can also be used for the other multiplier bits. In general, this recoding results in a larger number of 0 bits, which is an advantage for some algorithms. More important is that the sign bit is treated the same as the digit bits, which simplifies the algorithm.

Recoding Algorithm.   The recoding can occur bit by bit during the multiplication. When a multiplier bit is 1, it is considered as $2 + {}^-1$. The operation for $^-1$, a subtraction, takes place during the current cycle, while the operation for 2 is interpreted as an addition during the next cycle. The fact that this addition must take place is recorded in the *multiplier balance* bit.

When at the start of a cycle the balance is 0, a multiplier bit 0 causes no action and a multiplier bit 1 causes a subtraction, as described above. When the balance is 1, a multiplier bit 1 causes no action, since the addition for the balance compensates the subtraction for the multiplier bit. The balance remains 1 in this case. When, however, the multiplier bit is 0, the balance leads to an addition and the new balance becomes 0.

Table 3-8A summarizes the recoding rules. Where in *POSMPY* the actions for 0s and 1s were quite different, they are now more symmetrical.

MR[J]	OLD BALANCE	RECODING	OPERATION	NEW BALANCE
0	0	0	NONE	0
0	1	1	ADDITION	0
1	0	$^-1$	SUBTRACTION	1
1	1	0	NONE	1

A. SIMPLE RECODING

MR[(J-1),J]	OLD BALANCE	RECODING	OPERATION	NEW BALANCE
0 0	0	0	NONE	0
0 0	1	1	ADDITION	0
0 1	0	1	ADDITION	0
0 1	1	0	NONE	1
1 0	0	0	NONE	0
1 0	1	$^-1$	SUBTRACTION	1
1 1	0	$^-1$	SUBTRACTION	1
1 1	1	0	NONE	1

B. RECODING FOR MINIMAL ARITHMETIC

Table 3-8   Coding of the multiplier with 1, 0, and $^-1$.

*RECODE*1, Program 3-9, shows the principle of the recoding, when applied in parallel. Table 3-10 shows an example of recoding for 1, 0, and ⁻1, as well as examples of types of recoding to be discussed later.

```
    ∇ OUT←RECODE1 IN
[1]  OUT←(1↓IN,0)-IN
    ∇
```

Program 3-9   Recoding for 1, 0, and ⁻1.

```
    RECODE1 0 1 1 0 0 1 1 1
1  0  ⁻1  0  1  0  0  ⁻1

    RECODE1 0 0 0 1 0 1 0 0
0  0  1  ⁻1  1  ⁻1  0  0

    ⍝ RECODING FOR 1, 0, AND ⁻1

    RECODE1X 0 1 1 0 0 1 1 1
1  0  ⁻1  0  1  0  0  ⁻1

    RECODE1X 0 0 0 1 0 1 0 0
0  0  0  1  0  1  0  0

    ⍝ RECODING FOR MINIMAL ARITHMETIC

    RECODE2 0 1 1 0 0 1 1 1
2  ⁻2  2  ⁻1

    ⍝ RECODING FOR 2, 1, 0, ⁻1, ⁻2

    RECODE3 0 0 1 1 0 0 1 1 1
2  ⁻3  ⁻1

    ⍝ RECODING FOR 4, 3, 2, 1, 0, ⁻1, ⁻2, ⁻3, ⁻4
```

Table 3-10   Examples of recoding.

Multiplier with 1-bit Shift

Figure 3-11 shows the block diagram of a multiplier for positive and negative operands. Program 3-12 shows the corresponding algorithm *ONEMPY* and Table 3-13 shows an example of its action.

Serial Recoding.   In *ONEMPY* the multiplier is recoded 1 bit at a time, and the balance must be remembered, from cycle to cycle. Table 3-8A shows that the new balance is equal to the current multiplier bit. Therefore, it is sufficient to remember the current multiplier bit during the next cycle and to use it during that cycle as balance. The balance is stored in register W, which can be considered as an extension of register Q or as a multiplier buffer. Prior to the multiplication there is no balance. Therefore, W is set to 0 at the start of the multiplication, as is shown in line 6 of *ONEMPY*.

Multiple Selection.   The function *TWOFOLD* determines which multiple of the multiplicand should be used. This selection is based upon the active multiplier bit in the rightmost bit of Q and the balance in W. *TWOFOLD* represents in essence the complementer shown in Figure 2-1, supplemented with the generation of the carry-in and the specialized control required by the multiplier.

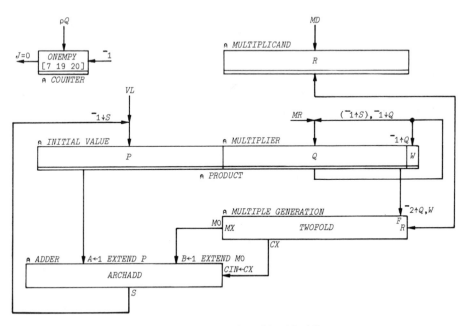

Figure 3-11   Multiplier with 1-bit shift.

```
     ∇ ONEMPY
[1]    ⍝ PROLOGUE
[2]    P←VL
[3]    Q←MR
[4]    R←MD
[5]    ⍝ MULTIPLICATION
[6]    W←0
[7]    J←ρQ
[8]    ⍝ MULTIPLE GENERATION
[9]  CONT:M0←R TWOFOLD ¯2↑Q,W
[10]   ⍝ ADDITION
[11]   A←1 EXTEND P
[12]   B←1 EXTEND M0
[13]   CIN←CX
[14]   ARCHADD
[15]   W←¯1↑Q
[16]   P←¯1↓S
[17]   Q←(¯1↑S),¯1↓Q
[18]   ⍝ COUNT
[19]   J←J-1
[20]   →(J≠0)/CONT
[21]   ⍝ EPILOGUE
[22]   PD←P,Q
     ∇
```

```
     ∇ MX←R TWOFOLD F
[1]    ⍝ DECISION
[2]    ONE←F[0]≠F[1]
[3]    ⍝ COMPLEMENT
[4]    COM←F[0]≠R
[5]    ⍝ SELECTION
[6]    MX←ONE∧COM
[7]    ⍝ CARRY-IN
[8]    CX←F[0]∧ONE
     ∇
```

```
     ⍝ REFERENCE:                          PROGRAM:
     ⍝ ARCHADD    ADDER ARCHITECTURE        2-5
     ⍝ EXTEND     OPERAND EXTENSION         3-3
```

Program 3-12   Multiplier with 1-bit shift.

Adder Length. The adder of *ONEMPY* is 1 bit longer than the adder of *POSMPY* to accommodate the maximum negative number of the 2's-complement range. In *POSMPY* the sign of the sum, which is always positive, is extended as the sum enters P. In *ONEMPY* such an extension would give the wrong result when the maximum negative number is complemented. The effect of the maximum negative number can also be seen from Table 3-2, where the left two product bits are always alike, except when both multiplier and multiplicand are maximum negative.

Shift. Following the addition, the new partial product bits are placed in P and the leftmost bit of Q, as shown in *ONEMPY*, lines 16 and 17. The completed part of the partial product and the remaining multiplier bits are placed 1 bit to the right in Q and W as shown in lines 15 and 17. The right shift of partial product and multiplier is thus achieved by reading into the desired register positions with a 1-bit displacement.

Shift Register. The right shift of the content of Q and W can also be performed within the register itself. A register that has the added function of such an internal shift is called a *shift register*. The description of *ONEMPY*, lines 15 and 17, may also be interpreted as such a shift register. The choice between these implementation details need not be made in the initial algorithm.

Shifting in P. In *ONEMPY* the new content of P is always obtained from the adder output. When the multiplicand is neither added nor subtracted, however, the content of P can simply be shifted 1 bit to the right. If the time allotted for this shift is equal to that for the addition, there is no particular advantage in using a shift register for P. If, however, a shift cycle is shorter than an add cycle, a speed advantage may be obtained.

Recoding for Optimum Shift. The recoding of the multiplier according to Table 3-8A tends to give a large number of 0 digits. In case of an isolated 0 or 1, however, the recoding introduces both an addition and a subtraction. Thus, 0 1 0 1 0 1 0 1, which would involve four additions without the recoding, is recoded to 1 ⁻1 1 ⁻1 1 ⁻1 1 ⁻1, which requires four additions and four subtractions. Therefore, when an optimum shift over 0 is required, the recoding algorithm should be modified such that only one action occurs for an isolated 0 or 1. Table 3-8B shows the rules for such a recoding, and Table 3-10 shows an example. The corresponding modification of *TWOFOLD* is shown in Program 3-16.

Multiplier Application. An example of a multiplier with a fast shift register for P and modified recoding is the PDP11/45 floating-point multiplier. The shift cycle of this multiplier is four times faster than its add cycle.

Multiplier Trace. Table 3-13 compares the actions of *ONEMPY* with *POSMPY*, Section 3-2, and *SHIFTMPY*, to be discussed in Section 3-4. The content of the pertinent registers and the properly aligned adder inputs and output are traced.

The printout of Table 3-13 is obtained by introducing in *ARCHADD* a function similar to *PRINTADD*. Each time *ARCHADD* is called by *POSMPY* or *ONEMPY*, a compact printout of the desired information is obtained.

A trace can also be obtained quite simply with the trace functions of the APL implementations. In that case, the printout is not compact and not aligned. Such a trace will often be quite satisfactory, however. The function used here shows how with little effort a complete record of an operation can be obtained.

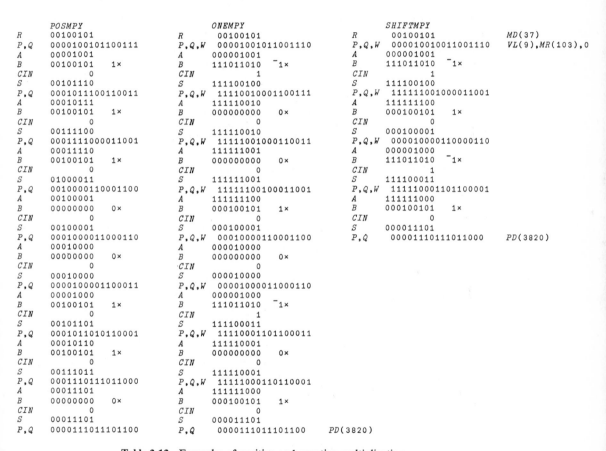

Table 3-13 Examples of positive and negative multiplication.

3-4 MULTIPLIER WITH VARIABLE SHIFT

In the previous section, either a regular or a fast cycle was taken when the recoded multiplier digit is 0. It is even more effective to read the multiplier and partial product into P, Q, and W with such a displacement that the next multiplier digit is either 1 or $^-$1. Thus, multiplier digits that are 0 are passed by and no shift cycles are required.

Shifting over Zeros.   When the multiplier bits are not recoded, the average shift is 2 bits. Therefore, shifting over 0s reduces the number of multiplication cycles by one half.

Limited Shifting.   The average shift of 2 bits assumes that every displacement is allowed. In practice, however, the possible displacements will be limited, because of the expense involved. A large number of displacements requires many 'and' circuits as input to P, Q, and W. The first row of Table 3-14 shows that the average shift length improves less and less as the number of displacements increases. Therefore, the number of shift possibilities usually is kept small.

MAXIMUM PERMISSIBLE SHIFT:	2	3	6	∞
SHIFT ONLY OVER 0	1.50	1.75	1.98	2.00
SHIFT OVER 1 AND 0	1.75	2.25	2.90	3.00

Table 3-14   Average shift length in bits.

Shifting over Zeros and Ones.   The recoding of Table 3-8A makes it also possible to shift over groups of 1s, since these will be, for the most part, changed to 0s. When all displacements are allowed, the average shift is now 3. Hence, the number of operations can be brought back to a third.

When the number of displacements again is limited, the average shift that can be obtained is shown in the second row of Table 3-14.

Random and Realistic Digit Distribution.   The numbers of Table 3-14 are obtained for a random distribution of 0s and 1s. As stated in Chapter 2, integer operands are likely to have a string of leading 0s or 1s. These strings improve the the average shift length.

Some multipliers use the fact that the leftmost multiplier bits are likely to be identical. Thus the System/370 Model 158 integer multiplier shifts 4 bits each time 4 equal multiplier bits are encountered. The System/370 Model 168 tests for the equality of the left 17 multiplier bits. This equality is particularly likely in view of the half-word operands, which may be used in System/370.

Variable-Shift Multiplier

Figure 3-15 and *SHIFTMPY*, Program 3-16, describe a multiplier that displaces the partial product with a minimum of 1 bit and a maximum of 4 bits. The use of the multiplier is illustrated in Table 3-13. The multiplier uses the recoding of Table 3-8B in the multiple selection of *TWOFOLDX*. The amount of displacement is determined by the function *DISPLACE*.

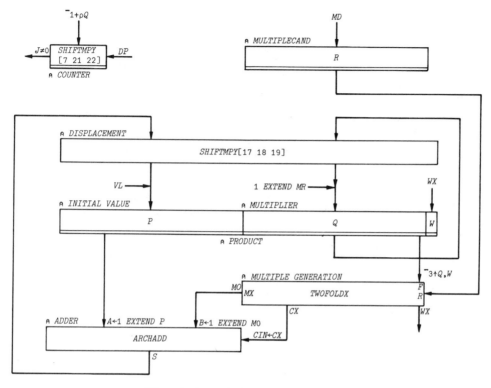

Figure 3-15 Variable shift multiplier.

Multiple Selection. *TWOFOLDX* shows that the multiple selection as such is not appreciably complicated by the recoding for maximum shift. Only the new balance, which formerly was just the old multiplier bit, is now determined by an 'and-or' condition, as shown in line 10 of *TWOFOLDX*.

Since the multiple selection uses 2 multiplier bits, the multiplier must now be extended by 1 bit. Hence, Q is made 1 bit longer in *SHIFTMPY* than was the case in *ONEMPY*. The extension of the multiplier also assures that the product has the proper sign, since the last multiplicand multiple will now be the same as for *ONEMPY*.

Displacement. The function *DISPLACE* indicates the desired displacement by means of the vector *DP*. The displacement is determined by the rightmost transition from 0 to 1, or reverse, in the new values of Q and W. The displacement should not shift the multiplier beyond its leftmost digit; that is, the count J may not become negative. If, for instance, J is 1 prior to the addition, only a 1-bit displacement is allowed. In that case, $DP[3]$ is made 1 in line 3 of *DISPLACE*, and all other bits of *DP* become 0. Lines 18 and 19 of *SHIFTMPY* are now equivalent to lines 16 and 17 of *ONEMPY*.

```
        ∇ SHIFTMPY                              ∇ MX←R TWOFOLDX F
[1]       ⍝ PROLOGUE                     [1]      ⍝ DECISION
[2]       P←VL                           [2]      ONE←F[1]≠F[2]
[3]       Q←1 EXTEND MR                  [3]      ⍝ COMPLEMENT
[4]       R←MD                           [4]      COM←F[0]≠R
[5]       ⍝ MULTIPLICATION               [5]      ⍝ SELECTION
[6]       W←0                            [6]      MX←ONE∧COM
[7]       J←¯1+ρQ                        [7]      ⍝ CARRY-IN
[8]       ⍝ MULTIPLE GENERATION          [8]      CX←F[0]∧ONE
[9]     CONT:M0←R TWOFOLDX ¯3↑Q,W        [9]      ⍝ NEW BALANCE
[10]      ⍝ ADDITION                     [10]     WX←(F[0]∧F[1])∨(F[0]∧F[2])∨F[1]∧F[2]
[11]      A←1 EXTEND P                          ∇
[12]      B←1 EXTEND M0
[13]      CIN←CX
[14]      ARCHADD
[15]      W←WX
[16]      ⍝ DISPLACEMENT
[17]      DP←DISPLACE(¯1+¯4↑Q),WX
[18]      P←(DP[0]∧¯4↓S[0 0 0],S)∨(DP[1]∧¯3↓S[0 0],S)∨(DP[2]∧¯2↓S[0],S)∨DP[3]∧¯1↓S
[19]      Q←(DP[0]∧(¯4↑S),¯4↓Q)∨(DP[1]∧(¯3↑S),¯3↓Q)∨(DP[2]∧(¯2↑S),¯2↓Q)∨DP[3]∧(¯1↑S),¯1↓Q
[20]      ⍝ COUNT
[21]      J←J-(DP[0]×3)+(DP[1]×2)+DP[2]+1
[22]      →(J≠0)/CONT
[23]      ⍝ EPILOGUE
[24]      PD←¯1↓P,Q
        ∇


        ∇ DP←DISPLACE F
[1]       ⍝ DISPLACEMENT DECISION
[2]       DP←4ρ0
[3]       DP[3]←(J=1)∨F[2]≠F[3]
[4]       DP[2]←(~DP[3])∧(J=2)∨F[1]≠F[2]
[5]       DP[1]←(~∨/DP[2 3])∧(J=3)∨F[0]≠F[1]
[6]       DP[0]←~∨/DP[1 2 3]
        ∇


        ⍝ REFERENCE:                                        PROGRAM:
        ⍝ ARCHADD       ADDER ARCHITECTURE                    2-5
        ⍝ EXTEND        OPERAND EXTENSION                     3-3
```

Program 3-16   Variable shift multiplier.

Multiplier Speed and Cost. *SHIFTMPY* is about 2.1 times faster than *ONEMPY*, assuming all operand bits are significant and assuming a lengthening of the cycle by 10% as a result of the variable displacement. When only half the operand bits are significant, the speed improvement over *ONEMPY* is a factor of 2.8. The amount of equipment, however, has increased by about 40%, owing to the four-way displacement.

These estimates are independent of the operand lengths. As a rough measure, four nands per register position are assumed and nine nands per adder position. The other counts can be obtained directly from the programs.

3-5 MULTIPLIER WITH FIXED SHIFT

As an alternative to the variable shift, the fixed shift of 1 of *ONEMPY* can be increased to 2, 3, or more bits. The shift mechanism is now simple and a shift decision is not necessary, since the same shift is used each cycle. The multiplier can be regarded as represented in binary-coded base 4 or base 8 notation. Or, to put it differently, the multiplier is processed with 2 or 3 bits in series–parallel.

Generation of Multiples of the Multiplicand.   When the multiplier is processed with 2 or 3 bits at a time, the corresponding multiples of the multiplicand should be available. These multiples can be generated in advance or during the multiply cycles. When generated in advance, the multiples are stored in registers or storage. When generated during the multiply cycles, a shifter can be used to obtain multiples that are a power of 2 and a complementer to obtain negative multiples. The two methods may be combined by storing only a few multiples and obtaining the others by shifting and complementing.

Babbage proposed for his decimal multiplier to store all nine multiples of the multiplicand and to generate them by repeated addition. When time is not critical, as for the Hewlett-Packard 9100A, the multiples can be generated when needed, also using repeated addition. The System/370 Model 155 floating-point multiplier generates and stores in advance the multiples 2, 3, and 6, and uses a 1-bit displacement to obtain the multiples 4, 6, and 12. The multiplier is processed 4 bits at a time by using up to three of these multiples in succession.

The System/370 Model 158 multiplier also uses a fixed 4-bit shift but obtains the multiplicand multiples by table look-up. For each 4 multiplicand bits the 4 low-order and the 4 high-order multiple bits are obtained from a table stored in an individual component. The multiple is assembled as two words, which both must be added to the partial product. Similarly, the TI SN74284 and SN74285 provide the product bits of a 4-bit multiplier and a 4-bit multiplicand. Several of these modules can be used in parallel to match the multiplicand length.

Multiplier with 2-bit Shift

For a fixed shift of 2 bits, the desired multiples are specified by Table 3-17A. The multiplier is thought to be extended by a balance bit, $MR[J + 1]$. Table 3-17A can be obtained by applying the principle of Table 3-8A twice in succession. Table 3-17A can also be obtained directly by noticing that two multiplier bits, representing the digit 0, 1, 2, or 3, can be coded as 0, 1, 4-2, or 4-1. The 4

MR[(J-1),J,J+1]	RECODING		MR[(J-2),(J-1),J,J+1]	RECODING
0 0 0	0		0 0 0 0	0
0 0 1	1		0 0 0 1	1
0 1 0	1		0 0 1 0	1
0 1 1	-2		0 0 1 1	2
1 0 0	-2		0 1 0 0	2
1 0 1	-1		0 1 0 1	3
1 1 0	-1		0 1 1 0	3
1 1 1	0		0 1 1 1	4
			1 0 0 0	-4
			1 0 0 1	-3
			1 0 1 0	-3
			1 0 1 1	-2
			1 1 0 0	-2
			1 1 0 1	-1
			1 1 1 0	-1
			1 1 1 1	0

A. 2-BIT SHIFT   B. 3-BIT SHIFT

Table 3-17   Coding of the multiplier for a fixed shift.

is counted as a balance of 1 in the next cycle. If there was already a balance, then 0, 1, 2, and 3 are coded as 1, 2, 4-1, and 4. The last two digits again give a balance of 1. An example of 2-bit encoding is shown in Table 3-10.

Figure 3-18 shows the block diagram for a 2-bit multiplier. *TWOMPY*, Program 3-19, describes this multiplier and an example of a multiplication is shown in Table 3-20. The function *FOURFOLD* produces the multiple of the multiplicand as specified by Table 3-17A. *TWOFOLD* incorporates a complementer and a 1-bit shifter. Thus, a variable displacement of the multiplicand is introduced instead of the variable displacement of the partial product and multiplier.

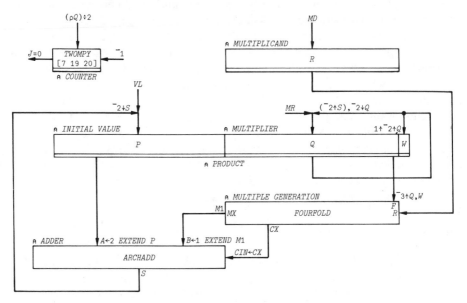

Figure 3-18   Multiplier with 2-bit shift.

Multiplier Cost and Speed.   *TWOMPY* is about twice as fast as *ONEMPY*, since 2 multiplier bits are processed per cycle, and the datapath is not noticeably lengthened. The increase in the cost of TWOMPY over ONEMPY is about 10%. Hence, *TWOMPY* compares favorably with *SHIFTMPY*, which explains why the fixed shift is normally preferred over the variable shift.

Three-Bit Shift

A fixed shift of 3 bits requires the multiplicand multiples 0 through 7. The multiples 4, 5, 6, and 7 again can be obtained as 8-4, 8-3, 8-2, and 8-1, as shown in Table 3-17B. The multiple 8 is used as a balance in the next cycle.

Multiple 3 cannot be obtained by shifting. This multiple can be obtained when needed by employing the multiples 1 and 2 in two successive cycles. This solution degrades the performance by about 25% and complicates the algorithm. The

```
        ∇ TWOMPY
  [1]   ⍝ PROLOGUE
  [2]   P←VL
  [3]   Q←MR
  [4]   R←MD
  [5]   ⍝ MULTIPLICATION
  [6]   W←0
  [7]   J←(⍴Q)÷2
  [8]   ⍝ MULTIPLE GENERATION
  [9]   CONT:M1←R FOURFOLD ¯3↑Q,W
  [10]  ⍝ ADDITION
  [11]  A←2 EXTEND P
  [12]  B←1 EXTEND M1
  [13]  CIN←CX
  [14]  ARCHADD
  [15]  W←1↑¯2↑Q
  [16]  P←¯2↓S
  [17]  Q←(¯2↑S),¯2↓Q
  [18]  ⍝ COUNT
  [19]  J←J-1
  [20]  →(J≠0)/CONT
  [21]  ⍝ EPILOGUE
  [22]  PD←P,Q
        ∇
```

```
        ∇ MX←R FOURFOLD F
  [1]   ⍝ DECISION
  [2]   ONE←F[1]≠F[2]
  [3]   TWO←((~F[0])∧F[1]∧F[2])∨F[0]∧(~F[1])∧~F[2]
  [4]   ⍝ COMPLEMENT
  [5]   COM←F[0]≠R
  [6]   ⍝ SELECTION
  [7]   MX←(ONE∧COM[0],COM)∨TWO∧COM,F[0]
  [8]   ⍝ CARRY-IN
  [9]   CX←F[0]∧ONE∨TWO
        ∇
```

```
  ⍝ REFERENCE:                                              PROGRAM:
  ⍝ ARCHADD      ADDER ARCHITECTURE                         2-5
  ⍝ EXTEND       OPERAND EXTENSION                          3-3
```

Program 3-19   Multiplier with 2-bit shift.

Table 3-20   Examples of multiplying with 2 bits simultaneously.

```
      TWOMPY                                         TWOMPY
R        00100101          MD(37)         R             00100101           MD(37)
P,Q,W    0000100101100110  VL(9),MR(103),0  P,Q,W     00001001100110010   VL(9),MR(¯103),0
A        0000001001                         A         0000001001
B        1111011010   ¯1×                   B         0000100101    1×
CIN           1                             CIN           0
S        1111100100                         S         0000101110
P,Q,W    11111001000110011  P,Q,W           00001011101001100
A        1111111001                         A         0000001011
B        0001001010   2×                    B         1110110101   ¯2×
CIN           0                             CIN           1
S        0001000011                         S         1111000001
P,Q,W    00010000110001100  P,Q,W           11110000011010011
A        0000010000                         A         1111110000
B        1110110101   ¯2×                   B         0001001010    2×
CIN           1                             CIN           0
S        1111000110                         S         0000111010
P,Q,W    11110001101100011  P,Q,W           00001110100110100
A        1111110001                         A         0000001110
B        0001001010   2×                    B         1110110101   ¯2×
CIN           0                             CIN           1
S        0000111011                         S         1111000100
P,Q      0000111011101100   PD(3820)        P,Q        1111000100100110   PD(¯3802)
```

multiple can also be made in advance in a separate cycle and stored in a register. Most attractive, however, is to make the multiple in a combinational tripling circuit attached to the multiplicand register. This last method is used in the 12-bit multiplier, which is discussed in Section 3-6.

Further Development of the Algorithm.   The datapath and control for the 2-bit multiplier *TWOMPY* are further discussed in Chapters 5 and 6. The reader will not lose any continuity if he proceeds directly to the first sections of those chapters and returns to the remainder of this chapter later.

3-6 MULTIPLIERS WITH MULTIPLE ADDERS

The multiplication cycles of the previous algorithms can, in principle, be performed simultaneously. Thus, one could unroll *ONEMPY* as an algorithm with N adders comparable to the unrolling of *RIPPLE*, Program 2-17. Such a circuit is, of course, extensive. Since it is built from regular circuits, it can be constructed relatively inexpensively, however, with integrated components. Therefore, circuits with multiple adders are being considered more and more (Habibi and Wintz, 1970; Kamal and Ghannam, 1972).

The use of multiple adders can be combined with a recoding of the multiplier. Accordingly, the number of times that the multiplicand must be added is divided by 2 or 3.

The multiplicand multiples can be added by a set of carry-save adders followed by a carry-propagation adder. The propagation of the carry strongly influences the speed of the multiplier. We can therefore distinguish between multipliers with immediate and with delayed carry propagation.

Immediate Carry Propagation

The multiplier *EIGHTMPY* of Figure 3-21 and Program 3-22 uses the principle of *TWOMPY* four times. The total shift is therefore 8 bits. The 8 multiplier bits are used in four groups of 2 bits, each coded according to Table 3-17A, using 2 multiplier bits and a balance. The resulting four multiples of the multiplicand must be added to the partial product. For this addition three carry-save adders, *ARCH-SAVE*, Program 2-36, are used. Each carry-save adder reduces the number of operands by one. The last two operands are joined in a carry-propagation adder *ARCHADD*, which yields the new partial product.

The carry-save adders are shifted 2 bits with respect to each other and have a length of $N + 1$ bits. The propagation adder is $N + 8$ bits long. The low-order bits of this adder may operate slowly, since their operands are available early. For the remaining part a carry speed-up circuit is desirable. The last bit of the carry-save adders can be made less expensive by observing that two of the three operands have been extended (MacSorley, 1961, p. 78).

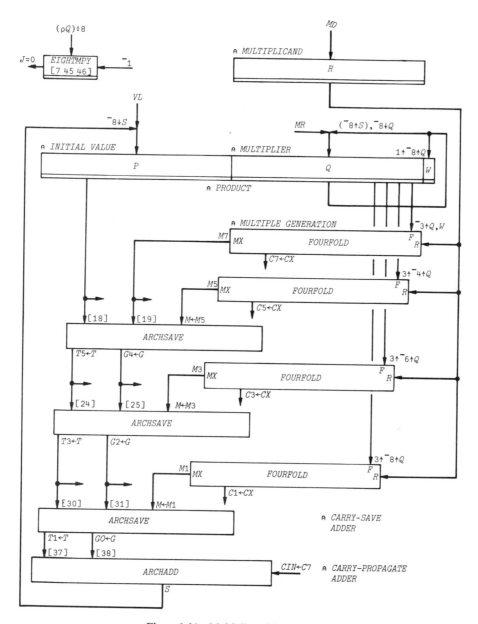

Figure 3-21 Multiplier with 8-bit shift.

Multiplier Speed and Cost.   The 8-bit multiplier is only about six times as fast as a 1-bit multiplier, since the combinatoric path is increased with one third by the levels of the carry-save adders. The cost of *EIGHTMPY* is about three times that of *ONEMPY*.

```
        ∇ EIGHTMPY
[1]     ⍝ PROLOGUE
[2]     P←VL
[3]     Q←MR
[4]     R←MD
[5]     ⍝ MULTIPLICATION
[6]     W←0
[7]     J←(⍴Q)÷8
[8]     ⍝ MULTIPLE GENERATION
[9]     CONT:M7←R FOURFOLD ¯3↑Q,W
[10]    C7←CX
[11]    M5←R FOURFOLD 3↑¯4↑Q
[12]    C5←CX
[13]    M3←R FOURFOLD 3↑¯6↑Q
[14]    C3←CX
[15]    M1←R FOURFOLD 3↑¯8↑Q
[16]    C1←CX
[17]    ⍝ CARRY-SAVE ADDITION
[18]    K←3 EXTEND ¯2↑P
[19]    L←2 EXTEND ¯2↓M7
[20]    M←M5
[21]    ARCHSAVE
[22]    T5←T
[23]    G4←G
[24]    K←2 EXTEND ¯2↓T5
[25]    L←1 EXTEND ¯1↓G4
[26]    M←M3
[27]    ARCHSAVE
[28]    T3←T
[29]    G2←G
[30]    K←2 EXTEND ¯2↓T3
[31]    L←1 EXTEND ¯1↓G2
[32]    M←M1
[33]    ARCHSAVE
[34]    T1←T
[35]    G0←G
[36]    ⍝ CARRY-PROPAGATE ADDITION
[37]    A←1 EXTEND T1,(¯2↑T3),(¯2↑T5),¯2↑P
[38]    B←G0,C1,(¯1↑G2),C3,(¯1↑G4),C5,¯2↑M7
[39]    CIN←C7
[40]    ARCHADD
[41]    W←1↑¯8↑Q
[42]    P←¯8↓S
[43]    Q←(¯8↑S),¯8↓Q
[44]    ⍝ COUNT
[45]    J←J-1
[46]    →(J≠0)/CONT
[47]    ⍝ EPILOGUE
[48]    PD←P,Q
        ∇
```

⍝ REFERENCE:		PROGRAM:
⍝ ARCHADD	ADDER ARCHITECTURE	2-5
⍝ ARCHSAVE	CARRY-SAVE ADDER ARCHITECTURE	2-36
⍝ EXTEND	OPERAND EXTENSION	3-3
⍝ FOURFOLD	MULTIPLICAND SELECTION FOR 2-BIT SHIFT	3-19

Program 3-22   Multiplier with 8-bit shift.

Array Multiplier.   The carry-save adders of *EIGHTMPY* have a regular pattern. This regularity can be extended by joining lines 3 and 4 of the circuit *FOURFOLD* with a carry-save adder. Thus, for each bit position a unit circuit, or *cell*, arises. This cell has as inputs 2 bits of the multiplicand in *R*, one multiplier bit from *Q*, and the outputs *T* and *G* from the preceding cell. The signals *ONE* and *TWO* of *FOURFOLD* are made once per multiple and are also inputs of each

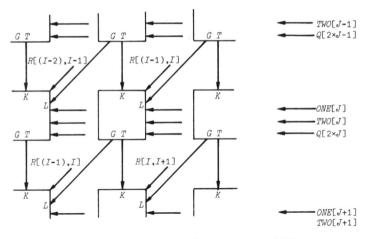

Figure 3-23 Network of cells in an array multiplier.

cell for that multiple. As outputs a T and G are again generated. Thus, the cell has seven inputs and two outputs. Figure 3-23 shows such a cell with respect to its neighbors. A multiplier that is constructed to a large extent from a network of identical cells is called an *array multiplier*.

In *EIGHTMPY* a cellular construction can be used for the adders of lines 27 and 33. With some modification these cells can also be used for line 21. When the cells are relatively inexpensive, the network can be expanded. The number of multiplier bits used per cycle increases each time by 2. Thus, one can eventually do the entire multiplication in one cycle (Pezaris, 1971).

The cell of Figure 3-23 has nine connections. Since wires take up a relatively large amount of space on an integrated circuit, it may be desirable to reduce this number. Starting with *ONEMPY*, the number of connections can be brought back to seven at the expense of a doubling of the number of cells. When only positive operands are used, *POSMPY* can be taken as a starting point, which results in only six connections per cell.

Adder Cascade. When a large number of carry-save adders follow each other, one speaks of a *cascade* of adders. The time necessary for passing through this cascade is a determining factor of the multiplier speed. This time can be reduced by simultaneously adding a larger number of multiples per bit position (Dadda, 1965; Schwartzlander, 1973). Also, the adders may be grouped more advantageously, as is demonstrated in the following example.

Delayed Carry Propagation

A multiplier that postpones the carry propagation until the end of the multiplication is shown in Figure 3-24 and described in *TWELVEMPY*, Program 3-25.

In the given example, 12 multiplier bits are used simultaneously by selecting four multiples of the multiplicand. Each multiple corresponds to 3 multiplier bits, that are coded according to Table 3-17B.

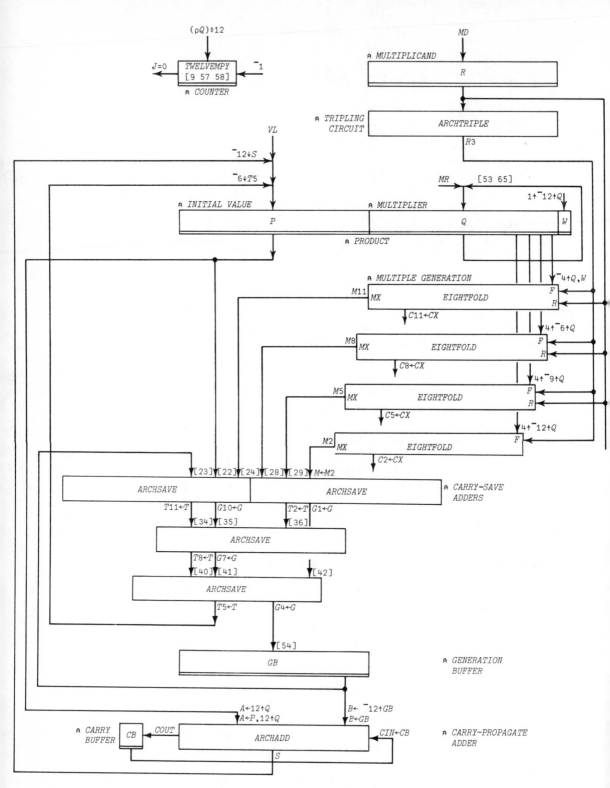

Figure 3-24 Multiplier with 12-bit shift and delayed carry propagation.

```
        ∇ TWELVEMPY
[1]     ⍀ PROLOGUE
[2]     P←VL
[3]     Q←MR
[4]     R←MD
[5]     ⍀ MULTIPLICATION
[6]     GB←(12+⍴P)⍴0
[7]     CB←0
[8]     W←0
[9]     J←(⍴Q)÷12
[10]    ⍀ TRIPLE MULTIPLICAND
[11]    R3←ARCHTRIPLE R
[12]    ⍀ MULTIPLE GENERATION
[13]    CONT:M11←R EIGHTFOLD ¯4↑Q,W
[14]    C11←CX
[15]    M8←R EIGHTFOLD 4↑¯6↑Q
[16]    C8←CX
[17]    M5←R EIGHTFOLD 4↑¯9↑Q
[18]    C5←CX
[19]    M2←R EIGHTFOLD 4↑¯12↑Q
[20]    C2←CX
[21]    ⍀ CARRY-SAVE ADDITION
[22]    K←2 EXTEND P
[23]    L←2 EXTEND ¯12↓GB
[24]    M←M11
[25]    ARCHSAVE
[26]    T11←T
[27]    G10←G
[28]    K←6 EXTEND ¯6↓M8
[29]    L←3 EXTEND ¯3↓M5
[30]    M←M2
[31]    ARCHSAVE
[32]    T2←T
[33]    G1←G
[34]    K←9 EXTEND ¯3↓T11
[35]    L←8 EXTEND ¯2↓G10
[36]    M←T2,¯6↑M8
[37]    ARCHSAVE
[38]    T8←T
[39]    G7←G
[40]    K←1 EXTEND ¯3↓T8
[41]    L←¯2↓G7
[42]    M←G1,C2,¯3↑M5
[43]    ARCHSAVE
[44]    T5←T
[45]    G4←G
[46]
```

```
[46]    ⍀ PARTIAL PROPAGATION
[47]    A←12↑Q
[48]    B←¯12↑GB
[49]    CIN←CB
[50]    ARCHADD
[51]    W←1↑¯12↑Q
[52]    P←¯6↓T5
[53]    Q←(¯6↑T5),(¯3↑T8),(¯3↑T11),¯12↓S,12↓Q
[54]    GB←1↓G4,C5,(¯2↑G7),C8,(¯2↑G10),C11
[55]    CB←COUT
[56]    ⍀ COUNT
[57]    J←J-1
[58]    →(J≠0)/CONT
[59]    ⍀ FINAL PROPAGATION
[60]    A←P,12↑Q
[61]    B←GB
[62]    CIN←CB
[63]    ARCHADD
[64]    P←¯12↓S
[65]    Q←(¯12↑S),12↓Q
[66]    ⍀ EPILOGUE
[67]    PD←P,Q
        ∇
```

```
        ∇ MX←R EIGHTFOLD F;MULT
[1]     ⍀ DECISION
[2]     MULT←+/ ¯4 2 1 1 ×F
[3]     ⍀ SELECTION
[4]     MX←((2+⍴R)⍴2)⊤(MULT×TWOC R)-MULT<0
[5]     ⍀ CARRY-IN
[6]     CX←MULT<0
        ∇
```

```
        ⍀ REFERENCE:                                    PROGRAM:
        ⍀ ARCHADD      ADDER ARCHITECTURE                2-5
        ⍀ ARCHSAVE     CARRY-SAVE ADDER ARCHITECTURE     2-36
        ⍀ ARCHTRIPLE   TRIPLER ARCHITECTURE              2-53
        ⍀ EXTEND       OPERAND EXTENSION                 3-3
```

Program 3-25   Multiplier with 12-bit shift.

Carry Generation Buffer.   The carry-save adders reduce the partial product and multiplicand multiples to a generated carry $G4$ and a transmission $T5$. The generated carry is temporarily stored in the generation buffer, register GB, while the transmission is placed in registers P and Q.

Adder Tree.   Since the partial product is now represented by a generation and transmission, a total of six operands must be added. This addition is accomplished by first using two carry-save adders in parallel, which reduce the number of operands from six to four, and subsequently placing two carry-save adders in series, which results in one transmission and one generated carry.

The number of carry-save adders that are passed in series is reduced from four to three by placing two adders in parallel. This arrangement of the carry-save adders is an example of an *adder tree* (Wallace, 1964). In general, a large number of multiples can be added with less delay by using such a tree. The regular construction of the cascade of adders, illustrated in Figure 3-21, however, is disturbed.

Partial Carry Propagation.   In *TWELVEMPY* the rightmost bits of the multiples need only pass through a part of the adder tree, while the leftmost bits are again extended, as in *EIGHTMPY*. The rightmost 12 bits of transmission and generation do not take part in further additions. They are added in the carry-propagation adder during the following cycle and their sum is placed in Q. This is described in *TWELVEMPY*, lines 47 through 55.

During the first multiplication cycle there is not yet a generated carry. Hence, *GB* is set to 0 in line 6. The adder actually adds 0 to the high-order part of the multiplier during this first cycle, when it routinely performs a 12-bit addition in lines 47 and following.

Final Carry Propagation.   When the entire multiplier has been processed, the remaining transmission and generation must still be summed in the carry-propagation adder. This is shown in lines 60 through 65.

Multiple Generation.   *EIGHTFOLD* generates the multiplicand multiples according to the rules of Table 3-17B. In contrast to *TWOFOLD* and *FOUR-FOLD*, Programs 3-12 and 3-19, the description of *EIGHTFOLD* is on an architectural level, giving the function of the circuit but not the implementation details.

Line 2 of *EIGHTFOLD* summarizes Table 3-17B by noting that the four columns of this table, when assigned the weights $^-4, 2, 1$, and 1, yield the factor to be used. Line 4 applies this factor to the multiplicand. The rightmost term of line 4 assures that the multiple is obtained in 1's complement, as will be the case for the implementation. The carry-in, specified in line 6, will again change the 1's complement to the 2's complement.

The specification of *EIGHTFOLD* would have been simpler with *MX* in 2's complement and the carry-in 0. In that case, however, the internal functioning of the multiplier would change when *EIGHTFOLD* is replaced by an actual implementation. Hence, the designer would no longer be certain that the design is correct.

Multiplier Speed and Cost.   The delayed propagation makes it possible to reduce the number of levels of each cycle by about one half as compared to the immediate propagation. An extra carry-propagate cycle, however, is introduced. Hence, the speed advantage over *ONEMPY* is about a factor of 16, assuming an operand length of 48 bits. The cost is between four and five times that of *ONEMPY*.

Multiplier Application. The IBM 7030 used the basic approach of *TWELVE-MPY* (Bloch, 1962). The System/360 Model 91 processes 12 multiplier bits simultaneously by generating six multiples corresponding to two multiplier bits each, using the recoding of *FOURFOLD*. The six multiples are reduced to a transmission and generation with a carry-save adder tree similar to the tree used in *TWELVEMPY*. These two results are now combined in two carry-save adders with the transmission and generation that have resulted from the previous multiplication cycles. A single tree could have reduced the eight inputs in fewer levels to two outputs. The carry-save adder outputs are stored in registers, however, such that the successive cycles overlap each other. Thus the cycle time is effectively reduced (Anderson et al., 1967).

3-7 EVALUATION OF MULTIPLIERS

Table 3-26 shows a summary of the multiplier algorithms discussed in this chapter. The rightmost column in this table gives a rough comparison of the performance of these multipliers. The figures depend upon the number of multiplier cycles and the time required for each cycle. The figures are derived for 48 bit operands. One cycle through the circuits of *POSMPY* is taken as unity. This time includes the delay through the combinational path, including the adder time, and the time required for reading into the registers.

The relative speed for the multiplier for positive operands, *POSMPY*, would be 48. Since in all cases, positive and negative operands are assumed, the use of *POSMPY* requires added cycles for the complementing of operands and results. An average of two complementing cycles has been assumed, which gives a relative speed of 50 for this adder type.

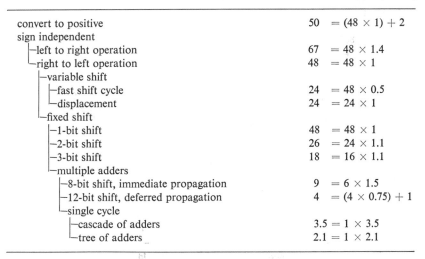

convert to positive	50	$= (48 \times 1) + 2$
sign independent		
⎯left to right operation	67	$= 48 \times 1.4$
⎯right to left operation	48	$= 48 \times 1$
⎯variable shift		
⎯fast shift cycle	24	$= 48 \times 0.5$
⎯displacement	24	$= 24 \times 1$
⎯fixed shift		
⎯1-bit shift	48	$= 48 \times 1$
⎯2-bit shift	26	$= 24 \times 1.1$
⎯3-bit shift	18	$= 16 \times 1.1$
⎯multiple adders		
⎯8-bit shift, immediate propagation	9	$= 6 \times 1.5$
⎯12-bit shift, deferred propagation	4	$= (4 \times 0.75) + 1$
⎯single cycle		
⎯cascade of adders	3.5	$= 1 \times 3.5$
⎯tree of adders	2.1	$= 1 \times 2.1$

Table 3-26 Summary of multipliers.

When processing the multiplier from left to right, a longer adder is required. It is estimated that this adder increases the basic cycle by 40%; hence, the relative speed is shown as 67.

For each multiplier, the relative speed is derived by a formula of the form $N \times L$, where N is the number of cycles and L the relative length of the cycles. These figures are no more than a first approximation. They may vary considerably, owing to the system environment of the multiplier and the realization used for the components.

REFERENCES

ANDERSON, S. F., J. G. EARLE, R. E. GOLDSCHMIDT, and D. M. POWERS: "The IBM System/360 Model 91: Floating-Point Execution Unit." *IBM Journal of Research and Development*, vol. 11, no. 1, pp. 34–53 (January, 1967).

BLOCH, E.: "The Central Processing Unit." In W. BUCHHOLZ: *Planning a Computer System*, pp. 202–207. McGraw-Hill, New York, 1962. See also Bell and Newell pp. 421–439).

BOOTH, A. D.: "A Signed Binary Multiplication Technique." *Quarterly Journal of Applied Mathematics*, vol. 4, pt. 2, pp. 236–240 (1951).

DADDA, L.: "Some Schemes for a Fast Multiplier." *Alta Frequenza*, vol. 34, pp. 346–356 (May, 1965).

HABIBI, A., and P. A. WINTZ: "Fast Multipliers." *IEEE Transactions on Computers*, vol. C-19, no. 2, pp. 153–157 (February, 1970).

KAMAL, A. A., and M. A. N. GHANNAM: "High-Speed Multiplication Systems." *IEEE Transactions on Computers*, vol. C-21, no. 9, pp. 1017–1021 (September, 1972).

MACSORLEY, O. L.: "High-Speed Arithmetic in Binary Computers." *Proceedings of the IRE*, vol. 49, no. 1, pp. 67–91 (January, 1961).

PEZARIS, S. D.: "A 40-ns 17-Bit by 17-Bit Array Multiplier." *IEEE Transactions on Computers*, vol. C-20, no. 4, pp. 442–447 (April, 1971).

SCHWARTZLANDER, E. E., JR.: "The Quasi-serial Multiplier." *IEEE Transactions on Computers*, vol. C-22, no. 4, pp. 317–321 (April, 1973).

WALLACE, C. S.: "A Suggestion for a Fast Multiplier." *IEEE Transactions on Electronic Computers*, vol. EC-13, no. 2, pp. 14–17 (February, 1964).

EXERCISES

3-1   Rewrite *ARCHMPYX*, Program 3-3, without the function *EXTEND*, for the case that *VL*, *MR*, and *MD* each have the length N and *PD* has the length $2 \times N$.

3-2   Restate *ARCHMPY*, Program 3-1, in the form *ARCHMPYP*, suggested by von Neumann, which interprets the 2's-complement operands as positive integers without extension. A correction is applied to the product when the operands are negative.

3-3 Give the architecture *ARCHMPYD* for unsigned decimal operands.

3-4 Determine the multiplier architecture *ARCHMPY1* for 1's-complement notation.

3-5 Give the architecture *ARCHMPYF* for a multiplier that interprets the multiplicand, multiplier, and product as fractions represented in signed-magnitude representation, all with a single length.

3-6 Determine *RECODE2* and *RECODE3*, corresponding to *RECODE1*, Program 3-9, which recode a multiplier in groups of 2 and 3 bits, respectively. Also, determine *RECODE1X*, which recodes a multiplier for minimal arithmetic.

3-7 Give the architectural form, similar to *EIGHTFOLD*, Program 3-25, for *TWOFOLD* and *FOURFOLD*, Programs 3-12 and 3-19.

3-8 Give the implementation form for *EIGHTFOLD*, which matches that of *TWOFOLD* and *FOURFOLD*.

3-9 Starting with *TWOMPY* and *EIGHTMPY*, determine the algorithm *FOURMPY*, which uses 4 multiplier bits simultaneously.

3-10 Design the implementation *THREEMPY*, which uses 3 multiplier bits simultaneously and has deferred carry propagation. What speed value would you assign to this multiplier according to the rules of Table 3-26?

3-11 Determine a less-expensive implementation for *ARCHSAVE*, Program 2-36, when it is known that the left N bits of K are identical and the left N bits of L also are identical. For an application, see *TWELVEMPY*, Program 3-25, lines 34 and 35.

3-12 Use *DECADD*, Exercise 2-18, and proceed from *POSMPY*, Program 3-6, to determine the multiplier *DECMPY* for positive decimal numbers.

3-13 Determine a multiplier implementation for signed-magnitude notation. Observe the architecture of Exercise 3-5. Use the inner cycle of *POSMPY*, preceded or followed by expressions for the sign handling.

3-14 Design an initial algorithm for a multiplier, as used in the PDP11/40, that converts the 2's-complement operands to signed-magnitude, then applies the principle of *POSMPY*, and finally converts the result to 2's-complement form. The multiplier should adhere to *ARCHMPY*.

3-15 Design an initial algorithm for a multiplier that satisfies *ARCHMPY* and processes the multiplier bits from left to right.

3-16 Modify *ONEMPY*, Program 3-12, such that the multiplier recoding for optimum shift of Table 3-8B is used and, in case of a recoded multiplier bit 0, a shift in P is used rather than a pass through the adder.

3-17   Determine an algorithm for the number of multiply cycles that a given multiplier MR requires. Assume that a variable displacement with a maximum of N bits is allowed and MR is recoded according to Table 3-8B.

3-18   Design a multiplier that uses some of the methods of the System/370 Model 158 multiplier for $ARCHMPY$ with 32 bit operands.

The multiples are obtained from read-only stores. Each store contains 256 words of 8 bits. The 8-bit address for the store is formed by 4 multiplier bits and 4 multiplicand bits. The addressed word contains the corresponding 8-bit product. This product is treated as two groups of 4 bits, which are joined with the outputs of the other read-only stores to two words.

The carry propagation is deferred until the end of the multiplication. Each cycle the generation and transmission of the partial product are combined with the two words that represent the selected multiple. This occurs in a table-look-up carry-save adder, which again makes use of a number of parallel read-only memories. Four corresponding pairs of adjacent operand bits address one such read-only store. The word addressed by these 8 bits contains the 2 low-order sum bits and the 2 high-order sum bits. Thus, the four operands are reduced to two results.

A regular adder may be used for the final carry propagation.

Derive the functions that generate the desired content of the read-only stores.

3-19   Give a multiplier implementation that resembles the multiplier of the CDC 6600.

Operands are positive and 48 bits long. The left 24 bits of the multiplier MR are multiplied with the multiplicand MD, in parallel with the multiplication of the right 24 bits of MR with MD.

Each of the two multiplications requires four cycles and processes 6 multiplier bits per cycle without carry propagation.

The 6 multiplier bits are subdivided in three groups of 2 bits each, each of which can select zero, one, two, or three times MD. The multiples $2 \times MD$ and $3 \times MD$ are generated prior to the addition cycles. The three selected multiples and the generation and transmission of the partial product are added in three cascaded carry-save adders.

The four results from the two parallel procedures are added in a final cycle. Two carry-save adders reduce the number of operands from four to two, and a carry-propagate adder derives the final result.

3-20   Design a selective multiplier test $QUIZMPY$ and give meaningful test cases.

4 DIVISION

Division is derived from multiplication and is defined as the determination of the *quotient* that multiplied by the *divisor* produces the *dividend*.

In contrast to multiplication, the division operation is not architecturally commutative. Since it is not always possible to find an integer quotient for an integer divisor and dividend, division leads either to the extension of the number concept with *fractions*, or to the definition of a *remainder*. In the latter case, division is the inverse of cumulative multiplication.

In machine arithmetic, the quotient is usually considered as a fraction when the divisor and the dividend are also fractions. This is in particular the case for floating-point arithmetic. The architecture should in that case determine if, and if so how, the quotient must be rounded.

If the operands are integers, the results of the division are usually integers as well, so that a quotient and a remainder are obtained. The remainder has a magnitude that is smaller than the divisor and has the same sign as the dividend unless it is zero.

Division may be performed by repeatedly subtracting the divisor from the dividend and recording the number of subtractions as the quotient. As the division progresses, these quantities are called *partial dividend*, or partial remainder, and *partial quotient*. When the division is completed, the partial dividend becomes the remainder.

Organization of the Chapter

The architecture of the systems component that performs division, the *divider*, is discussed in Section 4-1. The basic algorithm for a divider, comparable to manual division, is presented in Section 4-2. The basic algorithm applies only to positive operands and takes more than one cycle per quotient digit. Division for positive operands is relatively prominent, however, since many dividers convert to and from positive operands to use such an algorithm. Hence, in Sections 4-3 and 4-4 the basic algorithm is improved, such that one quotient digit per cycle is obtained. In Section 4-5 the algorithm is expanded to permit direct use of both positive and negative operands.

Higher performance for the divider can be obtained with algorithms that derive several result bits per cycle. Thus, Section 4-6 describes shifting over groups of dividend bits, whereas Section 4-7 discusses the use of multiples to obtain even larger shifts. In both cases a variable amount of shift is assumed. Section 4-8 discusses the use of multiples to obtain a fixed shift of 2 bits per cycle.

For the algorithm described in Section 4-5, the datapath is developed in Chapter 5 and the control in Chapter 6. Therefore, the reader may wish to proceed to those chapters immediately following Section 4-5 and return to the remaining sections later.

4-1 ARCHITECTURE OF THE DIVIDER

In this text, division of integers resulting in a quotient and a remainder will be discussed.

Architecture in Words

The different implementations must fulfill an architecture, which can be put in words as follows. A dividend DD, of ρDD bits, is divided by a divisor DR, of ρDR bits, and results in a quotient QT, of $(\rho DD) - \rho DR$ bits, and a remainder RM, of ρDR bits. All numbers are integers, represented in binary with 2's-complement notation. When the quotient exceeds the range of representation, or if it is undefined, as in division by zero, the division overflow signal $OFDV$ is made 1. In that case, the value of the quotient and remainder is undetermined. In all other cases, $OFDV$ is made 0.

Architecture in APL

An architecture in APL is given in $ARCHDIV$, Program 4-1. This description assumes, as does the verbal description, that the concept of division is known.

The actual division takes place in line 1 of $ARCHDIV$ and results in the integer $QUOTIENT$. This quotient is used in line 2 for the determination of the integer $REMAINDER$. In lines 3 and 4 these numbers are represented with 2's-complement notation as the vectors QT and RM. Finally, the overflow signal $OFVD$ is determined in line 5.

$QUOTIENT$ is the integer part of the algebraic quotient. Line 1 of $ARCHDIV$ shows that this integer part is obtained by first determining the absolute value of

```
     ∇ ARCHDIV;QUOTIENT;REMAINDER
[1]    QUOTIENT←(¯1*DD[0]≠DR[0])×⌊|(TWOC DD)÷(TWOC DR)+0=∨/DR
[2]    REMAINDER←(TWOC DD)-QUOTIENT×TWOC DR
[3]    QT←(((ρDD)-ρDR)ρ2)⊤QUOTIENT
[4]    RM←((ρDR)ρ2)⊤REMAINDER
[5]    OFDV←(QUOTIENT≠TWOC QT)∨0=∨/DR
     ∇
```

```
     ⍝ REFERENCE:                                      PROGRAM:
     ⍝ TWOC          2-COMPLEMENT INTERPRETATION          3-1
```

Program 4-1 Divider architecture.

the quotient, then taking the largest integer less than this absolute value, and finally restoring the correct sign. The expression in line 1 also contains a provision to prevent division by 0.

Absolute Value. The *absolute value* of the quotient is determined by the operator |. Where the traditional indication for absolute value makes use of two vertical stripes, APL uses only one stripe. This notation harmonizes with other monadic operators, such as the minus sign. The traditional indication actually mixes the absolute-value operation with priority determination, as with parentheses. In APL, these aims are kept separate.

Floor and Ceiling. The operator *floor*, ⌊, obtains the largest integer equal to, or less than, a given operand. For a negative operand the floor is thus, in absolute value, larger than the operand itself. ⌊3.14 is equal to 3, whereas ⌊¯3.14 is equal to ¯4. Therefore, the integer part of the quotient is obtained by taking the absolute value first and the floor next. Because the quotient is thus truncated toward zero, the remainder has the sign of the dividend. For 2's-complement notation, one could also give the remainder the sign of the divisor, so that continued division with the remainder gives a positive low-order quotient (Chinal, 1972).

In contrast to the floor, the operator *ceiling*, ⌈, obtains the smallest integer larger than or equal to the operand. Thus ⌈3.14 is 4 and ⌈¯3.14 is ¯3.

Quotient Sign. The sign of the quotient is determined from the sign of the dividend and divisor. Therefore, in line 1 of *ARCHDIV*, the exclusive-or of the signs is used as the exponent of ¯1, and the result is multiplied with the integer part of the absolute value of the quotient.

Division by Zero. The rightmost part of line 1 contains an expression that determines if division by 0 occurs. If so, then 1 is added to the value of the divisor such that the algorithm can be continued without further problems. In line 5 it is again noted that the divisor is 0, and *OFDV* is consequently set to 1.

The continuation of the algorithm in case of a zero divisor ensures that the result vectors *QT* and *RM* are defined. Although the value of these vectors is undetermined when *OFDV* is 1, they should still have a proper length, as indeed they have in the hardware. This case is particularly important when *ARCHDIV* is used for simulation.

Operand Length. The lengths of the operands in the algorithms of this chapter are again kept variable to help in verifying the correctness of these algorithms, as was also the case in Chapter 3.

Verifying Architecture

The architecture of *ARCHDIV* is *constructive*: for a given dividend and divisor, a quotient and remainder are obtained. An architecture need not be constructive, however, but may limit itself to the conditions which the results of the operation—here quotient and remainder—must satisfy. Such an architecture will be called *verifying*. The two types of architecture can also be characterized as generative versus assertive.

CHECKDIV, Program 4-2, shows the verifying architecture of the divider. It simply states the arithmetic definition of division. The program checks if a quotient and remainder fit a given dividend and divisor. If so, then the signal *YES* is 1; otherwise, the signal is 0.

```
       ∇ YES←CHECKDIV;CQT;CRM;COF
  [1]     ⍝ QUOTIENT
  [2]     CQT←OFDV∨(TWOC DD)=(TWOC RM)+(TWOC DR)×TWOC QT
  [3]     ⍝ REMAINDER
  [4]     CRM←OFDV∨(~∨/RM)∨(DD[0]=RM[0])∧(|TWOC DR)>|TWOC RM
  [5]     ⍝ OVERFLOW
  [6]     COF←OFDV=(|TWOC DD)≥(|TWOC DR)×(DD[0]≠DR[0])+2*⁻1+(⍴DD)-⍴DR
  [7]     YES←CQT∧CRM∧COF
       ∇

         ⍝ REFERENCE:                                    PROGRAM:
         ⍝ TWOC        2-COMPLEMENT INTERPRETATION          3-1
```

Program 4-2   Verifying divider architecture.

Lines 2 and 4 of *CHECKDIV* correspond to the arithmetic definition of quotient and remainder. Line 6 concerns the overflow, which occurs for division by 0 or for a quotient that requires more bits than the representation provides. To determine the overflow, the divisor is multiplied by the largest representable quotient. When this product is less than the dividend, it is not possible to represent the quotient.

The verifying architecture has the advantage that it can specify a 'don't-care' condition. Thus, *CHECKDIV* specifies properly that the quotient and remainder are arbitrary in case of an overflow. The constructive architecture *ARCHDIV*, however, does not specify this fact—it must be stated apart from the algorithm. Indeed, a constructive algorithm cannot express the concept of arbitrariness. Even the question-mark operator of APL, originally introduced for this purpose, yields a specific result, although this result will differ upon each invocation. *CHECKDIV* is therefore particularly suited to verify the action of an implementation.

The constructive architecture, in contrast, has the advantage that it can be substituted for the implementation in a simulation, such as the use of *ARCHADD* in *ONEMPY*. Also, the results of a constructive architecture are demonstrable, which is in particular desirable for a new design.

4-2 BASIC DIVIDER ALGORITHM

Since the arithmetic definition of division is not constructive, it does not help in finding the quotient and remainder. At best it tells us to compare successively all multiples of the divisor to the dividend. This process is far too slow. Again, however, the positional notation may be used to determine the answer digit by digit. This is the method of manual division, Table 4-3.

```
                 BINARY           DECIMAL EQUIVALENT

             1100111 QT                 103
          +------------             +----
DR  100101|111011101100 DD         37|3820
             100101                   2368  ←  64×37
          ------                      ----
             101101                   1452
             100101                   1184  ←  32×37
          ------                      ----
            1000011                    268
             100101                    148  ←   4×37
          ------                       ---
             111100                    120
             100101                     74  ←   2×37
          ------                        --
             101110                     46
             100101                     37  ←   1×37
          ------                         --
                1001 RM                  9
```

Table 4-3 Manual division.

As the division progresses, the dividend becomes shorter and the quotient longer. Therefore, it is attractive to place these two variables jointly in a pair of registers, as was the case with the partial product and multiplier in multiplication. During the division, the dividend and quotient are shifted to the left. Thus, the same register positions are again connected to the adder and the quotient digit is always entered at the right. In contrast to multiplication, the shift direction cannot be reversed. This is a consequence of the sequential character of the basic divide algorithm and makes division fundamentally more complicated than multiplication.

The basic algorithm assumes positive operands. The divisor is subtracted until the partial dividend turns from positive to negative. For base 2, this process is characteristically simplified: the subtraction takes place or it does not.

Restoring Divider

The basic algorithm for positive operands is illustrated in Figure 4-4 and described by *POSDIV*, Program 4-5. The partial dividend must be compared to the divisor. A comparison, however, requires nearly as much time and hardware as an addition. It is therefore attractive to subtract the divisor immediately from the partial dividend and to examine the sign of the result. The subtraction occurs in lines 8 through 13 of *POSDIV*. The sign of the result is determined in line 14

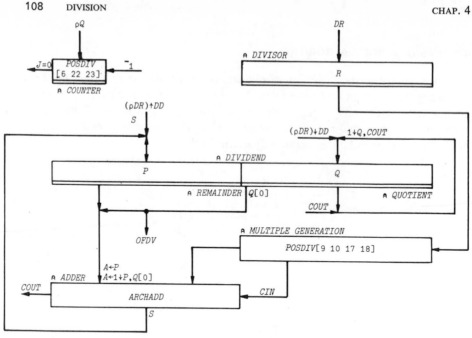

Figure 4-4   Restoring divider.

```
      ∇ POSDIV
[1]    ⍝ PROLOGUE                    [15]   ⍝ RESTORATION
[2]    P←(ρDR)↑DD                    [16]   A←P
[3]    Q←(ρDR)↓DD                    [17]   B←R
[4]    R←DR                          [18]   CIN←0
[5]    ⍝ DIVISION                    [19]   ARCHADD
[6]    J←ρQ                          [20]   P←S
[7]    ⍝ REDUCTION                   [21]   ⍝ COUNT
[8]    CONT:A←1↓P,Q[0]               [22]   END:J←J-1
[9]    B←~R                          [23]   →(J≠0)/CONT
[10]   CIN←1                         [24]   ⍝ EPILOGUE
[11]   ARCHADD                       [25]   RM←P
[12]   P←S                           [26]   QT←Q
[13]   Q←1↓Q,COUT                    [27]   OFDV←Q[0]
[14]   →COUT/END                            ∇
[15]
```

        ⍝ REFERENCE: PROGRAM:
        ⍝ ARCHADD   ADDER ARCHITECTURE   2-5

Program 4-5   Restoring divider.

from the carry-out *COUT*. The two operands have opposite signs. Therefore, the result will be positive or negative depending on whether *COUT* is 1 or 0.

    When the partial dividend is positive, the quotient digit is 1 and the cycle is finished. The quotient digit is recorded in line 13 by extending the quotient in Q with *COUT*. When the partial dividend is negative, the quotient digit is recorded as 0. The subtraction actually should not have taken place in this case. The dividend is now restored by an addition, hence the name *restoring division*. The restore decision occurs in line 14, the addition in lines 16 through 20.

Overflow Condition. Line 27 of *POSDIV* verifies if the quotient correctly represents the result of the division. If the dividend is too large with respect to the divisor, the first cycle will produce a positive result and the leftmost quotient digit will be recorded as 1. At the end of the division, this quotient digit appears as the sign bit in position $Q[0]$. For a zero divisor the result of the first subtraction also is positive and results in 1 in position $Q[0]$. Therefore, a negative quotient is a necessary and sufficient indication of an overflow condition.

Divider Speed. The number of division cycles is $N + M$, with N the number of quotient bits and M the number of 0s in the quotient. Since positive numbers usually begin with a string of 0s, the number of cycles is on the average more than one and one-half times N. In contrast, the simplest multiplication algorithm requires only N cycles.

Divider Application. Restoring division was proposed in the designs of Babbage. Many early processors, such as the IBM 604, used this principle, as well as the Hewlett-Packard 9100A.

A numerical example of the restoring division is given in Table 4-6.

```
        POSDIV
R       00100101          DR(37)
P,Q     0000111011101100  DD(3820)
A       00011101        _
B       11011010  ‾1×
CIN            1
S       11111000
P,Q     1111100011011000       P,Q     0001000011000110
A       11111000               A       00100001        _
B       00100101  1×           B       11011010  ‾1×
CIN            0               CIN            1
S       00011101               S       11111100
P,Q     0001110111011000       P,Q     1111110010001100
A       00111011        _      A       11111100
B       11011010  ‾1×          B       00100101  1×
CIN            1               CIN            0
S       00010110               S       00100001
P,Q     0001011010110001       P,Q     0010000110001100
A       00101101               A       01000011
B       11011010  ‾1×          B       11011010  ‾1×
CIN            1               CIN            1
S       00001000               S       00011110
P,Q     0000100001100011       P,Q     0001111000011001
A       00010000        _      A       00111100        _
B       11011010  ‾1×          B       11011010  ‾1×
CIN            1               CIN            1
S       11101011               S       00010111
P,Q     1110101111000110       P,Q     0001011100110011
A       11101011               A       00101110        _
B       00100101  1×           B       11011010  ‾1×
CIN            0               CIN            1
S       00010000               S       00001001
P,Q     0001000011000110       P,Q     0000100101100111   RM(9),QT(103)
                               OFDV
                                  0
```

Table 4-6 Example of restoring division.

Robertson Diagram

The different divide algorithms can be illustrated with a diagram proposed by Robertson (1958). The *Robertson diagram* for the restoring division is shown in Figure 4-7. The value of the divisor, *DSR*, is taken as the unit of length in the diagram. Along the horizontal axis is marked the value of the partial dividend relative to *DSR* at the start of cycle *J*, *DVD*[*J*]. On the vertical axis, the value of the partial dividend at the end of that cycle is noted. This dividend value, in turn, is the start value for cycle *J* + 1, that is, *DVD*[*J* + 1].

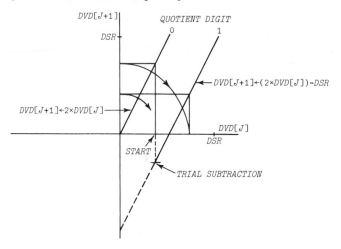

Figure 4-7   Robertson diagram for restoring division.

The Robertson diagram expresses graphically the relation that holds throughout division, the *invariant* of division: the new partial dividend equals the old partial dividend minus the divisor times the quotient digit.

The value of the partial dividend is noted as it is seen at the adder input. Therefore, when the quotient digit is 1, the relation between $DVD[J + 1]$ and $DVD[J]$ is given by $DVD[J + 1] \leftarrow (2 \times DVD[J]) - DSR$. The factor 2 is introduced by the 1-bit shift. For quotient digit 0, the relation is $DVD[J + 1] \leftarrow 2 \times DVD[J]$. Both cases are shown as lines in the diagram.

The trial subtraction determines the intersection with the line for quotient bit 1. If this intersection indicates a negative partial dividend, then the intersection with the line for quotient bit 0 is chosen. Once the new partial dividend is found on the vertical axis, this value can again be marked on the horizontal axis to find the following quotient bit. This is indicated in Figure 4-7 by the quarter circle. Since all operands are positive, only the right half of the diagram is used.

4-3   NONPERFORMING DIVIDER

The restore cycle of *POSDIV* may be eliminated by making the restore decision before the result of the adder is placed in *P*. Rather than restoring an undesirable reduction, the reduction is not performed: hence the somewhat startling name, *nonperforming division.*

The nonperforming divider is shown in Figure 4-8 and described by *POSNON-DIV*, Program 4-9. The essence of the algorithm is found in line 12. Depending upon the sign of the adder output, as indicated by *COUT*, either the reduced or the shifted value of the partial dividend is placed in *P*.

Divider Speed and Cost. *POSNONDIV* compares favorably in speed with *POSDIV*, since the restore cycles are eliminated. Moreover, when the carry-out *COUT* is available halfway through the adder cycle, as for the carry prediction methods of Section 2-9, the reduction cycle can be shortened when *COUT* is 0, thus resulting in an even greater time improvement. This advantage, however, is only realized when a variable cycle time is used.

The equipment for *POSNONDIV* is about the same as for *POSDIV*, since the adder output selection circuit of *POSNONDIV*, line 12, may be traded for the adder input selection circuits of *POSDIV*, lines 8, 9, 16, and 17. In practice, however, the inputs of lines 9, 16, and 17 are often required anyway for addition and subtraction. In that case the output selection circuit may represent an added investment and may even lengthen the adder cycle. Detailed considerations such as these may detract from the apparent advantages of *POSNONDIV* and may ultimately cause the algorithm to be rejected. Hence, in the next section another alternative to the restoring divider is given.

4-4 NONRESTORING DIVIDER

The restoring division is slowed down by the restore cycle. This shortcoming can be overcome by allowing a negative as well as a positive partial dividend and restoring only the final partial dividend, the remainder, to a positive value. This is the principle of the *nonrestoring division*, as discussed by von Neumann. A corresponding divider is shown in Figure 4-10 and in *POSONEDIV*, Program 4-11.

The nonrestoring division will be described in this section for positive operands; in Section 4-5, the algorithm will be changed so that both signs are allowed.

Dividend Reduction. In nonrestoring division, a negative partial dividend is not restored to positive, but rather used as it is in the next cycle. The absolute value of the partial dividend is now reduced in every divide cycle by either adding the divisor to it or subtracting the divisor from it.

Lines 8 through 13 of *POSONEDIV* describe the core of nonrestoring division. The algorithm is complicated in comparison to lines 8 through 13 of *POSDIV* because the divisor is now subtracted from a positive partial dividend and added to a negative partial dividend.

Quotient Digits. The partial dividend determines which quotient bit is recorded each cycle. When the partial dividend is positive, the divisor is subtracted from

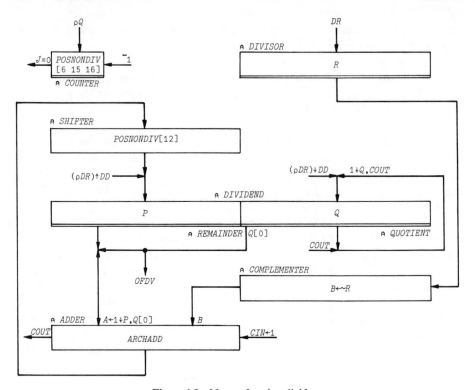

Figure 4-8   Nonperforming divider.

```
      ∇ POSNONDIV
[1]    ⍝ PROLOGUE
[2]    P←(ρDR)↑DD
[3]    Q←(ρDR)↓DD
[4]    R←DR
[5]    ⍝ DIVISION
[6]    J←ρQ
[7]    ⍝ REDUCTION
[8]  CONT:A←1↓P,Q[0]
[9]    B←~R
[10]   CIN←1
[11]   ARCHADD
[12]   P←(COUT∧S)∨(~COUT)∧1↓P,Q[0]
[13]   Q←1↓Q,COUT
[14]   ⍝ COUNT
[15]   J←J-1
[16]   →(J≠0)/CONT
[17]   ⍝ EPILOGUE
[18]   RM←P
[19]   QT←Q
[20]   OFDV←Q[0]
      ∇
```

```
      ⍝ REFERENCE:                              PROGRAM:
      ⍝ ARCHADD      ADDER ARCHITECTURE         2-5
```

Program 4-9   Nonperforming divider.

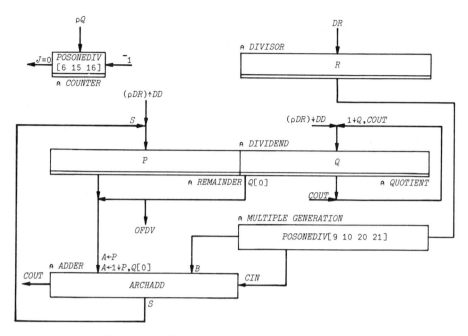

Figure 4-10   Nonrestoring divider for positive operands.

```
     ∇ POSONEDIV
[1]     ⍝ PROLOGUE                    [17]    ⍝ REMAINDER CORRECTION
[2]     P←(ρDR)↑DD                    [18]    →COUT/END
[3]     Q←(ρDR)↓DD                    [19]    A←P
[4]     R←DR                          [20]    B←R
[5]     ⍝ DIVISION                    [21]    CIN←0
[6]     J←ρQ                          [22]    ARCHADD
[7]     ⍝ REDUCTION                   [23]    P←S
[8]  CONT:A←1↓P,Q[0]                  [24]    ⍝ EPILOGUE
[9]     B←P[0]=R                      [25]  END:RM←P
[10]    CIN←~P[0]                     [26]    QT←Q
[11]    ARCHADD                       [27]    OFDV←Q[0]
[12]    P←S                              ∇
[13]    Q←1↓Q,COUT
[14]    ⍝ COUNT
[15]    J←J-1
[16]    →(J≠0)/CONT
[17]
```

⍝ REFERENCE:	PROGRAM:
⍝ ARCHADD ADDER ARCHITECTURE	2-5

Program 4-11   Nonrestoring divider for positive operands.

the dividend. Therefore, the old dividend equals the sum of the new dividend and one times the divisor. The quotient digit to be recorded is thus 1.

When the partial dividend is negative, the divisor is added. Now the old dividend equals the new dividend decreased by one times the divisor and the quotient digit to be recorded is ⁻1. Thus, a positive dividend at the end of a cycle gives a quotient digit 1 for the next cycle; a negative dividend gives a quotient digit ⁻1.

Recoding of the Quotient. The quotient is obtained in a coding, which uses the digits 1 and $^-1$. This coding must now be converted to binary notation. Let X be the number represented by the 1s, with 0 in the position of each $^-1$, and Y the 1's-complement of X. Then $-Y$ is the number formed by the $^-1$s. Since Y is the 1's-complement of X, it is $(2 * N) - (1 + X)$. The quotient is now $X - Y$, or $X + 1 + X - 2 * N$. The last term falls outside the representation range, so the quotient is $1 + 2 \times X$.

As the example of Table 4-12 shows, the quotient can now be formed by recording the digits 1 multiplied by a factor 2, hence shifted one place to the left, while the digits $^-1$ are not recorded and thus leave a 0 one place to the left of the original $^-1$.

Generated quotient digits	1	$^-1$	1	1	$^-1$	$^-1$	1	1	
X, quotient digits $= 1$	1	0	1	1	0	0	1	1	179
Y, quotient digits $= {}^-1$	0	1	0	0	1	1	0	0	76
$X - Y$, correct quotient	0	1	1	0	0	1	1	1	103
X shifted one place left	0	1	1	0	0	1	1	0	102
Recorded quotient digits	0	1	1	0	0	1	1	1	103

Table 4-12 Example of the recoding of quotient digits.

The 1-bit shift to the left makes it desirable to know the quotient digit one cycle earlier. This knowledge is available since the sign of the partial dividend at the end of a cycle determines the quotient digit for the next cycle. Therefore, the quotient digit can be recorded at the end of the preceding cycle and thus is shifted one place to the left.

The quotient digit that belongs to the first cycle should be placed to the left of the highest quotient bit and thus is not recorded.

After the last cycle, a 1 should always be recorded, according to the formula. If for that cycle, not the digit 1, but a digit based upon the sign of the sum is again recorded, the quotient will be 1 too small in case of a negative remainder. This shortage is taken into consideration by the remainder correction.

Remainder Correction. At the end of the divide cycles, the partial dividend becomes the remainder. The remainder must be positive. When it is negative, the *remainder correction* cycle, which adds the divisor to the remainder, is inserted, as shown in lines 19 through 23 of *POSONEDIV*. These lines correspond to lines 16 through 20 of *POSDIV*. The remainder correction effectively reduces the quotient by 1. Since for a negative partial dividend the quotient was already recorded as 1 too small, no further action is necessary.

Divider Speed and Cost. The nonrestoring divider is comparable in cost to *POSDIV* and *POSNONDIV*. The divider is aimed at a fixed reduction cycle and is in such an environment competitive in speed with *POSNONDIV*. A disadvantage of *POSONEDIV* is the time and complexity of the remainder correction cycle.

4-5 DIVIDER FOR POSITIVE AND NEGATIVE OPERANDS

The division of negative operands may be accomplished with the algorithms described in the preceding sections. In that case, a negative dividend or divisor is complemented prior to the division and the quotient and remainder are complemented after the division as needed. In this chapter, however, no conversion to positive will be assumed. The resulting algorithms are more general and at least as efficient as those reverting to positive operands. Also, the algorithms for positive operands can be obtained more readily from those which permit both signs than the reverse.

The introduction of negative operands has a greater influence on the division algorithm than the removal of the restore cycle. For a negative dividend a negative remainder is required; a positive remainder would have been simpler for 2's-complement notation.

The algorithm for positive and negative nonrestoring division is *ONEDIV*, Program 4-14, illustrated by the block diagram of Figure 4-13. In comparison with the preceding algorithms, the remainder correction and the overflow condition are more complex; also, a quotient correction is introduced.

Adder Length. The most negative number that can be represented with a given number of bits in 2's-complement form has no representable opposite. For 4 bits this number is $^-8$. Its opposite is 8, which cannot be represented with 4 bits. Since this number, or its opposite, may appear during division, the adder must be extended by 1 bit to make sure that the sign of the result is properly recognized.

Recording of the Dividend Sign. The algorithm requires a separate recording of the dividend sign. The original dividend sign is stored in register U, the momentary partial dividend sign in register W.

Recording of the Quotient. During the reduction cycle, the divisor is either added to, or subtracted from, the partial dividend such that the absolute value of the partial dividend decreases. Line 11 of *ONEDIV* shows that the sign of the divisor $R[0]$ is used in the complement decision. Therefore, the reduction is effectively independent of the sign of the divisor. For a negative divisor, however, the quotient should be the complement of what is generated for a positive divisor. Therefore, the quotient digits are inverted when the divisor is negative, as shown in line 15 of *ONEDIV*. Consequently, the 1's complement of the quotient is obtained. To get the 2's-complement form, 1 should be added to the quotient. This addition occurs during the quotient correction cycle.

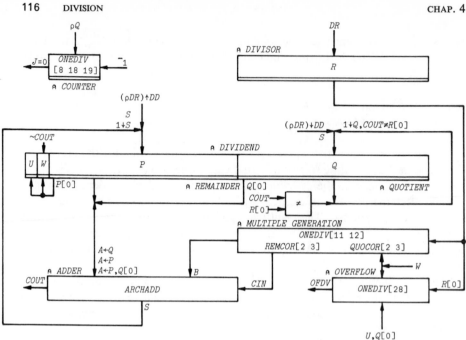

Figure 4-13   Nonrestoring divider.

Remainder Correction.   The remainder should have the sign of the original dividend, unless the remainder is zero. This requirement determines in lines 21 and 23 of *ONEDIV* if the remainder must be corrected. The remainder correction makes use of the function *REMCOR*, which is an extension of the remainder correction of *POSONEDIV*, lines 19 through 23.

When a partial dividend becomes zero, the last partial dividend will be negative and equal to the divisor in magnitude. This case is illustrated in Table 4-15B. When the original dividend is negative, this partial dividend looks like the final remainder. The correct remainder, however, is 0. Therefore, a negative remainder is first made positive by *REMCOR* in line 22 of *ONEDIV*. Next, line 23 checks if the remainder is 0 or, on the basis of the original sign *U*, must remain positive. If so, the remainder is correct; otherwise, a second remainder correction is applied by *REMCOR* in line 24.

Quotient Correction.   *POSONEDIV* shows that for a positive remainder the quotient is recorded correctly, even if this positive remainder is obtained by a remainder correction. This rule applies also for a negative dividend, provided the divisor is positive. In the discussion of *POSONEDIV*, it was further shown that for a negative remainder, the quotient would be 1 too small. Therefore, a final negative remainder obtained for a negative dividend and positive divisor has a quotient that is recorded as 1 too small.

When the divisor is negative, the quotient is recorded in 1's-complement form, and 1 must be added to obtain the 2's-complement form, as stated above. Therefore, in case of a positive or zero remainder and negative divisor, a *quotient correc-*

```
      ∇ ONEDIV                              [20]  ⍝ REMAINDER CORRECTION
[1]     ⍝ PROLOGUE                          [21]  →(~W)/RMC
[2]     P←(ρDR)↑DD                          [22]  REMCOR
[3]     Q←(ρDR)↓DD                          [23]  RMC:→(~U∧V/P)/QTC
[4]     R←DR                                [24]  REMCOR
[5]     ⍝ DIVISION                          [25]  ⍝ QUOTIENT CORRECTION
[6]     U←P[0]                              [26]  QTC:QUOCOR
[7]     W←P[0]                              [27]  ⍝ OVERFLOW
[8]     J←ρQ                                [28]  OFLO←U≠R[0]≠Q[0]∨~W
[9]     ⍝ REDUCTION                         [29]  ⍝ EPILOGUE
[10]  CONT:A←P,Q[0]                         [30]  RM←P
[11]    B←(W=R[0])≠1 EXTEND R               [31]  QT←Q
[12]    CIN←W=R[0]                          [32]  OFDV←OFLO
[13]    ARCHADD                                 ∇
[14]    P←1↓S
[15]    Q←1↓Q,COUT≠R[0]
[16]    W←~COUT
[17]    ⍝ COUNT
[18]    J←J-1
[19]    →(J≠0)/CONT
[20]


      ∇ REMCOR                              ∇ QUOCOR
[1]     A←P                             [1]   A←Q
[2]     B←(W=R[0])≠R                    [2]   B←0
[3]     CIN←W=R[0]                      [3]   CIN←W≠R[0]
[4]     ARCHADD                         [4]   ARCHADD
[5]     P←S                             [5]   Q←S
[6]     W←~COUT                         [6]   W←~COUT
      ∇                                    ∇


      ⍝ REFERENCE:                                        PROGRAM:
      ⍝ ARCHADD        ADDER ARCHITECTURE                  2-5
      ⍝ EXTEND         OPERAND EXTENSION                   3-3
```

Program 4-14   Nonrestoring divider.

tion of 1 is required. In the case of a negative divisor and negative remainder, however, the quotient that was recorded was 1 too small. Hence, its inverse produces the desired 2's-complement, and no further quotient correction is required. In summary, quotient correction is required when the sign of the remainder is unequal to the sign of the divisor (Rhyne, 1971).

The quotient correction is performed in *ONEDIV* by the function *QUOCOR*. The quotient correction cycle is always taken. The value of the correction, however, is 1 or 0, depending on the correction condition, which determines the carry-in in line 3 of *QUOCOR*. The algorithm can be accelerated by omitting the correction with 0.

Overflow Condition.   The algorithm recognizes the overflow in the same manner as for the restoring division. The overflow is noticed because the quotient exceeds the representation range and has a quotient sign that does not match the divisor and dividend sign. This situation is recognized in line 28 by comparing the sign of the quotient with the original dividend sign U and the divisor sign $R[0]$, also taking a zero quotient into account.

When a partial dividend becomes so large that its digits enter the sign position, the quotient may get the opposite sign. This case can be eliminated by constantly preserving the correct sign of the result of the reduction, even if this result can no longer be placed in its entirety in the allotted dividend space. With the dividend sign thus correctly preserved, the sign of the quotient becomes a necessary and sufficient criterion for the overflow.

The correct sign of the partial dividend is recorded on the basis of *COUT* in *W*. This occurs in *ONEDIV*, line 16, and in *REMCOR* and *QUOCOR*, line 6. When in a test or complement decision the sign of the dividend is required, as in *ONEDIV*, line 21, *W* is used and not the highest bit of *P*.

A zero quotient can be tested in the same way as a zero remainder. In line 23, an 'or' circuit was necessary for the remainder. For the quotient a cheaper solution is found in line 28. The zero test is only important when a negative quotient is normally expected: thus, for a negative dividend and a positive divisor, or vice versa. For such operands, a zero quotient is always obtained from a quotient correction of $^-1$. In that case, and only in that case, the carry-out from the quotient correction cycle is 1. This fact is used via *W* in the overflow test.

Divider Speed and Cost. The increase in cost due to the negative operands, which are permitted in *ONEDIV*, over the cost of the algorithms for positive operands is quite small. Although the complexity of the algorithms has increased, the circuits that handle this complexity are incidental in nature and not repeated for all operand bits. The increase in time is due to the correction cycles. The performance can be improved by invoking the quotient correction cycle only when needed. Also the two remainder correction cycles can be reduced to one, as mentioned in Exercise 4-5. These alternatives are all marginal as far as cost and speed are concerned.

This cost comparison, as well as the others in this chapter, can only be crude, since much depends upon the degree to which the registers, the adder, the adder inputs, and the complementer are shared with the addition and multiplication processes.

Conversion to Positive Operands. The use of an algorithm for positive operands associated with the pre- and postcomplementing of the actual operands and results is quite prominent. Thus, the PDP11/45; the System/370 Models 155, 158, 165, and 168; and the CDC 6600 integer dividers all convert operands to positive.

A comparison of pre- and postcomplementing with the algorithm *ONEDIV* shows that in particular the dividend complement cycles are eliminated in *ONEDIV*. The divisor complementing occurs in *ONEDIV* as part of the reduction cycle, a practice that can easily be traded with precomplementing. The quotient is recorded in 1's-complement form, which is comparable to the postcomplementing of the quotient, in particular since a quotient correction cycle is still required. The remainder correction cycles are comparable to the postcorrection of the remainder.

This comparison suggests that several intermediate choices can be made between the two extreme alternatives. Thus the System/370 Models 155 and 158 convert only the dividend to positive; they develop the quotient directly in 1's-complement form, as in *ONEDIV*.

Verification

ONEDIV is illustrated by the examples of Table 4-15. A single example is, however, unsatisfactory since many special cases can occur. Therefore, in Table 4-16, all possible divisions of a 4-bit dividend by a 2-bit divisor are tabulated.

```
        ONEDIV                                            ONEDIV
R        00100101              DR(37)           R          00100101              DR(37)
W,P,Q    00000111011101100  W,DD(3820)         W,P,Q      00000100101000000  W,DD(2368)
A        000011101  _                          A          000010010
B        111011010   1×                        B          111011010   ‾1×
CIN              1                             CIN                1
S        111111000                             S          111101101
W,P,Q    11111100011011000                     W,P,Q      11110110110000000
A        111110001                             A          111011011
B        000100101   1×                        B          000100101   1×
CIN              0                             CIN                0
S        000010110                             S          000000000
W,P,Q    00001011010110001                     W,P,Q      00000000000000001
A        000101101  _                          A          000000000
B        111011010   1×                        B          111011010   ‾1×
CIN              1                             CIN                1
S        000001000                             S          111011011
W,P,Q    00000100001100011                     W,P,Q      11101101100000010
A        000010000  _                          A          110110110
B        111011010   1×                        B          000100101   1×
CIN              1                             CIN                0
S        111101011                             S          111011011
W,P,Q    11110101111000110                     W,P,Q      11101101100000100
A        111010111                             A          110110110
B        000100101   1×                        B          000100101   1×
CIN              0                             CIN                0
S        111111100                             S          111011011
W,P,Q    11111110010001100                     W,P,Q      11101101100001000
A        111111001                             A          110110110
B        000100101   1×                        B          000100101   1×
CIN              0                             CIN                0
S        000011110                             S          111011011
W,P,Q    00001111000011001                     W,P,Q      11101101100010000
A        000111100  _                          A          110110110
B        111011010   1×                        B          000100101   1×
CIN              1                             CIN                0
S        000010111                             S          111011011
W,P,Q    00001011100110011                     W,P,Q      11101101100100000
A        000101110  _                          A          110110110
B        111011010   1×                        B          000100101   1×
CIN              1                             CIN                0
S        000001001                             S          111011011
W,P,Q    00000100101100111                     W,P,Q      11101101101000000
A               01100111                       A          11011011
CIN              0      QUOCOR                 B          00100101   1×      REMCOR
S               01100111                       CIN                0
P,Q      0000100101100111  RM(9),QT(103)       S          00000000
        OFDV                                   W,P,Q      00000000001000000
0                                              A               01000000
                                               CIN              0      QUOCOR
                                               S               01000000
                                               P,Q       0000000001000000  RM(0),QT(64)
                                                         OFDV
                                               0

     ⋀ A.                                           ⋀ B.
```

Table 4-15   Examples of nonrestoring division.

Exhaustive Divider Test. The tabulation of Table 4-16 is obtained from *ONEDIV* and is identical to the results of *ARCHDIV*. Thus, the algorithm is verified for all 4-bit dividends with 2-bit divisors. When the comparison is programmed, *CHECKDIV* is more suitable as the comparison algorithm, as shown in *TESTDIV*, Program 4-17.

OFDV	RM	QT ← DD ÷ DR		← ÷
*	00	00 ← 0000 ÷ 00	0	0 ← 0 ÷ 0
	00	00 ← 0000 ÷ 01	0	0 ← 0 ÷ 1
	00	00 ← 0000 ÷ 10	0	0 ← 0 ÷ $^-$2
	00	00 ← 0000 ÷ 11	0	0 ← 0 ÷ $^-$1
*	01	01 ← 0001 ÷ 00	1	1 ← 1 ÷ 0
	00	01 ← 0001 ÷ 01	0	1 ← 1 ÷ 1
	01	00 ← 0001 ÷ 10	1	0 ← 1 ÷ $^-$2
	00	11 ← 0001 ÷ 11	$^-$0	$^-$1 ← 1 ÷ $^-$1
*	10	10 ← 0010 ÷ 00	$^-$2	$^-$2 ← 2 ÷ 0
*	00	10 ← 0010 ÷ 01	0	$^-$2 ← 2 ÷ 1
	00	11 ← 0010 ÷ 10	0	$^-$1 ← 2 ÷ $^-$2
	00	10 ← 0010 ÷ 11	0	$^-$2 ← 2 ÷ $^-$1
*	11	11 ← 0011 ÷ 00	$^-$1	$^-$1 ← 3 ÷ 0
*	00	11 ← 0011 ÷ 01	0	$^-$1 ← 3 ÷ 1
	01	11 ← 0011 ÷ 10	1	$^-$1 ← 3 ÷ $^-$2
*	00	01 ← 0011 ÷ 11	0	1 ← 3 ÷ $^-$1
*	00	00 ← 0100 ÷ 00	0	0 ← 4 ÷ 0
*	00	00 ← 0100 ÷ 01	0	0 ← 4 ÷ 1
	00	10 ← 0100 ÷ 10	0	$^-$2 ← 4 ÷ $^-$2
*	00	00 ← 0100 ÷ 11	0	0 ← 4 ÷ $^-$1
*	01	01 ← 0101 ÷ 00	1	1 ← 5 ÷ 0
*	00	01 ← 0101 ÷ 01	0	1 ← 5 ÷ 1
	01	10 ← 0101 ÷ 10	1	$^-$2 ← 5 ÷ $^-$2
*	00	11 ← 0101 ÷ 11	0	$^-$1 ← 5 ÷ $^-$1
*	10	10 ← 0110 ÷ 00	$^-$2	$^-$2 ← 6 ÷ 0
*	00	10 ← 0110 ÷ 01	0	$^-$2 ← 6 ÷ 1
*	00	01 ← 0110 ÷ 10	0	1 ← 6 ÷ $^-$2
*	00	10 ← 0110 ÷ 11	0	$^-$2 ← 6 ÷ $^-$1
*	11	11 ← 0111 ÷ 00	$^-$1	$^-$1 ← 7 ÷ 0
*	00	11 ← 0111 ÷ 01	0	$^-$1 ← 7 ÷ 1
*	01	01 ← 0111 ÷ 10	1	1 ← 7 ÷ $^-$2
*	00	01 ← 0111 ÷ 11	0	1 ← 7 ÷ $^-$1

OFDV	RM	QT ← DD ÷ DR		← ÷
*	00	00 ← 1000 ÷ 00	0	0 ← $^-$8 ÷ 0
*	00	00 ← 1000 ÷ 01	0	0 ← $^-$8 ÷ 1
*	00	00 ← 1000 ÷ 10	0	0 ← $^-$8 ÷ $^-$2
*	00	00 ← 1000 ÷ 11	0	0 ← $^-$8 ÷ $^-$1
*	01	01 ← 1001 ÷ 00	1	1 ← $^-$7 ÷ 0
*	00	01 ← 1001 ÷ 01	0	1 ← $^-$7 ÷ 1
*	11	11 ← 1001 ÷ 10	$^-$1	$^-$1 ← $^-$7 ÷ $^-$2
*	00	11 ← 1001 ÷ 11	0	$^-$1 ← $^-$7 ÷ $^-$1
*	10	10 ← 1010 ÷ 00	$^-$2	$^-$2 ← $^-$6 ÷ 0
*	00	10 ← 1010 ÷ 01	0	$^-$2 ← $^-$6 ÷ 1
*	00	11 ← 1010 ÷ 10	0	$^-$1 ← $^-$6 ÷ $^-$2
*	00	10 ← 1010 ÷ 11	0	$^-$2 ← $^-$6 ÷ $^-$1
*	11	11 ← 1011 ÷ 00	$^-$1	$^-$1 ← $^-$5 ÷ 0
*	00	11 ← 1011 ÷ 01	0	$^-$1 ← $^-$5 ÷ 1
*	11	10 ← 1011 ÷ 10	$^-$1	$^-$2 ← $^-$5 ÷ $^-$2
*	00	01 ← 1011 ÷ 11	0	1 ← $^-$5 ÷ $^-$1
*	00	00 ← 1100 ÷ 00	0	0 ← $^-$4 ÷ 0
*	00	00 ← 1100 ÷ 01	0	0 ← $^-$4 ÷ 1
*	00	10 ← 1100 ÷ 10	0	$^-$2 ← $^-$4 ÷ $^-$2
*	00	00 ← 1100 ÷ 11	0	0 ← $^-$4 ÷ $^-$1
*	01	01 ← 1101 ÷ 00	1	1 ← $^-$3 ÷ 0
*	00	01 ← 1101 ÷ 01	0	1 ← $^-$3 ÷ 1
	11	01 ← 1101 ÷ 10	$^-$1	1 ← $^-$3 ÷ $^-$2
*	00	11 ← 1101 ÷ 11	0	$^-$1 ← $^-$3 ÷ $^-$1
*	10	10 ← 1110 ÷ 00	$^-$2	$^-$2 ← $^-$2 ÷ 0
	00	10 ← 1110 ÷ 01	0	$^-$2 ← $^-$2 ÷ 1
	00	01 ← 1110 ÷ 10	0	1 ← $^-$2 ÷ $^-$2
*	00	10 ← 1110 ÷ 11	0	$^-$2 ← $^-$2 ÷ $^-$1
*	11	11 ← 1111 ÷ 00	$^-$1	$^-$1 ← $^-$1 ÷ 0
	00	11 ← 1111 ÷ 01	0	$^-$1 ← $^-$1 ÷ 1
	11	00 ← 1111 ÷ 10	$^-$1	0 ← $^-$1 ÷ $^-$2
	00	01 ← 1111 ÷ 11	0	1 ← $^-$1 ÷ $^-$1

Table 4-16 All divisions with 4-bit dividend and 2-bit divisor.

Although the tabulation of Table 4-16 is not a complete test, it has the advantage of containing a large number of special cases that the division algorithm must satisfy. Thus, from the 32 cases in which the first 2 bits of *DD* are unequal, only two give no overflow. The tabulation also shows the lack of symmetry between positive and negative numbers, caused by the maximum negative number, here $^-$2, which has no representable complement.

Selective Divider Test. For a divisor larger than 2 or 3 bits, the exhaustive approach quickly requires too much machine time, since increasing the divisor and quotient length by 1 causes the test time to grow with a factor of 8.

Having tested an algorithm for short operands by no means guarantees its proper operation for larger operands. Therefore, other tests should be used. For an algorithm such as *ONEDIV*, with several branches and a domain for overflow and no-overflow, it is attractive to develop a number of test cases. The test cases

```
     ∇ TESTDIV X;VX
[1]    ⍝ N[0]←DIVISOR LENGTH, N[1]←QUOTIENT LENGTH
[2]    ⍝ CONSTRUCTION OF OPERANDS
[3]   CONT:VX←((+/N[0 0 1])⍴2)⊤X
[4]    DD←(-N[0])↓VX
[5]    DR←(-N[0])↑VX
[6]    ⍝ POS←1 FOR POSITIVE OPERANDS
[7]    →(~POS)/COMP
[8]    DD← 0 0 ,DD
[9]    DR←0,DR
[10]   ⍝ ALGORITHM TO BE TESTED
[11]  COMP:POSONEDIV
[12]   ⍝ TEST
[13]   →CHECKDIV/RIGHT
[14]   ⍝ PRINT
[15]   PRINTDIV;' WRONG'
[16]   ARCHDIV
[17]   PRINTDIV;' RIGHT'
[18]   ⍝ END TEST
[19]  RIGHT:X←X-1
[20]   →(X≥0)/CONT
[21]   'READY'
     ∇

     ∇ CHAR←PRINTDIV
[1]    CHAR←'01 *←÷QTRM'[(OFDV+2), 2 6 7 2 ,QT, 2 8 9 2 ,RM, 2 4 2 ,DD, 2 5 2 ,DR]
     ∇

       ⍝ REFERENCE:                                           PROGRAM:
       ⍝ ARCHDIV        DIVIDER ARCHITECTURE                    4-1
       ⍝ CHECKDIV       VERIFYING DIVIDER ARCHITECTURE          4-2
```

Program 4-17 Exhaustive divider test.

can exercise the various branch conditions as well as the domain boundaries, as mentioned in Section 2-15.

QUIZDIV, Program 4-18, shows the procedure used for a selective test. The program also shows typical sets of operands for the test. The first set, *BRANCHDIV*, tests all paths through the algorithm. The other sets, *ZERODIV* and *MAXDIV*, test the actions for zero operands and for overflow. Some of the latter tests are also contained in *BRANCHDIV*, to make that test more revealing. *BRANCHDIV* starts with a division whose intermediate results are known from Table 4-15 to see if the divider works at all.

These test cases are not only useful for the initial algorithm, but also for transformations of this algorithm, to be discussed in Chapters 5 and 6. They even prove quite valuable in testing the physical implementation of the design.

Robertson Diagram

The Robertson diagram for the nonrestoring division is shown in Figure 4-19. All four quadrants are used. In comparison to Figure 4-7, the line for quotient 0 is absent and a line for quotient ¯1 is introduced.

Further Development of the Algorithm. In Section 5-3 a datapath is derived for the nonrestoring divider *ONEDIV* and in Sections 6-1 and 6-2 the control for such a datapath is described. The reader can proceed directly to Chapters 5 and 6 if he so desires.

```
      ∇ QUIZDIV X;VX
[1]    ⍝ N[0]←DIVISOR LENGTH, N[1]←QUOTIENT LENGTH
[2]    ⍝ CONSTRUCTION OF OPERANDS
[3]    CONT:DD←((+/N)ρ2)⊤X[0]
[4]    DR←(N[0]ρ2)⊤X[1]
[5]    ⍝ ALGORITHM TO BE TESTED
[6]    ONEDIV
[7]    ⍝ TEST
[8]    →CHECKDIV/RIGHT
[9]    ⍝ PRINT
[10]   PRINTDIV;' WRONG'
[11]   ARCHDIV
[12]   PRINTDIV;' RIGHT'
[13]   ' '
[14]   ⍝ END TEST
[15]  RIGHT:X←2↓X
[16]   →(0≠ρX)/CONT
[17]   'READY'
      ∇
```

```
      BRANCHDIV
3820   37  ¯36  120  2368  37  16512  ¯128  ¯1  0  16511  ¯128  ¯8130  ¯127  ¯16383  ¯128
      ZERODIV
0  0   0  1  0  127  0  ¯128  0  ¯1  1  0  ¯65536  0  65535  0  ¯1  0
      MAXDIV
16255  127  16256  127  16511  ¯128  16512  ¯128  ¯16382  127  ¯16383  127  ¯16383  ¯128
                                                                          ¯16384  ¯128
```

```
      ⍝ TEST CASES FOR 8-BIT OPERANDS

      ⍝ REFERENCE:                                          PROGRAM:
      ⍝ ARCHDIV       DIVIDER ARCHITECTURE                  4-1
      ⍝ CHECKDIV      VERIFYING DIVIDER ARCHITECTURE        4-2
      ⍝ PRINTDIV      DIVIDER DATA DISPLAY                  4-17
```

Program 4-18   Selective divider test.

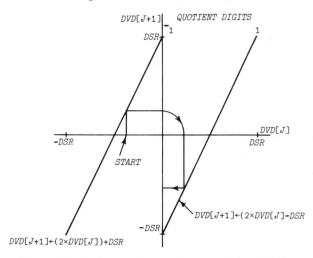

Figure 4-19   Robertson diagram for nonrestoring division.

4-6 SHIFTING OVER ONES AND ZEROS

The possibility of shifting over a series of 0s or 1s during multiplication suggests a similar acceleration for division. Such a method was found in 1958 by Sweeney (MacSorley, 1961), Robertson (1958), and Tocher (1958), independent of one another, and is therefore called *S-R-T division*. Afterward, it proved that this method had already been published in 1956 by Nadler.

A shift over a group of bits can be considered as a series of shifts of 1 bit each. The first shift is linked to a subtraction or addition and produces a quotient bit of 1 or -1. The following shifts occur without processing and have a quotient bit of 0.

Normalization of the Divisor. *SHIFTDIV*, Program 4-20, represents the algorithm for shifting over 0s and 1s. In this algorithm the divisor is assumed to be normalized. An operand is *normalized* when its left 2 bits are unequal. For *DSR*, the value of a normalized divisor, $1 > DSR \geq 0.5$ or $-0.5 > DSR \geq -1$ either holds. The divisor is interpreted here as a fraction. Because of the normalization, the size of the divisor is approximately known. The partial dividend can now be shifted until it corresponds in size to the divisor. Only the left bits of the partial dividend need be inspected during this shift.

The alignment of dividend and divisor might also be possible without normalization of the divisor. In that case, however, the divisor and partial dividend must be

```
       ∇ SHIFTDIV                              [26]   ⍝ REMAINDER CORRECTION
[1]      ⍝ PROLOGUE                            [27]   RCR:→(~W)/RMC
[2]      P←(ρDR)↑DD                            [28]   REMCOR
[3]      Q←(ρDR)↓DD                            [29]   RMC:→(~U∧∨/P)/QTC
[4]      R←DR                                  [30]   REMCOR
[5]      ⍝ DIVISION                            [31]   ⍝ QUOTIENT CORRECTION
[6]      U←P[0]                                [32]   QTC:QUOCOR
[7]      W←P[0]                                [33]   ⍝ OVERFLOW
[8]      J←ρQ                                  [34]   OFLO←OFLO∨U≠R[0]≠Q[0]∨~W
[9]      ⍝ NORMALIZATION                       [35]   ⍝ REMAINDER SCALING
[10]     NM←DIVNORM                            [36]   P←(NMρP[0]),(-NM)↓P
[11]     ⍝ MULTIPLE GENERATION                 [37]   ⍝ EPILOGUE
[12]     CONT:M0←R TWOSELECT 4↑W,P             [38]   RM←P
[13]     ⍝ REDUCTION                           [39]   QT←Q
[14]     A←1↓P,Q[0]                            [40]   OFDV←OFLO
[15]     B←(W=M0[0])≠M0                               ∇
[16]     CIN←W=M0[0]
[17]     ARCHADD
[18]     ⍝ DISPLACEMENT
[19]     DP←J⌊1⌈(1↓S,1↓Q)⍳~S[0]                       ∇ NM←DIVNORM
[20]     P←(DP-1)↓S,1↓DP↑Q                     [1]      NM←¯1+R⍳~R[0]
[21]     Q←DP↓Q,COUT≠R[0]=ONE,(DP-1)ρ0         [2]      OFLO←NM≥P⍳~P[0]
[22]     W←~COUT                               [3]      P←NM↓P,NM↑Q
[23]     ⍝ COUNT                               [4]      Q←NM↓Q,NMρ0
[24]     J←J-DP                                [5]      R←NM↓R,NMρ0
[25]     →(J≠0)/CONT                           [6]      OFLO←OFLO∨R[0]=R[1]
[26]                                                   ∇


       ∇ MX←R TWOSELECT F
[1]      ⍝ DECISION
[2]      ONE←4≠F⍳~F[0]
[3]      ⍝ SELECTION
[4]      MX←ONE∧R
       ∇

       ⍝ REFERENCE:                                   PROGRAM:
       ⍝ ARCHADD      ADDER ARCHITECTURE              2-5
       ⍝ QUOCOR       QUOTIENT CORRECTION             4-14
       ⍝ REMCOR       REMAINDER CORRECTION            4-14
```

Program 4-20 Divider with shift over zeros and ones.

compared over their full lengths. This comparison takes just as long as a reduction cycle and thus offers no advantage.

When the divisor is not normalized, a normalization step is required prior to the reduction cycles. The divisor is shifted left until $R[0]$ is unequal to $R[1]$. The dividend must be shifted an equal amount so that the quotient remains unchanged. If the dividend loses significant digits during this shift, an overflow condition appears. These shifts are shown in the function *DIVNORM*. They reduce the efficiency of the algorithm in time and equipment. When the operands are usually normalized, however, as is the case in floating-point arithmetic, the time disadvantage disappears.

The representation of 0 cannot be normalized. Division by 0 gives an overflow, however, and has arbitrary quotient and remainder. Therefore, this case is signaled in line 6 of *DIVNORM* and the division continues routinely.

The number of bits that must be shifted during the normalization *NM* is determined in line 1 of *DIVNORM*. The APL description is kept at the architectural level. An implementation will have to be worked out later.

Index of. In *DIVNORM* the operator *index of* is used, represented by the dyadically used Greek letter iota, $\imath$. This operator determines where the elements of the right operand first appear in the left operand. The result of $0\ 0\ 0\ 1\ 1\ 0\ \imath\ 1$ is thus 3, the place of the leftmost 1. In *DIVNORM*, line 1, the position of the first significant digit is determined by the index of the inverse of the leftmost bit. This amount is reduced by 1 to obtain the normalization amount *NM*.

Shifting. The shift decision is summarized in Table 4-21, which corresponds to *SHIFTDIV*, line 19. Again the description is given at a high level and the hardware to be used should be detailed later. Line 19 assumes that all possible shifts are available. In a later step of the design, the number of bits that are shifted per cycle is likely to be limited in view of the cost of the displacement circuit, analogous to the considerations mentioned in multiplication.

$P[0\ 1\ 2]$	ACTION	QUOTIENT BIT
0 0 0	SHIFT	$R[0]$
0 0 1	REDUCTION	$COUT{\neq}R[0]$
- - -	- - - -	- - - -
1 1 0	REDUCTION	$COUT{\neq}R[0]$
1 1 1	SHIFT	$R[0]$

Table 4-21 Action of the reduction cycle.

Maximum and Minimum. In *SHIFTDIV*, line 19, the dyadically used symbols $\lfloor$ and $\lceil$ occur, which were encountered earlier in this chapter as the monadic floor and ceiling operators. In their dyadic use, these operators select the *minimum* and *maximum* of their operands, respectively. Thus, in *SHIFTDIV*, line 19, they assure that the displacement never becomes smaller than 1 or larger than the count value *J*.

Scaling of the Remainder. The division with shifting over 0s and 1s follows—apart from the shifts—the algorithm of *ONEDIV*. Hence, a remainder arises which corresponds to the normalized operands. In *SHIFTDIV*, line 36, this remainder is scaled to match the unnormalized operands. The normalization amount *NM* obtained in the preliminary action of line 10 remains stored during the division, to be used in this adjustment.

Examples of division with shifting over 0 and 1 are shown in Table 4-22.

```
        SHIFTDIV                                        SHIFTDIV
R       01001010                DR(37)          R       01001010                DR(37)
W,P,Q 00001110111011000 W,DD(3820)             W,P,Q 11110001000101000 W,DD(¯3820)
A       00111011                                A       11000100
B       11111111   0×                           B       00000000   0×
CIN          1                                  CIN          0
S       00111011                                S       11000100
W,P,Q 00011101110110000                         W,P,Q 11100010001010001
A       01110111                                A       10001000
B       10110101  ¯1×                           B       01001010   1×
CIN          1                                  CIN          0
S       00101101                                S       11010010
W,P,Q 0001011010101100001                       W,P,Q 11101001010100010
A       01011010                                A       10100101
B       10110101  ¯1×                           B       01001010   1×
CIN          1                                  CIN          0
S       00010000                                S       11101111
W,P,Q 0001000011000110                          W,P,Q 11101111010001001
A       01000011                                A       10111101
B       10110101  ¯1×                           B       01001010   1×
CIN          1                                  CIN          0
S       11111001                                S       00000111
W,P,Q 1110010000110011                          W,P,Q 0001110001001000
A       11001000                                A             00111000
B       01001010   1×      REMCOR               B             10110101  ¯1×      REMCOR
CIN          0                                  CIN                1
S       00010010                                S             11101110
W,P,Q 0000100100110011                          W,P,Q 11110111010011000
A             01100111                           A             10011000
CIN                0       QUOCOR               CIN                1      QUOCOR
S             01100111                           S             10011001
P,Q     0000100101100111   RM(9),QT(103)        P,Q     1111011110011001   RM(¯9),QT(¯103)
        OFDV                                            OFDV
0                                               0
```

Table 4-22 Examples of shifting over zeros and ones.

Divider Speed and Cost. The extra cost of *SHIFTDIV* over the simple non-restoring divider *ONEDIV* is in the displacement circuit. For a maximum displacement of 4 bits, the divider cost is already increased by about 40%, as was the case for the multiplier with variable displacement. The speed improvement for such a divider is a factor of 2.39. Table 4-26 shows this figure in relation to other displacements. These costs and speeds ignore the expense of normalization.

The alternatives discussed for the multiplier with variable displacement apply also to the divider. Thus, a fast shift register may be substituted for the variable displacement. This method is used in the PDP11/45 floating-point divider, which uses a shift cycle that is four times faster than the reduction cycle.

4-7 USE OF MULTIPLES WITH VARIABLE SHIFT

Robertson Diagram.   Figure 4-23A shows the Robertson diagram for division with shift over 0s and 1s. Next to the two lines for the nonrestoring division, corresponding to quotient digits 1 and $^-1$, a center line appears, which represents shifting without reduction, hence with quotient digit 0.

The Robertson diagram shows that for certain ratios of dividend and divisor there is no choice in quotient digit, while for other values there is a choice that

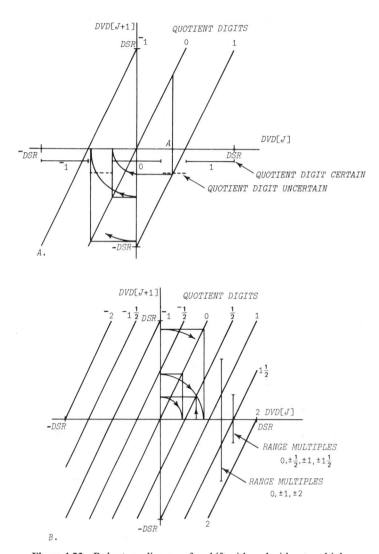

Figure 4-23   Robertson diagrams for shift with and without multiples.

depends on the absolute value of the dividend. Thus, the quotient digit to be used for the divisor A in Figure 4-23A can be 0 or 1. If the criterion of Table 4-21 leads to the choice of 0, then the following cycle will undoubtedly produce a quotient digit 1 and thus require an addition or subtraction. If, on the contrary, 1 was chosen, then a number of quotient digits 0 could follow, which is equivalent to a large shift. The Robertson diagram further shows that the choice of quotient digit 0 is never necessary, whereas 1 and $^-1$ are at times mandatory.

Tolerant Algorithm.   The choice in the multiple to be used in the reduction shows that the nonrestoring division is a *tolerant algorithm*. This tolerance is caused by the recoding of the quotient digits, which, for instance, makes the two quotient digits 0 1 equivalent to 1 $^-1$. The tolerance of the algorithm may be exploited to obtain large strings of 0s or 1s, resulting in large shifts and few divide cycles. *SHIFTDIV* may therefore be expanded by:

(a) Giving more alternatives for the quotient digits by providing more multiples of the divisor.
(b) Selecting the quotient digit in such a way that the number of shifts is optimized.

In the Robertson diagram of Figure 4-23B, the lines for a positive and negative quotient of magnitude 0.5, 1.5, and 2 are drawn next to the familiar lines for 0, 1, and $^-1$. For each point on the horizontal axis, that is, each value of $DVD[J]$, there are now several alternatives, each of which leads to a different value for $DVD[J + 1]$. Of these, the smallest value is the most favorable.

Available Multiples.   The multiples 0.5 and 2 of the divisor are easily obtained by a shift. As in multiplication, however, three times the divisor can also be made available. From this, by means of a shift, one and one half and three fourths of the divisor can be obtained.

MULTDIV, Program 4-24, is a division algorithm that uses the multiples one-and-one-half, one, three-fourths, and one-half times the divisor. The design follows that for *SHIFTDIV*. In line 14 the function *MANYSELECT* is called, which produces the correct multiple.

A Priori Multiple Selection.   The multiple to be used in the reduction can be determined a priori or a posteriori. *MANYSELECT* makes use of the first possibility. The left 6 bits of the dividend and the left 5 bits of the divisor are inspected for this purpose. Since normalization and shifting precede the selection, normally only 3 bits of each are significant, as shown in lines 4 and 5. The matrix *TABMANY* specifies the multiple to be used. The numbers in the matrix are converted to integers by enlarging the multiples four times. Thus, one and one half is represented by 6. The multiple two would only come out favorably once and therefore is not used.

Lines 2 and 3 of *MANYSELECT* determine if the dividend is properly aligned. When too many high-order bits are significant, the normal divisor, represented by

```
      ∇ MULTDIV                              [29]  ⍝ REMAINDER CORRECTION
 [1]    ⍝ PROLOGUE                           [30]  RCR:→(~W)/RMC
 [2]    P←(ρDR)↑DD                           [31]  REMCOR
 [3]    Q←(ρDR)↓DD                           [32]  RMC:→(~U∧∨/P)/QTC
 [4]    R←DR                                 [33]  REMCOR
 [5]    ⍝ DIVISION                           [34]  ⍝ QUOTIENT  CORRECTION
 [6]    U←P[0]                               [35]  QTC:QUOCOR
 [7]    W←P[0]                               [36]  ⍝ OVERFLOW
 [8]    J←ρQ                                 [37]  OFLO←OFLO∨U≠R[0]≠Q[0]∨~W
 [9]    ⍝ NORMALIZATION                      [38]  ⍝ REMAINDER SCALING
[10]    NM←DIVNORM                           [39]  P←(NMρP[0]),(-NM)↓P
[11]    ⍝ TRIPLE DIVISOR                     [40]  ⍝ EPILOGUE
[12]    R3←ARCHTRIPLE R                      [41]  RM←P
[13]    ⍝ MULTIPLE GENERATION                [42]  QT←Q
[14]  CONT:M0←R MANYSELECT 7↑W,P,Q           [43]  OFDV←OFLO
[15]    ⍝ REDUCTION                                ∇
[16]    A←P,Q[0 1 2]
[17]    B←(W=M0[0])≠M0
[18]    CIN←W=M0[0]
[19]    ARCHADD
[20]    ⍝ DISPLACEMENT
[21]    DP←J⌊1⌈¯2+(S,3↓Q)⍳~S[0]
[22]    P←(ρP)↑DP↓S,3↓Q
[23]    QD←,(DPρ2)⊤(MULT×(2⋆DP-3)×¯1⋆W)-~COUT
[24]    Q←DP↓(¯3↑S),3↓Q,QD≠R[0]
[25]    W←~COUT
[26]    ⍝ COUNT
[27]    J←J-DP
[28]    →(J≠0)CONT
[29]
```

```
      ∇ MX←R MANYSELECT F;DSOR;DDND                   TABMANY
 [1]    ⍝ DECISION                             4  4  3  3  3  2  2  2
 [2]    MULT←+/ 4 4 6 × 1 2 3 =F⍳~F[0]         4  4  4  3  3  3  2  2
 [3]    →(MULT≠6)/CONT                         4  4  4  4  3  3  3  3
 [4]    DSOR←R[0]≠R[2 3 4]                     6  4  4  4  4  4  3  3
 [5]    DDND←F[0]≠F[4 5 6]                     6  6  4  4  4  4  4  3
 [6]    MULT←TABMANY[2⊥DDND;2⊥DSOR]            6  6  4  4  4  4  4  4
 [7]    ⍝ END OF COUNT CORRECTION              6  6  6  6  4  4  4  4
 [8]  CONT:MULT←(MULT×J>0)+(4×J=0)+(MULT=3)×J=1 6  6  6  6  4  4  4  4
 [9]    NHF←MULT=6
[10]    ONE←MULT=4
[11]    TQR←MULT=3
[12]    HLF←MULT=2
[13]    ⍝ SELECTION
[14]    MX←(NHF∧R3,0)∨(ONE∧R[0],R, 0 0)∨(TQR∧R3[0],R3)∨HLF∧R[0 0],R,0
      ∇
```

```
      ⍝ REFERENCE:                                       PROGRAM:
      ⍝ ARCHADD      ADDER ARCHITECTURE                  2-5
      ⍝ ARCHTRIPLE   TRIPLER ARCHITECTURE                2-53
      ⍝ DIVNORM      PRENORMALIZATION FOR DIVISION       4-20
      ⍝ QUOCOR       QUOTIENT CORRECTION                 4-14
      ⍝ REMCOR       REMAINDER CORRECTION                4-14
```

Program 4-24 Divider using multiples and variable shift.

the number 4, is used. When not enough bits are significant, the multiple 0 is used, which causes the partial dividend to be shifted without reduction.

A Posteriori Multiple Selection.   In the a posteriori choice, all multiples are used in just as many adders and the adder output with the highest number of connected high-order 0s or 1s is selected. A more economical intermediate form selects first the two most promising multiples and decides subsequently on the basis of the two results.

An example of a posteriori selection is the CDC 6600 divider, which reduces its positive partial dividend with one, two, and three times the divisor in three separate adders, then selects the smallest positive result, using an early carry-out as an indication.

Recording of Quotient Digits. The quotient digits are determined by the same principle as in *ONEDIV* or *SHIFTDIV*, except that several bits are required to record the quotient digits for the multiples one and one half or three fourths. *MULTDIV*, line 23, gives the coding of the quotient digits. They enter Q in line 24.

Line 8 of *MANYSELECT* sees to it that at the end of the division no more quotient digits are generated than can be placed in Q. Furthermore, *TABMANY* has been determined such that following a three-fourths multiple, Q can always be shifted three places, while for all other multiples, the shift is at least two places. Therefore, the quotient digits can be recorded independent of each other.

The numerical example of Table 4-25A illustrates how the correct choice of multiples drastically reduces the number of division cycles.

Divider Speed and Cost. In Table 4-26 the effect of the different multiples and choice criteria is shown (MacSorley, 1961, p. 91). Again a limited number of dis-

```
        MULTDIV                                    TWODIV
R        01001010              DR(37)      R        01001010              DR(37)
W,P,Q 00001110111011000 W,DD(3820)         W,P,Q 00001110111011000 W,DD(3820)
A        00011101110                       A        0001110111
B        11111111111    0×                 B        1101101011    ⁻2×
CIN            1                           CIN            1
S        00011101110                       S        1111100011
W,P,Q 00011101110110000                    W,P,Q 11110001101100001
A        00111011101                       A        1110001101
B        11001000011    ⁻6×                B        0010010100    2×
CIN            1                           CIN            0
S        00000100001                       S        0000100001
W,P,Q 0001000011000110                     W,P,Q 00010000110000110
A        00100001100                       A        0010000110
B        11011010111    ⁻4×                B        1101101011    ⁻2×
CIN            1                           CIN            1
S        11111100100                       S        1111110010
W,P,Q 11100100001100111                    W,P,Q 11111001000011001
A        11001000                          A        1111001000
B        01001010    1×      REMCOR        B        0001001010    1×
CIN            0                           CIN
S        00010010                          S        0000010010
W,P,Q 00001001001100111                    W,P,Q 00001001001100111
A            01100111                      A            01100111
CIN            0      QUOCOR               CIN            0      QUOCOR
S            01100111                      S            01100111
P,Q      0000100101100111  RM(9),QT(103)   P,Q      0000100101100111  RM(9),QT(103)
         OFDV                                       OFDV
0                                          0
           ₐ A.                                       B.
```

Table 4-25 Example of the use of multiples.

MAXIMUM PERMISSIBLE SHIFT	4	6	8	∞
SHIFT OVER 0	1.76	1.83	1.85	1.86
SHIFT OVER 0 AND 1	2.39	2.54	2.64	2.66
MULTIPLES .5,1, AND 2	2.53	2.78	2.84	2.86
MULTIPLES .75 AND 1.5	3.07	3.55	3.72	3.77

Table 4-26 Average shift length in bits.

placements is likely to be used, in view of the noticeable cost and the diminishing return in performance that each added displacement involves. The cost of using many multiples is found mainly in the multiple selection circuit. Also, the generation of triple the divisor is costly, but the tripling circuit may be shared with high-speed multiply equipment. As a result, *MULTDIV* is about three times as fast as *ONEDIV*, for an added cost of about 90%.

Divider Application. An example of the use of multiples in a divider is the IBM 7030, which used one, one-and-one-half, and three-fourths times the divisor with a maximum shift of 6 bits.

4-8 USE OF MULTIPLES WITH FIXED SHIFT

As in multiplication, a fixed shift of 2 or 3 bits offers a simpler organization than a variable shift. Figure 4-27 and *TWODIV*, Program 4-28, show such an algorithm, and Table 4-25B illustrates its use.

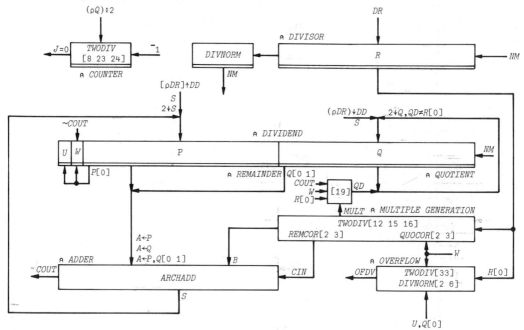

Figure 4-27 Divider with 2-bit shift.

Divider with Two-Bit Shift

TWODIV has a constant shift of 2 bits. In the reduction cycle the dividend is reduced by zero, one, or two times the divisor. The divisor is assumed to be normalized.

The choice of the multiple is determined by *FOURSELECT* and the table *TAB4*. Thee times the divisor is not needed. The two quotient bits can be recorded simply, as appears from *TWODIV*, lines 19 and 20.

```
      ∇ TWODIV                                  [25]  ⍝ REMAINDER CORRECTION
[1]     ⍝ PROLOGUE                              [26]  →(~W)/RMC
[2]     P←(ρDR)↑DD                              [27]  REMCOR
[3]     Q←(ρDR)↓DD                              [28]  RMC:→(~U∧∨/P)/QTC
[4]     R←DR                                    [29]  REMCOR
[5]     ⍝ DIVISION                              [30]  ⍝ QUOTIENT CORRECTION
[6]     U←P[0]                                  [31]  QTC:QUOCOR
[7]     W←P[0]                                  [32]  ⍝ OVERFLOW
[8]     J←(ρQ)÷2                                [33]  OFLO←OFLO∨R[0]≠Q[0]∨~W
[9]     ⍝ NORMALIZATION                         [34]  ⍝ REMAINDER SCALING
[10]    NM←DIVNORM                              [35]  P←(NMρP[0]),(-NM)↓P
[11]    ⍝ MULTIPLE GENERATION                   [36]  ⍝ EPILOGUE
[12]    CONT:M1←R FOURSELECT 7↑W,P              [37]  RM←P
[13]    ⍝ REDUCTION                             [38]  QT←Q
[14]    A←P,Q[0 1]                              [39]  OFDV←OFLO
[15]    B←(W=M1[0])≠M1                             ∇
[16]    CIN←W=M1[0]
[17]    ARCHADD
[18]    P←2↓S
[19]    QD←, 2 2 ⊤(MULT×⁻1↑W)-~COUT
[20]    Q←2↓Q,QD≠R[0]
[21]    W←~COUT
[22]    ⍝ COUNT
[23]    J←J-1
[24]    →(J≠0)/CONT
[25]
```

```
      ∇ MX←R FOURSELECT F;DSOR;DDND
[1]     ⍝ DECISION
[2]     MULT←2
[3]     →(3>F⍳~F[0])/CONT
[4]     DSOR←R[0]≠R[2 3 4]
[5]     DDND←F[0]≠F[3 4 5 6]
[6]     MULT←TAB4[2⊥DDND;2⊥DSOR]
[7]     CONT:ONE←MULT=1
[8]     TWO←MULT=2
[9]     ⍝ SELECTION
[10]    MX←(ONE∧R[0 0],R)∨TWO∧R[0],R,0
```

TAB4

```
0 0 0 0 0 0 0 0
0 0 0 0 0 0 0 0
1 1 1 1 0 0 0 0
1 1 1 1 0 0 0 0
1 1 1 1 1 1 1 1
1 1 1 1 1 1 1 1
2 1 1 1 1 1 1 1
2 2 1 1 1 1 1 1
2 2 2 2 1 1 1 1
2 2 2 2 1 1 1 1
2 2 2 2 2 2 1 1
2 2 2 2 2 2 2 2
2 2 2 2 2 2 2 2
2 2 2 2 2 2 2 2
2 2 2 2 2 2 2 2
```

```
⍝ REFERENCE:                                              PROGRAM:
⍝ ARCHADD    ADDER ARCHITECTURE                           2-5
⍝ DIVNORM    PRENORMALIZATION FOR DIVISION                4-20
⍝ QUOCOR     QUOTIENT CORRECTION                          4-14
⍝ REMCOR     REMAINDER CORRECTION                         4-14
```

Program 4-28 Divider with 2-bit shift.

Divider Speed and Cost. The greatest simplification in hardware of *TWODIV*, as compared to *MULTDIV*, is the standard shift of 2 bits. Hence, the decision and selection circuits for the displacement are not represented in *TWODIV*. As a result, *TWODIV* is twice as fast as *ONEDIV* but only 15% more expensive, again ignoring the cost of normalization.

Array Divider

An array divider can be obtained in the same manner as for an array multiplier by 'unrolling' the reduction loop of an algorithm such as *ONEDIV*. In contrast to multiplication, however, the multiples used in the rows of the array are not independent of each other. The multiple to be used depends upon the sign of the partial dividend developed in the preceding row.

When each row of the array incorporates a carry-propagate adder, the progress through the array is quite slow. The carry-propagate adders may, however, be replaced by a cascade of carry-save adders. The partial dividend is then represented in each row by a generation and transmission. The sign of this partial dividend can be determined by a carry-prediction circuit, as described in Section 2-9 (Cappa and Hamacher, 1972).

Divider Speed and Cost. The interdependence of the rows of the divider array make the speed improvement of the array divider over a divider with a single adder, such as *ONEDIV*, rather limited. Only the time for the carry assimilation and the reading into the register is saved between the rows of the array. Hence, about a factor of 2 in performance may be achieved. The cost of the divider is only reasonable when the array elements are obtained as an integrated circuit at relatively low cost. Unfortunately, the carry-prediction circuit disturbs the regular pattern of the array.

Iterative Division

Division can also be performed by successive approximation, using Newton's iterative method. This method requires repeated multiplications and is only competitive when these are performed at high speed. Since the quotient is approximated, no remainder is obtained as a final partial dividend.

Iterative division was used in the System/360 Model 91 (Anderson et al., 1967). The reader is referred to the literature for a discussion of this method (Ahmad, 1973).

Construction of Algorithms

The different algorithms of this chapter have much in common. Lines 25 through 39 of *TWODIV*, for example, are the same as lines 29 through 43 of *MULTDIV* and lines 26 through 40 of *SHIFTDIV*. In *ONEDIV* the corresponding lines are simpler, since the scaling of the remainder may be omitted, whereas in *POSONEDIV* the negative sign of the operands also need not be considered.

It is important to maintain this common appearance in the design. Thus, the essential differences are often limited to a few lines or functions. This helps the understanding and accelerates the testing of the algorithms.

REFERENCES

AHMAD, M.: "Iterative Schemes for High Speed Division." *The Computer Journal*, vol. 15, no. 4, pp. 333–336 (November, 1972).

ANDERSON, S. F., J. G. EARLE, R. E. GOLDSCHMIDT, and D. M. POWERS: "The IBM System/360 Model 91: Floating-Point Execution Unit." *IBM Journal of Research and Development*, vol. 11, no. 1, pp. 34–53 (January, 1967).

CAPPA, M., and V. C. HAMACHER: "An Augmented Iterative Array for High-Speed Binary Division." *IEEE Transactions on Computers*, vol. C-22, no. 2, pp. 172–175 (February, 1973).

CHINAL, J. P.: "Some Comments on Postcorrections for Nonrestoring Division." *IEEE Transactions on Computers*, vol. C-21, no. 12, pp. 1385–1394 (December, 1972).

MACSORLEY, O. L.: "High-Speed Arithmetic in Binary Computers." *Proceedings of the IRE*, vol. 49, no. 1, pp. 67–91 (January, 1961).

NADLER, M.: "A High-Speed Electronic Arithmetic Unit for Automatic Computing Machines." *Acta Technica* (Prague), vol. 6, pp. 464–478 (1956).

RHYNE, V. T.: "A Simple Postcorrection for Nonrestoring Division." *IEEE Transactions on Computers*, vol. C-20, no. 2, pp. 213–214 (February, 1971).

ROBERTSON, J. E.: "A New Class of Digital Division Methods." *IRE Transactions on Electronic Computers*, vol. 7, no. 3, pp. 218–222 (September, 1958).

TOCHER, K. D.: "Techniques of Multiplication and Division for Automatic Binary Computers." *Quarterly Journal of Mechanics and Applied Mathematics*, vol. 11, pt. 3, pp. 364–384 (1958).

EXERCISES

4-1   Give the division architecture *ARCHDIVD*, which differs from *ARCHDIV* by determining in line 1 the value of the remainder and in line 2 the value of the quotient.

4-2   Give the constructive and verifying divider architecture *ARCHDIV*1 and *CHECKDIV*1 for operands represented in 1's-complement form.

4-3   Give the constructive and verifying divider architecture *ARCHDIVF* and *CHECKDIVF* for single-length operands represented with signed magnitude and interpreted as fractions. No remainder is to be preserved.

4-4   Start with *POSDIV* and *ONEDIV* and derive the algorithm *NEGDIV*, which is a restoring division for positive and negative operands.

4-5   Determine an algorithm for nonrestoring division *ONEDIVS* that has only a single remainder correction cycle. Use the multiple 0 in the reduction, when W, P, and the leftmost bit of Q are all 0, to avoid the case that the partial dividend becomes negative with an absolute value equal to the absolute value of the divisor. Proceeding from *ONEDIV*, it is only necessary to add the multiple 0 and modify the remainder correction conditions.

4-6   Design a divider *COMPDIV*, for positive and negative operands, that precomplements the dividend and then uses nonrestoring division.

4-7   Design a divider *COMPNONDIV* for positive and negative operands that precomplements the dividend and then uses nonperforming division.

4-8   Why can the operands of the reduction cycle of *SHIFTDIV* be shorter than in *ONEDIV*?

4-9   Design the implementation of a circuit that displaces the contents of P and Q in parallel by 1, 2, 3, or 4 bits. Make the implementation correspond to lines 19 through 21 of *SHIFTDIV*, except for the maximum of 4 bits.

4-10 Design a divider similar to the PDP11/45 floating-point divider that uses the algorithm of *SHIFTDIV* but with a 1-bit displacement followed by fast shifts in the registers P and Q.

4-11 Design a divider for positive operands that follows the CDC 6600 approach. Use a fixed 2-bit shift with a posteriori selection of one, two, and three times the divisor subtracted from the partial dividend.

4-12 Determine the combinational circuit with *ONE* and *TWO* as outputs and the bits of R, W, and P as inputs, as specified by *TWODIV* and *FOURSELECT*, Program 4-28.

4-13 Use the signals W, *COUT*, *ONE*, and *TWO* (not *MULT*) as inputs and determine the combinational circuit for *QD*, as specified in *TWODIV*, line 19. Which of the circuits of Exercises 4-12 and 4-13 should be fast? How would you improve the speed of this part of the design?

4-14 Assume that in *TWODIV* the normalization and scaling are performed only with 2-bit resolution, such that the left 2 bits of R may still be equal after normalization. Change *FOURSELECT* and *TAB4* such that the division will still be correct in this case.

4-15 Write an auxiliary program that determines for each of the values of *DSOR* and *DDND* of *MANYSELECT* the minimum shift that each of the multiples produces. Determine on the basis of these data:
      (a)   Whether *TABMANY* is optimal.
      (b)   How *TABMANY* changes if the multiple three fourths is not available.

(c)   How the average minimum shift changes if *TABMANY* is reduced to a 4 by 4 matrix.

4-16   How are the statistics of Table 4-26 improved when it is known that the left half of the quotient digits are identical?

4-17   Design, starting with *MULTDIV*, a divider that uses the multiples 2, 1, and $\frac{1}{2}$. Use the data of Exercise 4-15b to obtain a suitable multiple selection.

4-18   Modify *ONEDIV* by replacing the carry-propagate adder with a carry-save adder and a prediction circuit for the carry-out. Propagate the carry during the final correction cycles. How does this adder compare in speed and cost with *ONEDIV*?

4-19   Determine an initial algorithm *IMPNORM* that is equivalent to *ARCH-NORM*, Program 4-29, such that the number of cycles involved never exceeds $(\rho OD2) \div 2$.

```
        ∇  OUT←ARCHNORM IN;NM
[1]        NM←¯1+IN ι~IN[0]
[2]        OUT←NM↓IN,NMρ0
        ∇
```

Program 4-29   Normalization architecture.

4-20   Determine a set of test cases for testing *MULTDIV*, Program 4-24, with *QUIZDIV*, Program 4-18.

4-21   Define a divider architecture, in which the remainder has the sign of the divisor. Change *ONEDIV*, so that it adheres to this architecture.

5 DATAPATH

Previous chapters emphasized the finding of the proper algorithm for a given operation. Multiplication and division were transformed to a multitude of additions; addition, in turn, was transformed to a multitude of logical operations such as 'and,' 'or,' and 'not.' In some cases the operation could be transformed to a purely combinational circuit. In other cases, a succession of steps was expedient, such as the cycles of a multiplication. For each of these steps, equipment and time are required. A good design will use both efficiently.

To achieve an efficient design, the algorithms of the previous chapters must be ordered in space and time. This ordering, which is the subject of this chapter, will separate the equipment, which is assumed to be available, from the use of this equipment by internal control.

Processing Unit

The part of a digital system that executes the instructions is the processing unit. The fetching and interpretation of instructions is done in the instruction unit, or *I-box*, which will be discussed in Chapter 7. The unit that performs the operations, such as addition, multiplication, and division, is the execution unit, or *E-box*.

Datapath and Control. The part of the execution unit in which data are transported and transformed is called the *datapath*. The central part of the datapath comprising the adder and associated combinational units is called the *arithmetic and logic unit*, or *ALU*. The datapath around the ALU will be described in this chapter. The remaining part of the execution unit serves to control the datapath. This control mechanism is discussed in Chapter 6.

Organization of the Chapter

For a proper perspective the architecture of an instruction repertoire is discussed in Section 5-1. Subsequently, the characteristics of a datapath are considered. These characteristics are illustrated in Sections 5-2 and 5-3, with specialized datapaths for addition, multiplication, and division. The datapaths are combined in Section 5-3 to a common datapath which can serve for all these operations. Several implementations of this common datapath are described. The first of these implementations uses a parallel organization, gaining speed at the expense of equipment. The implementations described in Sections 5-4 through 5-8 use an increasingly serial organization, thereby reducing the equipment involved.

The selection of the data to be processed by the serial datapath is treated as an initial algorithm in Sections 5-4 through 5-6. A datapath for this data selection is introduced in Section 5-7.

In the early sections of this chapter, some specialized functions are used in the datapath, which make the datapath relatively efficient and simple to control. These functions are removed in Section 5-8, resulting in a more austere datapath, which requires a more elaborate control.

The last sections of this chapter may be skipped in a first reading.

5-1 ARCHITECTURE OF OPERATIONS

The precise location of the operands and results, in main storage or in a local store, is not important for the execution unit. The fetching and storing of data will be discussed in Chapters 7 and 8. For the moment it will be assumed that the data are already located in directly accessible registers. This permits a typical set of operations of System/360 to be reduced to a list, as shown in *OPERATION*, Program 5-1.

General Pattern for Operations. *OPERATION* shows that in System/360 the monadic and dyadic operations follow the pattern $RL1 \leftarrow OD1 \oplus OD2$. $OD1$ is here called the *first operand* and $OD2$ the *second operand; RL1* is the result and $\oplus$ is an arbitrary operator. The source of the operands, a register or main storage, does not affect the names.

Fixed-length multiplication and division of System/360 do not quite fit the given pattern. A double-length product is developed to obtain greater precision, while in division a remainder as well as a quotient is generated. These results are considered to consist of the two parts $RL1$ and $RL2$, as shown in *OPERATION*, lines 24, 25, 30, and 31. Also, in division a double-length dividend is used, which is comprised of the two operands $OD2$ and $OD3$, as shown in line 28.

Operators

Operators can be divided into data-handling, logical, and arithmetic operators. In *OPERATION* some of these operators are shown. The choice between the

```
     ∇ OPERATION
[1]    →(POS,NEG,LOAD,COMP,AND,SUB,OR,XOR,LOAD,SUB,ADD,SUB,MPY,DIV,ADD,
                                            SUB)[2⊥INST[4 5 6 7]]
[2]    ⍝ DATA HANDLING
[3]    POS:RL1←(32ρ2)⊤|TWOC OD2
[4]     →0
[5]    NEG:RL1←(32ρ2)⊤-|TWOC OD2
[6]     →0
[7]    COMP:RL1←(32ρ2)⊤-TWOC OD2
[8]     →0
[9]    LOAD:RL1←OD2
[10]    →0
[11]   ⍝ LOGIC
[12]   AND:RL1←OD1∧OD2
[13]    →0
[14]   OR:RL1←OD1∨OD2
[15]    →0
[16]   XOR:RL1←OD1≠OD2
[17]    →0
[18]   ⍝ ARITHMETIC
[19]   ADD:RL1←(32ρ2)⊤(2⊥OD1)+2⊥OD2
[20]    →0
[21]   SUB:RL1←(32ρ2)⊤(2⊥OD1)-2⊥OD2
[22]    →0
[23]   MPY:PD←(64ρ2)⊤(TWOC OD1)×TWOC OD2
[24]    RL1←32↑PD
[25]    RL2←32↓PD
[26]    →0
[27]   DIV:DR←OD1
[28]    DD←OD2,OD3
[29]    ARCHDIV
[30]    RL1←QT
[31]    RL2←RM
     ∇
```

```
     ⍝ REFERENCE:                                        PROGRAM:
     ⍝ ARCHDIV        DIVIDER ARCHITECTURE                 4-1
     ⍝ TWOC           2-COMPLEMENT INTERPRETATION          3-1
```

Program 5-1   Architecture of operations.

operations is determined in line 1 by instruction bits 4 through 7. For the 16 operation codes represented by these four bits only 11 distinct operations are required. Codes that specify the same operation differ in details that fall outside the scope of the operation as far as the datapath is concerned.

Data Handling.   This group of operators comprises the Load and the Store operators. At the time of loading the sign of the operand can be changed. Thus, a number can be fetched unchanged with Load, as in line 9 of *OPERATION*, while in line 3 the absolute value of the number is fetched with Load Positive, in line 5 the negative absolute value with Load Negative, and in line 7 the value with opposite sign with Load Complement.

Since the operands are represented in 2's-complement form, the corresponding interpretation function *TWOC*, Program 3-1, is used in these specifications. The encode operator ⊤ gives the 2's-complement when used with a binary base vector.

32-bit operands are assumed. The absolute-value operator, the monadic |, changes the sign of its argument to positive.

Logic. The most important logical operators are And, Or, and Exclusive-or in lines 12, 14, and 16, respectively.

Arithmetic. The arithmetic operators are Add, Subtract, Multiply, and Divide, shown in lines 19, 21, 23, and 27, respectively. A comparison is made by means of a subtraction. The multiplication is not cumulative. For the division, the architecture *ARCHDIV*, Program 4-1, is used.

Instruction Repertoire. Appendix B shows the complete instruction repertoire of System/360. *OPERATION* corresponds with the second column of the *RR* format. The table shows that the various formats noticeably influence the number of instructions. The operation Load occurs four times because of differences in operand format. The choice in operand location further doubles the number of instructions. This number is augmented even further by the Move operations for variable-length operands, which, in essence, are Load operations.

As mentioned before, the majority of format variations fall outside the concern of the execution unit proper. Thus, the half-word operands can be treated as full-word operands by extending the sign bit with 16 bits, prior to entering the execution unit.

5-2 SPECIALIZED DATAPATH

The implementation algorithms of Chapters 2, 3, and 4 give a good impression of the equipment required for the corresponding operations. The initial algorithms, however, do not constitute a direct description of the equipment. To obtain such a description the components of a datapath will be reviewed first. Subsequently, the operations of Chapters 2 and 3 will be described in terms of their use of a datapath.

Components of a Datapath. A datapath consists of three types of components, which also can be recognized in the block diagram for the datapath.

The first component type is the *combinational circuit*, such as an adder, or complementer (Appendix D). The combinational circuit is represented in the block diagram by a rectangle. Usually, the width of the rectangle indicates the amount of equipment represented. Also, the relative placement may be illustrative, as in Figure 3-21.

A second component type is the *sequential circuit*, such as a register or counter. The sequential circuit is also shown as a rectangle but is distinguished from the combinational circuit by a double bottom line.

Finally, the *connections* between the components are shown in the block diagram as lines. Each line may represent a multitude of parallel signals.

Illustration of a Datapath by a Block Diagram. The illustrative character of the block diagram has an inner contradiction: the more that is shown, the less clear the drawing becomes. Because of this, some connections may not be shown over their full length. It also is not profitable to work out the relative size and placement in too great a detail. These omissions result in incompleteness. The use of a language such as APL, however, may make the diagram complete again. Each component is now described by an expression, or, if this would be too space-consuming, by a name or line number reference, which may be explained elsewhere by a diagram or function. Thus, the adder of Figure 3-5 refers to the function *ARCHADD*, while other combinational circuits of Figure 3-5 are explained by expressions of *POSMPY*.

```
     ∇ IMPPOS                                    ∇ IMPMIN
[1]    ⍙ PROLOGUE                           [1]    ⍙ PROLOGUE
[2]    R←OD2                                [2]    P←OD1
[3]    ⍙ ABSOLUTE VALUE                     [3]    R←OD2
[4]    A←(⍴R)⍴0                             [4]    ⍙ SUBTRACTION
[5]    B←R[0]≠R                             [5]    A←P
[6]    CIN←R[0]                             [6]    B←~R
[7]    ARCHADD                              [7]    CIN←1
[8]    P←S                                  [8]    ARCHADD
[9]    ⍙ EPILOGUE                           [9]    P←S
[10]   RL1←P                                [10]   ⍙ EPILOGUE
     ∇                                      [11]   RL1←P
                                                 ∇

      ⍙ REFERENCE:                                            PROGRAM:
      ⍙ ARCHADD        ADDER ARCHITECTURE                      2-5
```

Program 5-2   Implementation of Load Positive and Subtract.

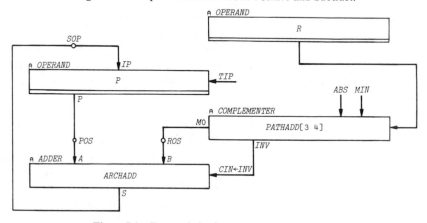

Figure 5-3   Datapath for load and add operations.

When the lines and rectangles of the drawing are omitted, a set of expressions remains which in itself describes the equipment completely. The drawing is formally superfluous, therefore, and merely helps to provide insight. The gain in understanding, however, more than justifies the effort of the drawing.

Description of Datapath in APL

In this section, the APL description of a datapath is presented. The datapath will be derived from the initial algorithms for the functions to be performed. As a first example, a datapath capable of the load and add operations will be described. These operations include sign handling and subtraction. They are represented by *OPERATION* lines 3, 5, 7, 9, 19, and 21.

Datapath for Load and Add Operations.   Since the six load and add operations are very similar, only two representative operations will be discussed in detail. Program 5-2 gives the initial algorithms *IMPPOS* and *IMPMIN* for the implementation of the load with absolute-value and subtract operations. They correspond to Load Positive and Subtract, as described in lines 3 and 21 of *OPERATION*. In these initial algorithms lines 4 through 8 and 5 through 9 represent the equipment that the designer has in mind for each of these operations. In both cases an adder with a complementer as one of its inputs is postulated. These requirements can be satisfied by a datapath, as illustrated by the block diagram of Figure 5-3 and described by *PATHADD*, Program 5-4.

Gates.   In this example the datapath must be used for the various data-handling operations. Hence, the signals used in the datapath must be selected to suit the operation. For example, the *A* input of the adder should be zero in *IMPPOS*, but it should be connected to *P* in *IMPMIN*. Also, the signals that enter the *B* and *CIN* inputs of the adder differ in these two cases.

The selection of a signal can be accomplished simply by an 'and' connection with a control signal. Such an 'and' circuit is called a *gate*, and the control signal

```
      ∇ PATHADD                          ∇ DECLADD
[1]     ⍝ ADDER INPUTS              [1]     ⍝ OPERAND REGISTERS
[2]     A←Y[POS]∧P                  [2]     P←(ρOD1)ρ0
[3]     INV←Y[MIN]≠Y[ABS]∧R[0]      [3]     R←(ρOD1)ρ0
[4]     M0←INV≠R                          ∇
[5]     B←Y[ROS]∧M0
[6]     CIN←INV
[7]     ⍝ ADDER
[8]     ARCHADD
[9]     ⍝ REGISTER INPUTS
[10]    IP←Y[SOP]∧S
[11]    ⍝ REGISTERS
[12]    P←(Y[TIP]∧IP)∨(~Y[TIP])∧P
      ∇
```

```
      ⍝ REFERENCE:                                      PROGRAM:
      ⍝ ARCHADD      ADDER ARCHITECTURE                   2-5
```

Program 5-4   Datapath for load and add operations.

is called the *gate signal*. If a group of signals, such as those specified by a vector, is to be selected, a common gate signal can be used to control the gates of each of these signals.

In Figure 5-3, therefore, gates have been introduced at the adder and register inputs, as indicated by the small circles in the connecting lines.

To the corresponding expressions for A, B, and S in *PATHADD*, the gate signals are also introduced. For instance, the gate signal $Y[POS]$ controls the connection of P to the A input of the adder. For the absolute-value algorithm, $Y[POS]$ should be 0; for the subtraction algorithm, it should be 1.

Gate Vector.   Since there are many gate signals in a datapath, they have been collected in a *gate vector* Y. The final allocation of the bits of this vector can be postponed by using names like *POS* and *ABS* for the bit positions. These names have the added advantage of being mnemonic—calling their purpose to remembrance.

In this text the names of the input gates of the adder generally end with S, and the gates in the output of the adder generally start with S. Gates associated with register P use the letter P. The names *ABS* and *MIN* are derived from 'absolute value' and 'minus.' No effort has been made to be too particular about these names, since each designer has his own preferences.

GATECODE, Program 5-5, shows a possible assignment of the bits of the gate vector. In this assignment, *POS* has the value 0 and *ABS* has the value 12. Hence, the gate signals $Y[POS]$ and $Y[ABS]$ are the first and the thirteenth bits of Y.

```
        ∇ GATECODE
[1]     ⍝ ADDER INPUT GATES              [15]    ⍝ CONTROL GATES
[2]     POS←0                            [16]    ABS←12
[3]     ROS←1                            [17]    MIN←13
[4]     MOS←2                            [18]    BOS←14
[5]     LOS←3                            [19]    TOK←15
[6]     KOS←4                            [20]    SKH←16
[7]     DOS←5                            [21]    ⍝ REGISTER READ-IN SIGNALS
[8]     ⍝ REGISTER INPUT GATES           [22]    TIB←17
[9]     SOP←6                            [23]    TIP←18
[10]    SOM←7                            [24]    TIQ←19
[11]    KOK←8                            [25]    TIU←20
[12]    COW←9                            [26]    TIV←21
[13]    MOR←10                           [27]    TIW←22
[14]    DOR←11                           [28]    TIJ←23
[15]                                             ∇
```

Program 5-5   Assignment of gate signals to the gate vector.

Modification Signals.   The gates $Y[MIN]$ and $Y[ABS]$ are not used to pass an operand. Rather, in combination with $R[0]$, the sign of R, they form in line 3 of *PATHADD* the signal *INV*, which governs the inversion of R. This type of gate signal, the *modification signal*, changes the action of the datapath rather than the flow through the datapath. Therefore, the term 'gate signal' must be taken in the general sense of a *control signal*.

The inversion control described by line 3 of *PATHADD* permits all the complements required by the load and add operations. The gates $Y[ROS]$ and $Y[SOP]$ in lines 5 and 10 of *PATHADD* are not necessary for the load and add operations.

Since the designer intends to use the datapath for additional operations, however, he has as a general procedure placed gates at all critical points. At this stage it is wise to be liberal with gates. Later it will be relatively simple to decide if a gate is actually needed and to remove the unnecessary gates.

Registers.   In APL an assigned value remains available until it is changed by a subsequent expression. The equipment that corresponds to such an action is a register. Since a variable may moreover appear simultaneously on the left and the right of an assignment symbol, the registers would have to incorporate two storage elements for each bit. Such a register is called *doubly latched*.

In an actual implementation a much more frugal use of registers is made than would be suggested by the naive interpretation of the APL statements. For example, the signals *ONE*, *TWO*, and *COM* in *TWOMPY*, Program 3-19, need not be stored at all. Moreover, in *TWOMPY*, *P* is intended to be a doubly latched register. One could also use a single latch for register *P* and another for the adder output *S*. The program does not tell us which alternative is chosen.

Identification of Registers.   The ambiguity in the use of registers is quite proper for an initial algorithm, since the designer is not concerned with these details at that point. For the datapath description, however, the use of registers is a central issue and the description should be clear about it. This is done by declaring the registers in a separate function, by listing the registers in the datapath as a group, and by giving separate names to the input and the output of a doubly latched register. The latter convention indicates that the input affects the output not immediately, as is the case for a single latch.

In *PATHADD*, *P* is intended to be built with a double latch. To indicate this intention, *P* is listed in line 12 of *PATHADD* as a register, and the input signal *IP* is distinguished from the output *P* in the datapath. *R* is treated as an input of the datapath. Its nature can be decided later.

Description of a Register.   The working of the register is for the moment indicated in a simple manner, as shown in line 12 of *PATHADD*. If line 12 were translated into a circuit, the register would actually be in danger of not setting correctly because of the delays in the circuit elements; it contains a *hazard*. In Chapter 8 the inner working of various types of registers will be discussed further. The current description has the nature of an architecture.

Read-in Signals.   The signal *Y[TIP]*, when 1, sets the content of register *P* according to the input *IP*. When *Y[TIP]* is 0, the value of *P* remains unchanged. Such a signal is called a *read-in signal*. It is the third type of gate signal which is found in the datapath.

Declaration of Registers.   Associated with a datapath description is the declaration of the registers used in this datapath. For *PATHADD*, this declaration is given by *DECLADD*, Program 5-4. The two registers *P* and *R* are declared in *DECLADD* by stating their dimension. The dimension is derived in this case from the operands $OD1$ and $OD2$. The contents of the registers are set to 0 as a matter of convenience, as was the case for the declaration of the carry in *RIPPLE*, Program 2-17.

The register declaration clarifies the use of the registers in the datapath. The declaration is also necessary when the datapath description is to be used as a function in a simulation. If, for instance, *PATHADD* is called, *P* must have the proper dimension even when the content of *P* is not used, as is the case for Load Positive.

Description of Combinational Circuits.   The expressions for the combinational circuits that are simultaneously active are placed on successive lines of APL programs. It may be possible to write these expressions all on a single line. This complexity is not necessary, however. The simultaneity can be deduced in the datapath program from the comments. The succession of the expressions indicates the flow of the information through the logical circuits. A variable is not found in any line preceding its assignment. Hence, the outputs of the combinational circuits need not be declared in advance, and the expressions that generate the outputs need only be executed once to simulate the action of the circuit.

Description of Sequential Circuits.   A sequential circuit can be described just as a combinational circuit. Here variables are used before they are set, however. An example is the adder *RIPASYNC*, Program 2-45. To simulate such a circuit, the expressions must be executed repeatedly until the circuit has come to a stable state. This involves the use of housekeeping expressions as is illustrated by the label and branch in *RIPASYNC* lines 13 and 18. Sequential circuits of this kind are rare in a datapath, since they are difficult to test and uncertain in their timing. Hence, they will not be considered here in further detail.

Block Diagram of a Datapath.   The two-dimensional form of the block diagram properly represents the concurrent nature of digital equipment. There is no pretense that one action should precede another, as is the case with a program.

The inputs and outputs of the blocks in the diagram are indicated by names or expressions. For the registers the name of the operand is mentioned in the block, and the output is indicated only when there is a selection of signals. The read-in signals of the registers are shown at the side of the block. When more than one signal enters at an input, an 'or' circuit is implied. This is indicated by bringing the signals together in one point.

The names of the gate signals are written next to the circle which represents the gate. The name is abbreviated by omitting the vector name *Y* and the square brackets of the index. Thus, *POS* represents *Y[POS]*. In actual practice the gates are often built as a part of the registers or adders. The block diagram indicates this by showing the gate signals as input to the block representing the circuit. This is shown in Figure 5-3 in the case of the complementer.

Gate Program

GATEPOS and *GATEMIN* are the programs that result from *IMPPOS* and *IMPMIN* when the datapath is available as a function. The function call to the datapath occurs in line 2 of the function *GATE*. *GATEPOS*, *GATEMIN*, and *GATE* are shown in Program 5-6.

```
        ∇ GATEPOS                              ∇ GATEMIN
  [1]      ⍝ PROLOGUE                    [1]      ⍝ PROLOGUE
  [2]      R←OD2                          [2]      P←OD1
  [3]      ⍝ ABSOLUTE VALUE               [3]      R←OD2
  [4]      GATE ROS,ABS,SOP,TIP           [4]      ⍝ SUBTRACTION
  [5]      ⍝ EPILOGUE                     [5]      GATE POS,ROS,MIN,SOP,TIP
  [6]      RL1←P                          [6]      ⍝ EPILOGUE
        ∇                                 [7]      RL1←P
                                              ∇

        ∇ GATE X
  [1]     Y←(⍳24)∊X
  [2]     PATHADD
        ∇

        ⍝ REFERENCE:                                      PROGRAM:
        ⍝ PATHADD      DATAPATH FOR LOAD AND ADD OPERATIONS    5-4
```

Program 5-6 Gate programs for Load Positive and Subtract.

Line 1 of *GATE* determines the gate vector *Y* from the specification given in the calling program. For *GATEPOS*, the gate signals *Y[ROS]*, *Y[ABS]*, *Y[SOP]*, and *Y[TIP]* are set to 1, while all other gate signals are set to 0.

Index Generator. Expression 1 of *GATE* uses the *index generator*, represented by the Greek letter iota, ι. The monadic form ιN generates a vector consisting of the first *N* integers. These are the numbers 0 up to *N* for index origin 0 and the numbers 1 up to and including *N* for index origin 1. Since this text uses index origin 0, $\iota 24$ is equivalent to the vector 0 1 2 3 . . . 23.

As indicated by its name, the index generator is useful in indexing. Thus, the seven elements of *A* starting at element 5 can be identified by $A[5 + \iota 7]$. The application of the iota is not restricted to indexing, however, as is illustrated by line 1 of *GATE*.

Membership. Line 1 of GATE also uses the *membership* operator, which is indicated by the Greek letter epsilon, ϵ. This dyadic operator forms a logical array with the same dimensions as the left operand. An element in this array will be 1 when the corresponding element of the left operand is a member of the set designated by the right operand; otherwise, the element is 0.

In line 1 of *GATE* a gate vector of 24 bits is formed. When *GATE* is called by line 4 of *GATEPOS*, the elements corresponding to *ROS*, *ABS*, *SOP*, and *TIP* will be 1 and all others 0. According to *GATECODE*, these are the elements 1, 12, 6, and 18, such that *Y* has the value indicated in Table 5-7.

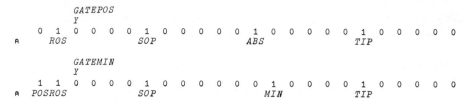

```
        GATEPOS
        Y
    0   1   0   0   0   0   1   0   0   0   0   0   1   0   0   0   0   0   1   0   0   0   0   0
ρ       ROS             SOP                 ABS                 TIP


        GATEMIN
        Y
    1   1   0   0   0   0   1   0   0   0   0   0   0   1   0   0   0   0   1   0   0   0   0   0
ρ   POSROS              SOP                     MIN             TIP
```

Table 5-7   Gate vectors for load positive and subtract.

Declaration of Gate Names.   Since the gates are specified by names, these names must be known to the system when the gate program is executed. Hence, it is necessary to execute the name declaration program *GATECODE* prior to the use of the gate programs.

Arithmetic and Logic Unit

The combinational part of *PATHADD*, comprising the adder and the complementer and their gates, constitutes the arithmetic and logic unit (ALU) of the datapath. The ALU is normally also able to perform the logical functions, as specified in *OPERATION*, lines 12, 14, and 16.

An example of an ALU capable of load, complement, add, subtract, and associated arithmetic operations, as well as all 16 logical connectives, is the TI SN74181. This ALU is built as one integrated circuit. The adder is 4 bits wide and uses the carry prediction given by *PRED*5, Program 2-26. A wider ALU can be obtained by using several units in parallel. The TI SN74182 can be used as a companion circuit to obtain carry prediction for groups of four similar to the principle discussed for *PREDICT*100, Program 2-28. The implementation of the TI SN74181 is described in Exercise 5-3.

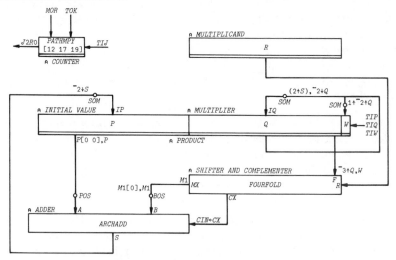

Figure 5-8   Datapath for multiplier.

Repeated Use of a Datapath

As a second example of the separation of an implementation into a datapath and a gate program, this procedure is applied to the 2-bit multiplier *TWOMPY*, Figure 3-18 and Program 3-19.

Datapath for Multiplier. The block diagram for the multiplier datapath is shown in Figure 5-8. The description of the datapath is given by *PATHMPY*, and the use of the datapath for the multiplication is described by *GATEMPY*, Program 5-9. The function *GATE* refers here in line 2 to *PATHMPY*.

The datapath *PATHMPY* can be obtained from *TWOMPY* by inserting gates in the expressions for the adder inputs and outputs and by associating inputs and read-in signals with the registers P, Q, W, and J. The combinational multiple-selection circuit *FOURFOLD* can be used unchanged. The extension of the operands P and $M1$ is shown here without use of the function *EXTEND*.

Decision in Datapath. During the multiplication, the datapath *PATHMPY* is used repeatedly. The first time, in line 6 of *GATEMPY*, W and J are set to their

```
     ∇ PATHMPY
[1]    ⍝ ADDER INPUTS
[2]    A←Y[POS]∧P[0 0],P
[3]    M1←R FOURFOLD ‾3↑Q,W
[4]    B←Y[BOS]∧M1[0],M1
[5]    CIN←CX
[6]    ⍝ ADDER
[7]    ARCHADD
[8]    ⍝ REGISTER INPUTS
[9]    IP←Y[SOM]∧‾2↓S
[10]   IQ←Y[SOM]∧(‾2↑S),‾2↓Q
[11]   IW←Y[SOM]∧1↑‾2↑Q
[12]   IJ←(Y[MOR]×(⍴Q)÷2)+Y[TOK]×J-1
[13]   ⍝ REGISTERS
[14]   P←(Y[TIP]∧IP)∨(~Y[TIP])∧P
[15]   Q←(Y[TIQ]∧IQ)∨(~Y[TIQ])∧Q
[16]   W←(Y[TIW]∧IW)∨(~Y[TIW])∧W
[17]   J←(Y[TIJ]×IJ)+(~Y[TIJ])×J
[18]   ⍝ TESTCONDITIONS
[19]   JZRO←J=0
     ∇
```

```
     ∇ DECLMPY
[1]    ⍝ MULTIPLIER/PRODUCT REGISTERS
[2]    P←(⍴MD)⍴0
[3]    Q←(⍴MR)⍴0
[4]    ⍝ MULTIPLICAND REGISTER
[5]    R←(⍴MD)⍴0
[6]    ⍝ MULTIPLIER BALANCE
[7]    W←0
[8]    ⍝ COUNTER
[9]    J←0
     ∇
```

```
     ∇ GATEMPY
[1]    ⍝ PROLOGUE
[2]    P←VL
[3]    Q←MR
[4]    R←MD
[5]    ⍝ MULTIPLICATION
[6]    GATE MOR,TIW,TIJ
[7] CONT:GATE POS,BOS,SOM,TOK,TIP,TIQ,TIW,TIJ
[8]    →(~JZRO)/CONT
[9]    ⍝ EPILOGUE
[10]   PD←P,Q
     ∇
```

```
     ∇ GATE X
[1]    Y←(⍳24)∊X
[2]    PATHMPY
     ∇
```

```
     ⍝ REFERENCE:                              PROGRAM:
     ⍝ ARCHADD       ADDER ARCHITECTURE         2-5
     ⍝ FOURFOLD      MULTIPLICAND SELECTION     3-19
```

Program 5-9 Datapath and gate program for multiplier.

initial value. During the subsequent calls of the datapath, in line 7, the multiplication cycles take place. The gate program determines the end of the multiplication by means of a decision, based upon the test signal *JZRO*.

Test Signals.   Each decision taken in a program like *TWOMPY* contains a combinational element, the *test signal*, here *JZRO*, and a sequential element, the *branch* to be taken, such as the choice between continuation and termination. The logic of the test signal, here *J* being 0, belongs to the datapath, as shown in line 19 of *PATHMPY*, while the use of the signal belongs to the control section, as shown in line 8 of *GATEMPY*. Hence, the communication between datapath and control consists in one direction in gate signals and in the other direction in test signals, as shown in Figure 5-10.

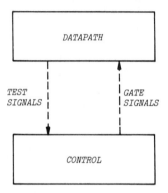

Figure 5-10   Relation of datapath and control.

In *GATEMPY* the branch is taken when *JZRO* is 0. This requires that ~*JZRO* be used as a test condition. In general, test signals may be used to specify a branch when 0 or when 1. The choice between these two options depends upon the organization of the gate program. The test signals are developed in the datapath independently of the polarity that may be required by the gate program. The control is expected to invert the signal as needed. Thus, the design of the logic of the datapath is separated from the development of the gate program.

Deferred Substitution.   The counter *J* and the adder *ARCHADD* are still defined arithmetically in *PATHMPY*. Eventually they will have to be replaced by the logic representing the actual circuits. As long as the designer is confident that these substitutions will cause no problems, in particular that they will not influence the other parts of the datapath, this substitution can be postponed, thus preserving compactness of expression and clarity of overview.

Separation of Space and Time.   The equipment of the datapath represents the spatial part of the algorithms of the previous chapters. The use of this equipment in time is determined by the control. Each part can be described by its own algorithm, such as the algorithms *PATHMPY* and *GATEMPY*. The design of a processing unit therefore results in a separation of space and time.

Register Transfer Concept.   The separation of space and time involves the use of storage elements, such as registers. Hence, the operation of a digital system can at this level be described by the transfer of information from register to register via the combinational circuits of the datapath. Languages that are intended to describe this level of the implementation are called *register transfer languages* (Schorr, 1964; Stabler, 1970). It is, however, more advantageous to use the same language for the various levels of architecture and implementation that are encountered in a design, thus eliminating the need for a special language at this point.

The DEC PDP16 register transfer modules are an example of equipment designed to facilitate the construction of a digital system with readymade components (Bell et al., 1972).

Further Development of the Datapath Control.   The following sections of this chapter will discuss the datapath in further detail. The reader may, however, wish to study the elementary control of the datapath at this point and can do so by proceeding to the first section of Chapter 6.

5-3 COMMON DATAPATH

The design of a common datapath will be illustrated by the requirements of the nonrestoring division, *ONEDIV*, Program 4-14. The example illustrates the decisions that the designer must make to use a datapath for several purposes. This design process will be further illustrated by combining the datapath for division with the datapaths for addition and multiplication.

Time and Space Sharing.   The initial algorithm determines in general the cost of the operation in equipment and time. The designer must now decide in detail which expressions of the initial algorithm are performed simultaneously in the datapath, hence in *space sharing*, and which expressions use the same equipment in succession, hence in *time sharing*. Thus, the choice between parallel and serial operation reappears at this point but is now applied to larger functional units.

Common Equipment.   It seems natural to perform the additions in line 13 of *ONEDIV* and in line 4 of the remainder correction *REMCOR* and the quotient correction *QUOCOR* by the same adder. In fact, the initial algorithm has already assumed this by expressing the addition of 0 or 1 in *QUOCOR* in terms of *ARCHADD* and not in terms of a counter. A and B have the dimension $1 + \rho P$ in lines 10 and 11 of *ONEDIV*, whereas they have the length ρP in *REMCOR* and *QUOCOR*. This implies a length of $1 + \rho P$ for the adder and requires a lengthening of the operands in *REMCOR* and *QUOCOR*.

The subtraction of *ONEDIV*, line 18, can also be performed by the adder of line 13. Line 18 must then be rewritten in terms of *ARCHADD*, and the dimension of the operands must conform to the common value. With some imagination the zero test of line 23 can also be performed by the adder. These two suggestions, however, save little in equipment. The use of the adder for the count of line 18 furthermore requires two passes through the adder for each reduction cycle. The reduction cycle is the most frequently executed cycle, the *inner loop*, of the algorithm. Lengthening the inner loop correspondingly lengthens the total operation time, which is very undesirable. Therefore, the design will assume a separate counter and zero tester.

A uniform function, such as *ARCHADD*, does not necessarily imply a single implementation. In the bit adder of Program 2-9, the same function is mentioned in lines 2 and 7, but it is intended to be built twice.

Further Development of the Divider Algorithm

ONEDIV will first be converted into the intermediate algorithm *IMPDIV*, Program 5-11, to make the choice in equipment more apparent. Such an intermediate step between initial algorithm and datapath can usually be omitted, however.

```
      ∇ IMPDIV                                        ∇ IMPIND
[1]      ∩ PROLOGUE                           [1]       U←P[0]
[2]      P←(ρDR)↑DD                           [2]       W←P[0]
[3]      Q←(ρDR)↓DD                           [3]       J←ρQ
[4]      R←DR                                          ∇
[5]      ∩ DIVISION
[6]      IMPIND
[7]      ∩ REDUCTION                                 ∇ IMPRED
[8]   CONT:IMPRED                             [1]       A←P,Q[0]
[9]      →(J≠0)/CONT                          [2]       B←(W=R[0])≠R[0],R
[10]     ∩ REMAINDER CORRECTION               [3]       CIN←W=R[0]
[11]     →(~W)/RMC                            [4]       ARCHADD
[12]     IMPRMC                               [5]       P←1↓S
[13]  RMC:→(~U∧∨/P)/QTC                       [6]       Q←1↓Q,COUT≠R[0]
[14]     IMPRMC                               [7]       W←~COUT
[15]     ∩ QUOTIENT CORRECTION                [8]       ∩ COUNT
[16]  QTC:IMPQTC                              [9]       J←J-1
[17]     ∩ EPILOGUE                                   ∇
[18]     RM←P
[19]     QT←Q
[20]     OFDV←OFLO
      ∇


      ∇ IMPRMC                                        ∇ IMPQTC
[1]      A←P[0],P                            [1]       A←Q[0],Q
[2]      B←(W=R[0])≠R[0],R                    [2]       B←(1+ρQ)ρ0
[3]      CIN←W=R[0]                           [3]       CIN←W≠R[0]
[4]      ARCHADD                              [4]       ARCHADD
[5]      P←1↓S                                [5]       Q←1↓S
[6]      W←~COUT                              [6]       W←~COUT
      ∇                                       [7]       ∩ OVERFLOW
                                              [8]       OFLO←U≠R[0]≠Q[0]∨~W
                                                       ∇


          ∩ REFERENCE:                                     PROGRAM:
          ∩ ARCHADD        ADDER ARCHITECTURE                 2-5
```

Program 5-11 Implementation form of divider.

Lengthening of Operands. *IMPDIV* shows the modification of *ONEDIV* into an algorithm using a common datapath. All distinct datapath actions are represented by separate functions, while *IMPDIV* gives the order in which these actions must take place. Thus, the initiation of the sign registers and the counter is performed by *IMPIND* and the reduction loop, including the count, by *IMPRED*. The remainder and quotient correction were already represented by the separate functions *REMCOR* and *QUOCOR*. These functions are now modified and represented by *IMPRMC* and *IMPQTC*.

The operands are lengthened to the dimension $N + 1$. The designer must decide in which direction he wants to lengthen the operands. Lengthening is to the left with the sign and to the right with 0. Here, the designer has chosen to extend to the left as illustrated in lines 1 and 2 of *IMPRMC* and *IMPQTC*.

Uniformity of Expression. The aim of obtaining common equipment is also expressed by making the various expressions as uniform as possible. For instance, when *IMPRMC* is used on line 12 of *IMPDIV*, the content of *W* is known to be 1. Hence, the expressions of *IMPRMC* could be simplified accordingly. This is not done, however, since *IMPRMC* can now be used on both lines 12 and 14. Furthermore, *IMPRMC*, lines 2, 3, 5, and 6, now match *IMPRED*, lines 2, 3, 5, and 7, which permits a common circuit in the ultimate datapath.

Verification of Modifications. The algorithm *IMPDIV* is logically equivalent to *ONEDIV*. For the designer it is of great value to verify this equivalence. Since he has assured himself of the correctness of *ONEDIV*, he would not like to lose this assurance through the modifications that have been made.

Local Verification. *IMPDIV* can be tested in its entirety as was the case with *ONEDIV*. It is more effective, however, to test just the substitutions made. For example, the lengthening of the operands of *REMCOR* to those of *IMPRMC* can be tested separately.

QUIZPATH, Program 5-12, shows a selective test for the datapath actions. The program follows the pattern of earlier test programs and should be self-explanatory. The number and size of the operands precludes an exhaustive test. Since the datapath is sufficiently regular, however, a well-selected set of operands will give a quite convincing verification.

A local verification is considerably more efficient than using only a global verification. On the other hand, the designer probably wants to see the algorithm work as an entity as well: hence the importance of preserving the ability to execute the description.

Datapath for Divider

The description of the datapath for the divider *PATHDIV*, Program 5-14, can now be derived from *IMPDIV*. The corresponding block diagram is shown in

```
     ∇ QUIZPATH X;COMPARAND
[1]    ⍝ N[0]←P AND R LENGTH, N[1]←Q LENGTH
[2]    ⍝ CONSTRUCTION OF OPERANDS
[3]  CONT:MAKEPQR
[4]    ⍝ COMPARISON PATH
[5]    QUOCOR
[6]    ⍝ SAVE RESULT
[7]    COMPARAND←J,U,W,P,Q,R
[8]    MAKEPQR
[9]    ⍝ PATH TO BE TESTED
[10]   IMPQTC
[11]   ⍝ TEST
[12]   →(∧/COMPARAND=J,U,W,P,Q,R)/END
[13]   ⍝ PRINT
[14]   J;' ';PRINT U,W,P,Q,R;' WRONG'
[15]   1↑COMPARAND;' ';PRINT 1↓COMPARAND;' RIGHT'
[16]   MAKEPQR
[17]   J;' ';PRINT U,W,P,Q,R;' OLD'
[18]   ' '
[19]   ⍝ END TEST
[20] END:X←5↓X
[21]   →(0≠⍴X)/CONT
[22]   'READY'
     ∇
```

```
     ∇ MAKEPQR
[1]    P←(N[0]⍴2)⊤X[0]
[2]    Q←(N[1]⍴2)⊤X[1]
[3]    R←(N[0]⍴2)⊤X[2]
[4]    U←2≤X[3]
[5]    W←2|X[3]
[6]    J←X[4]
     ∇
```

```
     ⍝ REFERENCE:                                                PROGRAM:
     ⍝ PRINT        COMPACT LOGICAL PRINTOUT                      2-49
```

Program 5-12   Selective datapath test.

Figure 5-13. This figure is a modification of Figure 4-13. Division is performed in this datapath by means of the function *GATEDIV*, Program 5-14.

Generation of Datapath.   *PATHDIV* is obtained by combining the expressions of *IMPDIV*, which assign a value to the same variable. Thus, *A* is specified in line 1 of *IMPRED*, *IMPRMC*, and *IMPQTC*. It proves that all three expressions are different. The three different expressions, preceded by a distinctive gate, are now combined with an 'or,' thus forming line 2 of *PATHDIV*. By continuing systematically in this manner, lines 2 through 12 of *PATHDIV* are obtained. In the process the inputs of registers, such as *IP*, are distinguished from the register values, such as *P*, as was the case in *PATHADD* and *PATHMPY*. All registers are listed as a group in lines 14 through 18 of *PATHDIV*. The test conditions are listed in lines 20 through 23, with each condition identified by a suitable name.

The block diagram of Figure 5-13 has been simplified by combining the combinational test circuits in one block. This is also realistic, because the circuits can in part be combined.

Multiplexer.   Figure 5-13 and line 2 of *PATHDIV* show that the *A* input to the adder has three sources. Each of these alternatives is selected by a gate. This type of and-or circuit is called a *multiplexer*. Because selection is a common occurrence in a datapath, the multiplexer is one of the typical datapath circuits. It appears in *PATHDIV* also for the input of Q in line 9 and for the single signals *CIN* and *IW* in lines 4 and 11.

Gate Program for Division.   In *GATEDIV* the sequence of *IMPDIV* is followed line for line. The datapath actions, however, are replaced by gate signal specifications. The function *GATE* calls in this case in line 2 upon the datapath function *PATHDIV*.

The decisions within the gate program require the test signals *RPOS* and *RCOR* besides the signal *JZRO*, which was already encountered in the multiplication. The test signal *OFLO* is not used in the division proper but is available to indicate whether an overflow has occurred during the division.

The substitution of the separate functions of *IMPDIV* by the common datapath *PATHDIV*, controlled by gate settings, can again be verified with *QUIZPATH*. Thus, the action of line 12 of *GATEDIV* can be compared with the action of *REMCOR*, Program 4-14, by introducing these expressions in lines 10 and 5 of *QUIZPATH*.

Specialized Datapath

High-performance processing units can be obtained by using several specialized datapaths side by side. The datapaths for multiplication and division, each usually geared to a fast algorithm, are used as individual units that perform their tasks concurrently. In that case, each unit requires a separate set of registers.

An example of a computer using several specialized processing units is the CDC 6600, which uses two add units, a shift unit, a logical unit, two multiply units, one divide unit, and two incrementers all capable of operating simultaneously (Thornton, 1970). Another example is the System/360 Model 91, which uses a separate floating-point unit, which in turn consists of an adder unit and a unit for multiplication and division (Tomasulo, 1967).

Most computers, however, use the same datapath for the various operations, and this common use will be discussed in the remainder of the chapter.

Common Datapath

The datapath for division resembles that for addition and multiplication. We shall now consider how these datapaths can be combined such that the instruction repertoire of *OPERATION* can be performed. The parallel nature of these datapaths will be maintained in this section. Thus, a datapath will be developed which resembles that of multiplication and division, having three operand registers. In the next section a datapath resembling that for addition, and having only two operand registers, will be considered.

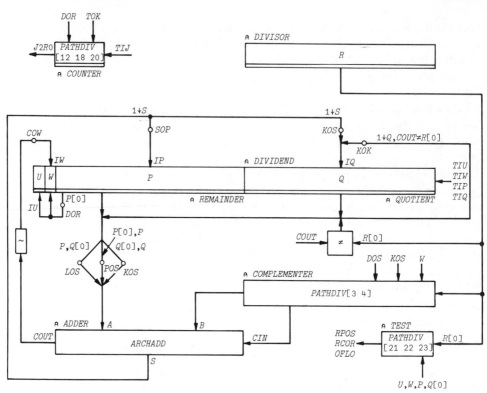

Figure 5-13   Datapath for divider.

As shown in Figure 5-15, the datapath for the divider requires only a limited extension to be suitable also for the other operations. This is not so surprising, since the designer intended his algorithms to be processed by a common datapath. Thus, the main registers, P, Q, and R, are in each case used for the operands, while the auxiliary 1-bit register W can be used in both multiplication and division.

The function *COMPAR*, which is a modification of *FOURFOLD*, Program 3-19, is used to complement and shift the second operand.

An APL description of the common datapath is shown in *PATHPAR*, Program 5-16. A comparison with *PATHADD*, *PATHMPY*, and *PATHDIV* shows that *PATHPAR* is obtained as a superposition of these three datapaths. The longest adder is required by *PATHMPY*. The length of the operands in the other datapaths is extended accordingly. The gates, which have been chosen judiciously, can be maintained in the operand expressions. Different operand selections are combined by a multiplexer, as shown for *IP* in line 9.

Since the gates for addition, multiplication, and division are preserved, the gate programs for these operations need not be changed. Line 2 of *GATE* now refers to *PATHPAR*.

```
    ∇ PATHDIV                                          ∇ DECLDIV
[1]   A ADDER INPUTS                             [1]    A DIVIDEND/QUOTIENT REGISTERS
[2]   A←(Y[POS]∧P[0],P)∨(Y[LOS]∧P,Q[0])∨Y[KOS]∧Q[0],Q  [2]    P←(ρDR)ρ0
[3]   B←Y[DOS]∧(W=R[0])≠R[0],R                   [3]    Q←((ρDD)-ρDR)ρ0
[4]   CIN←(Y[DOS]∧W=R[0])∨Y[KOS]∧W≠R[0]          [4]    A DIVIDER REGISTER
[5]   A ADDER                                    [5]    R←(ρDR)ρ0
[6]   ARCHADD                                    [6]    A SIGN BUFFERS
[7]   A REGISTER INPUTS                          [7]    U←0
[8]   IP←Y[SOP]∧1↓S                              [8]    W←0
[9]   IQ←(Y[KOK]∧1↓Q,COUT≠R[0])∨Y[KOS]∧1↓S       [9]    A COUNTER
[10]  IU←Y[DOR]∧P[0]                             [10]   J←0
[11]  IW←(Y[DOR]∧P[0])∨Y[COW]∧~COUT                     ∇
[12]  IJ←(Y[DOR]×ρQ)+Y[TOK]×J-1
[13]  A REGISTERS
[14]  P←(Y[TIP]∧IP)∨(~Y[TIP])∧P
[15]  Q←(Y[TIQ]∧IQ)∨(~Y[TIQ])∧Q
[16]  U←(Y[TIU]∧IU)∨(~Y[TIU])∧U
[17]  W←(Y[TIW]∧IW)∨(~Y[TIW])∧W
[18]  J←(Y[TIJ]×IJ)+(~Y[TIJ])×J
[19]  A TESTCONDITIONS
[20]  JZRO←J=0
[21]  RPOS←~W
[22]  RCOR←~U∧∨/P
[23]  OFLO←U≠R[0]≠Q[0]∨~W
    ∇
    ∇ GATEDIV                                         ∇ GATE X
[1]   A PROLOGUE                                  [1]   Y←(ι24)∈X
[2]   P←(ρDR)↑DD                                  [2]   PATHDIV
[3]   Q←(ρDR)↓DD                                        ∇
[4]   R←DR
[5]   A DIVISION
[6]   GATE DOR,TIU,TIW,TIJ
[7]   A REDUCTION
[8]   CONT:GATE LOS,DOS,SOP,KOK,COW,TOK,TIP,TIQ,TIW,TIJ
[9]   →(~JZRO)/CONT
[10]  A REMAINDER CORRECTION
[11]  →RPOS/RMC
[12]  GATE POS,DOS,SOP,COW,TIP,TIW
[13]  RMC:→RCOR/QTC
[14]  GATE POS,DOS,SOP,COW,TIP,TIW
[15]  A QUOTIENT CORRECTION
[16]  QTC:GATE KOS,COW,TIQ,TIW
[17]  A EPILOGUE
[18]  RM←P
[19]  QT←Q
[20]  OFDV←OFLO
    ∇

    A REFERENCE:                                 PROGRAM:
    A ARCHADD        ADDER ARCHITECTURE          2-5
```

Program 5-14 Datapath and gate program for divider.

5-4 SINGLE PARALLEL DATAPATH

The datapath of Figure 5-15 arises from the requirements of multiplication and division. As a result it contains three complete operand registers, P, Q, and R, and their associated paths. For the load and add operations Q is not used, however. Therefore, if it is desirable to reduce costs, it seems natural to eliminate Q and the paths leading to and from it. Such a decision of course substantially reduces

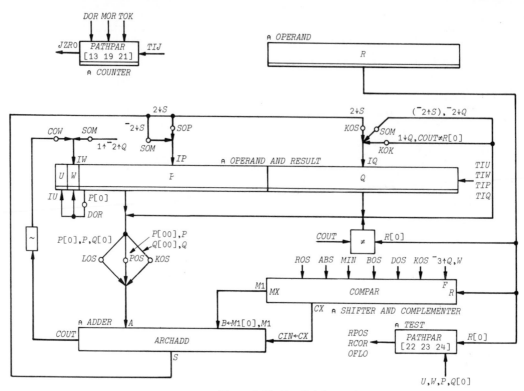

Figure 5-15   Parallel datapath.

the speed of multiplication and division. Since it leaves the load and add times unchanged it is particularly attractive if the load and add types of operations dominate in the average distribution of operation frequencies, the *operation mix*.

The block diagram of Figure 5-17 and *PATHSGL*, Program 5-18, describe a datapath with two operand sources, the *single datapath*. Register *R* has remained unchanged. The output of *R* is combined in the adder with a second path *LS*, which presents the content of *P* or *Q*. The selection of *P* and *Q* for this path is shown schematically at the top of Figure 5-17 and is described as an initial algorithm by *DATASGL*, Program 5-18.

Separation of Local Store

The reduction in equipment of the single datapath over the parallel datapath of Figure 5-15 may seem rather disappointing. The register *Q* is not actually eliminated but merely moved from one location to another. Nevertheless, this move is meaningful. *Q* was first an individual register with its own inputs and outputs. In the local store *Q* shares its inputs and outputs with those of other registers. These inputs and outputs are, moreover, of a standard and simple nature. A group of registers combined in this fashion is called a *local store* and will be

```
      ∇ PATHPAR
[1]     ⍝ ADDER INPUTS
[2]     A←(Y[POS]∧P[0 0],P)∨(Y[LOS]∧P[0],P,Q[0])∨Y[KOS]∧Q[0 0],Q
[3]     M1←R COMPAR ¯3↑Q,W
[4]     B←M1[0],M1
[5]     CIN←CX
[6]     ⍝ ADDER
[7]     ARCHADD
[8]     ⍝ REGISTER INPUTS
[9]     IP←(Y[SOP]∧2↓S)∨Y[SOM]∧¯2↓S
[10]    IQ←(Y[KOK]∧1↓Q,COUT≠R[0])∨(Y[KOS]∧2↓S)∨Y[SOM]∧(¯2↓S),¯2↓Q
[11]    IU←Y[DOR]∧P[0]
[12]    IW←(Y[DOR]∧P[0])∨(Y[COW]∧~COUT)∨Y[SOM]∧1↑¯2↓Q
[13]    IJ←(Y[DOR]×ρQ)+(Y[MOR]×(ρQ)÷2)+Y[TOK]×J-1
[14]    ⍝ REGISTERS
[15]    P←(Y[TIP]∧IP)∨(~Y[TIP])∧P
[16]    Q←(Y[TIQ]∧IQ)∨(~Y[TIQ])∧Q
[17]    U←(Y[TIU]∧IU)∨(~Y[TIU])∧U
[18]    W←(Y[TIW]∧IW)∨(~Y[TIW])∧W
[19]    J←(Y[TIJ]×IJ)+(~Y[TIJ])×J
[20]    ⍝ TESTCONDITIONS
[21]    JZRO←J=0
[22]    RPOS←~W
[23]    RCOR←~U∧∨/P
[24]    OFLO←U≠R[0]≠Q[0]∨~W
      ∇


      ∇ MX←R COMPAR F
[1]     ⍝ DECISION
[2]     ONE←Y[ROS]∨(Y[BOS]∧F[1]≠F[2])∨Y[DOS]
[3]     TWO←Y[BOS]∧((~F[0])∧F[1]∧F[2])∨F[0]∧(~F[1])∧~F[2]
[4]     INV←(Y[ROS]∧Y[MIN]≠Y[ABS]∧R[0])∨(Y[BOS]∧F[0])∨Y[DOS]∧F[2]=R[0]
[5]     ⍝ COMPLEMENT
[6]     COM←INV≠R
[7]     ⍝ SELECTION
[8]     MX←(ONE∧COM[0],COM)∨TWO∧COM,INV
[9]     ⍝ CARRY-IN
[10]    CX←(INV∧ONE∨TWO)∨Y[KOS]∧F[2]≠R[0]
      ∇
```

```
      ∇ DECLPAR                              ∇ GATE X
[1]     ⍝ OPERAND REGISTERS           [1]     Y←(⍳24)∈X
[2]     P←(ρOD1)ρ0                    [2]     PATHPAR
[3]     Q←(ρOD1)ρ0                          ∇
[4]     R←(ρOD2)ρ0
[5]     ⍝ BUFFER REGISTERS
[6]     U←0
[7]     W←0
[8]     ⍝ COUNTER
[9]     J←0
      ∇
```

```
        ⍝ REFERENCE:                              PROGRAM:
        ⍝ ARCHADD        ADDER ARCHITECTURE         2-5
```

Program 5-16   Parallel datapath.

discussed further in Chapter 8. Besides the content of P and Q, other information can also be placed in the local store, such as an instruction address or a data address. The more registers are joined in this fashion, the smaller the cost per bit, hence the larger the advantage of the local store.

Data Selection.   Each multiplication cycle and each reduction cycle of division is now required to use the datapath twice. Each use of the datapath is called a

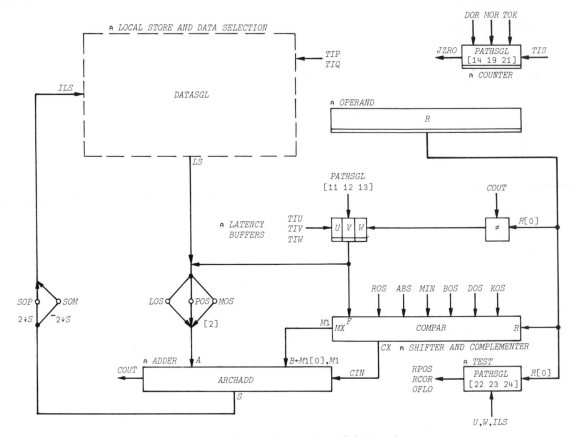

Figure 5-17   Single parallel datapath.

stroke. The selection of the proper information for each stroke from the local store is controlled by the signals *Y*[*TIP*] and *Y*[*TIQ*]. These signals no longer appear in *PATHSGL* but are used in the data-selection function *DATASGL*.

The gate programs for multiplication and division are extended with separate strokes for *P* and *Q*. The load and add operations are not affected by the change in datapath. Their gate programs are therefore still valid for *PATHSGL*.

Hidden Information.   The equipment saved by the elimination of the path to and from *Q* is in part offset by the complication of the pertinent algorithms. In the initial multiplication and division algorithms, all necessary information is assumed to be accessible. Since *P* and *Q* are no longer simultaneously present, the *P* stroke cannot make use of the information in *Q*, and vice versa. The necessary information will therefore have to be preserved in auxiliary registers. To this end, the auxiliary registers *U* and *W* of *PATHPAR* have been augmented with a third 1-bit register, *V*.

The fact that information is hidden, the *latency* of information, is a character-

```
      ∇ PATHSGL                                              ∇ DECLSGL
[1]     ⍝ ADDER INPUTS                               [1]      ⍝ OPERAND REGISTERS
[2]     A←(Y[POS]∧LS[0 0],LS)∨(Y[LOS]∧LS[0],LS,V)∨Y[MOS]∧U,V,LS   [2]  P←(ρOD1)ρ0
[3]     M1←R COMPAR U,V,W                            [3]      Q←(ρOD1)ρ0
[4]     B←M1[0],M1                                   [4]      R←(ρOD1)ρ0
[5]     CIN←CX                                       [5]      ⍝ LATENCY BUFFERS
[6]     ⍝ ADDER                                      [6]      U←0
[7]     ARCHADD                                      [7]      V←0
[8]     ⍝ LOCAL STORE INPUT                          [8]      W←0
[9]     ILS←(Y[SOP]∧2↓S)∨Y[SOM]∧¯2↑S                 [9]      ⍝ COUNTER
[10]    ⍝ REGISTER INPUTS                            [10]     J←0
[11]    IU←(Y[DOR]∧LS[0])∨Y[SOM]∧1↑¯2↑S                       ∇
[12]    IV←(Y[KOK]∧LS[0])∨(Y[COW]∧COUT≠R[0])∨Y[SOM]∧¯1↑S
[13]    IW←(Y[DOR]∧LS[0])∨(Y[COW]∧~COUT)∨Y[BOS]∧U
[14]    IJ←(Y[DOR]×ρLS)+(Y[MOR]×(ρLS)÷2)+Y[TOK]×J-1
[15]    ⍝ REGISTERS
[16]    U←(Y[TIU]∧IU)∨(~Y[TIU])∧U
[17]    V←(Y[TIV]∧IV)∨(~Y[TIV])∧V
[18]    W←(Y[TIW]∧IW)∨(~Y[TIW])∧W
[19]    J←(Y[TIJ]×IJ)+(~Y[TIJ])×J
[20]    ⍝ TESTCONDITIONS
[21]    JZRO←J=0
[22]    RPOS←~W
[23]    RCOR←~U∧v/ILS
[24]    OFLO←U≠R[0]≠ILS[0]∨~W
      ∇

      ∇ DATASGL
[1]     LS←(Y[TIP]∧P)∨Y[TIQ]∧Q
[2]     PATHSGL
[3]     P←(Y[TIP]∧ILS)∨(~Y[TIP])∧P
[4]     Q←(Y[TIQ]∧ILS)∨(~Y[TIQ])∧Q
      ∇

        ⍝ REFERENCE:                                 PROGRAM:
        ⍝ ARCHADD        ADDER ARCHITECTURE           2-5
        ⍝ COMPAR         PARALLEL MULTIPLE SELECTION  5-16
```

Program 5-18   Single parallel datapath.

istic of series operation. Since P and Q are now handled in series, this characteristic appears here for the first time.

Transformation of Datapath

The datapath $PATHPAR$ is the simplest form of a common datapath. It is therefore a good starting point to obtain the less expensive, but more complex, single parallel datapath $PATHSGL$.

Once the designer has decided to use U, V, and W as auxiliary registers, he can proceed systematically through $PATHPAR$, to obtain $PATHSGL$. All references to P and Q are replaced by references to LS, while the hidden information is now obtained from U, V, or W.

In multiplication, the active multiplier bits are placed in U, V, and W during the Q stroke. During the subsequent P stroke, the proper multiple can be selected by using the content of these registers, as shown in line 3 of $PATHSGL$. At the end of the P stroke, the 2 rightmost bits of the sum are in turn placed in U and V such that they can be placed in the 2 leftmost bits of Q during the next stroke. Thus, U

and V enable the right shift of P and Q. Line 2 of *PATHSGL*, as controlled by $Y[MOS]$, and lines 11 and 12, as controlled by $Y[SOM]$, illustrate this case.

In division, U and W keep their original function of sign registers. V is now used during the P stroke to save the new quotient bit such that it can be placed in Q during the next stroke. During the Q stroke, V, in turn, is used to store the left bit of Q, which is to be shifted into P. The first action is controlled by the gate $Y[COW]$ and the second by $Y[KOK]$, as shown in line 12 of *PATHSGL*.

Transformation of Gate Programs

The gate program *SGLMPY* and *SGLDIV*, Program 5-19, for multiplication and division in the single parallel datapath, can be obtained by transforming the

```
        ∇ SGLMPY                                             ∇ GATE X
[1]       ⍝ PROLOGUE                                  [1]      Y←(⍳24)∊X
[2]       P←VL                                        [2]      DATASGL
[3]       Q←MR                                               ∇
[4]       R←MD
[5]       ⍝ MULTIPLICATION
[6]       GATE POS,SOM,MOR,TIQ,TIU,TIV,TIW,TIJ
[7]       ⍝ STROKE P
[8]     CONT:GATE POS,BOS,SOM,TOK,TIP,TIU,TIV,TIW,TIJ
[9]       ⍝ STROKE Q
[10]      GATE MOS,SOM,TIQ,TIU,TIV
[11]      →(~JZRO)/CONT
[12]      ⍝ EPILOGUE
[13]      PD←P,Q
        ∇


        ∇ SGLDIV
[1]       ⍝ PROLOGUE
[2]       P←(ρDR)↑DD
[3]       Q←(ρDR)↓DD
[4]       R←DR
[5]       ⍝ DIVISION
[6]       GATE POS,SOP,DOR,TIP,TIU,TIW,TIJ
[7]       ⍝ REDUCTION
[8]       ⍝ STROKE Q
[9]     CONT:GATE LOS,SOP,KOK,TOK,TIQ,TIV,TIJ
[10]      ⍝ STROKE P
[11]      GATE LOS,DOS,SOP,COW,TIP,TIV,TIW
[12]      →(~JZRO)/CONT
[13]      ⍝ BUFFER STROKE
[14]      GATE LOS,SOP,TIQ
[15]      ⍝ REMAINDER CORRECTION
[16]      →RPOS/RMC
[17]      GATE POS,DOS,SOP,COW,TIP,TIW
[18]    RMC:→RCOR/QTC
[19]      GATE POS,DOS,SOP,COW,TIP,TIW
[20]      ⍝ QUOTIENT CORRECTION
[21]    QTC:GATE POS,KOS,SOP,COW,TIQ,TIW
[22]      ⍝ EPILOGUE
[23]      RM←P
[24]      QT←Q
[25]      OFDV←OFLO
        ∇


        ⍝ REFERENCE:                                          PROGRAM:
        ⍝ PATHSGL        SINGLE PARALLEL DATAPATH                5-18
```

Program 5-19   Gate programs for single datapath.

corresponding gateprograms *GATEMPY* and *GATEDIV* for the common datapath. The overall flow of the programs remains unchanged. The actions, which involve a single register, such as the remainder correction, lines 12 and 14 of *GATEDIV*, also are in the first instance unchanged, as shown by lines 17 and 19 of *SGLDIV*. Actions involving both P and Q are split into two strokes, as illustrated by the reduction cycle of division, lines 8 through 11 of *SGLDIV*. Also, the effects of buffering and precession should be taken in account.

Buffering. In the shifts of the partial product and the partial dividend, U and V are used as buffer registers. In the initial multiplication algorithm, W already had such a function. A *buffer* is, in principle, a delay mechanism. Therefore, it requires an extra stroke, either to fill it in advance, as in line 6 of *SGLMPY* and *GATEMPY*, or to empty it at the end, as for the quotient digit of the division, line 14 of *SGLDIV*.

Buffer Strokes. Besides the doubling of multiplication and division cycles, the single datapath therefore also requires extra buffer strokes. With care the designer can often combine these strokes with other preparatory or concluding actions. Thus, U and V are set in line 6 of *SGLMPY* at the same time as W.

Precession. The content of P and Q, as processed by *PATHSGL*, no longer matches cycle for cycle the content of these registers as processed by *PATHPAR*. During the first Q stroke of the dividend reduction, for instance, the first quotient digit is not yet known and a 0 is introduced instead in the low-order position of Q. The actual first quotient digit is entered during the next Q cycle. The extra 0 moves through the register Q and is eliminated at the end of the reduction cycles during the buffer stroke of *SGLDIV*, line 14. This progression of extraneous information through the register can be described as a *precession* action.

In multiplication, the precession concerns 2 bits, which move left to right at the rate of 2 bits per cycle. Here the extra bits have the value of the multiplier sign.

Transformation Test. Owing to the precession, the transition from *PATHPAR* or *IMPDIV* to *PATHSGL* cannot be tested for single datapath actions in multiplication and division. Rather, the full multiplication or all the reduction cycles of division must be tested as an entity. This test can, of course, be shortened by the use of a small dimension for P and Q. The remainder and quotient correction can still be verified as individual datapath actions, however.

Modular Construction. A *slice* of a single parallel datapath can be constructed as one integrated circuit, including the ALU, the operand registers, the multiplexers and the local store. An example is the Intel 3002, which provides a 2-bit-wide slice of such a datapath, with two operand registers and eleven local store registers. These slices can be placed in parallel to obtain the desired operand length. As in the case of an integrated ALU circuit, a separate carry-predict circuit can be connected across the adder. The slice, of course, does not contain the specialized sign and overflow circuits.

5-5 BASIC SERIES–PARALLEL DATAPATH

The single datapath is slower and more complex than the fully parallel implementation of the datapath. The only motive for such an organization is a reduction in cost. This cost reduction can be obtained through elimination of some circuits in the datapath and through the economy of the local store. The total required capacity of the storage locations is influenced only to a minor degree by the organization form. The same consequences are true in an even larger measure when the operands are processed a part at a time: the *series–parallel datapath.*

The load and add operations, which were not affected by the transition from parallel to single datapaths, need to be revised for use in the series–parallel datapaths. They will be discussed here first with a datapath that is limited to this type of operation. In the next section this datapath will be extended so that it can also be used for multiplication and division.

Storage Reflection.   The series operation is particularly inexpensive when the local store can be combined with main storage. Such a use of main storage locations for internal register space is called *storage reflection.*

From an architectural point of view, main store should not be influenced by storage reflection. Hence, separately addressable storage locations should be made available to the implementation. Since these storage locations are fabricated as part of the larger unit, however, they are relatively inexpensive. This approach was used in the System/360 Model 30. The advent of relatively inexpensive local stores built as integrated circuits has made storage reflection less attractive, however.

Data Width.   The number of bits that are processed in parallel is called the *width* of the datapath. For example, *PATHPAR*, operating on full-word operands in a System/360 architecture, would have a width of 32.

The registers, multiplexers, and adders each consist of many identical circuits, commonly controlled. Thus, they form the most orderly part of the datapath. These can be reduced easily by decreasing the width of the datapath in a series–parallel organization. When, for instance, the operands are processed with four strokes in series, the width of this part of the datapath can be reduced to one fourth of its original size.

The parts of the datapath that are inherently 1 bit wide, such as the registers U, V, and W and the test circuits, are much more difficult to remove by a series organization. In fact, their number is more likely to increase as a result of this type of organization, as will be apparent in this section and the next. In Section 5-8, it will be shown how this complexity can, in turn, be traded for control.

A serial approach becomes attractive when the operands are variable in length, hence more difficult to process as a unit, or when the operands occupy several storage locations, since the storage width is small. For the smaller and less expensive core storages, this width used to be limited, for instance, to 8 or 16 bits. For operands of 32 or 48 bits, this data width required a serial organization. For 16-bit operands, as found in minicomputers, a parallel organization could still be maintained with a 16-bit store, which also explains the popularity of the 16-bit minicomputer. Since the transistor storages, which have replaced core storage as the standard storage technology, can be made less expensively in parallel, the parallel organization has become more popular, even for low-cost machines.

The five original models of System/360, Models 30, 40, 50, 60, and 70, had, for example, a data width of 8, 8, 32, 56, and 64 bits, respectively (Stevens, 1964). The data width of the System/370 Models 125, 135, 145, 158, and 168 is 16, 16, 16, 32, and 64 bits.

Series–Parallel Addition

PATHSERAD, Program 5-21, and Figure 5-20 illustrate a datapath for the load and add operations. The buffering and data selection introduced by this organization will be discussed in turn.

Carry Buffer.   As was shown in Figure 2-12, a series addition requires a carry buffer. Similarly, a series–parallel adder will require a buffer for the carry-out of the parallel group to be stored, such that it can be used as the carry-in for the next group of bits. Lines 12 and 15 of *PATHSERADD* show that *COUT* is saved in the register *CB*, and line 6 shows that the content of this register is used to determine *CIN*. During the first stroke *CIN* is not determined by *CB* but by the condition that was used in the parallel implementation. A characteristic control signal of a series implementation is *SKL*, the gate signal that identifies the low-order stroke.

The carry buffer arises from cutting the addition into strokes and the need to propagate the carry between the strokes. Therefore, the buffer is characterized as a *propagation* buffer, rather than a *latency* buffer, which makes hidden information available, as encountered above.

Sign Buffer.   In the series–parallel datapath, not only *P* and *Q*, but also *R*, are located in the local store. Hence, the sign of the operand in *R* is not directly available during series operation. Since this sign is required during absolute-value operations, it must be stored in a latency buffer. Register *V* is used for this purpose.

Use of Local Store.   Figure 5-20 shows that all operands are obtained from a common local store. The gate programs for the load and add operations, Program 5-22, indicate how the operands are placed in this local store. The number of sections, or bytes, of the operands is indicated by *PL* and the width of the datapath by *SL*. Normally, the width of the datapath is a submultiple of the operand length. The ability to vary both *PL* and *SL* is a major help in testing the datapath and gate programs.

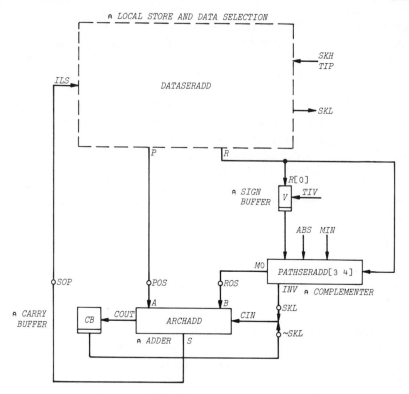

Figure 5-20 Series-parallel datapath for load and add operations.

Operand $OD2$ is placed at the PL locations beginning with location $RADR$; operand $OD1$ and the result $RL1$ start at location $PADR$, as shown in $SERMIN$ lines 2, 3, and 8. $SERADDCODE$, Program 5-21, shows a possible assignment of the local store locations and the corresponding operand and datawidth dimensions.

Data Selection. $DATASERADD$, Program 5-21, selects the bytes that are required by the datapath. This selection is for the moment kept separate from the datapath and described as an initial algorithm. One byte is selected from the $OD2$ locations, starting with address $RADR$, and presented to the R side of the datapath each time $DATASERADD$ is used. Also, 1 byte from the $OD1$ locations starting with $PADR$ is presented to the P side of the datapath.

Operands are selected from right to left to ensure proper propagation of the carry. Because the data selection has been kept general with respect to the number of strokes required for one path through the operand, a signal must be provided to indicate the end of the operand. Thus, $DATASERADD$ generates the signal of $DLN0$, which is 1 when the residual operand length is not 0. This signal is used in the gate program to control the operand loop. The data selection also generates the signal SKL, indicating the low-order stroke. It is used in line 6 of $PATH$-$SERADD$ to select the proper carry-in.

The data selection is controlled by the gate SKH. This gate causes $DATA$-

```
     ∇ PATHSERADD                          ∇ SERADDCODE
[1]    ⍝ ADDER INPUTS                 [1]    ⍝ DATAWIDTH
[2]    A←Y[POS]∧P                     [2]    SL←8
[3]    INV←Y[MIN]≠Y[ABS]∧V            [3]    ⍝ NUMBER OF BYTES PER OPERAND
[4]    MO←INV≠R                       [4]    PL←4
[5]    B←Y[ROS]∧MO                    [5]    ⍝ ADDRESS ASSIGNMENT
[6]    CIN←(SKL∧INV)∨(~SKL)∧CB        [6]    RADR←4
[7]    ⍝ ADDER                        [7]    PADR←12
[8]    ARCHADD                          ∇
[9]    ⍝ LOCAL STORE INPUT
[10]   ILS←Y[SOP]∧S
[11]   ⍝ REGISTER INPUTS
[12]   ICB←COUT                         ∇ DECLSERADD
[13]   IV←R[0]                       [1]    ⍝ CARRY BUFFER
[14]   ⍝ REGISTERS                   [2]    CB←0
[15]   CB←(Y[TIB]∧ICB)∨(~Y[TIB])∧CB  [3]    ⍝ LATENCY BUFFER
[16]   V←(Y[TIV]∧IV)∨(~Y[TIV])∧V     [4]    V←0
     ∇                                  ∇

     ∇ DATASERADD                        ∇ DECLDATASERADD
[1]    ⍝ SELECT                      [1]    ⍝ LOCAL STORE
[2]    DL←(~Y[SKH])×PL|DL-1          [2]    LOCALSTORE←((4×PL),SL)⍴0
[3]    ⍝ FETCH DATA                  [3]    ⍝ DATA REGISTERS
[4]    P←LOCALSTORE[PADR+DL;]        [4]    P←SL⍴0
[5]    R←LOCALSTORE[RADR+DL;]        [5]    R←SL⍴0
[6]    ⍝ TESTCONDITIONS               ∇
[7]    SKL←DL=PL-1
[8]    DLN0←DL≠0
[9]    ⍝ DATAPATH ACTION
[10]   PATHSERADD
[11]   ⍝ STORE DATA
[12]   →(~Y[TIP])/0
[13]   LOCALSTORE[PADR+DL;]←ILS
     ∇

       ⍝ REFERENCE:                        PROGRAM:
       ⍝ ARCHADD      ADDER ARCHITECTURE      2-5
```

Program 5-21 Series-parallel datapath for load and add operations.

```
     ∇ SERPOS                            ∇ GATE X
[1]    ⍝ PROLOGUE                    [1]    Y←(⍳24)∈X
[2]    LOCALSTORE[RADR+⍳PL;]←(PL,SL)⍴OD2  [2]    PATHSERADD
[3]    ⍝ DETERMINE SIGN                   ∇
[4]    GATE TIV,SKH
[5]    ⍝ ABSOLUTE VALUE
[6]  SKP:GATE ROS,ABS,SOP,TIB,TIP
[7]    →DLN0/SKP
[8]    ⍝ EPILOGUE
[9]    RL1←,LOCALSTORE[PADR+⍳PL;]
     ∇

     ∇ SERMIN
[1]    ⍝ PROLOGUE
[2]    LOCALSTORE[PADR+⍳PL;]←(PL,SL)⍴OD1
[3]    LOCALSTORE[RADR+⍳PL;]←(PL,SL)⍴OD2
[4]    ⍝ SUBTRACTION
[5]  SKP:GATE POS,ROS,MIN,SOP,TIB,TIP
[6]    →DLN0/SKP
[7]    ⍝ EPILOGUE
[8]    RL1←,LOCALSTORE[PADR+⍳PL;]
     ∇

       ⍝ REFERENCE:                                    PROGRAM:
       ⍝ PATHSERADD   SERIES-PARALLEL DATAPATH FOR ADDITION    5-21
```

Program 5-22 Gate programs for series-parallel Load Positive and Subtract.

SERADD to select the leftmost section of an operand. This control is used to obtain the sign of an operand by selecting the leftmost part of that operand. The control also assures that the data selection will select the rightmost operand section during the next stroke.

Gate Program for Series–Parallel Load and Add Operations. Lines 5 and 6 of *SERMIN* show that the operand stroke is repeated until all bytes have been processed. The Load Positive operation *SERPOS* requires an extra cycle, line 4, to fetch the operand sign and record it in register *V*.

5-6 GENERAL SERIES–PARALLEL DATAPATH

An extension of the series–parallel datapath for load and add operations to one that can handle multiplication and division as well yields the datapath of Figure 5-24, described by *PATHSER*, Program 5-25. The extension incorporates the features found in *PATHSGL*. Furthermore, two buffer registers, *BIN* and *BOUT*, are added to allow a right and left shift in multiplication and division.

Relative Shift of Operands and Results. Figure 5-23 shows schematically the relative position of the operands *A* and *B* and the sum *S* of the adder in addition, multiplication, and the various parts of division. Two strokes per operand are assumed, marked by the letter *L* for the left stroke and the letter *R* for the right stroke.

Operand Buffer. During the reduction cycle of division, the partial dividend, entering the *A* input of the adder from *P*, is shifted 1 bit to the left with respect to

```
ADDITION, RCOR AND QCOR                    MULTIPLICATION

A ==LLLLLLLLRRRRRRRR  POS, KOS       A ==LLLLLLLLLRRRRRRRR  ROS
B ==LLLLLLLLLRRRRRRRR  ROS, DOS      B ==LLLLLLLLLRRRRRRRR  ONE
`S ==LLLLLLLLLRRRRRRRR  SOP           B =LLLLLLLLLRRRRRRRR=  TWO
                                     S LLLLLLLLLRRRRRRRR==  SOM


REDUCTION OF DIVISION

A =LLLLLLLLLRRRRRRRR=  LOS
B ==LLLLLLLLLRRRRRRRR  DOS
S ==LLLLLLLLLRRRRRRRR  SOP


TWO STROKES PER OPERAND
```

Figure 5-23 Relative displacement of operands and results.

the sum S and the divisor, entering the B input of the adder from R. Therefore, the left bit of P, $P[0]$, must be saved to participate in the next stroke. To this end, $P[0]$ is saved in the incoming buffer BIN, in $PATHSER$, line 11. During the next stroke, the content of BIN is used in line 2 to extend P to the right.

The same procedure and the same buffer are used during multiplication, where the multiplicand, entering the adder from R via $COMSER$, may be shifted 1 bit to the left with respect to the partial product, entering the adder from P. Here the extension is shown in $COMSER$, line 6.

Result Buffer. During multiplication, the content of P and Q must be shifted two places to the right. Accordingly, the operand bits are fetched 2 bits to the left of the location where the corresponding result bits are returned. Therefore, the first byte cannot return to storage until the next byte is fetched. This implies the use of a buffer, the outgoing buffer $BOUT$.

BIN and $BOUT$ are both latency buffers. The length of BIN equals the amount of the left shift, in this case 1 bit. The length of $BOUT$ unfortunately equals the data width minus the amount of right shift. Therefore, $BOUT$ has about the same length as the data width.

In line 12 of $PATHSER$, the sum bits are placed in $BOUT$. During the next stroke they are again fetched from $BOUT$, as shown in line 9. At that time, the remaining result bits are available, which are concatenated with the bits in $BOUT$.

Latency Buffers. U, V, and W are still used as latency buffers for the multiplier bits. Since $BOUT$ now handles the shift from P into Q, U and V are no longer used for that purpose. This explains a number of detailed differences between $PATHSER$ and $PATHSGL$.

The sign of the divisor must be known during the reduction cycles. It is stored in V in the same manner as for the absolute-value operation, using lines 16 and 25 of $PATHSER$.

Dynamic Test. Since the content of P is no longer available all at once, the test for P equal to zero must be performed dynamically rather than statically. The zero-buffer ZB is introduced for this purpose. During each stroke the adder output is tested for all 0s. The outcome of this test is combined with the result of preceding strokes as stored in ZB, as shown in line 14 of $PATHSER$. During the low-order stroke, the propagation buffer ZB is set to 0.

Adder Extension. The adders used in the parallel and single datapaths are 2 bits longer than the operands, to accommodate the operand extensions in multiplication and division. This extension is preserved in the series adder of $PATHSER$. The full adder length is only used during the last stroke of a cycle. For the other strokes the adder would more appropriately have matched the byte length. Thus, the carry-out of the adder for those strokes should match the byte length. Hence, the circuit of line 13 uses as input to the carry buffer the carry that enters the second adder position.

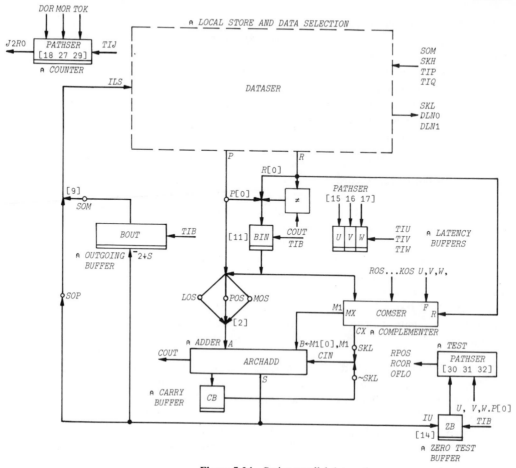

Figure 5-24   Series-parallel datapath.

The System/360 Model 40 illustrates the adder extension. Its 8-bit adder is when necessary extended with 3 bits.

Data Selection.   *DATASER*, Program 5-26, shows the data selection for the series–parallel datapath. *DATASER* has the same properties as *DATASERADD*. The gates *Y[TIP]* and *Y[TIQ]* now determine which operand enters the datapath as the *P* byte, as shown in *DATASER*, line 5.

As an extra function, a delay is introduced in returning the results of the partial product. This delay is required by the buffering in *BOUT*. The delay is obtained by the branch in line 14, which skips line 15 during multiplication. As a result, the write operation refers to the location from which the operands were fetched during the preceding stroke.

Gate Programs for Series–Parallel Multiplication and Division.   Program 5-27 shows the gate programs *SERMPY* and *SERDIV*, for multiplication and division

```
        ∇ PATHSER
[1]      � ADDER INPUTS
[2]      A←(Y[POS]∧P[0 0],P)∨(Y[LOS]∧P[0],P,BIN)∨Y[MOS]∧(¯2↓P[0 0],P),2↑BOUT
[3]      M1←R COMSER U,V,W
[4]      B←M1[0],M1
[5]      CIN←(SKL∧CX)∨(~SKL)∧CB
[6]      � ADDER
[7]      ARCHADD
[8]      � LOCAL STORE INPUT
[9]      ILS←(Y[SOP]∧2↓S)∨Y[SOM]∧( 2↑S),2↓BOUT
[10]     � REGISTER INPUTS
[11]     IBIN←(Y[KOK]∧P[0])∨(Y[COW]∧COUT≠R[0])∨Y[BOS]∧R[0]
[12]     IBOUT← ¯2↓S
[13]     ICB←S[1]≠A[1]≠B[1]
[14]     IZB←~∨/S,~ZB∨SKL
[15]     IU←(Y[DOR]∧P[0])∨Y[SOM]∧1↓ 2↑P
[16]     IV←((~Y[SOM])∧R[0])∨Y[SOM]∧¯1↑P
[17]     IW←(Y[DOR]∧P[0])∨(Y[COW]∧~COUT)∨Y[SOM]∧U
[18]     IJ←(Y[DOR]×PL×SL)+(Y[MOR]×PL×SL÷2)+Y[TOK]×J-1          ∇ DECLSER
[19]     � REGISTERS                                      [1]   � INCOMING BUFFER
[20]     BIN←(Y[TIB]∧IBIN)∨(~Y[TIB])∧BIN                       [2]   BIN←0
[21]     BOUT←(Y[TIB]∧IBOUT)∨(~Y[TIB])∧BOUT                    [3]   � OUTGOING BUFFER
[22]     CB←(Y[TIB]∧ICB)∨(~Y[TIB])∧CB                          [4]   BOUT←SLρ0
[23]     ZB←(Y[TIB]∧IZB)∨(~Y[TIB])∧ZB                          [5]   � CARRY BUFFER
[24]     U←(Y[TIU]∧IU)∨(~Y[TIU])∧U                             [6]   CB←0
[25]     V←(Y[TIV]∧IV)∨(~Y[TIV])∧V                             [7]   � ZERO TEST BUFFER
[26]     W←(Y[TIW]∧IW)∨(~Y[TIW])∧W                             [8]   ZB←0
[27]     J←(Y[TIJ]×IJ)+(~Y[TIJ])×J                             [9]   � LATENCY BUFFERS
[28]     � TESTCONDITIONS                                 [10]  U←0
[29]     JZRO←J=0                                              [11]  V←0
[30]     RPOS←~W                                               [12]  W←0
[31]     RCOR←~U∧~ZB                                           [13]  � COUNTER
[32]     OFLO←U≠V≠ILS[0]∨~W                                    [14]  J←0
        ∇                                                          ∇


        ∇ MX←R COMSER F
[1]      � DECISION
[2]      ONE←Y[ROS]∨(Y[BOS]∧F[1]≠F[2])∨Y[DOS]
[3]      TWO←Y[BOS]∧((~F[0])∧F[1]∧F[2])∨F[0]∧(~F[1])∧~F[2]
[4]      INV←(Y[ROS]∧Y[MIN]≠Y[ABS]∧F[1])∨(Y[BOS]∧F[0])∨Y[DOS]∧F[1]=F[2]
[5]      � COMPLEMENT
[6]      COM←INV≠R,BIN
[7]      � SELECTION
[8]      MX←(ONE∧¯1↓COM[0],COM)∨TWO∧COM
[9]      � CARRY-IN
[10]     CX←(INV∧ONE∨TWO)∨Y[KOS]∧F[1]≠F[2]
        ∇


        � REFERENCE:                                     PROGRAM:
        � ARCHADD        ADDER ARCHITECTURE               2-5
```

Program 5-25 Series-parallel datapath.

using the datapath *PATHSER*. The gate programs for the load and add types of operations of Program 5-22 are also valid for *PATHSER*.

Lines 10 and 13 of *SERMPY* and lines 11 and 19 of *SERDIV* illustrate how the signal *DLN0* can be used to repeat a given gate setting until the end of the operand is reached. Line 8 of *SERMPY* and line 9 of *SERDIV* show that the first stroke may differ from the subsequent strokes.

In lines 14, 23, 27, and 31 of *SERDIV*, the signal *DLN1* is used. *DLN1* is generated in *DATASER*, line 10, and indicates that the last operand section is not yet reached. *DLN1* is used to obtain a special gate setting for the last operand

```
      ∇ DATASER;LSADR;BADR                        ∇ SERCODE
 [1]     ⍝ SELECT                           [1]     ⍝ DATAWIDTH
 [2]     DL←(~Y[SKH])×PL|DL-1               [2]     SL←8
 [3]     ⍝ FETCH DATA                       [3]     ⍝ NUMBER OF BYTES PER OPERAND
 [4]     LSADR←(Y[TIP]×PADR)+(Y[TIQ]×QADR)+DL  [4]   PL←4
 [5]     P←LOCALSTORE[LSADR;]               [5]     ⍝ ADDRESS ASSIGNMENT
 [6]     R←LOCALSTORE[RADR+DL;]             [6]     RADR←4
 [7]     ⍝ TESTCONDITIONS                   [7]     PADR←12
 [8]     SKL←DL=PL-1                        [8]     QADR←16
 [9]     DLN0←DL≠0                          ∇
[10]     DLN1←DL≠1
[11]     ⍝ DATAPATH ACTION
[12]     PATHSER
[13]     ⍝ BUFFER DECISION
[14]     →Y[SOM]/WRITE-1
[15]     BADR←LSADR                         ∇ DECLDATASER
[16]     ⍝ STORE DATA                       [1]     ⍝ LOCAL STORE
[17]     →(~Y[TIP]∨Y[TIQ])/WRITE+1          [2]     LOCALSTORE←((8×PL),SL)⍴0
[18]  WRITE:LOCALSTORE[BADR;]←ILS           [3]     ⍝ DATA REGISTERS
[19]     ⍝ BUFFER FOR DELAYED STORE         [4]     P←SL⍴0
[20]     BADR←LSADR                         [5]     R←SL⍴0
      ∇                                     ∇


         ⍝ REFERENCE:                               PROGRAM:
         ⍝ PATHSER    SERIES-PARALLEL DATAPATH          5-25
```

Program 5-26   Data selection for series-parallel datapath.

section, as shown in lines 15, 24, 28, and 32 of *SERDIV*. The programs also show in line 6 the use of *SKH* to obtain the sign.

The emptying of the outgoing buffer *BOUT* takes place in line 16 of *SERMPY*.

5-7 DATAPATH FOR DATA SELECTION

In the preceding sections the data selection from the local store has been described at a high level. In this section an implementation form for this equipment is given. The data selection will be described here for the load and add operations. It applies also to multiplication and division, however, and will be used for that purpose in Section 5-8.

Access to Local Store

In the single and serial datapaths it was assumed that the desired data could be fetched from, and stored in, the local store in one cycle. Only very large systems permit such an action. Thus, in System/370, Model 168 four fetches and one store can be performed simultaneously in the local store. Most local stores, however, permit only one access at a time. The data selection must therefore take as many cycles as are required by the nature of the local store.

```
     ∇ SERMPY                                  ∇ SERDIV
[1]    A PROLOGUE                      [1]       A PROLOGUE
[2]    P←VL                            [2]       P←(ρDR)↑DD
[3]    Q←MR                            [3]       Q←(ρDR)↓DD
[4]    R←MD                            [4]       R←DR
[5]    A MULTIPLICATION                [5]       A DIVISION
[6]    GATE MOR,TIU,TIW,TIJ,SKH        [6]       GATE DOR,POS,SOP,TIB,TIP,TIU,TIV,TIW,TIJ,SKH
[7]    A STROKE Q                      [7]       A REDUCTION
[8]  CONT:GATE MOS,SOM,TOK,TIB,TIQ,TIU,TIV,TIW,TIJ  [8]  A STROKE Q
[9]  SKQ:GATE POS,SOM,TIB,TIQ         [9]     CONT:GATE LOS,SOP,KOK,TOK,TIB,TIQ,TIJ
[10]   →DLN0/SKQ                       [10]    SKQ:GATE LOS,SOP,KOK,TIB,TIQ
[11]   A STROKE P                      [11]      →DLN0/SKQ
[12] SKP:GATE POS,BOS,SOM,TIB,TIP      [12]      A STROKE P
[13]   →DLN0/SKP                       [13]    SKP:GATE LOS,SOP,KOK,DOS,TIB,TIP
[14]   →(~JZRO)/CONT                   [14]      →DLN1/SKP
[15]   A BUFFER STROKE                 [15]      GATE LOS,SOP,DOS,COW,TIB,TIP,TIW
[16]   GATE MOS,SOM                    [16]      →(~JZRO)/CONT
[17]   A EPILOGUE                      [17]      A BUFFER STROKE
[18]   PD←P,Q                          [18]    SKB:GATE LOS,SOP,KOK,TIB,TIQ
     ∇                                 [19]      →DLN0/SKB
                                       [20]      A REMAINDER CORRECTION
     ∇ GATE X                          [21]      →RPOS/RMC
[1]    Y←(ι24)εX                       [22]    RC1:GATE POS,SOP,DOS,TIB,TIP
[2]    DATASER                         [23]      →DLN1/RC1
     ∇                                 [24]      GATE POS,SOP,DOS,COW,TIB,TIP,TIW
                                       [25]    RMC:→RCOR/QTC
                                       [26]    RC2:GATE POS,SOP,DOS,TIB,TIP
                                       [27]      →DLN1/RC2
                                       [28]      GATE POS,SOP,DOS,COW,TIB,TIP,TIW
                                       [29]      A QUOTIENT CORRECTION
                                       [30]    QTC:GATE POS,SOP,KOS,TIB,TIQ
                                       [31]      →DLN1/QTC
                                       [32]      GATE POS,SOP,KOS,COW,TIB,TIQ,TIW
                                       [33]      A EPILOGUE
                                       [34]      RM←P
                                       [35]      QT←Q
                                       [36]      OFDV←OFLO
                                            ∇
```

```
A REFERENCE:                                    PROGRAM:
A DATASER       DATA SELECTION FOR SERIES-PARALLEL 5-26
```

Program 5-27 Gate programs for series-parallel multiplication
and division.

Sequential Read and Write. In the various data-selection functions, a local
store read and write were considered part of a datapath cycle. Such a procedure
is possible with the split cycle of core storage, as will be mentioned in Chapter 8.
For a local store made from integrated circuits, however, separate cycles for reading
and writing must be used. The duration of these storage cycles is moreover comparable to a datapath cycle. Therefore, separate read and write cycles must be
taken, even if they refer to the same location.

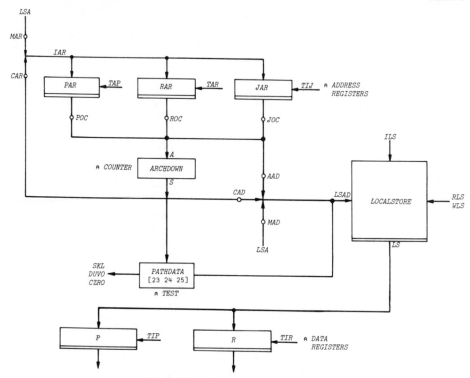

Figure 5-28   Datapath for data selection.

Direct or Buffered Access.   Depending upon the timing characteristics of the local store and the datapath, the data read from the store may, or may not, be processed in the datapath at the conclusion of the read cycle. Similarly, a datapath action may, or may not, be concluded with the writing of the result in the local store. For this section, the latter case will be assumed. This implies that the inputs to the datapath are supplied by two buffer registers, the registers P and R. The input to the local store, on the other hand, need not be buffered.

Data-Selection Implementation

Figure 5-28 and *PATHDATA*, Program 5-29, describe a simple addressing and buffering mechanism for the local store, which also incorporates an implementation of the counter for the multiply and divide cycles. The datapath contains the address registers PAR and RAR for the P and R operands and the associated data registers P and R. Also, a register JAR for the count J is provided.

Since processing is from right to left, the addresses must be reduced by 1 after each stroke. The counter *ARCHDOWN*, Program 2-52, is used for this purpose. The initial values of the addresses are supplied by the control. The register values and the decremented value, as obtained from the counter, can be used to address the local store.

```
        ∇ PATHDATA                                    ∇ DECLDATA
[1]     ⋒ COUNTER INPUTS                      [1]     ⋒ ADDRESS REGISTERS
[2]     A←(Y[POC]∧PAR)∨(Y[ROC]∧RAR)∨Y[JOC]∧JAR [2]     PAR←6ρ0
[3]     ⋒ COUNTER                             [3]     RAR←6ρ0
[4]     ARCHDOWN                              [4]     JAR←6ρ0
[5]     ⋒ REGISTER INPUTS                     [5]     ⋒ LOCAL STORE
[6]     IAR←(Y[MAR]∧Y[LSA])∨Y[CAR]∧S          [6]     LOCALSTORE←((8×PL),SL)ρ0
[7]     ⋒ ADDRESS REGISTERS                   [7]     ⋒ DATA REGISTERS
[8]     PAR←(Y[TAP]∧IAR)∨(~Y[TAP])∧PAR        [8]     P←SLρ0
[9]     RAR←(Y[TAR]∧IAR)∨(~Y[TAR])∧RAR        [9]     R←SLρ0
[10]    JAR←(Y[TIJ]∧IAR)∨(~Y[TIJ])∧JAR                ∇
[11]    ⋒ LOCAL STORE ADDRESS
[12]    LSADR←(Y[MAD]∧Y[LSA])∨(Y[AAD]∧A)∨Y[CAD]∧S
[13]    ⋒ FETCH DATA
[14]    →(~Y[RLS])/READ+1
[15]    READ:LS←LOCALSTORE[2⊥LSADR;]
[16]    ⋒ DATA REGISTERS
[17]    P←(Y[TIP]∧LS)∨(~Y[TIP])∧P
[18]    R←(Y[TIR]∧LS)∨(~Y[TIR])∧R
[19]    ⋒ STORE DATA
[20]    →(~Y[WLS])/WRITE+1
[21]    WRITE:LOCALSTORE[2⊥LSADR;]←ILS
[22]    ⋒ TESTCONDITIONS
[23]    SKL←∧/⁻2↑LSADR
[24]    DLN0←∨/⁻2↑LSADR
[25]    CZRO←∨/S
        ∇

        ⋒ REFERENCE:                              PROGRAM:
        ⋒ ARCHDOWN    DECREMENTING COUNTER ARCHITECTURE   2-52
```

Program 5-29 Datapath for data selection.

Gate Programs Using the Data-Selection Implementation

The gate programs for Load Positive and Subtract using *PATHDATA* for the data selection are shown in Program 5-30. Since there is a considerable turnover in the gates to be used in this section and the next, a new code assignment is used, as specified by *GATECODEX*. The gate programs are lengthened by the extra actions required for the local store, as compared to those shown in Program 5-22. The gate programs are, furthermore, complicated by the addressing control.

Read and Write Control. A typical processing cycle, such as *SERMIN*, line 5, is now replaced by the three actions shown in *DATAMIN*, lines 8, 9, and 10. Lines 8 and 9 fetch the operands, and line 10 processes the data and stores the result. Furthermore, another set of actions, lines 5, 6, and 7, is required to initiate the addresses. Thus, one line in *SERMIN* has expanded sixfold. When only one operand participates, as for Load Positive, the number of cycles is reduced accordingly. The gate program indicates the desired storage action by the read gate $Y[RLS]$ and the write gate $Y[WLS]$.

Addressing Control. The control can supply an address to *PATHDATA* by encoding the address as a set of gates. Bits 22 through 27 of Y, identified by the name *LSA*, are used to address local store under control of the gate $Y[MAD]$, or as input to the address registers under control of $Y[MAR]$. The value of bits 22 through 27 of Y is specified by indicating in the gate program which bits should be 1. These groups of bits are again indicated symbolically by names such as PAD and RAD. The low-order byte of an operand is specified by adding the group of gates LAD. Thus, the rightmost byte of $OD2$ is specified by both RAD and LAD. The assignments of the storage addresses is given by $GATECODEX$, lines 29 through 33.

The assignment implies a value of 4 for PL, the number of bytes per operand. Different values can of course be obtained by changing $GATECODEX$.

5-8 SIMPLIFIED SERIES–PARALLEL
DATAPATH

The general series–parallel datapath $PATHSER$ has increased noticeably in complexity over the datapath for the load and add operations, $PATHSERADD$, owing to the requirements for multiplication and division. This increase is caused

```
      ∇ DATAPOS
[1]    ⍝ PROLOGUE
[2]    LOCALSTORE[RADR+⍳PL;]←(PL,SL)ρOD2
[3]    ⍝ DETERMINE SIGN
[4]    GATE RAD,MCL,RLS,TIR
[5]    ⍝ ABSOLUTE VALUE
[6]    GATE RAD,LAD,MAR,TAR,MAD,RLS,TIR,TIV
[7]    GATE ROS,ABS,SOP,TIB,PAD,LAD,TAP,MAD,MAR,WLS
[8]   SKP:GATE ROC,CAR,TAR,CAD,RLS,TIR
[9]    GATE ROS,ABS,SOP,TIB,POC,CAR,TAP,CAD,WLS
[10]   →DLN0/SKP
[11]   ⍝ EPILOGUE
[12]   RL1←,LOCALSTORE[PADR+⍳PL;]
      ∇

      ∇ DATAMIN
[1]    ⍝ PROLOGUE
[2]    LOCALSTORE[PADR+⍳PL;]←(PL,SL)ρOD1
[3]    LOCALSTORE[RADR+⍳PL;]←(PL,SL)ρOD2
[4]    ⍝ SUBTRACTION
[5]    GATE PAD,LAD,MAR,TAP,MAD,RLS,TIP
[6]    GATE RAD,LAD,MAR,TAR,MAD,RLS,TIR
[7]    GATE POS,ROS,MIN,SOP,TIB,POC,AAD,WLS
[8]   SKP:GATE POC,CAR,TAP,CAD,RLS,TIP
[9]    GATE ROC,CAR,TAR,CAD,RLS,TIR
[10]   GATE POS,ROS,MIN,SOP,TIB,POC,AAD,WLS
[11]   →DLN0/SKP
[12]   ⍝ EPILOGUE
[13]   RL1←,LOCALSTORE[PADR+⍳PL;]
      ∇

      ∇ GATE X
[1]    Y←(⍳40)∊X
[2]    PATHSERADD
[3]    PATHDATA
      ∇

      ⍝ REFERENCE:                                        PROGRAM:
      ⍝ PATHSERADD   SERIES-PARALLEL DATAPATH FOR ADDITION   5-21
      ⍝ PATHDATA     DATAPATH FOR DATA SELECTION             5-29
```

Program 5-30 Gate programs using the data selection implementation.

```
          ∇ GATECODEX
   [1]    ⍝ ADDER INPUT GATES
   [2]    POS←0
   [3]    ROS←1
   [4]    ⍝ COUNTER INPUT GATES
   [5]    POC←2
   [6]    ROC←3
   [7]    JOC←4
   [8]    ⍝ REGISTER INPUT GATES
   [9]    SOP←5
   [10]   SOM←6
   [11]   MAR←7
   [12]   CAR←8
   [13]   ⍝ CONTROL GATES
   [14]   ABS←9
   [15]   MIN←10
   [16]   CMP←11
   [17]   NSL←12
   [18]   ⍝ REGISTER READ-IN SIGNALS
   [19]   TAP←13
   [20]   TAR←14
   [21]   TIB←15
   [22]   TIP←16
   [23]   TIR←17
   [24]   TIU←18
   [25]   TIV←19
   [26]   TIW←20
   [27]   TIJ←21
   [28]   ⍝ ADDRESS VALUES
   [29]   LSA←22+⍳6
   [30]   LAD← 26 27
   [31]   PAD← 24 25
   [32]   QAD←23
   [33]   RAD←25
   [34]   ⍝ ADDRESS GATES
   [35]   MAD←28
   [36]   AAD←29
   [37]   CAD←30
   [38]   ⍝ LOCAL STORE CONTROL
   [39]   RLS←31
   [40]   WLS←32
   [41]   ⍝ GROUP NAMES
   [42]   LOWP←PAD,LAD,MAR,TAP,MAD,RLS,TIP
   [43]   NEXTP←POC,CAR,TAP,CAD,RLS,TIP
   [44]   LOWQ←QAD,LAD,MAR,TAP,MAD,RLS,TIP
   [45]   LOWR←RAD,LAD,MAR,TAR,MAD,RLS,TIR
   [46]   NEXTR←ROC,CAR,TAR,CAD,RLS,TIR
          ∇
```

Program 5-30 Cont.

by the many special controls that are incorporated in the datapath, such as the multiple selection and the quotient digit recording. This specialized control may, however, be handled by the internal control and thus be removed from the datapath. As a rule, this shift from datapath to control manifests itself in increased processing time. Thus, again, there is a trade of time versus space.

Datapath Implementation

Figure 5-31 and *PATHSIM*, Program 5-32, show a simple general datapath. The datapath resembles *PATHSERADD* extended with the outgoing buffer *BOUT* and a set of registers, which convey the status of the datapath to the control.

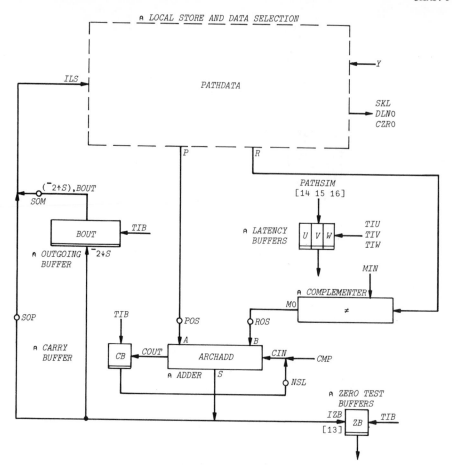

Figure 5-31 Simple general datapath.

Shift Provision.   A good part of the complexity of *PATHSER* can be attributed to the left and right shifts of the operands and results in multiplication and division. *PATHSIM* has no provisions for a left shift. Instead, a separate pass through the datapath is taken, in which the operand is added to itself, hence shifted 1 bit to the left.

The left shift is required for the multiple 2 of the multiplicand. This shift is performed prior to the multiplication and the shifted multiplicand is placed in the local store. Thus, the price for this extra action is paid only once. The left shift is also required for the quotient and partial dividend during the reduction cycles of division. Here the time penalty is paid each cycle.

A right shift cannot be performed by a simple ALU. Hence, the outgoing buffer *BOUT* has been included as a special provision. The output signals from *BOUT* are combined with those from the adder in such a way that the 2-bit shift to the right required by the multiplication algorithm is obtained.

```
      ∇ PATHSIM                                    ∇ DECLSIM
[1]     ⋀ ADDER INPUTS                     [1]       ⋀ OUTGOING BUFFER
[2]     A←Y[POS]⋀P                         [2]       BOUT←(SL-2)ρ0
[3]     M0←Y[MIN]≠R                        [3]       ⋀ CARRY BUFFER
[4]     B←Y[ROS]⋀M0                        [4]       CB←0
[5]     CIN←Y[CMP]∨Y[NSL]⋀CB               [5]       ⋀ ZERO TEST BUFFER
[6]     ⋀ ADDER                            [6]       ZB←0
[7]     ARCHADD                            [7]       ⋀ LATENCY BUFFERS
[8]     ⋀ LOCAL STORE INPUT                [8]       U←0
[9]     ILS←(Y[SOP]⋀S)∨Y[SOM]⋀(¯2↑S),BOUT  [9]       V←0
[10]    ⋀ REGISTER INPUTS                  [10]      W←0
[11]    IBOUT←¯2↑S                                 ∇
[12]    ICB←COUT
[13]    IZB←~∨/S,Y[NSL]⋀~ZB
[14]    IU←((~Y[SOM])⋀P[0])∨Y[SOM]⋀1↑¯2↑S
[15]    IV←((~Y[SOM])⋀R[0])∨Y[SOM]⋀¯1↑S
[16]    IW←((~Y[SOM])⋀S[0])∨Y[SOM]⋀U
[17]    ⋀ REGISTERS
[18]    BOUT←(Y[TIB]⋀IBOUT)∨(~Y[TIB])⋀BOUT
[19]    CB←(Y[TIB]⋀ICB)∨(~Y[TIB])⋀CB
[20]    ZB←(Y[TIB]⋀IZB)∨(~Y[TIB])⋀ZB
[21]    U←(Y[TIU]⋀IU)∨(~Y[TIU])⋀U
[22]    V←(Y[TIV]⋀IV)∨(~Y[TIV])⋀V
[23]    W←(Y[TIW]⋀IW)∨(~Y[TIW])⋀W
      ∇

        ⋀ REFERENCE:                                PROGRAM:
        ⋀ ARCHADD      ADDER ARCHITECTURE              2-5
```

Program 5-32 Simple general datapath.

Staticizers.   The simple datapath has eliminated most of the special controls found in *PATHSER*. The registers, such as *U, V,* and *W,* are now used to present the status of the datapath to the control rather than affecting the operation of the datapath directly. Registers that preserve the datapath status are called *staticizers,* or test registers. The staticizers bring some order in the various control conditions. Nevertheless, the inputs to these registers still have a certain 'ad hoc' character.

Gate Programs for the Simple Datapath

When *PATHSIM* is combined with *PATHDATA* a simple processor organization is obtained. In this organization the address registers are as prominent as the data registers, as is typical for a series processor (Brooks and Iverson, 1969).

The use of the series processor will be described for the Load Positive operation and for the reduction cycles of division.

The gate specifications for *PATHDATA* are quite lengthy and repetitive, as is clear from *DATAPOS* and *DATAMIN*. Hence, the gate programs of this section use some gate names that identify frequently occurring groups of gates. These groups are identified in *GATECODEX*, lines 42 and following.

Sign Control in Gate Program.   *SIMPOS,* Program 5-33, shows the gate program for Load Positive using the data-selection implementation of *PATHDATA* and the simple datapath *PATHSIM. SIMPOS* illustrates how a control circuit in the datapath, here the inversion control of *PATHSERADD,* line 3, can be elimi-

```
        ∇ SIMPOS
[1]     ⍝ PROLOGUE
[2]     LOCALSTORE[RADR+⍳PL;]←(PL,SL)⍴OD2
[3]     ⍝ DETERMINE SIGN
[4]     GATE RAD,MAD,RLS,TIR
[5]     ⍝ ABSOLUTE VALUE
[6]     GATE LOWR,TIV
[7]     →V/COMP
[8]     GATE ROS,SOP,TIB,PAD,LAD,MAR,TAP,MAD,WLS
[9]     SKP:GATE NEXTR
[10]    GATE ROS,SOP,TIB,POC,CAR,TAP,CAD,WLS
[11]    →DLN0/SKP
[12]    →END
[13]    COMP:GATE ROS,MIN,CMP,SOP,TIB,PAD,LAD,MAR,TAP,MAD,WLS
[14]    SKPC:GATE NEXTR
[15]    GATE ROS,MIN,NSL,SOP,TIB,POC,CAR,TAP,CAD,WLS
[16]    →DLN0/SKPC
[17]    ⍝ EPILOGUE
[18]    END:RL1←,LOCALSTORE[PADR+⍳PL;]
        ∇


        ∇ GATE X
[1]     Y←(⍳40)∊X
[2]     PATHSIM
[3]     PATHDATA
        ∇


        ⍝ REFERENCE:                                         PROGRAM:
        ⍝ PATHDATA      DATAPATH FOR DATA SELECTION           5-29
        ⍝ PATHSIM       SIMPLE SERIES DATAPATH                5-32
```

Program 5-33   Gate program for simple series Load Positive.

nated by performing that function in the control. *SIMPOS* takes in line 7 a branch on the value of V, which represents the operand sign. The gate program for positive sign just moves the operand $OD1$ from the R to the P locations, as shown in lines 8 through 12. The gate program for negative sign complements the operand $OD1$ as it is moved in lines 13 through 16 to the result locations.

SIMPOS is considerably longer than *DATAPOS* because of these two separate routines. The routines may, however, be shared with the other load operations, thus making the gate program more efficient.

SIMPOS also illustrates the control of the carry-in from the gate program, as opposed from the direct control by the data selection. The gate program now specifies that a stroke is not the low-order stroke with the gate *NSL* as in *SIMPOS*, line 15. The signal $Y[NSL]$ is used in the datapath to propagate the carry and the zero test.

Shift by Addition.   Because of the length of the gate programs for the simple datapath, only the reduction part of the division will be shown in *SIMRED*, Program 5-34. This program illustrates the use of the datapath to obtain a left shift. For this left shift, the dividend and quotient are added to themselves by reading the local store into both P and R.

The shift uses a separate set of strokes. During that process the quotient digit is entered in the low-order position of Q.

The precession that occurred for *SGLDIV* and *SERDIV* is also present in *SIMRED*. Thus, the content of the partial dividend and quotient should match

```
      ∇ SIMRED                                                    ∇ GATE X
[1]      ⍝ DETERMINE QUOTIENT DIGIT                          [1]     Y←(⍳40)∊X
[2]      GATE LOWQ,TIR                                       [2]     PATHSIM
[3]     →V/DRN                                               [3]     PATHDATA
[4]      GATE POS,ROS,NSL,SOP,TIB,POC,AAD,WLS                  ∇
[5]      ⍝ SHIFT Q
[6]   SKQ:GATE NEXTP,TIR
[7]      GATE POS,ROS,NSL,SOP,TIB,POC,AAD,WLS
[8]     →(~SKL)/SKQ
[9]     →SKP
[10]  DRN:→CB/DRN+3
[11]     GATE POS,ROS,CMP,SOP,TIB,POC,AAD,WLS
[12]    →SKQ
[13]     GATE POS,ROS,SOP,TIB,POC,AAD,WLS
[14]    →SKQ
[15]     ⍝ SHIFT P
[16]  SKP:GATE NEXTP,TIR
[17]     GATE POS,ROS,NSL,SOP,TIB,POC,AAD,WLS,TIW
[18]    →(~SKL)/SKP
[19]    →W/DDN
[20]    →(~V)/SUB
[21]     ⍝ ADD DIVISOR
[22]  ADD:GATE LOWP
[23]     GATE LOWR
[24]     GATE POS,ROS,SOP,TIB,POC,AAD,WLS
[25]  SKPA:GATE NEXTP
[26]     GATE NEXTR
[27]     GATE POS,ROS,NSL,SOP,TIB,POC,AAD,WLS
[28]    →(~SKL)/SKPA
[29]    →CNT
[30]  DDN:→V/ADD
[31]     ⍝ SUBTRACT DIVISOR
[32]  SUB:GATE LOWP
[33]     GATE LOWR
[34]     GATE POS,ROS,MIN,CMP,SOP,TIB,POC,AAD,WLS
[35]  SKPS:GATE NEXTP
[36]     GATE NEXTR
[37]     GATE POS,ROS,MIN,NSL,SOP,TIB,POC,AAD,WLS
[38]    →(~SKL)/SKPS
[39]     ⍝ COUNT
[40]  CNT:GATE JOC,CAR,TIJ
      ∇
```

```
      ⍝ REFERENCE:                                           PROGRAM:
      ⍝ PATHDATA      DATAPATH FOR DATA SELECTION            5-29
      ⍝ PATHSIM       SIMPLE SERIES DATAPATH                 5-32
```

Program 5-34 Gate program for simple series dividend reduction.

that for the single datapath and can be compared with a suitably modified version
of *QUIZDIV*.

The shift of the partial dividend requires a temporary extension of this dividend
and of the divisor by 1 bit. This requirement follows from the extensions shown
in the initial algorithm *ONEDIV*, Program 4-14, lines 10 and 11. Since an extension
with a single bit is not easily attained in the datapath, the dividend and divisor are,
instead, extended by a full byte in the local store. This extension takes place prior
to the reduction cycles, hence is not shown in *SIMRED*.

Speed and Cost Comparison. Table 5-35 shows the relative performance
and cost for the fully parallel datapath, the single datapath, and the series datapaths. Assuming 32-bit operands and an 8-bit series datapath, a factor 4 is obtained
for addition and a factor 8 for multiplication and division between the parallel
organization and the series operation. The simple series datapath gives another

	RELATIVE TIME FOR ADD MULTIPLY DIVIDE			RELATIVE COST
PATHPAR	1	17	35	1400
PATHSGL	1	33	68	950
PATHSER	4	130	269	350
PATHSIM	4	149	465	200

SAME TIME ASSUMED FOR DATASELECTION

NO TIME CALCULATED FOR GATEPROGRAM DECISIONS

NO DATA SELECTION COST COUNTED

Table 5-35 Speed and cost comparison of datapaths.

decrease in performance, owing to the extra shift actions. Variations from these figures are caused by the loading and emptying of buffers, which may or may not be combined with extra start and end cycles. The series datapath can in itself be faster than the parallel datapath because of the reduced length of the adder.

The cost of the parallel unit as shown in Figure 5-15 can be estimated at 1400 nands for 32-bit operands. The corresponding cost of the series unit of Figure 5-24 handling 8 bits at a time would be 350 nands, exclusive of the local store positions. The cost improvement is about four times as opposed to a speed reduction of four to eight times. In contrast, the cost of the simple datapath of Figure 5-31 is about 200 nands.

As stated earlier, the cost can be influenced considerably by the use of a local or main storage unit for P, Q, and R. Also, the cost of the data selection should be taken into account, which for $PATHDATA$ is about 250 nands. Finally, the larger number of gates and strokes that the series datapaths require tends to make the control more expensive.

REFERENCES

BELL, C. G., J. GRASON, and A. NEWELL: *Designing Computers and Digital Systems, Using PDP16 Register Transfer Modules*. Digital Press, Digital Equipment Corporation, Maynard, Mass., 1972.

BROOKS, F. P. JR., and K. E. IVERSON: *Automatic Data Processing: System/360 Edition*, pp. 255–262. Wiley, New York, 1969.

SCHORR, H.: "Computer-Aided Digital System Design and Analysis Using a Register Transfer Language." *IEEE Transactions on Electronic Computers*, vol. EC-13, no. 12, pp. 730–737 (December, 1964).

STABLER, E. P.: "System Description Languages." *IEEE Transactions on Computers*, vol. C-19, no. 12, pp. 1160–1173 (December, 1970).

STEVENS, W. Y.: "The Structure of System/360, Part II, System Implementation." *IBM Systems Journal*, vol. 3, no. 2, pp. 136–143 (1964). Reprinted in Bell and Newell pp. 602–606.

THORNTON, J. E.: *Design of a Computer, The Control Data* 6600, pp. 57–111. Scott, Foresman, Glenview, Ill., 1970.

TOMASULO, R. M.: "An Efficient Algorithm for Exploiting Multiple Arithmetic Units." *IBM Journal of Research and Development*, vol. 11, no. 1, pp. 25–33 (January, 1967).

EXERCISES

5-1 Give the gate programs *GATELOAD*, *GATENEG*, and *GATEPLUS*, which, respectively, fetch an operand unaltered, fetch it with negative absolute value, and add two operands, as specified in *OPERATION*, Program 5-1, lines 9, 5, and 19. Use the datapath *PATHPAR*, Program 5-16.

5-2 Determine the gate programs *SERLOAD*, *SERNEG*, and *SERPLUS*, which perform the same operations as in Exercise 5-1, using the datapath *PATH-SERADD*, Program 5-21.

5-3 *IMP*74181, Program 5-36, gives the implementation approach of the TI SN74181 ALU. Give the architecture of this unit in a form comparable to that of *OPERATION*, Program 5-1.

```
        ∇ POST←IMP74181 PRE;MODE;F;A;B;CIN;G;GT;C;S;COUT
  [1]     ⍝ GATES
  [2]     MODE←PRE[8]
  [3]     F←PRE[13 11 10 9]
  [4]     ⍝ ADDER INPUTS
  [5]     A←PRE[19 21 23 2]
  [6]     B←PRE[18 20 22 1]
  [7]     CIN←~PRE[7]
  [8]     ⍝ TRANSMISSION AND GENERATION
  [9]     GT←A∨(F[3]∧B)∨F[2]∧~B
  [10]    G←(A∧F[0]∧B)∨A∧F[1]∧~B
  [11]    ⍝ CARRY PREDICTION
  [12]    C←G PRED5 GT
  [13]    ⍝ CARRY ASSIMILATION
  [14]    S←G≠GT≠1↓C∨~MODE
  [15]    COUT←1↑C
  [16]    ⍝ ADDER OUTPUTS
  [17]    POST←PRE
  [18]    POST[12 11 10 9]←S
  [19]    POST[16]←~COUT
  [20]    ⍝ GROUP TRANSMISSION AND GENERATION
  [21]    POST[15]←∧/GT
  [22]    POST[17]←G[0]∨(GT[0]∧G[1])∨(∧/GT[0 1],G[2])∨∧/GT[0 1 2],G[3]
  [23]    ⍝ EQUALITY
  [24]    POST[14]←∧/A=B
  [25]    ⍝ POWER CONNECTIONS
  [26]    ⍝ PRE[12]←GROUND
  [27]    ⍝ PRE[0]←SUPPLY VOLTAGE, PIN 24
        ∇

        ⍝ REFERENCE:                              PROGRAM:
        ⍝ PRED5         5-BIT CARRY PREDICTION       2-26
```

Program 5-36 Implementation of TI SN74181 ALU.

5-4 Design a datapath capable of the load, logic, and add types of operations of *OPERATION*, Program 5-1, which uses *IMP*74181, Program 5-35, as a building stone. Assume that the operands have a length of 4 bits. Give the gate programs for Load Positive and Subtract for use with this datapath.

5-5   Repeat the assignment of Exercise 5-4 with the assumption that the operand length is a multiple of 4 bits. Use a serial organization.

5-6   Develop *PATHMPY*1, which embodies the initial algorithm *ONEMPY*, Program 3-12. Is it necessary to change *GATEMPY*, Program 5-9?

5-7   Determine the general datapath *PATHSGL*1, which allows multiplication based upon *ONEMPY*, Program 3-12, as well as the load, add, and divide operations. Give the gate program for multiplication in this datapath.

5-8   What changes can be made in *DATASER* and *SERMPY*, Programs 5-26 and 5-27, if it is known that the operands are 32 bits wide and the datapath width is 16?

5-9   Replace *ARCHADD* by *ARCHWORK* in the various datapaths. Design *ARCHWORK* such that it performs the And, Or, and Exclusive-or operations required by *OPERATION*, Program 5-1, lines 12, 14, and 16, as well as the operations that are performed by *ARCHADD*. Introduce new gates as needed.

5-10   Modify *QUIZPATH*, Program 5-12, such that it can test the actions of a serial datapath.

5-11   Perform the separate remainder and quotient correction actions, as specified by *REMCOR* and *QUOCOR*, Program 4-14, with the simple serial datapath *PATHSIM*, Program 5-32.

5-12   Perform subtraction in the simple serial datapath *PATHSIM*, Program 5-32.

5-13   Give the gate program *DATAMPY* for multiplication in the serial datapath *PATHSER*, Program 5-25, using the data-selection implementation of *PATHDATA*, Program 5-29.

5-14   Design a parallel datapath *PATHNORM* and a gate program *GATENORM*, which perform the initial algorithm *IMPNORM* of Exercise 4-19, as well as the load and add operations of *PATHSERADD*, Program 5-21.

5-15   Transform the parallel datapath of Exercise 5-14 into a serial datapath *PATHSERNORM* and determine the corresponding gate program *SERNORM*. This datapath should be able to perform the load and add operations of *PATHSERADD*, Program 5-21.

5-16   Remove the zero-test buffer *ZB* and its input circuits from the simple datapath and give the gate program for performing the zero test in a separate set of strokes.

5-17   Remove the *J* counter *JAR* from the data-selection implementation. Assume that the count resides in local store and give the gate program for the count reduction and zero test.

5-18 Give the data-selection datapath for a local store that can combine reading with processing but not writing and processing. Illustrate the use of this data selection and the serial datapath for the subtract operation.

5-19 Assume that the data selection for the single datapath can combine neither reading nor writing with processing. Discuss the changes that this would require and give the gate program for multiplication.

6 INTERNAL CONTROL

In Chapter 5 the initial implementation algorithms of Chapters 2 through 4 have been transformed into a datapath and a gate program. The datapath represents the equipment necessary to perform an operation, and the gate program describes the control of this equipment. The description of the datapath is such that it can be readily realized once the circuit elements that are to be used as building stones are known. The gate program, on the other hand, still needs further development. It is the purpose of this chapter to describe the methods by which the control of a datapath, the *internal control*, can be implemented.

Figure 6-1 shows a flow diagram of the design process that is followed in this text. The architecture of an operation is first satisfied by an initial implementation algorithm. The initial algorithms are not necessarily suggested by the architecture. The subsequent development of the implementation algorithms, however, has a more evolutionary character, as does the separation of time and space resulting in datapath and gate program.

The gate programs form the specification of the internal control. Hence, the process of the previous chapters repeats itself. A control architecture is postulated and its implementation is worked out. Since the latter step has been treated at length in preceding chapters, it will only be briefly sketched. The main emphasis of this chapter will be to find the proper control architecture.

Nature of Internal Control

In Chapter 5, the control of a datapath was reduced to the opening of gates, the modification of the action of combinational circuits, and the activation of sequential circuits as specified by the gate program. The datapath, in turn, supplied test signals that determine the flow of the gate program. The gate program thus

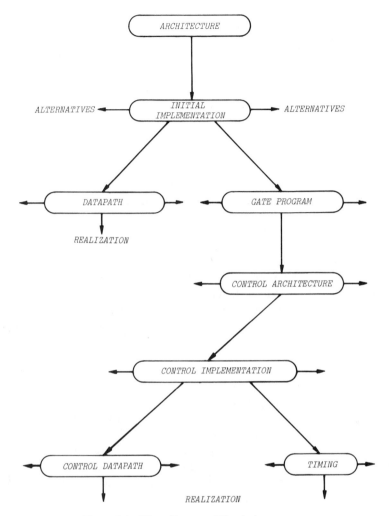

Figure 6-1   Flow diagram of the design process.

expressed the control of the datapath on a conveniently high level. In this chapter, the equipment required to implement the gate program will be considered.

The control equipment has three tasks, similar to those encountered in Chapter 1 in the control of the computer:

(a) The expressions of the gate program must be executed in order.
(b) On the basis of the test signals, the order must be changed.
(c) For each expression, the desired gate signals must be made 1.

The various solutions for these three tasks determine the nature of the control. The solutions are mainly distinguished by the type of coding that is used and will be discussed below. First, however, the general organization of the control will be described briefly.

Microprogramming.   Each expression of a gate program represents a state of the control. The specification of the gate signals that should be 1, and the specification of the state transitions that are to be made, are jointly called a *microinstruction*. The microinstruction can be identified by a number, called the *microaddress*.

These names are derived from the concept of *microprogramming* developed by Wilkes in 1951. Microprogramming assumes the use of an addressable store, the *microstore*, as the source of the microinstructions. Each microinstruction occupies one word in the microstore, the *microword*. Wilkes has pointed out that the idea of a microstore can be recognized in Babbage's designs.

Hard-Wired Control.   The gate program can also be considered as the specification of a sequential circuit. The gate signals are the outputs of this circuit and the test signals form its inputs. The control circuit can be built in a variety of ways from this specification by using combinational circuits, such as 'and,' 'or,' and nand circuits, and sequential circuits, such as registers and counters. The control is now determined by the fixed interconnections of these components, as opposed to being determined by the content of a microstore; hence it is called *hard-wired control*.

Organization of the Chapter

In Section 6-1, a simple microprogramming structure will be presented, which permits the control of the parallel datapaths described in Chapter 5. Both the architecture and a possible implementation of this control will be described. The hard-wired control of these datapaths will be discussed in Section 6-2. The various alternatives in specifying a microprogramming control are considered in Section 6-3 and a more elaborate structure is presented. A microprogramming organization, which very much resembles a regular computer organization, the vertical microprogram, is described in Section 6-4.

6-1   HORIZONTAL MICROPROGRAMMING CONTROL

Figure 6-2 shows the format of an elementary microinstruction. The format comprises three groups of bits, or *fields*. The right field, bits 16 through 39, is the *gate field*. The bits of this field set the gate signals, such as $Y[ABS]$ and $Y[TIP]$ of the datapaths of Chapter 5, to 0 or 1. The left field, bits 0 through 4, is the *test field*. In this field, a test signal, such as $JZRO$ or $RPOS$, can be specified, as well as its desired polarity. Finally, bits 5 through 15 form the *address field*. This field is used as the microaddress when the test condition is met.

Figure 6-2 Microinstruction format.

Architecture of Microprogramming

The architecture of a control that uses the microinstruction of Figure 6-2 is illustrated in Figure 6-3 and described by *ARCHMICRO,* Program 6-4.

The microstore *MICROSTORE* is addressed in line 2 of *ARCHMICRO* by the microaddress *MADR* and yields the microword *MWORD,* to be used as microinstruction. In line 4 the gate field of the microinstruction determines the setting of the gate vector *Y* such that an action can take place in a datapath, such as *PATHPAR.* In the meantime, *MADR* is incremented by 1 in line 8. Also, in line 11 the value of the test signal specified in the test field is determined. If the test is met, the content of the address field will be used in line 13 as the new value of *MADR.* If not, the incremented value of *MADR* is used. The control cycle repeats itself by fetching a new microinstruction with the new value of *MADR.*

Field Assignment. *MICROFIELD,* Program 6-4, shows the assignment of the fields *YES, TST, ADR,* and *GATES* of the microinstruction, as used in *ARCHMICRO.* This reference by name has the advantage of separating the bit assignment from the microprogramming architecture. It also makes the architecture more readable.

Gate Signals. The gates of the datapath are controlled directly by the gate field of the microinstruction. Such a direct control is called *horizontal microprogramming.* As an alternative to horizontal microprogramming, the gate field may be partially or completely encoded, as will be discussed in Sections 6-3 and 6-4.

Test Conditions. Bits 1 through 4, the field *TST,* specify the test signal to be sampled. Sixteen test signals are possible in this implementation, of which seven have been used up until now. One of these seven signals is constantly 1 and therefore connotes the idea of 'always.' Bit 0, the *YES* bit, determines whether the condition is met if the test signal is 0 or 1.

End Test. In line 15 of *ARCHMICRO* address 2047, which has all address bits 1, is used as an end condition. A branch to this address terminates the execution of the program and therefore stops the machine. This end test is mainly meaningful in the development of the microstorage content. In a finished machine, it will only be used for maintainance purposes, if at all.

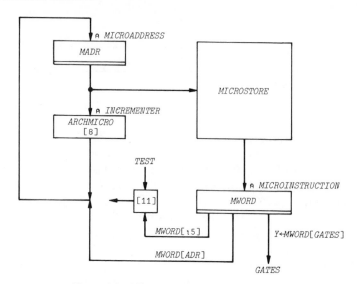

Figure 6-3   Microprogramming organization.

Microstorage Content.   Table 6-5 shows the content of the microstore for the operations that have been described up to this point. The functions of Program 6-6 use this microstore.

The operations of Chapter 5 each use one or more microinstructions. The start of each microprogram has been assigned a symbolic address, as indicated by the function *MADRCODE* of Program 6-6. Table 6-5 shows to the left of the microstore printout the symbolic addresses and to the right the corresponding absolute addresses. The use of symbolic addresses gives greater freedom in assembling the content of the microstore. Table 6-5 also identifies the microinstruction fields and the individual gate signals. Thus, the correspondence between the gate program and the content of the microstore can be visually verified.

Microprogram Routines.   Load Positive and Subtract each require only one microinstruction, just as their gate program specified only one gate setting. The microinstruction therefore specifies an unconditional branch to address 2047, indicating the end of the microprogram. At a later stage of the design, of course, this address will be replaced by an address that allows the computer operation to continue.

The multiplier test conditions that were part of *GATEMPY* are now handled by the control. Hence, only the initial content of the registers and the starting address of the microprogram need be specified by *MICROMPY*. Thus, the initial algorithm is reduced via the gate program to a calling program which contains only the original prologue and epilogue and the microprogram call.

The two gate settings of *GATEMPY* are expanded to the three microinstructions starting at *MADRMPY*. The third instruction only serves to stop the operation or, later, to branch to the continuation routine. This extra instruction gives an indi-

```
       ∇ ARCHMICRO MADR;TEST                        ∇ MICROFIELD
[1]      ⍝ READ MICROSTORE                  [1]       ⍝ TEST FIELD
[2]      CONT:MWORD←MICROSTORE[2⊥MADR;]     [2]       YES←0
[3]      ⍝ GATES                            [3]       TST←1+⍳4
[4]      Y←MWORD[GATES]                     [4]       ⍝ MICROADDRESS
[5]      ⍝ DATAPATH ACTION                  [5]       ADR←5+⍳11
[6]      PATHPAR                            [6]       ⍝ GATE FIELD
[7]      ⍝ INCREMENT ADDRESS                [7]       GATES←16+⍳24
[8]      MADR←(11⍴2)⊤1+2⊥MADR               ∇
[9]      ⍝ BRANCH CONDITION
[10]     TEST←1,JZRO,RPOS,RCOR,OFLO,DLN0,DLN1,9⍴0
[11]     →(MWORD[YES]≠TEST[2⊥MWORD[TST]])/END
[12]     ⍝ NEW ADDRESS
[13]     MADR←MWORD[ADR]
[14]     ⍝ END CONDITION
[15]     END:→(~∧/MADR)/CONT
       ∇


         ⍝ REFERENCE:                                   PROGRAM:
         ⍝ PATHPAR     PARALLEL DATAPATH                  5-16
```

Program 6-4   Microprogramming architecture.

```
            YES
            ↓TST ADR         ,GATES
MADRPOS     100001111111111101000010000010000010000   0              POS
MADRMIN     100001111111111111000010000001000010000   1              MIN
MADRMPY     000000000000000000000000010000000000011   2  INITIATION  MPY
            000010000000011100000010000001100110011   3  ADDITION    MPY
            100001111111111000000000000000000000000   4  END         MPY
MADRDIV     000000000000000000000000001000000001011   5  INITIATION  DIV
            000010000000110000101101100001001100011   6  REDUCTION   DIV
            100100000001010000000000000000000000000   7  BRANCH      DIV
            100110000010111000011001000000000100010   8  REMCOR1     DIV
            100000000001011100001100100000000100010   9  REMCOR2     DIV
            000110000001001000000000000000000000000  10  BRANCH      DIV
            100001111111111000010000100000000010010  11  QUOCOR      DIV
```

Table 6-5   Content of horizontal microstore.

cation that the microprogramming architecture of *ARCHMICRO* may occasionally have insufficient branching ability. The microprogram for division further
illustrates this problem. That microprogram will be discussed in Section 6-3 as
more powerful microprogramming structures are considered.

     Verification of the Microstorage Content.   In principle, an addition or multi-
plication can now be simulated entirely from the microprogram. Because of the
many functions that are involved, such a simulation tends to be time-consuming.
Certainly, a full check of the correct action of a multiplication could not reasonably
be performed in this manner. As stated earlier, however, the correctness of algorithms can better be checked in a step-by-step manner. In particular, the content
of *MICROSTORE* need only be checked against the content of the gate program
from which it is derived.

     Automatic Generation of the Microstorage Content.   At this stage of the design,
the amount of detail has grown noticeably. Whereas the gate program involved 24
distinct gates, now the simple microstore already contains an array of 12 by 40

```
        ∇ MICROPOS                          ∇ MICROMIN
[1]       ⍝ PROLOGUE                  [1]     ⍝ PROLOGUE
[2]       R←OD2                       [2]     P←OD1
[3]       ⍝ ABSOLUTE VALUE            [3]     R←OD2
[4]       ARCHMICRO MADRPOS           [4]     ⍝ SUBTRACTION
[5]       ⍝ EPILOGUE                  [5]     ARCHMICRO MADRMIN
[6]       RL1←P                       [6]     ⍝ EPILOGUE
        ∇                            [7]     RL1←P
                                           ∇


        ∇ MICROMPY                          ∇ MICRODIV
[1]       ⍝ PROLOGUE                  [1]     ⍝ PROLOGUE
[2]       P←VL                        [2]     P←(ρDR)↑DD
[3]       Q←MR                        [3]     Q←(ρDR)↓DD
[4]       R←MD                        [4]     R←DR
[5]       ⍝ MULTIPLICATION            [5]     ⍝ DIVISION
[6]       ARCHMICRO MADRMPY           [6]     ARCHMICRO MADRDIV
[7]       ⍝ EPILOGUE                  [7]     ⍝ EPILOGUE
[8]       PD←P,Q                      [8]     RM←P
        ∇                            [9]     QT←Q
                                     [10]    OFDV←OFLO
                                           ∇


        ∇ MADRCODE
[1]       ⍝ MICROADDRESS ASSIGNMENT
[2]       ⍝ ABSOLUTE VALUE
[3]       MADRPOS←11ρ0
[4]       ⍝ SUBTRACTION
[5]       MADRMIN←(11ρ2)⊤1
[6]       ⍝ MULTIPLICATION
[7]       MADRMPY←(11ρ2)⊤2
[8]       ⍝ DIVISION
[9]       MADRDIV←(11ρ2)⊤5
        ∇

        ⍝ REFERENCE:                                     PROGRAM:
        ⍝ ARCHMICRO   MICROPROGRAMMING ARCHITECTURE        6-4
```

Program 6-6   Microprogram calls.

bits, while for a complete design, the number of microwords will be an order of magnitude larger again.

The increase in detail is typical for the progression of the design from architecture via implementation to realization. To cope with this increase in detail, various automatic design tools may be introduced. Thus, it is possible to generate the contents of a microword or a portion of the microstore automatically from the gate program. As stated in Section 2-13, such an automatic generation constitutes a static verification of the content of the microstore.

It also is possible to proceed in the reverse direction and automatically reconstruct from the microword the original gate program. Thus, the designer can satisfy himself that the transition from gate program to microstorage content is performed correctly.

Implementation of Microprogramming

The datapath of the implementation of the microprogramming control is shown in Figure 6-7 and described by *PATHMICRO*, Program 6-8. Because of the simple organization there is no need for an initial algorithm and the datapath can be obtained directly from the architecture.

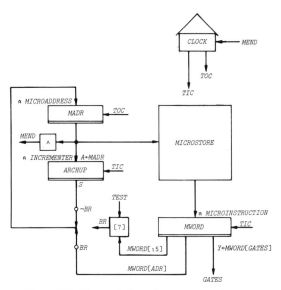

Figure 6-7 Datapath for microprogramming.

```
      ∇ PATHMICRO                                    ∇ CLOCK
 [1]    ค COUNTER INPUT                         [1]    CONT:TIC←1
 [2]    A←MADR                                  [2]    ค CONTROL ACTION
 [3]    ค COUNTER                               [3]    PATHMICRO
 [4]    ARCHUP                                  [4]    ค DATAPATH ACTION
 [5]    ค BRANCH CONDITION                      [5]    PATHPAR
 [6]    TEST←1,JZRO,RPOS,RCOR,OFLO,DLN0,DLN1,9ρ0 [6]   ค WAIT P1 NSEC
 [7]    BR←MWORD[YES]=TEST[2⊥MWORD[TST]]        [7]    TIC←0
 [8]    ค REGISTER INPUTS                       [8]    ค WAIT P2 NSEC
 [9]    IMADR←((~BR)∧S)∨BR∧MWORD[ADR]           [9]    TOC←1
[10]    ค FETCH MICROWORD                      [10]    ค CONTROL ACTION
[11]    →(~TIC)/READ+1                         [11]    PATHMICRO
[12]    READ:IMWORD←MICROSTORE[2⊥MADR;]        [12]    ค WAIT P3 NSEC
[13]    ค REGISTERS                            [13]    TOC←0
[14]    MADR←(TOC∧IMADR)∨(~TOC)∧MADR           [14]    ค WAIT P4 NSEC
[15]    MWORD←(TIC∧IMWORD)∨(~TIC)∧MWORD        [15]    →(~MEND)/CONT
[16]    ค GATES                                        ∇
[17]    Y←MWORD[GATES]
[18]    ค TESTCONDITION
[19]    MEND←∧/MADR
        ∇


      ∇ DECLMICRO
 [1]    ค MICROADDRESS REGISTER
 [2]    MADR←11ρ0
 [3]    ค MICROWORD REGISTER
 [4]    MWORD←40ρ0
        ∇

        ค REFERENCE:                                    PROGRAM:
        ค ARCHUP      INCREMENTING COUNTER ARCHITECTURE   2-51
        ค PATHPAR     PARALLEL DATAPATH                   5-16
```

Program 6-8 Microprogramming implementation.

Clock. The gate program for this datapath is reduced to the opening of the gates by *TIC* and *TOC* in an alternating sequence. These gate signals are generated by the circuit *CLOCK*. *CLOCK* can be considered to be available as a circuit element. Therefore, the regression of a datapath, which requires gate signals for its control, the gate signals in turn requiring a datapath, ends at this point.

CLOCK shows that for every datapath action two control actions are required.

Timing Signals. Since *TIC* and *TOC* are derived directly from the clock and are always present, they are called *timing signals*. *CLOCK* contains the length of

191

the timing signals *TIC* and *TOC* and the delay between the occurrence of these signals. This information is given in the comment and is not simulated.

Verification of the Implementation. *PATHMICRO* can now be verified against *ARCHMICRO*. In particular, selective tests can be made for the proper setting of the gate vector *Y* and the generation of the proper microaddress for the various test signals. For this purpose an auxiliary program can be used, which replaces *PATHPAR* in both programs and supplies the desired test signals. An example of such a program is given in Section 6-2.

When *PATHMICRO* is used instead of *ARCHMICRO* in the execution of an operation, the call of *ARCHMICRO* in Program 6-6 should be replaced by a specification of *MADR* and a call of *CLOCK*. Although interesting as an added test, the most effective test of the correctness of *PATHMICRO* is in its comparison with *ARCHMICRO*.

6-2 HARD-WIRED CONTROL

Microprogramming is less suitable for a very fast implementation. The microstore may add too much time to the elementary machine cycle. Also, fast equipment often uses several specialized processing units in parallel. Each of these requires its own control. The use of a separate store for each control tends to require too large an investment for the size of storage involved.

Since a hard-wired control is particularly suited for a specialized processing unit, its design will be illustrated with a specialized division unit. Two designs will be described. In the first design, the gate signals and internal states of the gate program are easily recognized. In the second design, a larger degree of encoding is used.

Decoded Control

Decoded Address.   In contrast to the binary addressing used in microprogramming, an address using a 1-out-of-*N* code is quite feasible for a specialized control. Such a code minimizes the equipment for address incrementation and word selection.

The circuit of Figure 6-9, described by *CTLDIV*, Program 6-10, shows a specialized division control. The circuit contains five flip-flops *DFF*, each of which represents a control state. At most, one flip-flop output will be 1 at a given moment.

Gate Control Matrix.   The flip-flops control the gate signals by means of a diode matrix, indicated schematically in Figure 6-9. Hence, there is no longer a need for the microword register.

The Whirlwind computer of M.I.T. (1951) was one of the first computers that systematically used such a diode matrix for internal control.

Compression. *CTLDIV*, line 4, selects a row from the gate matrix. This expression uses the compression operator, /. The slash is used here as a dyadic operator in contrast to the use of the slash in conjunction with another operator in the reduction operations, first encountered in *PREDICT*100, Program 2-28. *Compression* eliminates from the right operand those elements that correspond to a 0 in the left operand. It selects from the right operand those elements that correspond to a 1 in the left operand. Thus 0 0 0 1 0 / 1 2 3 4 5 gives 4.

When applied to a matrix, each row of the matrix is compressed as specified by the left operand. To apply compression along another coordinate, the number of this coordinate should be specified to the right of the slash. Thus in *CTLDIV*, line 4, the compression is applied to the elements of the columns by stating /[0]. Since at most one element of *DFF* is 1, a row is selected from *GATEMATRIX*.

The compression operator has already been used in the branch statements of the various programs. In those statements, the left operand is either 0 or 1. As a result, the target of the branch is either the label or an empty vector. A branch to an empty vector is defined in APL as no branch, hence a continuation of the normal sequence. Thus, the conditional branch is obtained by the standard use of the compression operator.

Reduction of the Number of Gates. Since division is treated separate from other operations, the number of gates may now be reduced. Figure 6-9 already omits gates signals such as $Y[ABS]$, which do not appear in division. As a next step, the gate signals that are the same may be combined. Thus, $Y[LOS]$, $Y[KOK]$, and $Y[TOK]$ are identical, as can be seen readily from the diode matrix or the corresponding *GATEMATRIX* of Program 6-10. Furthermore, it may be observed that $Y[TIW]$ is always 1. Therefore, this gate is omitted and register W is made to read in each cycle.

Don't-Care Gates. The gate programs indicate when a gate signal must be 1. It is assumed that otherwise the gate signal is 0. There are, however, situations in which a gate signal may be arbitrary or *don't care*.

Examples of don't-care values occur for the gate signals that control the inputs to registers. When the read-in signal to the register is absent, the input signal is not used, and its gate signals may have any value. Thus, it can be seen from *PATH-DIV*, Program 5-14, that $Y[SOP]$ is don't care when $Y[TIP]$ is 0. As a consequence, $Y[SOP]$ can be permanently 1 and therefore can be removed from the datapath and gate control. By more indirect reasoning, $Y[TIJ]$ can also be eliminated. $Y[TIJ]$ controls the reading into the counter. The output of the counter is only used during the reduction cycles. In the subsequent correction cycles, the counter may have any value, and therefore the read-in signal $Y[TIJ]$ and the input gate signals may be don't care.

Don't cares should be used with care. Not only may they easily introduce errors in the design, but also the circuit may become harder to understand and

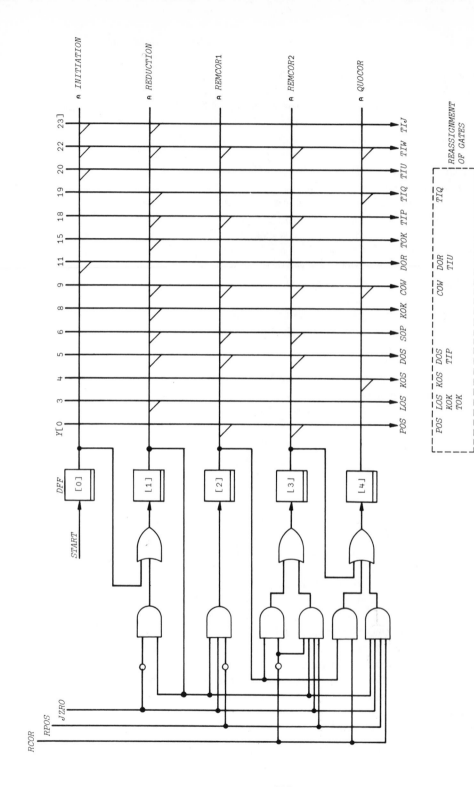

Figure 6-9 Decoded divider control.

```
      ∇ SPECDIV
[1]      ⍝ PROLOGUE
[2]      P←(ρDR)↑DD
[3]      Q←(ρDR)↓DD
[4]      R←DR
[5]      ⍝ CALL CONTROL
[6]      CTLDIV
[7]      ⍝ EPILOGUE
[8]      RM←P
[9]      QT←Q
[10]     OFDV←OFLO
      ∇
```

```
      ∇ CTLDIV                                    ∇ DECLCTLDIV
[1]      ⍝ START                          [1]      ⍝ CONTROL REGISTER
[2]      DFF← 1 0 0 0 0                    [2]      DFF←5ρ0
[3]      ⍝ GATES                               ∇
[4]      CONT:Y←,DFF/[0] GATEMATRIX
[5]      ⍝ DATAPATH ACTION
[6]      PATHDIV
[7]      ⍝ BRANCH CONDITIONS
[8]      IDFF[1]←DFF[0]∨DFF[1]∧~JZRO
[9]      IDFF[2]←DFF[1]∧JZRO∧~RPOS
[10]     IDFF[3]←(DFF[2]∧~RCOR)∨DFF[1]∧JZRO∧RPOS∧~RCOR
[11]     IDFF[4]←DFF[3]∨(DFF[2]∧RCOR)∨DFF[1]∧JZRO∧RPOS∧RCOR
[12]     ⍝ REGISTER
[13]     DFF←IDFF
[14]     ⍝ END CONDITION
[15]     →(∨/DFF)/CONT
      ∇
```

```
      GATEMATRIX
0 0 0 0 0 0 0 0 0 0 1 0 0 0 0 0 0 0 1 0 1 1
0 0 0 1 0 1 1 0 1 1 0 0 0 0 1 0 0 1 1 0 0 1 1
1 0 0 0 0 1 1 0 0 1 0 0 0 0 0 0 1 0 0 0 1 0
1 0 0 0 0 1 1 0 0 1 0 0 0 0 0 0 1 0 0 0 1 0
0 0 0 0 1 0 0 0 0 1 0 0 0 0 0 0 0 1 0 0 1 0
```

```
      ⍝ REFERENCE:                                        PROGRAM:
      ⍝ PATHDIV      DATAPATH FOR DIVIDER                  5-14
```

Program 6-10   Decoded divider control.

service. Signals that are not really used are a source of confusion. Also, the freedom to make alterations is noticeably restricted.

The number of gate signals is now reduced from 14 to 7. The reassigment of gate signals is given in *DIVCODE*, Program 6-13. Its effect is shown in the bottom line of Figure 6-9.

State Diagram of Control.   From *GATEDIV*, the gate program for division, the content of the diode matrix *GATEMATRIX* can be derived. *GATEDIV* also yields the state diagram for the control, shown in Figure 6-11.

In Figure 6-11 each circle identifies a state of the control. The names of the states refer to the actions of the gate program. The arrows indicate the transitions between the various states. The conditions for these transitions are shown next to the arrows.

Each control state is represented by a separate flip-flop in *CTLDIV*. The circuits that determine the transitions between these states are shown in the left part

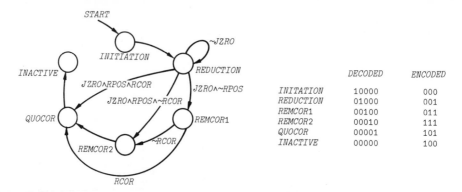

	DECODED	ENCODED
INITIATION	10000	000
REDUCTION	01000	001
REMCOR1	00100	011
REMCOR2	00010	111
QUOCOR	00001	101
INACTIVE	00000	100

Figure 6-11   State diagram of divider control.

of Figure 6-9 and are represented by lines 8 through 11 of *CTLDIV*. These 'and' and 'or' circuits directly match the statements next to the transitions in the state diagram.

Programmed Logic Array.   The hard-wired control, as illustrated by *CTLDIV*, can be implemented with a programmed logic array. A *programmed logic array* is normally realized as one integrated circuit. The inputs, here the test signals, are combined with a limited number of internal states by a *search* array of 'and' circuits. The outputs of the 'and's enter a *read* array of 'or' circuits. The outputs of the 'or's, in turn, activate a number of output signals, here the gate signals, and set the internal state.

An input signal may enter an 'and' with either the true or the inverse polarity or may not enter it at all. Thus, the and-or conditions of *CTLDIV*, lines 8 through 11, can readily be obtained.

The logic arrays are 'programmable,' in the sense that the inputs to the search and read arrays can be specified at a late moment in the design. A typical programmed logic array has 16 inputs, 20 outputs, 64 rows in the search and read arrays, and 8 internal flip-flops (Fleisher and Maissel, 1975). Logue et al. (1975) have implemented a terminal control unit with 7 programmed logic arrays using 18 inputs, 16 outputs, 70 rows, and 13 internal flip-flops.

Encoded Control

For the decoded control, a one-to-one correspondence exists between the diode matrix and the gate specifications of the gate program and between the flip-flops and the control states. The control circuit, however, can be reduced by encoding the control states and the gate control circuits.

Encoded Control States.   In *CTLDIV* the five active control states for division are represented by the five flip-flop outputs, using a 1-out-of-5 code. When all flip-flop outputs are 0, the control is inactive. These six control states can also be encoded with a 3-bit code. Sequential circuit theory indicates that if possible, it is desirable that adjacent control states have codes that differ in only one bit, thus with *distance* 1. Also, control states with the same output, such as *REMCOR*1 and *REMCOR*2, should preferably have distance 1.

In Figure 6-11 a 3-bit binary encoding of the control states is shown next to the coding used for *CTLDIV*. The resulting control circuit is shown in Figure 6-12 and described by *CTLDIVENC*, Program 6-13.

The flip-flops of *CTLDIVENC* are set-reset flip-flops, in contrast to the register, or D type, used in *CTLDIV*. The registers copy their input signals unchanged, as shown in *CTLDIV* line 13. For the set-reset flip-flop the 1 and the 0 state are controlled individually by set and reset signals, as shown in *CTLDIVENC* line 21. The next state of the control register is therefore determined in *CTLDIV* by one set of signals, lines 8 through 11, and in *CTLDIVENC* by two sets of signals, lines 15 through 19. In general the set-reset type flip-flop, as well as the *JK* type, is more economical in a hard-wired control circuit than the register type. The clarity of the design, however, suffers both from the encoding of the control states and from the use of the set-reset flip-flops.

Encoded Gate Control.   The diode matrix of *CTLDIV* is equivalent to a set of 'or' circuits. With binary-encoded control states, the gate signals, the outputs of the control, in general require an and-or circuit. Also, both polarities of the control flip-flops are used. With suitable encoding, however, most output circuits reduce to a single 'and' or 'or,' as shown in Figure 6-12. Thus, $Y[DOR]$ and $Y[TIU]$ are the inverse of $Y[COW]$. Since $Y[COW]$ is obtained directly from $DFF[2]$ the inverse signals can be taken from the opposite output $\sim DFF[2]$. Some outputs, such as $Y[TIQ]$ and $Y[KOS]$, are used in the setting of the control flip-flops.

Verification.   The correct action of a control of limited size, such as *CTLDIV-ENC*, can be tested exhaustively. *TESTGATE* and *TESTSTATE*, shown in Program 6-14, illustrate such a test. *TESTGATE* is inserted in *CTLDIVENC*, line 13, instead of *PATHDIV*. *TESTGATE* provides a printout of the gates that are 1 for each of the internal states. *TESTSTATE* is inserted just before the end test of *CTRDIVENC* and generates a complete transition table. Each row of this table represents a control state; the columns represent the eight possible values of the test signals as specified by *TESTSTATE* lines 12, 13 and 14.

The tests have been specialized for *CTLDIVENC*. It is possible, and in some cases desirable, to generalize these tests. The relative simplicity of the tests, however, makes it attractive for the designer to develop his test programs as he proceeds with his design.

Control Cost.   *CTLDIV* uses 5 flip-flops, 9 input circuits, and 4 'or' circuits in the matrix. *CTLDIVENC* uses 3 flip-flops, 6 set-reset circuits, and 4 output circuits. The reduction in circuits from *CTLDIV* to *CTLDIVENC* is marginal, while the loss in clarity is appreciable.

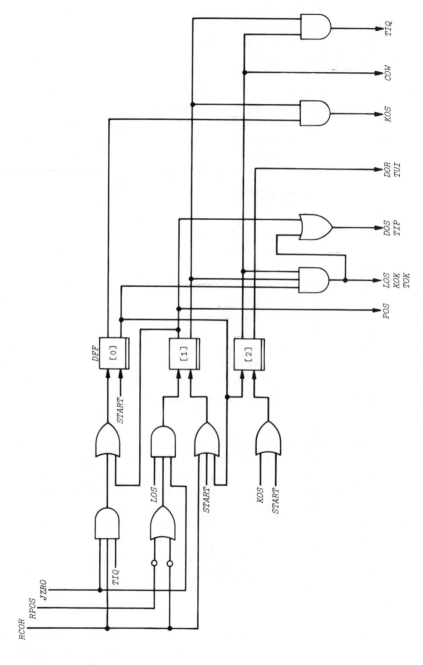

Figure 6-12 Encoded divider control.

```
     ∇ CTLDIVENC                                        ∇ DECLCTLDIVENC
[1]    ⍝ START                                   [1]     ⍝ CONTROL REGISTER
[2]    DFF← 0 0 0                                [2]     DFF←3ρ0
[3]    ⍝ GATES                                          ∇
[4]    Y[SOP,TIW,TIJ]←1
[5]  CONT:Y[POS]←DFF[1]                                 ∇ DIVCODE
[6]    Y[LOS,KOK,TOK]←(~DFF[0])∧(~DFF[1])∧DFF[2]   [1]    ⍝ ADDER INPUT GATES
[7]    Y[KOS]←DFF[0]∧~DFF[1]                      [2]     POS←1
[8]    Y[DOS,TIP]←DFF[1]∨Y[LOS]                   [3]     LOS←2
[9]    Y[COW]←DFF[2]                              [4]     KOS←5
[10]   Y[DOR,TIU]←~DFF[2]                         [5]     DOS←3
[11]   Y[TIQ]←(~DFF[1])∧DFF[2]                    [6]     ⍝ REGISTER INPUT GATES
[12]   ⍝ DATAPATH ACTION                          [7]     SOP←0
[13]   PATHDIV                                    [8]     KOK←2
[14]   ⍝ BRANCH CONDITIONS                        [9]     COW←6
[15]   SETDFF[0]←DFF[1]∨JZRO∧RPOS∧Y[TIQ]          [10]    DOR←4
[16]   SETDFF[1]←Y[LOS]∧JZRO∧(~RPOS)∨~RCOR        [11]    ⍝ CONTROL GATES
[17]   RESETDFF[1]←DFF[0]∨RCOR                    [12]    TOK←2
[18]   SETDFF[2]←~DFF[0]                          [13]    ⍝ REGISTER READ-IN SIGNALS
[19]   RESETDFF[2]←Y[KOS]                         [14]    TIP←3
[20]   ⍝ REGISTERS                                [15]    TIQ←7
[21]   DFF←SETDFF∨(~RESETDFF)∧DFF                 [16]    TIU←4
[22]   ⍝ END CONDITION                            [17]    TIW←0
[23]   →(~Y[KOS])/CONT                            [18]    TIJ←0
     ∇                                                  ∇
```

```
     ⍝ REFERENCE:                        PROGRAM:
     ⍝ PATHDIV     DATAPATH FOR DIVIDER  5-14
```

Program 6-13   Encoded divider control.

```
     ∇ TESTSTATE;Z                                           TRANSITION
[1]    ⍝ INSERT PRIOR TO END CONDITION IN CTLDIVENC     1  1  1  1  1  1  1  1
[2]    ⍝ ELIMINATE PATHDIV FORM CTLDIVENC               1  1  1  1  3  3  7  5
[3]    ⍝ INITIALISE WITH X←0 AND TRANSITION←8 8ρ8       7  5  7  5  7  5  7  5
[4]    ⍝ RECORDING OF TRANSITION                        7  5  7  5  7  5  7  5
[5]    TRANSITION[⌊X÷8;8|X]←2⊥DFF                        4  4  4  4  4  4  4  4
[6]    ⍝ INCREMENT                                      4  4  4  4  4  4  4  4
[7]    X←64|X+1                                         4  4  4  4  4  4  4  4
[8]    ⍝ CONTROL FLIP-FLOPS SET                         5  5  5  5  5  5  5  5
[9]    Z← 2 2 2 2 2 ⊤X
[10]   DFF←Z[0 1 2]
[11]   ⍝ TEST SIGNALS SET
[12]   JZRO←Z[3]
[13]   RPOS←Z[4]
[14]   RCOR←Z[5]
[15]   ⍝ ELIMINATION OF END CONTROL
[16]   Y[KOS]←0
     ∇
```

```
     ∇ TESTGATE
[1]    ⍝ INSERT INSTEAD OF PATHDIV IN CTLDIV OR CTLDIVENC
[2]    ⍝ PRINT GATEVECTOR
[3]    Y
[4]    ⍝ TEST SIGNALS FOR STRAIGHT PATH THROUGH CONTROL
[5]    JZRO←1
[6]    RPOS←0
[7]    RCOR←0
     ∇
```

Program 6-14   Exhaustive control tests.

Application of Sequential Circuit Theory.   Further marginal improvements may
be obtained by the use of sequential circuit theory. In that case the identity of the
flip-flops disappears, resulting in an even greater loss of clarity. This may explain
why sequential circuit theory has only limited application in computer design.

Hard-Wired Control Application.   The PDP11/20 uses hard-wired control, as does the PDP11/45 floating-point unit. The CDC 6600 also is a hard-wire controlled computer. Of System/360 and System/370 only Models 70 and 91 use hard-wired control. Except for the PDP11/20 all these examples represent high-performance models, which is indeed the main application area of hard-wired control. The high-performance CDC STAR-100 computer, however, uses microprogramming, indicating the importance of that technique even in the high-performance area.

6-3 ENCODED MICROPROGRAMMING CONTROL

The control organization of *ARCHMICRO*, which is used in Section 6-1 to explain the principle of microprogramming, is rather limited in the decisions that can be made and the number of gates that can be controlled.

The lack of power of *ARCHMICRO* is illustrated by the microprogram for division shown in words 5 through 11 of the microstore of Table 6-5. This program requires seven instructions, even though only five control states are involved. As shown in the state diagram of Figure 6-11, the state identifying the reduction cycles has transitions to itself and to three other states. Since the microinstruction allows only one branch, two extra microinstructions are required. These are the instructions in locations 7 and 10, which contain no gate settings. Also, it may be observed that the few operations of the first sections of Chapter 5 already use 24 gates. For a complete computer a few hundred gates may easily be required, which implies a very large word size.

In this section several modifications of the simple horizontal microprogramming structure will be discussed. These modifications involve a more effective specification of the instruction sequence and of the gate settings, usually resulting in the encoding of the specification. Hence, the resulting organization is called *encoded*, or *quasi-horizontal*, microprogramming.

The various design alternatives will be discussed by contrasting the organization of Section 6-1 with that of Figure 6-16, as described by *ARCHMICROENC*, Program 6-17. Figure 6-15 gives the microinstruction format for *ARCHMICRO-ENC*. The microinstruction is described in terms of the fields specified by *MICRO-ENCFIELD*, Program 6-17.

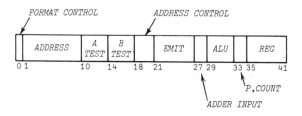

Figure 6-15   Encoded microinstruction format.

Instruction Sequence

A microstore may contain several hundred to several thousand words. In the example of *ARCHMICRO*, a capacity of 2048 words is assumed. This capacity requires a binary address of 11 bits. The operations that have been discussed up to now require only a small number of microwords. For a complete computer, however, the number will be increased considerably.

Explicit Successor Address. In *ARCHMICRO*, the normal successor address is obtained by incrementing the current microaddress with 1. As an alternative to this procedure, a separate address field can be used to indicate the normal successor. The additional address field extends the microwords and hence the microstorage bit capacity. When many unconditional branches occur in a microprogram, however, this solution will reduce the total number of microwords and may reduce the total number of bits involved.

In *ARCHMICRO* an explicit successor address would extend the microwords from 40 to 51 bits. The three instructions for multiplication, words 2 through 4 in Table 6-5, can then be replaced by two instructions, which reduces the number of bits from 120 to 102. If, more general, one unconditional branch occurs every five instructions, then the extension of the word is compensated by the reduction of the number of words.

ARCHMICROENC illustrates the use of an explicit successor address. The field *ADR*, bits 1 through 9, of the instruction supply the nine high-order address bits. The two low-order bits are specified separately in conjunction with the branch decisions.

Decision. The change in instruction sequence caused by a decision is, in essence, a conditional branch. Such a branch may be specified in a separate instruction, as is usually the case in the machine language. An implementation sequence requires many branches, however, as shown by the gate programs of Chapter 5. Therefore, a separate instruction would be too time-consuming. Hence, each instruction usually contains its own branch conditions, as is the case for *ARCHMICRO* and *ARCHMICROENC*.

Address Truncation. In *ARCHMICRO*, almost half of the instruction is used for the branch. To reduce this number of bits, a shorter address can be used, which replaces only the low-order bits of the microaddress when a branch address is formed. The branch is now restricted to the neighborhood of the current instruction. Such a reduction of the address size is called *address truncation*.

Multiple Tests. Often, more than one test is required for a given datapath action, such as the four-way branch in the division algorithm. The elementary solution takes several microwords for such a decision. As an alternative, several test fields and associated address fields may be introduced in the microinstruction. These multiple tests may be combined according to a ladder or a tree structure.

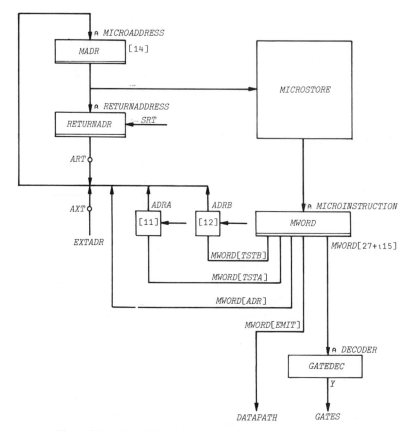

Figure 6-16 Encoded microprogramming organization.

In the *ladder* structure, the tests are performed conceptually in sequence. The first test that succeeds results in using the associated branch address. If no test succeeds, the normal successor address is used.

In the *tree* structure, each test contributes to the branch address. The various contributions may be added or superimposed with an 'or.'

For N tests, the ladder yields $N + 1$ possible addresses and the tree $2 * N$ addresses. With both structures, address truncation normally is used.

ARCHMICROENC illustrates the uses of two test fields: the *A*-test field, bits 10 through 13, and the *B*-test field, bits 14 through 17. *ARCHMICROENC* lines 11 and 12 show that these fields include a 4-bit test specification. The explicit successor address eliminates the need of an inversion control. The addresses associated with the tests are truncated down to a single bit each, and therefore need not appear in the microinstruction. *ADRA*, the result of the *A*-test, replaces microaddress bit 9; *ADRB*, the result of the *B*-test, replaces bit 10, as shown in *ARCHMICROENC* line 14. Since both tests include the constants 0 and 1, an unconditional branch with a full address can be specified.

```
      ∇ ARCHMICROENC MADR;TESTA;TESTB
[1]     ⍝ READ MICROSTORE
[2]   CONT:MWORD←MICROSTORE[2⊥MADR;]
[3]     ⍝ GATE DECODING
[4]     GATEDEC
[5]     ⍝ DATAPATH ACTION
[6]     PATHPAR
[7]     ⍝ STORE RETURN ADDRESS
[8]   RETURN:→(~Y[SRT])/RETURN+3
[9]     RETURNADR←MADR
[10]    ⍝ BRANCH CONDITION
[11]    ADRA←(0,1,JZRO,OFLO,DLN0,11ρ0)[2⊥MWORD[TSTA]]
[12]    ADRB←(0,1,RPOS,RCOR,DLN1,11ρ0)[2⊥MWORD[TSTB]]
[13]    ⍝ NEW ADDRESS
[14]    MADR←(Y[ART]∧RETURNADR)∨(Y[AXT]∧(5ρ0),EXTADR, 0 0)∨MWORD[ADR],ADRA,ADRB
[15]    ⍝ END CONDITION
[16]    →(~∧/MADR)/CONT
      ∇


      ∇ MICROENCFIELD                          ∇ GATECODEM
[1]     ⍝ FORMAT CONTROL                   [1]   ⍝ MICROADDRESS CONTROL
[2]     FORMAT←0                           [2]   ⍝ STORE RETURN ADDRESS
[3]     ⍝ MICROADDRESS                     [3]   SRT←24
[4]     ADR←1+⍳9                           [4]   ⍝ USE RETURN ADDRESS
[5]     ⍝ TEST FIELDS                      [5]   ART←25
[6]     TSTA←10+⍳4                         [6]   ⍝ USE EXTERNAL ADDRESS
[7]     TSTB←14+⍳4                         [7]   AXT←26
[8]     ⍝ MICROADDRESS CONTROL           ∇
[9]     ACT←18+⍳3
[10]    ⍝ EMIT FIELD
[11]    EMIT←21+⍳6
[12]    ⍝ ADDER INPUT FIELD
[13]    AFLD←27+⍳2
[14]    ⍝ ALU CONTROL AND REGISTER INPUT FIELDS
[15]    ALU←29+⍳4
[16]    PFLD←33
[17]    CNTFLD←34
[18]    ⍝ REGISTER READ-IN FIELD
[19]    REG←35+⍳7
      ∇


        ⍝ REFERENCE:                            PROGRAM:
        ⍝ GATEDEC        GATE DECODER           6-20
        ⍝ PATHPAR        PARALLEL DATAPATH       5-16
```

Program 6-17 Encoded microprogramming architecture.

External Branch Address. *OPERATION*, Program 5-1, employs in line 1 a multiple branch based upon the instruction bits 4 through 7. In a microprogram, such a multiple branch could be performed with a multitude of tests. It is simpler, however, to use the instruction code bits as part of the microaddress. This can be achieved by feeding a number of bits from the datapath to the microaddress under control of a gate. In this case, a test signal, as shown in Figure 5-10, should be understood to include selected data bits as well, as shown in Figure 6-18.

Return Address. A given sequence of microinstructions may be required at various places in a microprogram. Such a sequence can be treated as a subroutine, which only needs to reside once in storage. In returning from the subroutine, the

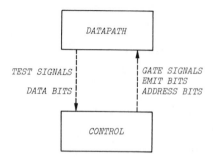

Figure 6-18   Relation of datapath to control.

location that called the routine must be known. To this end, a *return address* may be used. The calling program should set the return address, and the subroutine can employ it at the end of its execution.

The return address can be introduced simply in the microprogram organization by means of a register and a set of gates to fill it and to use its content. More-elaborate structures can be conceived, but actually the use of the simple return address is already quite limited.

ARCHMICROENC shows in lines 8 and 9 how the return address is stored under control of the gate *SRT*. In line 14, the return address, the explicit successor address, and the external branch address form the next microinstruction address. Usually the low-order return address bits are modified by the test fields such that the program does not return to the address at which the return address is stored.

Interrupt.   A microprogramming organization may also include an interrupt facility, similar to the one discussed in Chapter 1. This facility is particularly attractive when the processor must be able to handle input and output signals. The architecture of interruptions is further discussed in Chapter 7.

Microstorage Content.   Table 6-19 gives the content of the microstore, when used with the encoded microprogramming organization. The example shows that the locations of the various routines are intermixed as a result of the instruction sequencing organization. For the same reason two words are required for the reduction cycle of division. The number of extra branches that are executed in division is reduced from two to one, compared with the organization of *ARCH-MICRO*. The example also illustrates that the number of gate bits is reduced considerably. This reduction will be discussed next.

Gate-Signal Specification

ARCHMICROENC assumes a storage capacity of 2048 words. Therefore, adding 1 bit to the word length requires 2048 extra bits. As a consequence, the bits in the instruction must be used economically.

```
                                                  PFLD
                     FORMAT    TSTA     ACT        AFLD   |CNTFLD
                     ↓ADR_____↓↓↓↓TSTB↓↓↓EMIT__↓↓ALU_↓↓REG____
MADRPOS              0111111111000100010000000000001011001000000   0                      POS
MADRMIN              0111111111000100010000000000010110100100000   1                      MIN
MADRMPY              0000000001000000000000000000000010000000011   2   INITIATION  MPY
                     0000000000000000000000000000000000000000000   3   -
                     0000000001001000000000000000011010010110011   4   ADDITION    MPY
MADRDIV              0000000001000000000000000000000011000001011   5   INITIATION  DIV
                     0111111111000100010000000000000000000000000   6   END         MPY
                     0000000000000000000000000000000000000000000   7   -
                     0000000001000100010000000000101111110110011   8   REDUCTION   DIV
                     0000000001000100010000000000101111110110011   9   REDUCTION   DIV
                     0000000001100000011000000000011110100100010  10   REMCOR1     DIV
                     0000000011000000110000000000000000000000011  11   BRANCH      DIV
                     0000000001100000010000000000011110100100010  12   REMCOR2     DIV
                     0111111111000100010000000000111100000010010  13   QUOCOR      DIV
```

Figure 6-19 Content of encoded microstore.

As a first step toward greater bit efficiency the redundancy in the gate specifications may be removed. This involves the recognition of unnecessary and common gates, and the use of don't-care values, as explained in Section 6-2.

Once the designer is satisfied that he has the proper number of gates, the number of microword bits may be reduced by encoding the gate specifications. Thus, a departure is made from the straight horizontal code as proposed originally by Wilkes. In practice, this is almost always the case.

Two methods that may be used in a partially encoded microinstruction are the compression of gate signals and the reinterpretation of microword bits.

Compression of Gate Signals. One way of reducing the number of micro-word bits is to encode a group of gate signals. As an example, line 2 of *PATHPAR* shows that the gates $Y[POS]$, $Y[LOS]$, and $Y[KOS]$ are not intended to appear simultaneously. Hence, these three gate signals can be controlled by 2 bits of the microinstruction.

The decoding of the gate fields of *ARCHMICROENC* is given by *GATEDEC*, Program 6-20. Line 2 gives the decoding of *POS*, *LOS*, and *KOS*. Lines 4 through 13 show an encoding in which more than one output may be 1 at a given moment. Thus, when the microinstruction bits *ALU* are 0 1 1 1, representing the value 7, the gates $Y[ROS]$, $Y[ABS]$, and $Y[MIN]$ are all 1. Line 17 shows that the read-in signals of the registers are not encoded.

Since the specification of the gate decoder is at a high level, the details of the decoders are not shown. The implementation of decoders is described in Chapter 7.

Reinterpretation of Microword Bits. Another method of encoding reinterprets parts of the instruction bits under control of some of the remaining bits. Thus, the gate signals $Y[ROS]$, $Y[MIN]$, and $Y[ABS]$ do not appear in multiplication and division, while the gate signals $Y[TOK]$, $Y[KOK]$, and $Y[SOM]$ are absent in the load and add instructions. Therefore, *MWORD*[31] could be used to apply *MWORD* [17 29 28] either to the first group of gate signals or to the second group

```
      ∇ GATEDEC
[1]     ⍝ ADDER INPUT GATES
[2]     Y[POS,LOS,KOS]← 1 2 3 =2⊥MWORD[AFLD]
[3]     ⍝ ALU CONTROL AND REGISTER INPUT GATES
[4]     Y[MOR,DOR]← 2 3 =2⊥MWORD[ALU]
[5]     Y[ROS]←∨/ 4 5 6 7 =2⊥MWORD[ALU]
[6]     Y[ABS]←∨/ 5 7 =2⊥MWORD[ALU]
[7]     Y[MIN]←∨/ 6 7 =2⊥MWORD[ALU]
[8]     Y[SOM]←∨/ 8 9 10 11 =2⊥MWORD[ALU]
[9]     Y[MOS]←∨/ 9 11 =2⊥MWORD[ALU]
[10]    Y[BOS]←∨/ 10 11 =2⊥MWORD[ALU]
[11]    Y[DOS]←∨/ 14 15 =2⊥MWORD[ALU]
[12]    Y[KOK]←∨/ 13 15 =2⊥MWORD[ALU]
[13]    Y[COW]←∨/ 12 14 15 =2⊥MWORD[ALU]
[14]    Y[SOP]←MWORD[PFLD]
[15]    Y[TOK]←MWORD[CNTFLD]
[16]    ⍝ REGISTER READ-IN SIGNALS
[17]    Y[TIB,TIP,TIQ,TIU,TIV,TIW,TIJ]←MWORD[REG]
[18]    ⍝ MICRO-ADDRESS CONTROL
[19]    Y[SRT,ART,AXT]←MWORD[ACT]
      ∇
```

Program 6-20   Gate decoder.

of gate signals, thus saving two instruction bits. This procedure is illustrated in Program 6-21.

```
    ∇ REINTERPRETE
[1]   Y[ROS,MIN,ABS,TOK,KOK,SOM]←(MWORD[31]∧MWORD[17 29 28]),(~MWORD[31])∧MWORD[17 29 28]
    ∇
```

Program 6-21   Reinterpretation of microword bits.

Microinstruction Formats. As an extreme form of reinterpreting the bits of the microword, several microinstruction formats may be introduced. Thus, based upon a few format bits, all remaining bits of the microword may be reinterpreted, leading to different test, address, and gate fields and a different interpretation of each of these fields.

In *MICROENCFIELD*, line 2, bit 0 of the microinstruction is used as a format bit. When *MWORD*[0] is 0, the microinstruction is interpreted as shown in *ARCHMICROENC*. When *MWORD*[0] is 1, an alternative interpretation is given to the instruction bits. The alternative interpretation is not shown.

These methods of encoding reduce the number of possible combinations of gates. Unless the combinations are inherently mutually exclusive, the capabilities of the processing unit will be limited. Nevertheless, it is useful to assure the efficient use of the microstore (Grasselli and Montanari, 1970).

Since the microstores are usually available in preferred dimensions, the designer will aim at these values rather than at an absolute minimum.

Emission of Data from the Microword. It may be desirable to introduce constants, or bit configurations, from the microprogram into the datapath. Part of the gate field may be used for this purpose. Such a part is called an *emit field*. When it is considered inefficient to have such a field in all microwords, the field may be encoded with the gate signals.

The emit field of *ARCHMICROENC* is shown in Figure 6-15 and in *MICRO-ENCFIELD*, line 11. When the emit field is also used for the addressing of the local store, it coincides with the field *LSAD*, as used in the data-selection implementation of *PATHDATA*, Program 5-29.

Design Example. An example of the design of a microinstruction format is the procedure followed for the Hewlett-Packard 5345A electronic counter (Felsenstein, 1974).

In the initial design a horizontal microinstruction of 59 bits was used, which contained a 6-bit test field, a 7-bit successor address field, a 7-bit branch address field, and 39 directly specified gate bits.

In the second design phase, the branch address was eliminated and the successor address was shortened to 6 bits. The low-order address bit was supplied as a result of the test, similar to *ARCHMICROENC*. Furthermore, the content of the test field was identified with the successor address, thus eliminating the need for this field. This identification is peculiar to the equipment concerned and is by no means generally applicable. The microinstruction thus comprised a 6-bit address field and a 39-bit gate field, with a total of 45 bits.

In a third design phase, the address field and the gate signals were jointly encoded. A computer program was used which assigned optimum values to the don't cares. As a result, the microinstruction was reduced to 29 bits. Since storage was constructed, from modules that were effectively 8 bits wide, a 32-bit microword was used, leaving 3 spare bits.

Microprogramming Application. The encoded microprogram control is widely used. The PDP11 Models 5, 40, and 45 are examples of very limited encoding, approaching horizontal organization. Each uses 256 words, with 40 to 80 bits. Model 40 uses 56 bits, with 13 bits for addressing, 37 bits for datapath control, 3 bits for clock control, and 3 bits for bus control. There is an explicit successor address of 8 bits. Various test conditions can make the low-order address bits 1.

For System/360, Model 50 may serve as an example. In it, 2816 microwords are used. The word is 90 bits wide including two spare positions and 3 parity bits. There are two formats: the CPU mode and the input/output (I/O) mode format. The two formats differ in the interpretation of 22 gate field bits.

The 6 high-order address bits of the next instruction address are obtained from an address field of the microinstruction. The next 4 bits are obtained either from the microinstruction or as external bits from the datapath. The two low-order bits are set from two test fields of 6 and 5 bits each, similar to *ARCHMICROENC*. A total of 23 bits are used for address control. The gates are encoded with 1 to 5 bits and include 6 bits of local store control, a 4-bit emit field, 7 bits of adder input control, 3 bits of adder function control, and 6 staticizer control bits (Husson, 1970).

The System/370 Model 158 uses 8000 microwords of 72 bits each. The microword includes 3 parity bits, 18 address-control bits, 5 staticizer control bits, 8 emit bits, and 12 other gate fields of 1 to 5 bits. Twenty-two bits are under mode control. The next instruction address is determined by a 7-bit truncated address field, which covers either address bits 0 through 6 or 4 through 10. An external address can be entered in bits 7 through 10. Bits 11 and 12 are again specified by an A- and a B-test field. The microprogram uses a simple return address.

Microprogramming control, including address registers and branching control, is also available as one integrated circuit. An example is the Intel 3001, which gives the control for 512 microwords. The microstore itself can be obtained in a large variety of dimensions and technologies as integrated circuits.

6-4 VERTICAL MICROPROGRAMMING
CONTROL

In the horizontal microprogramming organization, each gate corresponds to 1 bit in the microword. In the quasi-horizontal microprogramming, groups of bits are encoded. The other extreme organization gives each unique set of gate values a separate code. The gate signals now are completely encoded. This procedure is called *vertical* microprogramming.

The vertical microprogramming organization has the appearance of a primitive computer. The operation repertoire of this computer is the list of different gate states of the datapaths.

Figure 6-23 and *ARCHMICROVER*, Program 6-24, show a simple vertical microprogram organization. The formats of the microinstructions are given in Figure 6-22. There is a branch format and a gate format. Because of the vertical organization, the microword length can be reduced to 18 bits. To make comparison easy, the organization of *ARCHMICROVER* is kept similar to that of *ARCH-MICRO* and *ARCHMICROENC*.

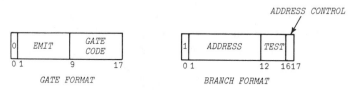

Figure 6-22 Vertical microinstruction formats.

Picocoding. Vertical microcoding requires a complete decoder, which translates gate codes into gate signals. Again, this decoding can be done in an orderly fashion with the aid of storage. Such a store is called a *picostore*, in contrast to the microstore. The gate code now selects a word from the picostore, and the bits of this word individually control a gate signal. This procedure is advantageous when a large number of gates is required for a large microprogram but only a relatively small number of different gate combinations occurs. Such a situation is especially suitable for a simple datapath, such as *PATHSIM*, Program 5-32.

If in *ARCHMICRO* the number of distinct control states is limited to 200, the word length can be reduced from $16 + 24$, or 40 bits, to $16 + 8$, or 24 bits. This saves 2048×16, or 32K bits. The picostore in this case would require 200 words of 24 bits; hence the net saving is about 27K bits.

Two-level Control. When one microinstruction is decoded into several successive picoinstructions, a two-level control organization arises. The initiative of the control now rests with the picocode, which interprets the microcode, which in turn interprets the machine code.

The System/370 Model 125 approaches the two-level control in its service processor. This service processor uses a vertical microcode with instructions of 1, 2, or 4 bytes of 8 bits each. The microstore capacity is 12K bytes. The picostore is almost fully horizontal, with 256 words of 60 bits (Schunemann, 1974).

Another example of two-level control is the Burroughs B700. Its vertical microinstruction has two formats of 16 bits. One format refers to a horizontal picoinstruction of 54 bits in a picostore of 4K words (Flynn, 1975).

The term *nanocoding* is also used for the second level of control.

Read-only Store

A store whose content is not changed is equivalent to a decoder circuit. Such a storage is called a *read-only memory*, or *ROM*. In contrast, a read-and-write random-access store is called a *RAM*. The control stores discussed in this chapter are in first instance read-only stores.

Realization of Read-only Storage. The read-only store can be implemented by a normal read–write storage. As an alternative, a realization form may be used in which writing can be performed only once, or in which writing is considerably more difficult than reading, the *programmable read-only store*, or *PROM*. Thus, writing may occur during the manufacturing process by applying a final mask to the integrated circuit, the *mask programmable* store; or, the content of the store may be written during the machine construction, the *field programmable* store.

The microstore also may have a storage medium that can be physically interchanged. The storage content is placed in the storage medium during the manufacturing process. This method was used in the capacitive and the inductive read-only store. Thus, the System/360 Model 30 had a microstore whose content was determined by punching on cards. The absence or presence of a hole was capacitively sensed. In System/370 a microstore made of integrated circuits is loaded from a plastic disc when power is turned on. Here the disc is made interchangeable.

Application of Writable Control Store. When writing is easily realized, the content of the microstore may be changed late in the design of the system. This gives greater freedom to the designer and proves in practice to be very effective in

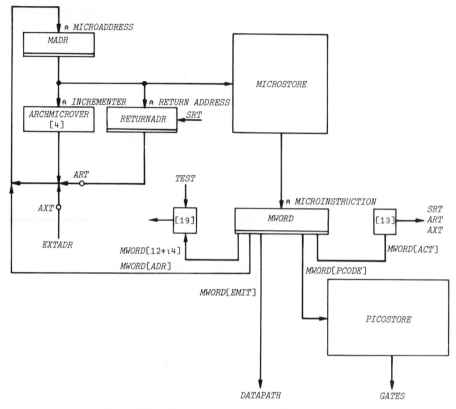

Figure 6-23 Vertical microprogramming organization.

improving the design schedule. Also, *engineering changes*, changes made after the design is in production, can be made relatively inexpensively. Finally, the content of the control store may be changed for diagnostic purposes. A special routine may be entered to provide system checkout as part of the power-on routine, or to provide fault location once a fault has been signaled.

The ability to change the microstore content easily allows a functional change of the equipment at a later date. Thus, a user could change his system according to his taste. The rigidity of the software, however, counteracts this pliability of the hardware.

Applicability of Microprogramming. The choice among the various types of microprogramming, including the use of a decoder instead of a storage unit, is determined by cost and performance. Besides the direct cost of the realization, the indirect cost must also be taken into account. One of the indirect advantages of microprogramming is its suitability to the automation of the design process, including easier verification and correction. Also, the design may be modified more readily for special applications. Finally, a small piece of equipment may implement a relatively elaborate architecture (Tucker, 1967; Rosin, 1969; Flynn, 1975).

210

```
      ∇ ARCHMICROVER MADR;TEST            ∇ MICROVERFIELD
[1]     ⍝ READ MICROSTORE           [1]     ⍝ FORMAT CONTROL
[2]     CONT:MWORD←MICROSTORE[2⊥MADR;]     [2]     FORMAT←0
[3]     ⍝ INCREMENT ADDRESS         [3]     ⍝ MICROADDRESS
[4]     MADR←(11ρ2)⊤1+2⊥MADR        [4]     ADR←1+⍳11
[5]     ⍝ TEST FOR BRANCH           [5]     ⍝ TEST FIELD
[6]     →MWORD[FORMAT]/MBRANCH      [6]     YES←12
[7]     ⍝ GATE DECODING             [7]     TST←13+⍳3
[8]     Y[⍳24]←PICOSTORE[2⊥MWORD[PCODE];]  [8]     ⍝ MICROADDRESS CONTROL
[9]     ⍝ DATAPATH ACTION           [9]     ACT←16+⍳2
[10]    PATHPAR                     [10]    ⍝ EMIT FIELD
[11]    →END                        [11]    EMIT←1+⍳8
[12]    ⍝ BRANCH                    [12]    ⍝ GATECODE
[13]  MBRANCH:Y[SRT,ART,AXT]← 1 2 3 =2⊥MWORD[ACT] [13]    PCODE←9+⍳9
[14]    ⍝ STORE RETURN ADDRESS              ∇
[15]  RETURN:→(~Y[SRT])/RETURN+3
[16]    RETURNADR←MADR
[17]    ⍝ BRANCH CONDITION
[18]    TEST←1,JZRO,RPOS,RCOR,OFLO,DLN0,DLN1,1ρ0
[19]    →(MWORD[YES]≠TEST[2⊥MWORD[TST]])/END
[20]    ⍝ NEW ADDRESS
[21]    MADR←(Y[ART]∧RETURNADR)∨(Y[AXT]∧(5ρ0),EXTADR, 0 0)∨MWORD[ADR]
[22]    ⍝ END CONDITION
[23]  END:→(~∧/MADR)/CONT
      ∇


      ⍝ REFERENCE:                      PROGRAM:
      ⍝ PATHPAR    PARALLEL DATAPATH       5-16
```

Program 6-24   Vertical microprogramming architecture.

Clock

The design of Figure 6-7 assumes a very simple pattern for the two timing signals, *TIC* and *TOC*. The time intervals for this pattern are not stated, since the delays of the circuit elements and the maximum number of levels of the datapath are not known. The time intervals also should match the delays that occur in the control itself. In particular, the time required for the reading of the microstore and the time required for the distribution of the timing signals should be taken into account. Finally, this system should match the storage cycle times. In particular, several elementary cycles may match one storage cycle. Thus, an elementary timing cycle for the machine may be found.

A schematic representation of the relation of the timing signals is shown in Figure 6-25. The figure shows that many actions must wait for the completion of the preceding action. Therefore, much equipment is active only part of the time. By using a larger degree of overlap, the equipment may be used more efficiently.

Timing of Gate Signals.   Figure 6-25 shows that not all gate signals have the same timing behavior. The gates that influence the datapath, like *ROS* and *ABS*, should be earlier than the read-in signals for the registers such as *TIP*. When the same logical signal is used for both purposes, as derived from the microcontrol, the gate signals must be modified to obtain the form suitable to its purpose. Such a modification may be performed in an 'and' circuit, combining the gate with a timing signal.

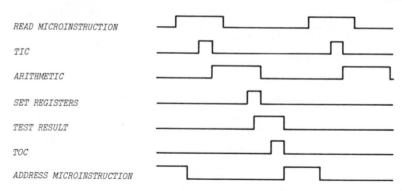

READ MICROINSTRUCTION

TIC

ARITHMETIC

SET REGISTERS

TEST RESULT

TOC

ADDRESS MICROINSTRUCTION

Figure 6-25   Relation of timing signals.

Timing of Test Signals.   In *PATHPAR* the test signals are derived from the register contents. As a result, the control must wait until the registers are set and the combinational test circuits take their final value, before the next control state can be determined. For many machines this procedure is far too slow. They determine the next machine state while the datapath action takes place. This overlap may be achieved by testing earlier in the datapath cycle, such as at the adder output, or by anticipating the result of the test by methods similar to those described in Chapter 8 for a pipeline organization. Even greater overlap is possible when the tests apply only to the datapath actions of preceding microinstructions.

The Sytem/370 Model 158, for example, fully overlaps the microstore and datapath actions. For the A-test, which controls the low-order address bit, both microwords are read and the proper word is chosen when the test value is known. Some test conditions are known in time for the B-test, some in time for the A-test, and some make neither test within one cycle and therefore have a two-cycle overlap.

In the design of the machine implementation, the clock appears rather late in the design cycle. In the design of the realization, the clock, in contrast, is one of the first major design subjects. As the implementer proceeds with his logical design, he will have to consult the designer of the realization to assure himself that the basic cycles and delays that are assumed match those of the realization.

REFERENCES

DAVIES, P. M.: "Readings in Microprogramming." *IBM Systems Journal*, vol. 11, no. 1, pp. 16–40 (1972).

FELSENSTEIN, R. E.: "An Example of State Machine Design." *Hewlett-Packard Journal*, vol. 25, no. 10, pp. 9–11 (June, 1974).

FLEISHER, H., and L. I. MAISSEL: "An Introduction to Array Logic." *IBM Journal of Research and Development*, vol. 19, no. 2, pp. 98–109 (March, 1975).

FLYNN, M. J.: "Microprogramming—Another Look at Internal Computer Control." *Proceedings of the IEEE*, vol. 63, no. 11, pp. 1554–1567 (November, 1975).

GRASSELLI, A., and U. MONTANARI: "On the Minimization of READ-ONLY Memories in Microprogrammed Digital Computers." *IEEE Transactions on Computers*, vol. C-19, no. 11, pp. 1111–1114 (November, 1970).

LOGUE, J. C., N. F. BRICKMAN, F. HOWLEY, J. W. JONES, and W. W. WU: "Hardware Implementation of a Small System in Programmable Logic Arrays." *IBM Journal of Research and Development*, vol. 19, no. 2, pp. 110–119 (March, 1975).

HUSSON, S. S.: *Microprogramming: Principles and Practices*. Prentice-Hall, Englewood Cliffs, N.J., 1970.

ROSIN, R. F.: "Contemporary Concepts of Microprogramming and Emulation." *Computing Surveys*, vol. 1, no. 4, pp. 197–212 (December, 1969).

SCHUNEMANN, C.: "Mikro- und Pico-Programmspeicher." In H. HASSELMEIER and W. SPRUTH: *Rechnerstrukturen*, pp. 36–74. R. Oldenbourg, Munich, 1974.

TUCKER, S. G.: "Microprogram control for System/360." *IBM Systems Journal*, vol. 6, no. 4, pp. 222–241 (1967).

WILKES, M. V.: *The Best Way to Design an Automatic Calculating Machine*, pp. 16–21. Report of Manchester University Computer Inaugural Conference, Manchester, July, 1951.

WILKES, M. V., and J. B. STRINGER: "Microprogramming and the Design of the Control Circuits in an Electronic Digital Computer." *Proceedings Cambridge Philosophical Society*, vol. 49, pt. 2, pp. 220–238 (April, 1953). Reprinted in C. G. Bell and A. Newell: *Computer Structures: Readings and Examples*, 335–340. McGraw-Hill, New York, 1971.

WILKES, M. V.: "The Growth and Interest in Microprogramming: A Literature Survey." *Computing Surveys*, vol. 1, no. 3, pp. 139–145 (1969).

EXERCISES

6-1   Determine for the control architecture *ARCHMICRO*, Program 6-4, the calling programs *MICROLOAD*, *MICRONEG*, and *MICROPLUS*, and the corresponding microcode content that matches the gate programs of Exercise 5-1. Assign the calling addresses *MADRLOAD*, *MADRNEG*, and *MADRPLUS*, respectively, and extend the microstore *MICROSTORE* as needed.

6-2   Give the content of *MICROSTORE* such that the series normalization of Exercise 5-15 can be performed by the microprogram organization *ARCH-MICRO*, Program 6-4.

6-3   Design a hard-wired control for the multiplication of *GATEMPY*, Program 5-9.

6-4   Reduce the specialized divider control of *CTLDIV*, Program 6-10, by replacing the diode matrix with an 'and-or' circuit.

6-5   Repeat Exercise 6-1 for the control architecture of *ARCHMICROENC*, Program 6-17.

6-6   Determine the content of *MICROSTORE*, Table 6-5, when the reduction in code bits of *REINTERPRETE*, Program 6-21, is introduced.

6-7   Change the test conditions of *ARCHMICROENC*, Program 6-17, such that no extra microinstructions are required for the division of *GATEDIV*, Program 5-14.

6-8   Design an encoded microprogram organization suited to the gate programs of Programs 5-33 and 5-34, which assume the simple datapath and the data-selection implementation of Programs 5-32 and 5-29.

6-9   Make a conversational function *MAKEMS* that can be introduced in *GATE*, Program 5-6, instead of the datapath call, such that upon execution of a gate program:
(a)   The gate-field bits of the microinstruction are properly set.
(b)   The user can indicate the location of the microword.
(c)   The user can indicate the value of the address field.
(d)   The user can indicate the test and its condition.
The microinstructions should be intended for *ARCHMICRO*, Program 6-4.

6-10   Repeat Exercise 6-9 for the microprogram organization of *ARCHMICRO-ENC*, Program 6-17.

6-11   Write a program *SHOWMS* that prints the names of the gates and tests and the decimal representation of the addresses that are specified by the words of *MICROSTORE*, as used with *ARCHMICRO*, Program 6-4. Use *SHOWMS* to verify the content of *MICROSTORE*.

6-12   Repeat Exercise 6-11 for the content of *MICROSTORE* as used with *ARCHMICROENC*, Program 6-17.

6-13   Write a program that determines, for a horizontal microstore:
(a)   Which gates are never used.
(b)   Which gates are always the same.

6-14   Give an implementation for *ARCHMICROENC*, Program 6-17.

6-15   Give an implementation for *ARCHMICROVER*, Program 6-24.

6-16   Determine the content of *MICROSTORE* and *PICOSTORE*, as used by *ARCHMICROVER*, Program 6-24, for the Load Absolute, Subtract, Multiply, and Divide operations.

6-17   Change the hard-wired control of *CTLDIV*, Program 6-10, to a control that resembles the original microprogramming proposal of Wilkes (1951):
(a)   The control states are identified by a binary code in a 3-bit register *DSTATE*.
(b)   The output of *DSTATE* is decoded to 5 lines.
(c)   A sequence matrix *SEQMATRIX* is used, which has the decoded output of *DSTATE*, as well as the signals *JZRO*, *RPOS*, and *RCOR* and their inverses as rows.
(d)   The columns of *SEQMATRIX* form the input of *DSTATE*.

7 SYSTEM CONTROL

System control sees to it that the operations of a system are performed in the right sequence and with the proper operands. The design process that was followed for such operations as addition, multiplication, and division can therefore be repeated for system control.

System control, when built as a separate entity, constitutes the instruction unit, or I-box. The I-box and the previously discussed execution unit, or E-box, together form a processor.

Figure 7-1 shows the relation of the instruction unit with the execution unit and storage. The figure shows the systems components that were originally presented in Figure 1-1 except for the input and the output. Input and output, however, are also handled by processors. Therefore, the design of system control completes the design of a processing unit.

PROCESSOR, Program 7-2, summarizes the architecture of a processor. *OPERATION*, line 5 of *PROCESSOR*, represents the execution of the operation specified in the instruction, as discussed in Chapter 5. In the present chapter, the actions relating to the instruction sequence, the fetching of the operands, and the storing of the results, as represented by *IFETCH*, *BRANCH*, *INTERRUPT*, *ODFETCH*, and *RLSTORE*, will be considered.

Organization of the Chapter

The architecture of system control is described in Section 7-1. The implementation of this architecture encompasses the design of the system organization and the design of individual system components.

The preceding chapters started with the components, such as an adder, and ended with the system organization, such as a microprogram processor. Since we

215

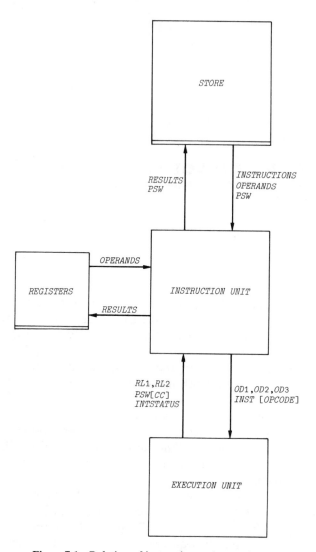

Figure 7-1 Relation of instruction and execution unit.

can be confident by now that a suitable implementation can be found for the components that are encountered in an overall system, the order of treatment is reversed in this chapter. This order better reflects the actual design procedure for a digital system. Hence, in Section 7-2 the organization of the system control implementation, including its datapath and gate programs, will be described. In Sections 7-3 through 7-6, the system components typical for system control, such as encoders, decoders, and priority circuits, are treated. The reader may also go first to Chapter 8 and return then to Sections 7-3 through 7-6.

```
      ∇ PROCESSOR;OD1;OD2;OD3;RL1;RL2;INST;INTSTATUS       ∇ DECLPROCESSOR
[1]     CONT:→INTERRUPT/CONT                          [1]    ⍝ MAIN STORE
[2]     IFETCH                                        [2]    STORE←(N,8)ρ0
[3]     →BRANCH/CONT                                  [3]    ⍝ GENERAL PURPOSE REGISTERS
[4]     ODFETCH                                       [4]    GPR← 16 32 ρ0
[5]     OPERATION                                     [5]    ⍝ PROGRAM STATUS WORD
[6]     RLSTORE                                       [6]    PSW←64ρ0
[7]     →CONT                                            ∇
      ∇

      ⍝ REFERENCE:                                          PROGRAM:
      ⍝ BRANCH       BRANCH ARCHITECTURE                      7-7
      ⍝ IFETCH       INSTRUCTION FETCH ARCHITECTURE           7-4
      ⍝ INTERRUPT    INTERRUPTION ARCHITECTURE                7-10
      ⍝ ODFETCH      OPERAND FETCH ARCHITECTURE               7-12
      ⍝ OPERATION    OPERATION REPERTOIRE ARCHITECTURE        5-1
      ⍝ RLSTORE      RESULT STORE ARCHITECTURE
```

Program 7-2   Processor architecture.

7-1 ARCHITECTURE OF SYSTEM CONTROL

The control of a computer uses instructions that are executed in a specified order. These instructions specify the operand and result locations as well as the operation to be performed. In this section, the architecture of the instruction sequence and operand fetch will be discussed. System/360 will again be taken as an example.

Instruction Sequence

Instructions are executed in the numerical order of their addresses. The instruction address must be incremented during the execution of the instruction with an amount that matches the length of the instruction.

The components of the I-box are shown in Figure 7-3. The instruction register *INST* is shown on the left side of this figure and the instruction address on the right side. The instruction address is placed with other control information in the *Program Status Word* (PSW) register. The field *IADR* of this register contains the instruction address. For ease of expression, the instruction address itself will be called *IADR*, as will be the case with the other fields of the PSW, shown in *PSW-FIELD*, Program 7-4.

Instruction Fetch.   *IFETCH*, Program 7-4, gives the architecture of the instruction addressing for the instruction formats of Figure 1-3. As stated in Chapter 1, the instruction length can be one, two, or three syllables. A *syllable* comprises 16 bits and is always located on an even-byte boundary. *IFETCH*, line 2, obtains bits 0 and 1 of the instruction from which it determines the instruction length. This length is recorded as the 2-bit *instruction length code, ILC*, which again is part of the PSW. The *ILC* is available to the program in case of an interrupt. The instruction *INST* is obtained in *IFETCH*, line 4, using *ILC*. Since this is an architectural description, the double reference to storage in lines 2 and 4 is no problem. In an implementation, of course only one reference need be made.

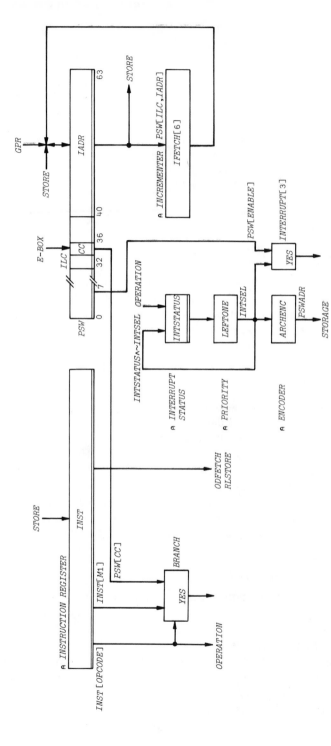

Figure 7-3 Instruction unit.

218

```
     ∇ IFETCH
[1]    ⍝ DETERMINE INSTRUCTION LENGTH
[2]    PSW[ILC]← 2 2 ⊤ 1 2 2 3[2⊥STORE[2⊥PSW[IADR]; 0 1]]
[3]    ⍝ FETCH INSTRUCTION
[4]    INST←,STORE[(2⊥PSW[IADR])+⍳2×2⊥PSW[ILC];]
[5]    ⍝ INCREMENT INSTRUCTION ADDRESS
[6]    PSW[IADR]←(24ρ2)⊤(2⊥PSW[IADR])+2×2⊥PSW[ILC]
     ∇


     ∇ PSWFIELD
[1]    ⍝ SIMPLIFIED ENABLE
[2]    ENABLE←7
[3]    ⍝ INSTRUCTION LENGTH CODE
[4]    ILC← 32 33
[5]    ⍝ CONDITION CODE
[6]    CC← 34 35
[7]    ⍝ INSTRUCTION ADDRESS
[8]    IADR←40+⍳24
     ∇
```

Program 7-4   Instruction fetch architecture.

Branch.   The elementary instruction order may be left when the instruction is a conditional branch. The operand address or the content of a register is used in this case as the new instruction address, the *branch address*. The branch will only be taken if the content of the condition code has the proper value.

Condition Code.   The *condition code*, *CC*, is located in the PSW. It has 2 bits with which it can indicate four states. These states are used to characterize the results of an operation. Table 7-5 shows the operations of Program 5-1, that change the condition code and the manner in which the condition code is set as a result of the operation. Operations that are not shown leave the condition code unchanged.

Table 7-5   CODING OF THE CONDITION CODE.

Operation	Condition Code			
	00	01	10	11
And	0	$\neq 0$	—	—
Or	0	$\neq 0$	—	—
Exclusive-or	0	$\neq 0$	—	—
Add	0	>0	<0	overflow
Subtract	0	>0	<0	overflow
Instruction bit	8	9	10	11

Condition.   Bits 8 through 11 of the conditional branch instruction each specify a value of the condition code for which a branch will succeed. This relation between instruction bits and condition code is shown at the bottom of Table 7-5. When all four bits are 1, the condition is always met, and the branch is uncondi- tional. When all four bits are 0, the branch is never taken. Figure 7-6 shows the instruction format of a conditional branch and *BRANCH*, Program 7-7, shows

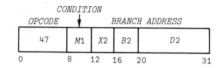

Figure 7-6 Conditional branch with *RX* format.

in line 5 the criterion that is used. Figure 7-8 expands the instruction fetch part of the instruction unit.

Branch Address.   *BRANCH* shows in lines 10 and 13 that the branch address is obtained from a register, or that the operand address is used as the branch address. The operand address is obtained as an *effective address* by adding the base address, index address, and displacement. The base address and index address reside in the general-purpose registers, *GPR*. The displacement is represented by a field of the instruction. The displacement *D2* and the specification of the base and index registers *B2* and *X2*, or the branch address register *R2*, are given by the instruction fields indicated by the indices of *INSTFIELD*, Program 7-7.

   EFFADR gives the architecture for the effective address calculation. The architecture is complicated by the rule that a register address 0000 indicates that the corresponding address component is 0. This is just one of many addressing complications. Other exceptions, such as the invalid address and the protected address, are ignored here.

```
     ∇ YES←BRANCH                                      ∇ INSTFIELD
[1]    ⍝ TEST OPERATION CODE                    [1]      ⍝ OPERATION CODE
[2]    YES←(2⊥INST[OPCODE])∊ 7 71               [2]      OPCODE←⍳8
[3]    →(~YES)/0                                 [3]      ⍝ REGISTER ADDRESS
[4]    ⍝ TEST CONDITION CODE                    [4]      R1←8+⍳4
[5]    YES←INST[M1[2⊥PSW[CC]]]                  [5]      R2←12+⍳4
[6]    →(~YES)/0                                 [6]      ⍝ STORAGE ADDRESS RX FORMAT
[7]    ⍝ FORMAT DECISION                        [7]      X2←12+⍳4
[8]    →INST[1]/RX                              [8]      B2←16+⍳4
[9]    ⍝ INSTRUCTION ADDRESS IN REGISTER       [9]      D2←20+⍳12
[10]   PSW[IADR]←8↓GPR[2⊥INST[R2];]            [10]     ⍝ STORAGE ADDRESS SS FORMAT
[11]   →0                                       [11]     L1←8+⍳4
[12]   ⍝ EFFECTIVE ADDRESS IS INSTRUCTION ADDRESS [12]  L2←12+⍳4
[13] RX:PSW[IADR]←EFFADR                        [13]     B1←16+⍳4
     ∇                                          [14]     D1←20+⍳12
                                                [15]     B2S←32+⍳4
     ∇ ADDRESS←EFFADR;BASE;INDEX;DISPLACEMENT   [16]     D2S←36+⍳12
[1]    BASE←2⊥(∨/INST[B2])∧8↓GPR[2⊥INST[B2];]   [17]     ⍝ IMMEDIATE OPERAND
[2]    INDEX←2⊥(∨/INST[X2])∧8↓GPR[2⊥INST[X2];]  [18]     I2←8+⍳8
[3]    DISPLACEMENT←2⊥INST[D2]                   [19]     ⍝ CONDITION MASK
[4]    ADDRESS←(24ρ2)⊤BASE+INDEX+DISPLACEMENT   [20]     M1←8+⍳4
     ∇                                              ∇
```

Program 7-7   Branch architecture.

Interruption

   As mentioned in Chapter 1, the instruction sequence can also be changed by an interruption. The concepts that are involved with an interruption will be discussed briefly at this point.

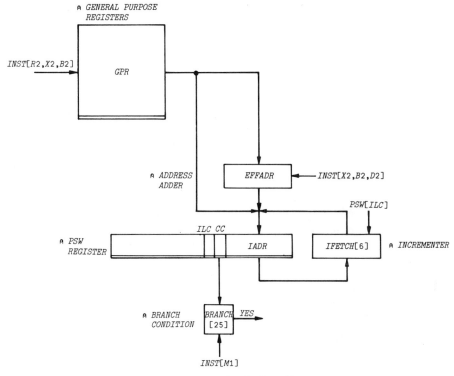

Figure 7-8   Instruction fetch architecture.

Cause of Interruption.   The cause of an interruption can be an exceptional event, such as division by 0, or an event that is difficult to predict, such as the completion of an input operation. These events are recorded in an *interrupt status* register. Figure 7-3 assumes an 8-bit status register *INTSTATUS*. Each bit in this register represents a class of interruption causes.

Moment of Interruption.   An interruption occurs normally after the completion of an instruction and prior to the execution of the next instruction. The interrupt is taken only when the computer is *enabled* for interruption. When an interrupt is taken, the succeeding interrupts usually are temporarily *disabled*. The disabling prevents interruptions from succeeding each other so rapidly that the program cannot pay proper attention to each of them. The enabling or disabling of an interruption is specified by a *mask* bit. In System/360 several mask bits are provided for the various interruption causes; in *PSWFIELD* the enabling function is simplified to one *ENABLE* bit.

Action of Interruption.   In System/360, the essential information for a program that is in execution is recorded in the program status word, the PSW. This information includes the instruction address, the condition code, the instruction length code, and the enable bit. Figure 7-9 shows the format of the PSW. The fields of the

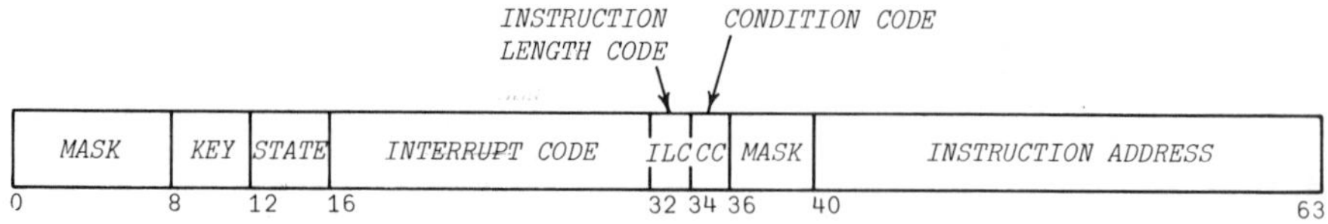

Figure 7-9 Program status word.

PSW that are not discussed in this text are left blank in the block diagrams. Also, the alternate PSW format, the extended control format, is not discussed.

The action of an interruption is shown in *INTERRUPT*, Program 7-10. This action involves the storing of the active PSW, the *old PSW*, in line 9, and the fetching of a PSW belonging to the interruption, the *new PSW*, in line 10. This interchange enables a new procedure to start at the instruction address which is found in the new PSW. Other interruptions can be disabled by setting the *ENABLE* bit of the new PSW to 0. When, eventually, the interrupted program is resumed, the old PSW is made active again. Thus, the program can be resumed as if no interruption has occurred.

```
      ∇ YES←INTERRUPT;INTSEL;PSWADR
[1]     ⍝ TEST STATUS AND ENABLE
[2]     INTSEL←LEFTONE INTSTATUS
[3]     YES←PSW[ENABLE]∧∨/INTSEL
[4]     →(~YES)/0
[5]     ⍝ UPDATE STATUS
[6]     INTSTATUS←INTSTATUS∧~INTSEL
[7]     ⍝ SWITCH PSW
[8]     PSWADR←ARCHENC INTSEL
[9]     STORE[(2⊥PSWADR, 0 0 0)+⍳8;]← 8 8 ⍴PSW
[10]    PSW←,STORE[64+(2⊥PSWADR, 0 0 0)+⍳8;]
      ∇

        ⍝ REFERENCE:                                          PROGRAM:
        ⍝ ARCHENC      ENCODER ARCHITECTURE                     7-19
        ⍝ LEFTONE      LEFTMOST-ONE ARCHITECTURE                7-30
```

Program 7-10 Interruption architecture.

INTERRUPT stores in line 9 the old PSW at the locations of *STORE* that start at address 0. In line 10 the new PSW is fetched from the locations starting at address 64. Line 9 includes a reshape operator, and line 10 a ravel since main storage has architecturally a wordlength of one byte. The encoding of the selected interruption as specified by the 8-bit vector *INTSEL* as the 3-bit address *PSWADR* in line 8 uses the encoder architecture *ARCHENC* to be discussed in Section 7-3.

Since each interruption class has its own locations for the old and the new PSW, all necessary information is made available to the system programmer.

Priority of Interruption. Since interruption causes may arise at arbitrary moments, two or more may be present at a given moment. This situation is even more to be expected, since some time will elapse between the moments at which an interrupt is allowed.

At the moment of interruption, the interruption causes are serviced in a fixed sequence, or leftmost-one priority. The function *LEFTONE*, Program 7-30, specifies this priority. This priority is an instance of the more general assignment problem, which will be discussed in Section 7-5.

Operand Fetch

System/360 operand addressing can, with some simplifications, be divided into five types. These types differ according to the location and nature of the operands. In particular, an operand can be located in a register or in main storage. In the latter case, the address is formed by indexing. Furthermore, the operand may have a fixed length of 2, 4, or 8 bytes, or a variable length.

For fixed-length operands, the addressing architecture is shown in Figure 7-11 and described by the functions *ODRR* and *ODRX* of Program 7-12. *ODRR* represents the *RR* format, with both operands in registers; *ODRX* represents the *RX* format, with one operand in a register and the other in storage. The function *ODRX* is simplified by assuming a constant operand length of 4 bytes. The function uses the effective address calculation *EFFADR* encountered in Program 7-7.

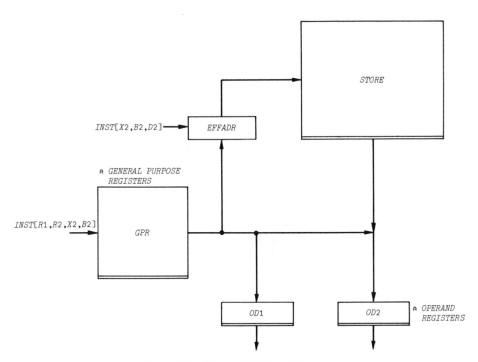

Figure 7-11 Operand fetch architecture.

```
      ∇ ODFETCH
[1]     →(RR,RR,RX,RX,RS,SI,SS,SS)[2⊥INST[0 1 3]]
[2]   RR:ODRR
[3]     →0
[4]   RX:ODRX
[5]     →0
[6]   RS:ODRS
[7]     →0
[8]   SI:ODSI
[9]     →0
[10]  SS:ODSS
      ∇
```

```
      ∇ ODRR
[1]     ⍝ FIRST OPERAND FROM REGISTER
[2]     OD1←GPR[2⊥INST[R1];]
[3]     ⍝ SECOND OPERAND FROM REGISTER
[4]     OD2←GPR[2⊥INST[R2];]
      ∇
```

```
      ∇ ODRX
[1]     ⍝ FIRST OPERAND FROM REGISTER
[2]     OD1←GPR[2⊥INST[R1];]
[3]     ⍝ SECOND OPERAND FROM STORAGE
[4]     OD2←,STORE[(2⊥EFFADR)+⍳4;]
      ∇
```

```
        ⍝ REFERENCE:                                          PROGRAM:
        ⍝ EFFADR        EFFECTIVE ADDRESS ARCHITECTURE           7-7
```

Program 7-12   Operand fetch architecture.

7-2   IMPLEMENTATION OF SYSTEM CONTROL

The architecture of system control mainly concerns decisions, which result in information movement. Therefore, the initial algorithms of the implementation can readily be derived from the architecture. This process will be described in this section for the instruction and operand fetch. Subsequently, the datapath and gate programs for these functions will be derived from the initial algorithms.

Instruction Fetch Implementation

Figure 7-13 and the functions *IFETCH*32 and *IMPBRANCH*, Program 7-14, show the implementation for the fetching of instructions according to the specifications of *IFETCH* and *BRANCH*. For this implementation a storage word length of 32 bits is assumed.

Instruction Buffer.   Since the instruction length is either 16, 32, or 48 bits, now and then 16 bits too many will be fetched from storage. This extra syllable is saved in the instruction buffer *BINST*, in *IFETCH*32 lines 6, 13, 20, and 28. *BINST* can be used for the next instruction, as in line 21, thus avoiding a second storage reference to the instruction location. The buffer activity bit *BINSTACT* indicates whether *BINST* is properly filled. Following a branch or interruption,

BINSTACT is set to 0, since the information in the instruction buffer is no longer relevant.

Instruction Address Incrementing. The instruction address *IADR* must be incremented by 2, 4, or 6, according to the instruction length. A specialized counter, *UPIADR*, in used in *IFETCH*32 lines 8, 15, 23, and 30, for this purpose. The counter is expressed in terms of *ARCHADD*, since eventually the adder of the instruction unit will be used for this purpose.

Effective Address Calculation. Program 7-14 also shows the implementation of the effective address computation *IMPEFFADR*. The architecture *EFFADR* specifies that the base, index, and displacement must be added to form the effective address. *IMPEFFADR* and Figure 7-13 show that a carry-save adder *ARCHSAVE* followed by a regular adder *ARCHADD* is used for this purpose. The carry-save adder only needs to be 12 bits wide, the width of the displacement. The carry-propagation adder is split into two parts to incorporate the carry-out of the carry-save adder at the right point.

Operand Fetch Implementation

IMPRR and *IMPRX*, Program 7-15, show the implementation of the operand fetch according to the specification of *ODRR* and *ODRX*. The equipment for this implementation is also shown in Figure 7-13. The description of the operand fetch implementation is simple because of its use of the function *IMPEFFADR*, which has been discussed above.

Use of Local Store. The general-purpose registers, *GPR*, used in *BRANCH*, *ODRR*, and *ODRX* are in the implementation assumed to be part of the local store. *IMPBRANCH*, *IMPRR*, and *IMPRX* show that the first locations of the local store are reserved for this purpose. Other registers of the architecture, such as the floating-point registers, can also be located in the local store, as well as registers known only to the implementation.

Reading from Storage. The functions *READLS* and *READMS* are used in the instruction and operand fetch implementations to obtain 32-bit words from the local store and the main store. The operand of these functions is the storage address. These functions are discussed in Chapter 8.

Alternative Implementations. The implementation of Figure 7-13 assumes an instruction register accommodating an instruction of 48 bits. The 48-bit instruction has two effective addresses, permitting storage-to-storage operations. The two effective addresses are computed in turn. As an alternative, the instruction register could be made 32 bits long, and the last syllable of a 48-bit instruction could be fetched after the first effective address is computed. This is just one example of the alternatives that can be considered in the design of the instruction unit.

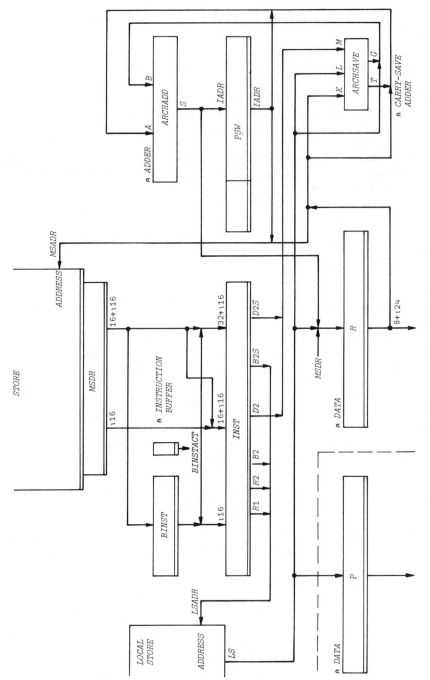

Figure 7-13 Instruction-unit implementation.

```
   ∇ IFETCH32
[1]   ⍝ TEST FOR ODD/EVEN SYLLABLE
[2]   →PSW[62]/ODD
[3]   ⍝ EVEN SYLLABLE
[4]   MSDR←READMS PSW[⁻2↓IADR]
[5]   INST[⍳32]←MSDR
[6]   BINST←MSDR[16+⍳16]
[7]   BINSTACT←~∨/MSDR[0 1]
[8]   UPIADR(∨/MSDR[0 1]),BINSTACT
[9]   →(~∧/INST[0 1])/0
[10]  ⍝ 48-BIT INSTRUCTION
[11]  MSDR←READMS PSW[⁻2↓IADR]
[12]  INST[32+⍳16]←MSDR[⍳16]
[13]  BINST←MSDR[16+⍳16]
[14]  BINSTACT←1
[15]  UPIADR 0 1
[16]  →0
[17]  ⍝ ODD SYLLABLE
[18]  ODD:→BINSTACT/CONT
[19]  MSDR←READMS PSW[⁻2↓IADR]
[20]  BINST←MSDR[16+⍳16]
[21]  CONT:INST[⍳16]←BINST
[22]  BINSTACT←0
[23]  UPIADR 0 1
[24]  →(~∨/INST[0 1])/0
[25]  ⍝ 32- OR 48-BIT INSTRUCTION
[26]  MSDR←READMS PSW[⁻2↓IADR]
[27]  INST[16+⍳32]←MSDR
[28]  BINST←MSDR[16+⍳16]
[29]  BINSTACT←~∧/INST[0 1]
[30]  UPIADR(∧/INST[0 1]),BINSTACT
   ∇
```

```
   ∇ YES←IMPBRANCH
[1]   ⍝ TEST OPERATION CODE
[2]   YES←∧/(~INST[0 2 3 4]),INST[5 6 7]
[3]   →(~YES)/0
[4]   ⍝ TEST CONDITION CODE
[5]   YES←CCTEST PSW[CC]
[6]   →(~YES)/0
[7]   BINSTACT←0
[8]   ⍝ FORMAT DECISION
[9]   →INST[1]/RX
[10]  ⍝ BRANCH ADDRESS IN REGISTER
[11]  LS←READLS INST[R2]
[12]  PSW[IADR]←LS[8+⍳24]
[13]  →0
[14]  ⍝ EFFECTIVE ADDRESS IS BRANCH ADDRESS
[15]  RX:PSW[IADR]←IMPEFFADR
   ∇
```

```
   ∇ UPIADR F
[1]   A←PSW[IADR]
[2]   B←(21⍴0),F,0
[3]   CIN←0
[4]   ARCHADD
[5]   PSW[IADR]←S
   ∇
```

```
   ∇ ADDRESS←IMPEFFADR
[1]   ⍝ BASE FROM REGISTER
[2]   R←32⍴0
[3]   →(~∨/INST[B2])/NOB
[4]   R←READLS INST[B2]
[5]   ⍝ INDEX FROM REGISTER
[6]   NOB:LS←32⍴0
[7]   →(~∨/INST[X2])/NOX
[8]   LS←READLS INST[X2]
[9]   ⍝ EFFECTIVE ADDRESS
[10]  NOX:ADDRESS←24⍴0
[11]  K←R[D2]
[12]  L←LS[D2]
[13]  M←INST[D2]
[14]  ARCHSAVE
[15]  A←T
[16]  B←1↓G,0
[17]  CIN←0
[18]  ARCHADD
[19]  ADDRESS[12+⍳12]←S
[20]  A←R[8+⍳12]
[21]  B←LS[8+⍳12]
[22]  CIN←COUT∨1↓G
[23]  ARCHADD
[24]  ADDRESS[⍳12]←S
   ∇
```

```
⍝ REFERENCE:                                      PROGRAM:
⍝ ARCHADD     ADDER ARCHITECTURE                    2-5
⍝ ARCHSAVE    CARRY-SAVE ADDER ARCHITECTURE         2-36
⍝ CCTEST      BRANCH CONDITION IMPLEMENTATION       7-38
⍝ READLS      READ FROM LOCAL STORE                 8-3
```

Program 7-14 Instruction fetch implementation.

227

```
      ∇ IMPRR
[1]     ⍝ FIRST OPERAND FROM REGISTER
[2]     P←READLS INST[R1]
[3]     ⍝ SECOND OPERAND FROM REGISTER
[4]     R←READLS INST[R2]
      ∇

      ∇ IMPRX
[1]     ⍝ EFFECTIVE ADDRESS
[2]     R←(8⍴0),IMPEFFADR
[3]     ⍝ FIRST OPERAND FROM REGISTER
[4]     P←READLS INST[R1]
[5]     ⍝ SECOND OPERAND FROM STORAGE
[6]     MSDR←READMS R[8+⍳22]
[7]     R←MSDR
      ∇
```

```
                                                                PROGRAM:
      ⍝ REFERENCE:
      ⍝ IMPEFFADR     EFFECTIVE ADDRESS IMPLEMENTATION           7-14
      ⍝ READLS        READ FROM LOCAL STORE                      8-3
      ⍝ READMS        READ FROM MAIN STORE                       8-4
```

Program 7-15   Operand fetch implementation.

Datapath and Gate Programs for
Instruction and Operand Fetch

The gate programs for the instruction fetch, the branch, and the operand fetches for the *RR* and *RX* formats are shown in Program 7-17. They control the instruction unit datapath *PATHIBOX*, Program 7-16, via the gates specified by *GATECODEI*, Program 7-16. The remarks made in Chapter 5 about the transition from an implementation description to a gate program are applicable again at this point. So are the remarks about the description of a datapath. They will not be repeated. The transition from a gate program to a microprogram as described in Chapter 6 can again be applied to these programs. Since it does not provide any new insight, it is not shown.

GATEBRANCH differs from earlier gate programs by incorporating the assignment target *YES* in the heading. Thus, *GATEBRANCH* matches the architecture *BRANCH* and the implementation *IMPBRANCH*. *GATEBRANCH* could replace *BRANCH* in line 3 of *PROCESSOR*, Program 7-2. When *PROCESSOR* and *GATEBRANCH* are eventually replaced by microcode, the test condition *BNCH* can be used to control the program flow.

Registers. *PATHIBOX* shows how parts of a register may be controlled separately. In particular, the three syllables of the instruction register *INST* have separate input signals in lines 22, 23, and 24 and read-in controls in lines 33, 34, and 35.

The registers *P* and *R* form the link between the I-box and the E-box. *R* is used in address computation, as in *GATERX*, line 6; hence it is described with the I-box. *P* contains the result of the E-box and therefore is described with that unit. The outputs of these registers, however, are also available to the other units. *PATHIBOX*, line 27, shows an input from the I-box to *P*.

```
      ∇ PATHIBOX
[1]     ⍝ ADDER INPUTS
[2]     K←Y[RUK]∧R[D2]
[3]     L←Y[SUL]∧LS[D2]
[4]     M←(Y[IUM]∧INST[D2])∨Y[RUM]∧INST[D2S]
[5]     ⍝ CARRY-SAVE ADDER
[6]     ARCHSAVE
[7]     ⍝ ADDER INPUTS
[8]     A←(Y[TUS]∧T)∨Y[PUS]∧PSW[¯12↑IADR]
[9]     B←(Y[GUS]∧1↓G,0)∨(9⍴0),INCIADR Y[UP1,UP2,UP3]
[10]    CIN←0
[11]    ⍝ RIGHT HALF OF ADDER
[12]    ARCHADD
[13]    SOUT[12+⍳12]←S
[14]    ⍝ ADDER INPUTS
[15]    A←(Y[RUS]∧R[8+⍳12])∨Y[WUS]∧PSW[12↑IADR]
[16]    B←Y[LUS]∧LS[8+⍳12]
[17]    CIN←COUT∨1↑G
[18]    ⍝ LEFT HALF OF ADDER
[19]    ARCHADD
[20]    SOUT[⍳12]←S
[21]    ⍝ REGISTER INPUTS
[22]    IINST[⍳16]←(Y[LIL]∧MSDR[⍳16])∨Y[BIL]∧BINST
[23]    IINST[16+⍳16]←(Y[LIM]∧MSDR[⍳16])∨Y[RIM]∧MSDR[16+⍳16]
[24]    IINST[32+⍳16]←(Y[LIR]∧MSDR[⍳16])∨Y[RIR]∧MSDR[16+⍳16]
[25]    IBINST←MSDR[16+⍳16]
[26]    IPSW[IADR]←(Y[SUI]∧SOUT)∨Y[LUI]∧LS[8+⍳24]
[27]    IP←Y[LOP]∧LS
[28]    IR←(Y[LOR]∧LS)∨(Y[MOR]∧MSDR)∨Y[SOR]∧(8⍴0),SOUT
[29]    ⍝ STORAGE ADDRESS
[30]    LSADR←(Y[R1L]∧INST[R1])∨(Y[R2L]∧INST[R2])∨(Y[B2L]∧INST[B2])∨Y[BSL]∧INST[B2S]
[31]    MSADR←(Y[RAM]∧R[8+⍳22])∨Y[PAM]∧PSW[¯2↓IADR]
[32]    ⍝ REGISTERS
[33]    INST[⍳16]←(Y[TIL]∧IINST[⍳16])∨(~Y[TIL])∧INST[⍳16]
[34]    INST[16+⍳16]←(Y[TIM]∧IINST[16+⍳16])∨(~Y[TIM])∧INST[16+⍳16]
[35]    INST[32+⍳16]←(Y[TIS]∧IINST[32+⍳16])∨(~Y[TIS])∧INST[32+⍳16]
[36]    BINST←(Y[TII]∧IBINST)∨(~Y[TII])∧BINST
[37]    PSW[IADR]←(Y[TIA]∧IPSW[IADR])∨(~Y[TIA])∧PSW[IADR]
[38]    R←(Y[TIR]∧IR)∨(~Y[TIR])∧R
[39]    ⍝ FETCH DATA
[40]    →(~Y[RLS])/READ+1
[41]  READ:LS←READLS LSADR
[42]    →(~Y[RMS])/READ+3
[43]    MSDR←READMS MSADR
[44]    ⍝ TESTCONDITIONS
[45]    BNCH←∧/(~INST[0 2 3 4]),INST[5 6 7],CCTEST PSW[CC]
[46]    BINSTACT←Y[TII]∨(~BNCH)∧BINSTACT
[47]    XZRO←~∨/INST[X2]
[48]    BZRO←~∨/INST[B2]
[49]    IODD←PSW[62]
[50]    ILC2←~∨/INST[0 1]
[51]    ILC6←∧/INST[0 1]
      ∇
```

⍝ REFERENCE:		PROGRAM:
⍝ ARCHADD	ADDER ARCHITECTURE	2-5
⍝ ARCHSAVE	CARRY-SAVE ADDER ARCHITECTURE	2-36
⍝ CCTEST	BRANCH-CONDITION IMPLEMENTATION	7-38
⍝ READLS	READ FROM LOCAL STORE	8-3
⍝ READMS	READ FROM MAIN STORE	8-4

Program 7-16 Datapath of instruction unit (Part 1).

```
      ∇ GATECODEI                              ∇ DECLIBOX
[1]     � ADDER INPUT GATES          [1]     � LOCAL STORE
[2]     RUK←0                             [2]     LOCALSTORE← 16 32 ⍴0
[3]     SUL←1                             [3]     � MAIN STORE
[4]     IUM←2                             [4]     STORE←(N,32)⍴0
[5]     RUM←3                             [5]     � INSTRUCTION REGISTER
[6]     TUS←4                             [6]     INST←48⍴0
[7]     PUS←5                             [7]     � INSTRUCTION BUFFER
[8]     GUS←6                             [8]     BINST←16⍴0
[9]     RUS←7                             [9]     � BUFFER ACTIVITY BIT
[10]    WUS←8                             [10]    BINSTACT←0
[11]    LUS←9                             [11]    � PROGRAM STATUS WORD REGISTER
[12]    � ADDER CONTROL GATES       [12]    PSW←64⍴0
[13]    UP1←10                            [13]    � OPERAND REGISTER
[14]    UP2←11                            [14]    R←32⍴0
[15]    UP3←12                                 ∇
[16]    � REGISTER INPUT GATES
[17]    LIL←13                                 ∇ OUT←INCIADR F
[18]    BIL←14                            [1]     � INCREMENT WITH 2 IF 1 SYLLABLE, ELSE 4
[19]    LIM←15                            [2]     OUT←F[0]∧(∨/MSDR[0 1]),(~∨/MSDR[0 1]),0
[20]    RIM←16                            [3]     � INCREMENT WITH 2
[21]    LIR←17                            [4]     OUT←OUT∨F[1]∧ 0 1 0
[22]    RIR←18                            [5]     � INCREMENT WITH 4 IF 3 SYLLABLES, ELSE 2
[23]    SUI←19                            [6]     OUT←OUT∨F[2]∧(∧/INST[0 1]),(~∧/INST[0 1]),0
[24]    LUI←20                                 ∇
[25]    LOP←21
[26]    LOR←22
[27]    MOR←23
[28]    SOR←24
[29]    � ADDRESS GATES
[30]    R1L←25
[31]    R2L←26
[32]    B2L←27
[33]    BSL←28
[34]    RAM←29
[35]    PAM←30
[36]    � REGISTER READ-IN SIGNALS
[37]    TIL←31
[38]    TIM←32
[39]    TIS←33
[40]    TII←34
[41]    TIA←35
[42]    TIP←36
[43]    TIR←37
[44]    � LOCAL AND MAIN STORE CONTROL
[45]    RLS←38
[46]    RMS←39
      ∇
```

Program 7-16   Datapath of instruction unit (Part 2).

Independence of Instruction Unit.   The implementation of Figure 7-13 assumes an independent I-box. It also is possible to make this unit coincide with a processing unit such as that described by *PATHSGL*, Program 5-18. In that case, *PATHSGL* will have to be extended with several registers and gates.

Interconnection of Datapaths and Control.   Figure 7-18 shows the interconnection of the datapaths for the I-box *PATHIBOX* and the E-box *PATHSGL*. The communication is in terms of the registers P and R rather than the operands and results, such as $OD1$, $OD2$, and $RL1$, as shown in Figure 7-1. The latter are part of the architectural specification but need not appear as an entity in the implementation as is illustrated by the serial datapath.

```
      ∇ GATEIFETCH
[1]    ⍝ TEST FOR ODD/EVEN SYLLABLE
[2]    →IODD/ODD
[3]    ⍝ EVEN SYLLABLE
[4]    GATE PAM,RMS
[5]    GATE PUS,UP1,WUS,SUI,TIA,LIL,RIM,TIL,TIM,TII
[6]    →(~ILC6)/0
[7]    ⍝ 48-BIT INSTRUCTION
[8]    GATE PAM,RMS
[9]    GATE PUS,UP2,WUS,SUI,TIA,LIR,TIS,TII
[10]   →0
[11]   ⍝ ODD SYLLABLE
[12]  ODD:→BINSTACT/CONT
[13]   GATE PAM,RMS
[14]   GATE MUB,TII
[15]  CONT:GATE PUS,UP2,WUS,SUI,TIA,BIL,TIL
[16]   →ILC2/0
[17]   ⍝ 32- OR 48-BIT INSTRUCTION
[18]   GATE PAM,RMS
[19]   GATE PUS,UP3,WUS,SUI,TIA,LIM,RIR,TIM,TIS,TII
      ∇

      ∇ YES←GATEBRANCH
[1]    ⍝ TEST BRANCH CONDITION
[2]    YES←BNCH
[3]    →(~BNCH)/0
[4]    ⍝ FORMAT DECISION
[5]    →(~ILC2)/RX
[6]    ⍝ BRANCH ADDRESS IN REGISTER
[7]    GATE R2L,RLS
[8]    GATE LUI,TIA
[9]    →0
[10]   ⍝ BASE FROM REGISTER
[11]  RX:→BZRO/NOB
[12]   GATE B2L,RLS
[13]   ⍝ INDEX FROM REGISTER
[14]   →XZRO/NOX
[15]   GATE LOR,TIR,R2L,RLS
[16]   ⍝ EFFECTIVE ADDRESS IS BRANCH ADDRESS
[17]  CONT:GATE RUK,SUL,IUM,TUS,GUS,RUS,SUI,TIA
[18]  NOB:→XZRO/NOBX
[19]   ⍝ SET BASE TO 0, INDEX FROM REGISTER
[20]   GATE TIR,R2L,RLS
[21]   →CONT
[22]   ⍝ ADDRESS WITHOUT X
[23]  NOX:GATE SUL,IUM,TUS,GUS,RUS,SUI,TIA
[24]   →0
[25]   ⍝ ADDRESS WITHOUT X AND B
[26]  NOBX:GATE IUM,TUS,GUS,RUS,SUI,TIA
      ∇

      ⍝ REFERENCE:                                    PROGRAM:
      ⍝ PATHIBOX        DATAPATH OF INSTRUCTION UNIT     7-16
```

Program 7-17   Gate programs for instruction and operand fetch (Part 1).

Figure 7-18 also shows the connection with storage and with microprogram control. When the microword of *ARCHMICRO* is sufficiently enlarged, so that it can control both the gates of *PATHSGL* and of *PATHIBOX*, with a different gate numbering, the processor can be run as an entity. An encoded microprogram organization such as *ARCHMICROENC* is more realistic, of course.

As has been stated repeatedly, the simulation of a whole unit is an exceptional procedure. The normal practice is to simulate and verify the parts against their architecture and to ascertain the proper interconnection at the architectural level.

```
        ∇ GATERR                                          ∇ GATE X
 [1]      ∧ FIRST OPERAND FROM REGISTER          [1]      Y←(ι40)∊X
 [2]      GATE R1L,RLS                           [2]      PATHIBOX
 [3]      ∧ SECOND OPERAND FROM REGISTER                ∇
 [4]      GATE LOP,TIP,R2L,RLS
 [5]      GATE LOR,TIR
        ∇


        ∇ GATERX
 [1]      ∧ BASE FROM REGISTER
 [2]      →BZRO/NOB
 [3]      GATE B2L,RLS
 [4]      ∧ INDEX FROM REGISTER
 [5]      →XZRO/NOX
 [6]      GATE LOR,TIR,R2L,RLS
 [7]      ∧ EFFECTIVE ADDRESS, FIRST OPERAND FROM REGISTER
 [8]      CONT:GATE RUK,SUL,IUM,TUS,GUS,RUS,LUS,SOR,TIR,R1L,RLS
 [9]      ∧ SECOND OPERAND FROM REGISTER
[10]      GATE LOP,TIP,RAM,RMS
[11]      GATE MOR,TIR
[12]      →0
[13]      NOB:→XZRO/NOBX
[14]      ∧ SET BASE TO 0, INDEX FROM REGISTER
[15]      GATE TIR,R2L,RLS
[16]      →CONT
[17]      ∧ ADDRESS WITHOUT X, FIRST OPERAND FROM REGISTER
[18]      NOX:GATE SUL,IUM,TUS,GUS,RUS,LUS,SOR,TIR,R1L,RLS
[19]      →CONT+2
[20]      ∧ ADDRESS WITHOUT X AND B, FIRST OPERAND FROM REGISTER
[21]      NOBX:GATE IUM,TUS,GUS,RUS,LUS,SOR,TIR,R1L,RLS
[22]      →CONT+2
        ∇
```

Program 7-17   Gate programs for instruction and operand fetch (Part 2).

Microprocessor.   Integrated circuit technology makes it possible to build a processor consisting of a local store, an E-box, and an I-box, as well as their internal control, as one integrated circuit. Such an implementation is called a *microprocessor*.

An example of a microprocessor is the Intel 8080, which has 8-bit datawidth, 8 local store registers of 8 bits each, and addressing for a 16-K store. The instruction repertoire allows binary and decimal load and add operations, including 16 bit arithmetic. An interrupt is provided for storage and I/O handling. The module has 40 pins. (See Appendix B, page 332.)

When storage, in the form of RAM and ROM modules, is connected to the microprocessor and proper connections are made to input and output devices, a *microcomputer* is obtained. The power of such a microcomputer is, however, limited by the width and speed of its datapath and storage. The datawidth is usually resticted to 8 bits by the number of pins that are available on the modules. The datapath and storage cycles are typically a few microseconds. This speed results from the type of technology that must be used to minimize the heat dissipation on the chip. Thus the processing power of the microprocessor is no match for that of the minicomputers or the conventional computers, which have a datawidth of 16 to 64 bits and a datapath cycle of several hundred nanoseconds down to 80 nanoseconds, as for the System/370 Model 168.

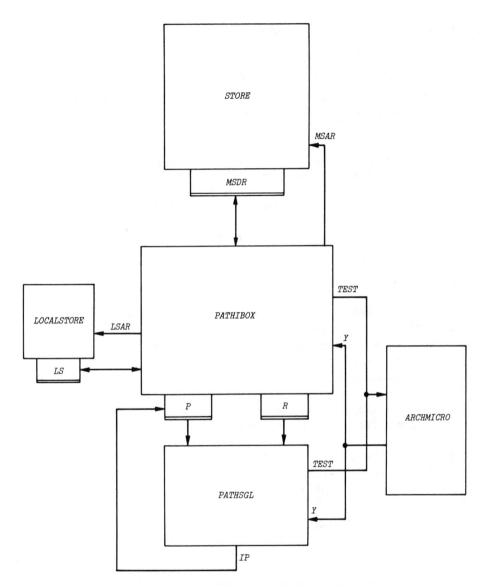

Figure 7-18   Parallel processor implementation.

```
     ∇ OUT←ARCHENC IN
[1]    OUT←((⌈2⍟⍴IN)⍴2)⊤IN⍳1
     ∇
```

Program 7-19   Encoder architecture.

System Components of System Control

With reading and writing to be discussed in Chapter 8, the specific implementation problems introduced by system control are:

    (a) The encoding of a number, as for the PSW address in *INTERRUPT*, line 8.
    (b) The decoding of a number, as for the operation code in *OPERATION*, Program 5-1, line 1, and in *BRANCH*, line 2; or for the register address in *BRANCH*, line 10.
    (c) The priority determination, as in *INTERRUPT*, line 2.
    (d) Special circuits, such as the condition code test in *BRANCH*, line 5.

The system components for these functions are discussed in Sections 7-3 through 7-6. The reader can, however, also proceed to Chapter 8, which again uses these system components, and return later to these sections.

7-3   ENCODING

ARCHENC, Program 7-19, shows the architecture of an *encoder*. In contrast to the APL encode operator $\top$, the object to be encoded is not a number but a representation. In fact, a number cannot reside as such in an implementation. It is always represented in one way or another.

The representation of the quantity to be encoded is assumed to be in the 1-out-of-N code. The result of the encoding is an unsigned binary representation. The architecture, therefore, first determines which input bit is 1, and subsequently encodes the index of this bit, using an appropriate number of binary digits.

One-Level Implementation.   *ENCODE*8, Program 7-21, and Figure 7-20 show a one-level encoder converting a 1-out-of-8 code to a 3-bit binary code. Only 3 'or' circuits with a total of 12 inputs are required.

Multilevel Implementation.   When the fan-in of the 'or' circuits is exceeded for a large number of inputs, a multilevel grouped approach becomes desirable. *ENCODE*64, Program 7-22, shows the circuit for the conversion from a 1-out-of-64 code to a 6-bit binary representation. A maximum fan-in of 8 is assumed. In total, 22 'or' circuits and 152 inputs are required.

The single-level approach would have required six 'or' circuits with 32 inputs each for this encoder. Replacing each of the 'or' circuits with four circuits with a fan-in of eight and a second-level circuit with a fan-in of four requires 30 'or' circuits and 216 inputs, which is more expensive than the solution of *ENCODE*64. The difference between these two approaches can be explained by characterizing *ENCODE*64 as a multiplicative approach and its alternative as a linear approach. The multiplicative approach will also prove to be advantageous in the implementation of the other control functions.

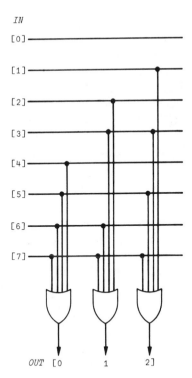

Figure 7-20   8-input encoder.

```
    ∇ OUT←ENCODE8 IN
[1]   OUT←(∨/IN[4 5 6 7]),(∨/IN[2 3 6 7]),∨/IN[1 3 5 7]
    ∇
```

Program 7-21   8-input encoder.

```
    ∇ OUT←ENCODE64 IN
[1]   OUT1←∨/ 8 8 ρIN
[2]   OUT2←∨/[0] 8 8 ρIN
[3]   OUT←(ENCODE8 OUT2),ENCODE8 OUT1
    ∇
```

Program 7-22   64-input encoder.

7-4 DECODING

A *decoder* changes an unsigned binary representation into a 1-out-of-N representation. *ARCHDEC*, Program 7-23, shows the APL function for the decoder
architecture.

```
    ∇ OUT←ARCHDEC IN
[1]   OUT←(ι2*ρIN)=2⊥IN
    ∇
```

Program 7-23   Decoder architecture.

The decoder is an important system component. The instruction list of Appendix B suggests that the operation code decoder for a complete computer can be appreciable in size. Even more important are the address decoders for storage units.

Encoding and decoding sometimes follow each other to reduce the number of signals to be transmitted and to achieve a common representation form. An example is the vector *INTSEL*, representing the selected interruption, which is encoded in line 8 of *INTERRUPT* and decoded again as part of storage addressing in lines 9 and 10.

The three main decoding methods are the simplex, matrix, and tree decoder.

Simplex Decoder

In the *simplex* decoder, each set of values of the input variables, or *code point*, uses a separate 'and' circuit. The 'and' circuit combines each input variable or its inverse.

Figure 7-24A illustrates a three-input simplex decoder and Program 7-25 gives its description.

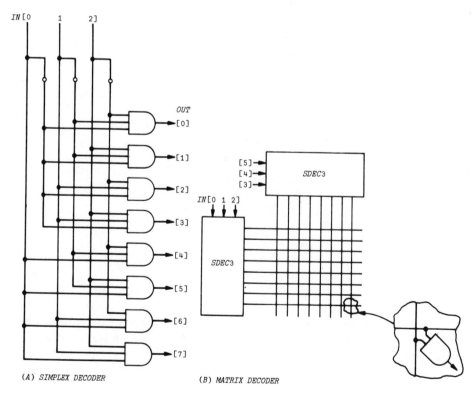

(A) *SIMPLEX DECODER*   (B) *MATRIX DECODER*

Figure 7-24 Simplex and matrix decoders.

```
    ∇ OUT←SDEC3Z IN
[1]   NIN←~IN                                       ∇ OUT←SDEC3Y IN
[2]   OUT←8ρ0                                  [1]    OUT←8ρ0
[3]   OUT[0]←NIN[0]∧NIN[1]∧NIN[2]              [2]    OUT[0]←IN∧.= 0 0 0
[4]   OUT[1]←NIN[0]∧NIN[1]∧IN[2]               [3]    OUT[1]←IN∧.= 0 0 1
[5]   OUT[2]←NIN[0]∧IN[1]∧NIN[2]               [4]    OUT[2]←IN∧.= 0 1 0
[6]   OUT[3]←NIN[0]∧IN[1]∧IN[2]                [5]    OUT[3]←IN∧.= 0 1 1
[7]   OUT[4]←IN[0]∧NIN[1]∧NIN[2]               [6]    OUT[4]←IN∧.= 1 0 0
[8]   OUT[5]←IN[0]∧NIN[1]∧IN[2]                [7]    OUT[5]←IN∧.= 1 0 1
[9]   OUT[6]←IN[0]∧IN[1]∧NIN[2]                [8]    OUT[6]←IN∧.= 1 1 0
[10]  OUT[7]←IN[0]∧IN[1]∧IN[2]                 [9]    OUT[7]←IN∧.= 1 1 1
    ∇                                             ∇

    ∇ OUT←SDEC3 IN
[1]   OUT←IN∧.= 2 2 2 ⊤ι8
    ∇
```

Program 7-25   3-input simplex decoder.

Description Methods. Program 7-25 gives three alternative descriptions for the simplex decoder. $SDEC3Z$ explicitly shows all eight three-input 'and's, as well as the inverters of the input IN.

Since the 'and's and 'or's of a set of signals and their inverse occur frequently, it may be desirable to have a shorter notation. $SDEC3Y$ illustrates such a notation for the three-input decoder. This notation uses the inner product of APL and uses 1 and 0 to specify a signal and its inverse.

Inner Product. The *inner product* is represented by the symbols $\wedge. =$ in $SDEC3Y$. More generally, the inner product consists of two diadic operators separated by a period (.).

The inner product is an extension of the classical vector product, which is written $+. \times$ in APL. The elements along the highest coordinate of the right operand are combined with the elements along the lowest coordinate of the left operand, using the right operator. Subsequently, the results are reduced to a single element, as specified by the left operator. In the case of matrix multiplication, the columns of the right operand are multiplied by the rows of the left operand, and summed to form one element of the result matrix.

In $SDEC3Y$ the elements of IN are first equated with a vector of 0s and 1s. This is equivalent to taking the inverse of the signals corresponding to a 0 and the true value of the signals corresponding to a 1. Subsequently, the 'and' of these results is taken.

$SDEC3$ obtains an even more compact notation by first generating the necessary matrix of 0s and 1s and then applying the inner product to this matrix. Although convenient to the expert, the description is cryptic to the novice. $SDEC3$ and $SDEC3Y$ are not explicit about the manner in which the inverse is generated. They also mingle operators that represent circuits, the 'and's, with operators that specify signals, the 'equal's. These descriptions therefore have the characteristic of an initial description, whereas $SDEC3Z$ best reflects the actual circuit.

In the operation code of System/360, listed in Appendix B, about 180 of the

256 code points are used. This would require 180 eight-input 'and' circuits, or a total of 1440 inputs. A complete decoder for N inputs has $2 * N$ 'and' circuits, $N \times 2 * N$ inputs, and a fan-in of N. It requires a fan-out of $2 * N - 1$ for the circuits driving the decoder. An address decoder might easily have 16 input signals. In that case, the fan-in and fan-out are clearly prohibitive.

Matrix Decoder

In the instruction list of System/360, a subdivision in classes can be recognized. Within each class a list of operations appears, which resembles the list in *OPERATION*, Program 5-1. This subdivision suggests a two-step decoding: (1) according to class, and (2) according to operations within a class. These two steps are the more meaningful because some decisions involve only the class of the operation, whereas for others the operation is of importance, and the class can be ignored.

Figure 7-24B illustrates this type of decoder. The circuits have two levels. The second level has the character of a matrix, in which columns and rows are connected by 'and' circuits. Hence, the name *matrix decoder*.

The example mentioned above now requires two simplex decoders each for a 1-out-of-16 representation, and subsequently 180 two-input 'and' circuits. In total, 212 circuits with 488 inputs are required. In comparison to the simplex decoder the number of 'and' circuits is increased. This is to be expected since the simplex decoder involves the minimum number of circuits: one for each output. The number of inputs, however, is drastically reduced, and so are the associated fan-in and fan-out.

The fan-in for a matrix decoder of N input signals is half the fan-in for the corresponding simplex decoder. The fan-out for the matrix decoder is about the square root of the fan-out required for the simplex decoder. The maximum fan-out of the matrix decoder occurs for the output of the first-level simplex decoders, and is $2 * N \div 2$.

Multilevel Matrix Decoder. The fan-in and fan-out of the two-level matrix decoder can be reduced even further by introducing more levels. Thus, a classical solution for core storage is a subdivision of the address in four parts. Two of these parts are decoded in one matrix decoder, as are the other two parts. Subsequently, the outputs from the two matrices are run as X and Y wires through the cores. Each core acts as an 'and' circuit, combining the signals on the X and Y wires.

A multilevel matrix decoder can best be designed by starting at the output and working toward the input. The number of output 'and's is always $2 * N$, the same as for the simplex decoder. For the matrix decoder these are two-input 'and' circuits. These inputs are fed from two lower-level decoders. Fan-out and circuit count are minimal when these two decoders are nearly equal in size. This minimum corresponds to the minimum circumference of a rectangle with a given surface, which is obtained for the square.

For the eight-input decoder of $MDEC8$, Program 7-26, level 3 is fed from two

```
     ∇ OUT←MDEC8 IN                          ∇ OUT←SDEC2 IN
[1]    ⍝ LEVEL 0              [1]    OUT←IN∧.= 2 2 ⊤⍳4
[2]    OUT10←SDEC2 IN[0 1]                    ∇
[3]    OUT11←SDEC2 IN[2 3]
[4]    OUT12←SDEC2 IN[4 5]
[5]    OUT13←SDEC2 IN[6 7]
[6]    ⍝ LEVEL 1
[7]    OUT20←,OUT10∘.∧OUT11
[8]    OUT21←,OUT12∘.∧OUT13
[9]    ⍝ LEVEL 2
[10]   OUT←,OUT20∘.∧OUT21
[11]   ⍝ LEVEL 3
     ∇
```

Program 7-26   8-input matrix decoder.

decoders with 16 outputs each. These in turn are each fed from two decoders with four outputs each. The decoders of level 1 are equivalent to simplex decoders.

Outer Product. The *outer product* of APL is represented by the symbols ∘.∧ in $MDEC8$. Of these three symbols the right one, here the 'and,' ∧, represents the actual operator and may be any dyadic operator. For the outer product, all elements of the right operand are combined with those of the left operand. The dimension of the resulting array is the concatenation of the dimensions of the operands. In $MDEC8$, line 10, an array of dimension 16 16 is thus formed from two 16-element vectors.

Matrix Decoder with Larger Fan-in. In the above examples the matrix is made from two-input 'and' circuits. The basic design concept, however, is not tied to this fan-in. Several lower-level decoders could be combined equally well with a set of 'and's of more than two inputs. The name 'matrix' would then no longer be appropriate, but this is immaterial.

The usefulness of a larger fan-in depends upon the realization costs. If only the number of circuits is decisive, the simplex decoder is the least expensive. If only the number of inputs is decisive, the multilevel matrix decoder with fan-in of two is the least expensive. If, on the other hand, circuits with a fan-in of a given maximum or less are considered equally expensive, then the matrix decoder with maximum fan-in would be less expensive and would require fewer levels than the two-input matrix.

Tree Decoder

In the design of a matrix decoder, the lower-level decoders feeding a given matrix are always made nearly equal in size, to minimize component cost. In the *tree* decoder, the opposite decision is taken: one of the inputs is derived from an input variable and its inverse; the other is derived from a decoder with half the number of outputs of the given level. Needless to say, the result is a more expensive decoder than the matrix decoder—in fan-out, number of inputs, number of circuits, and number of levels.

For the 8-input, 180-output decoder mentioned above, about 400 circuits would be required with 800 inputs. The fan-out would be about 100, and seven levels would be used. The tree decoder therefore has little to offer in an electronic design. It is, however, of interest as a relay circuit.

Relay Decoder.   As stated in Chapter 2, a relay contact is relatively inexpensive and fast when compared to a relay coil. There is, furthermore, scarcely any restriction on the fan-in. Consequently, the simplex decoder is quite attractive for a relay design. For relays, moreover, the elementary logical building blocks, such as 'and' and 'or,' are constructed from individual contacts as *composite* elements. Hence, the simplex decoder can be further simplified.

Figure 7-27A shows that the leftmost relay contacts of the simplex decoder are either the normally open or the normally closed contact for $IN[0]$. This entire set can be replaced by one contact pair. Proceeding further in this manner, the tree decoder of Figure 7-27B arises. Because of its appearance, the circuit has been called a *whiffle tree*.

Figure 7-27C shows for the sake of completeness the electronic equivalent of the relay decoder, and $TREEDEC8$, Program 7-28, describes a corresponding eight-input decoder.

Summary of Decoders.   Table 7-29 summarizes the various decoder types. For each level of an N-input decoder, the following properties hold: If the number of input variables involved in that level is J, and the fan-in is FIN, the number of circuits is $2 * J$, the number of circuit inputs is $FIN \times 2 * J$, and the number of decoders feeding this level is FIN.

The simplex decoder has only one level, which is fed by N signals and their inverse, each with fan-out $2 * N - 1$.

The tree decoder has $N - 1$ levels. Level $J - 1$ involves J variables and is fed by a signal and its inverse with fan-out $2 * J - 1$ and a $(J - 1)$-input decoder with fan-out 2.

The matrix decoder has $\lceil FIN \circledast N$ levels. The top level is fed by FIN decoders, with a maximum fan-out of $(2 * \lceil N \div FIN) * FIN - 1$.

Decoder Examples.   Although for a manufacturer the trade-off between speed and number of circuits is critical, the average user will mainly choose between decoders that are available as a unit. Much choice is offered here. Thus, the TI SN74S138 matches $SDEC3Z$ except for an additional enable gate.

The decoders have been illustrated here for a binary interpretation of the input codes. Often four inputs represent the 10 decimal digits and a decoder is built with just 10 outputs. The decoder is then specialized for the code used to represent the decimal digits, such as the TI SN74L42 for binary-coded decimal (BCD) and the TI SN74L43 for Excess-3.

Code Converters.   Some decoders have more than one output high for a given input and are more properly called *code converters*. A prominent example is the

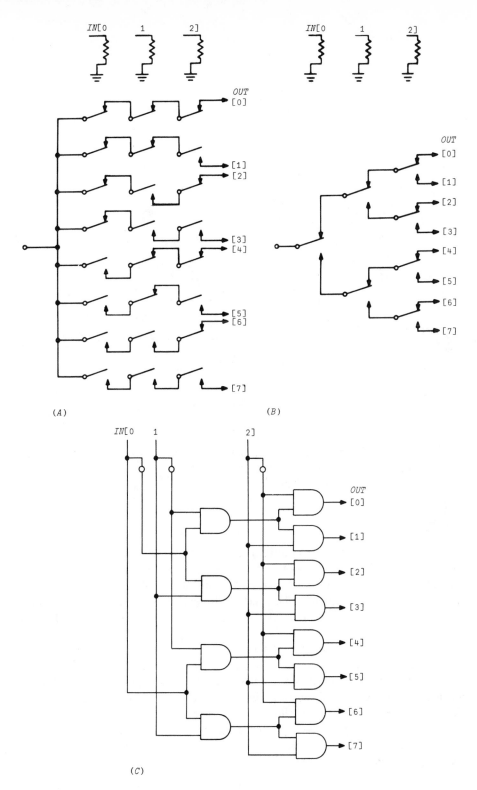

Figure 7-27 Tree decoders: (A) relay simplex decoder; (B) relay tree decoder; (C) 'and' tree decoder.

241

```
    ∇  OUT←TREEDEC8 IN
[1]     OUT1←,(IN[0]= 0 1)∘.∧IN[1]= 0 1
[2]     OUT2←,OUT1∘.∧IN[2]= 0 1
[3]     OUT3←,OUT2∘.∧IN[3]= 0 1
[4]     OUT4←,OUT3∘.∧IN[4]= 0 1
[5]     OUT5←,OUT4∘.∧IN[5]= 0 1
[6]     OUT6←,OUT5∘.∧IN[6]= 0 1
[7]     OUT←,OUT6∘.∧IN[7]= 0 1
    ∇
```

Program 7-28 8-input tree decoder.

INPUTS N	OUTPUTS	SIMPLEX ANDS	1 LEVEL INPUTS	FAN-IN	FAN-OUT	MATRIX ANDS	FAN-IN 2 INPUTS	FAN-OUT	LEVELS
2	4	4	8	2	2	4	8	2	1
3	8	8	24	3	4	12	24	4	2
4	16	16	64	4	8	24	48	4	2
6	64	64	384	6	32	88	176	8	3
8	256	256	2048	8	128	304	608	16	3
12	4096	4096	48K	12	2048	4272	8544	64	4

INPUTS N	OUTPUTS	MATRIX ANDS	FAN-IN 3 INPUTS	FAN-OUT	LEVELS	TREE ANDS	FAN-IN 2 INPUTS	FAN-OUT	LEVELS
2	4	4	8	2	1	4	8	2	1
3	8	8	24	4	1	12	24	4	2
4	16	20	56	8	2	28	56	8	3
6	64	76	236	16	2	124	248	32	5
8	256	276	824	64	2	508	1016	128	7
12	4096	4156	8350	256	3	8188	16376	2048	11

Table 7-29 Summary of decoders.

code converter, which provides the signals for a visual digit display (Exercise 7-12). Other examples are the converters that translate one character code to another. These components often use table look-up in a read-only store.

7-5 PRIORITY

The selection of one signal out of a set of possible candidates is called *priority* determination. The signal may indicate, for example, an interrupt request, such as *INTSTATUS* in *INTERRUPT*, Program 7-10, or the use of a section of storage, as will be discussed in Chapter 8. The selection depends upon the order of occurrence of the signals or upon the order of the locations that have been assigned to the signals.

The priority may be used to determine the order of service. Sometimes this service consists in removing an object, in which case the algorithm is called a *replacement* algorithm. Once the priority is used, a *reset* action may be required to indicate that the selected signal has been processed and to allow a fresh selection. Thus, in *INTERRUPT*, line 6, the selected interrupt status bit is turned off.

The term 'priority' is used here in a narrow sense. More generally, several levels of priority can be recognized, which divide the signals in classes rather than selecting one signal from the set.

Types of Priority. The most prominent priority algorithms are:

(a) Selection in order of location: the *leftmost one,* or fixed priority. This algorithm is used in *INTERRUPT* and described by *LEFTONE,* Program 7-30A.

(b) Selection by continuing in the order of the locations: the *round robin,* described in Program 7-30B.

```
      ∇ OUT←LEFTONE IN
  [1]    OUT←(ιρIN)=INι1
      ∇
        ⍝ A. LEFTMOST-ONE PRIORITY


      ∇ OUT←RROBIN IN;WHO
  [1]    WHO←LEFTONE(RBNPTR↓IN),RBNPTR↑IN
  [2]    OUT←((-RBNPTR)↑WHO),(-RBNPTR)↓WHO
  [3]    RBNPTR←(ρIN)|RBNPTR+(WHOι1)+∨/WHO
      ∇
        ⍝ B. ROUND-ROBIN PRIORITY
```

Program 7-30   Leftmost-one and round-robin priority.

(c) Selection in the order of occurrence: the *first come–first served* or *first in–first out* (*FIFO*) algorithm, described in Program 7-31.

```
      ∇ ARCHFIRSTIN IN
  [1]    LIST←LIST,2↓IN
  [2]    ROUT←ρIN
      ∇
        ⍝ FIFO INPUT


      ∇ ARCHLASTIN IN
  [1]    LIST←(2↓IN),LIST
  [2]    ROUT←ρIN
      ∇
        ⍝ LIFO INPUT


      ∇ OUT←ARCHFIRSTOUT
  [1]    OUT←(ROUTρ2)⊤1↑LIST
  [2]    LIST←1↓LIST
      ∇
        ⍝ FIFO OR LIFO OUTPUT
```

Program 7-31   FIFO and LIFO priority architecture.

(d) Selection in the order of nonoccurrence: the *least-recently-used,* or *LRU,* algorithm, described in Program 7-35.

(e) Selection in the inverse of the order of occurrence: the *last in–first out* (*LIFO*) algorithm, shown in Program 7-31.

Many more algorithms are possible. Sometimes a combination of algorithms is used, as is described in Chapter 8 for leftmost one and round robin.

The implementation of the leftmost-one and least-recently-used algorithms will be discussed below. The round-robin algorithm can be implemented by extending the leftmost-one implementation with a counter. The FIFO implementation is illustrated by the pipeline algorithm described in Chapter 8. The LIFO algorithm can be implemented in a similar way.

Leftmost-One Algorithm

For the implementation of the leftmost-one algorithm, the same design alternatives as found in the design of an adder are encountered. They will be briefly summarized here.

Algebraic Solution. For a small number of variables, a circuit such as that of Figure 7-32 can be obtained with methods like the minimization of Quine–McCluskey (Appendix D). These methods lend themselves to automation. APL programs can be provided as a design tool to give the decimal specification vector for an expression such as line 1 of *LEFTONE*, whereas other programs provide a Quine–McCluskey or a three-level nand solution for this decimal vector.

Basic Principle. Figure 7-33 shows a slice of a circuit that represents the idea behind the leftmost-one algorithm: an output is 1 if its input is 1 and no output

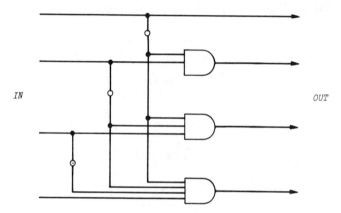

Figure 7-32   Leftmost-one circuit.

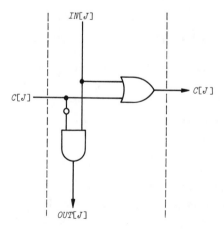

Figure 7-33   Basic element leftmost-one circuit.

to the left was 1. The circuit uses a carry C that has properties similar to the adder carry.

The basic principle results in a solution with many levels, comparable to the ripple adder implementation. By substituting the expressions for the lower levels in those of the following levels, the two-level solution of Figure 7-32 and *LEFTONE*4, Program 7-34, is obtained. This approach parallels that for the carry-predict adder *PREDICT*4, Program 2-26.

```
        ∇  OUT←LEFTONE4 IN
[1]     OUT← 0 0 0 0
[2]     OUT[0]←IN[0]
[3]     OUT[1]←IN[0 1]∧.= 0 1
[4]     OUT[2]←IN[0 1 2]∧.= 0 0 1
[5]     OUT[3]←IN∧.= 0 0 0 1
        ∇
```

Program 7-34   4-input leftmost-one implementation.

Multilevel Circuit.   For a large number of inputs the two-level solution is too expensive and the ripple solution too slow. An efficient solution can again be obtained by treating the input bits as groups, as in the larger, carry-predict adders. The design of such a circuit is left as an exercise for the reader (Exercise 7-10).

An example of a circuit element that follows *LEFTONE*4 is the TI SN74278. The circuit incorporates an input register. An extra input and output signal are provided for grouped priority determination.

An eight-input priority determination is combined with an eight-input encoder in the TI SN74148. The circuit has basically the architecture of *LEFTONE* followed by *ARCHENC*. In the implementation, the two functions are combined, however.

Least Recently Used Algorithm

ARCHLRU, Program 7-35, selects the least recently used element from a *usage list LIST*. *LIST* is updated by the algorithm *ARCHRU* each time an element is used. Together the two algorithms specify the architecture of the least-recently-used priority.

ARCHLRU simply selects the last item of the usage list *LIST* and encodes this number as a binary number. *ARCHRU* updates *LIST* by first removing the given value from the list and then placing it at the head of the list. *ARCHRU* may also

```
        ∇  ARCHRU IN
[1]     LIST←(2⊥IN),(LIST≠2⊥IN)/LIST
[2]     ROUT←ρIN
        ∇
            ⍝ RECENTLY-USED INPUT

        ∇  OUT←ARCHLRU
[1]     OUT←,(ROUTρ2)⊤¯1↑LIST
        ∇
            ⍝ LEAST-RECENTLY-USED OUTPUT
```

Program 7-35   Least-recently-used architecture.

be used as a reset function by specifying the least recently used element that was found by *ARCHLRU*.

In *ARCHRU*, line 1, the element of *LIST* that corresponds to *IN* produces a 0 in the compression vector; all other elements produce a 1. The particular element is thus eliminated from *LIST*. Subsequently, this element is concatenated at the left end of this vector, indicating its most recent use.

Implementation of LRU Algorithm.   In *IMPLRU* and *IMPRU*, Program 7-36, an implementation of the least recently used priority is shown. The implementation uses the logical matrix *LRUM*. The number of rows and columns of this matrix corresponds to the number of signals. When a signal occurs, the bits of the corresponding row of *LRUM* are set to 1 and the bits of the corresponding column are set to 0. At a given moment, the row with all bits equal to 0 indicates the least recently used row, hence the least recently occurring signal. In the example of *LRUM* in Program 7-36, this is row 4.

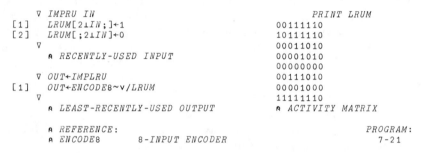

Program 7-36   Least-recently-used implementation.

The algorithm can be further refined by observing that the elements of the main diagonal of the matrix are always 0 and hence are superfluous. Also, pairs of bits that are symmetric with respect to this diagonal are always each other's inverse. Therefore, the only useful information in the matrix is the left lower or the right upper triangle next to the main diagonal. Thus, in the example of Program 7-36, the 64-bit matrix *LRUM* can be reduced to a triangle of 28 bits. The addressing of these bits becomes more involved, however.

7-6 SPECIAL CONTROL CIRCUITS

The implementation of special control circuits follows the principles discussed above. The condition code test, whose architecture is given in line 5 of *BRANCH*, is an example of such a circuit. Figure 7-37 gives an implementation for this architecture and *CCTEST*, Program 7-38, gives the corresponding APL expressions.

A switching algebra solution, manual or automated, will quickly result in the implementation of *CCTEST*. A thoughtful consideration of the specifications, however, usually is sufficient to suggest the desired solution. This is particularly

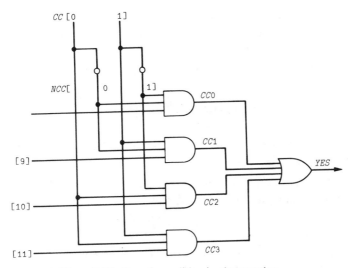

Figure 7-37   Branch condition implementation.

```
        ∇ YES←CCTEST CC
  [1]     NCC←~CC
  [2]     CC0←INST[8]∧NCC[0]∧NCC[1]
  [3]     CC1←INST[9]∧NCC[0]∧CC[1]
  [4]     CC2←INST[10]∧CC[0]∧NCC[1]
  [5]     CC3←INST[11]∧CC[0]∧CC[1]
  [6]     YES←CC0∨CC1∨CC2∨CC3
        ∇
```

Program 7-38   Branch condition implementation.

true when the specification is given with the implementation in mind, as is the case in this example.

EXERCISES

7-1   Give the architectural program *ODSI* which places the operands of the *SI* format in the registers *OD*1 and *OD*2, as suggested by Figure 1-3. The first operand uses base and displacement addressing; the second operand is immediate, comprising instruction bits 8 through 15. Both operands are one byte long.

7-2   Give the function *RLSTORE* of Program 7-2 which stores the results of an operation in the proper location for the *RR* and *RX* format.

7-3   Modify *IFETCH*32 and *IMPRX*, Programs 7-14 and 7-15, such that they match the datapath *PATHPAR*, Program 5-16. Determine the datapath *PATHIE* that can perform both the functions of *PATHPAR* and the instruction and operand fetch operations.

7-4   Design an implementation for *INTERRUPT*, Program 7-10. Use an extension of *PATHIBOX*, Program 7-16.

7-5   Design an I-box for a 16-bit-wide main store and local store and for a 16-bit-wide data-selection and serial datapath. Develop the gate programs for instruction and operand fetch.

7-6   Design the implementation *IMPSI* corresponding to the architecture *ODSI* of Exercise 7-1.

7-7   Determine the gate program *GATESI* derived from *IMPSI*, Exercise 7-6. Modify *PATHIBOX* as required.

7-8   Give the expressions for the two-level matrix decoder *MDEC*6, which corresponds to Figure 7-24B.

7-9   Give the APL expressions for a four-input tree decoder without using the outer product or the equality operator.

7-10 Determine the implementation *LEFTONE*64 that:
    (a)   Adheres to the architecture of *LEFTONE*.
    (b)   Has 64 as the dimension of the vectors *IN* and *OUT*.
    (c)   Has a maximum fan-in of five.
    (d)   Determines the output as much as possible in parallel.

7-11 Give an architecture and implementation for a 20-input decimal encoder.

7-12 Give the implementation for a BCD to seven-segment code converter the architecture of which is given by *ARCHBCD*7, Program 7-39.

```
     ∇ OUT←ARCHBCDTO7 IN
[1]    ∧ OUT←NORTH, NORTHEAST, SOUTHEAST, SOUTH, SOUTHWEST, NORTHWEST, CENTER
[2]    OUT←(7ρ2)⊤ 126 48 109 121 51 91 31 112 127 115[2⊥IN]
     ∇
```

Program 7-39   BCD to seven-segment code converter architecture.

7-13 Give an implementation of the round-robin priority of Program 7-30. Assume 8 input bits.

7-14 Give the implementation *IMPLRU*8 and *IMPRU*8 that uses only 28 bits of storage for eight users.

7-15 Rewrite *CCTEST*, Program 7-38, as a single expression by using the inner product.

7-16 Which modifications must be made to *PATHIBOX*, Program 7-16, such that it can communicate with *PATHPAR*, Program 5-16?

7-17 Give an architecture and an implementation for an encoder which generates an error signal when the input code is not 1-out-of-N.

8 STORAGE

Storage connects space and time. Hence, the separation of space and time mentioned in Chapter 5 involves the use of storage elements. In Chapter 5 and following, these storage elements were treated architecturally. In the present chapter, the implementation of the various stores that have been encountered will be considered. Particular attention will be given to the implementations that use several systems components for an architecturally single store.

Nature of Digital Storage

Storage can be defined as a piece of equipment that can absorb information and reproduce it unaltered later. In the analog technique, the faithfulness of recording and reproduction is an important quality criterion, as, for instance, it is in the tape recorder. This criterion is also of importance in the digital technique, but because of the discrete character of the digital technique, the terms *writing* and *reading* are used instead of recording and reproducing, and the term *reliability* instead of faithfulness.

A store is a special type of sequential switching circuit. The information read from the output of this circuit has the same content and form as the information, that was presented earlier to the input. A general sequential circuit can always be replaced by a functionally equivalent circuit consisting of a storage unit and a purely combinational circuit.

When storage is used only for reading, it is equivalent to a combinational decoding circuit, as in the case of the read-only store mentioned in Chapter 6.

Anthropomorphism. The term *memory* is often used for storage. Originally objections were raised against this term because of its anthropomorphism. Babbage has pointed out, however, that the use of terms, such as 'memory', 'read', 'know' and 'foresee', as applied to a computer, are just a matter of convenience and have no philosophical implications.

Although there is an analogy between storage and the human memory, there are, nevertheless, fundamental differences. First, a technical memory 'forgets' the old content perfectly when new information is entered, something humans find hard to do on command. Second, a technical memory has a *homogeneous* structure. The action of a storage location is independent of the use that is made of it. Human memory presents information more rapidly, as it is used more often. This property can be achieved in technical memories only when a number of storages of different speeds is combined in a *hierarchical* system.

Organization of the Chapter

In Section 8-1, the architecture of the various storage types is discussed. Since the implementation of storage is much influenced by the means of realization, that subject will be treated in Section 8-2 prior to the implementation. The discussion of storage implementation concerns its internal organization and its access. In Section 8-3, the implementation of single storage modules is discussed, while Sections 8-4 and 8-5 describe a modular and a hierarchical organization, respectively. Storage access may be single or multiple, as discussed in Section 8-6; it also may be buffered by a pipeline, as described in Section 8-7.

8-1 ARCHITECTURE OF STORAGE

In a complex digital system, information is stored at various places during shorter or longer periods. The storage types that are used to contain this information are discussed here first from an architectural point of view.

The minimal information capacity of a digital store is 1 bit. For all larger storage capacities, a distinction can be made between the number of bits that is read or written as a unit—the *word*—and the number of words that are contained in the storage—the storage *capacity*. The part of storage that is occupied by a given word is called the *location* of that word. In writing, a storage location is given a new content; in reading, the storage content remains unchanged. Therefore, reading is copying and writing is replacing. In reading and writing, the storage location concerned must be selected. The information that identifies the location to be selected is called the *address*.

Word Length.   The appearance of a storage location is determined only by the number of bits contained in that location, the *word length*. The meaning of the bits in that location are of no importance to the storage unit. One can distinguish storages with *fixed word length*, with the same number of bits for all locations, and storages with *variable word length*, whose locations contain different numbers of bits. In the latter case, the word length must either be stated with the address or be derived from the information in the storage unit.

Timing. When all bits of a word are read or written at the same moment, the storage is called *parallel*. When, in contrast, they are read or written in succession, the storage is called sequential, or *series*. Between these two extreme forms, the *series–parallel* solution is found.

Registers

The storage unit that contains 1 bit is the well-known *flip-flop*. The storage with a capacity of one word is the *register*. Figure 8-1 shows the symbolic representation of three storage types; Program 8-2 shows the APL description of these three types.

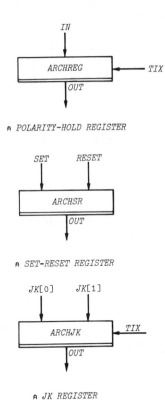

A *POLARITY-HOLD REGISTER*

A *SET-RESET REGISTER*

A *JK REGISTER*

Figure 8-1 Register types.

Polarity-hold Register. *ARCHREG* corresponds to the register type that has been used in the datapaths of the preceding chapters. The register copies the input when the read-in signal *TIX* is 1. It is therefore known as the *polarity-hold register*. The architecture provides a direct transfer of information when the read-in signal

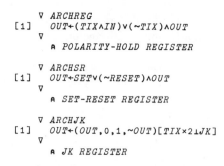

```
       ∇ ARCHREG
   [1]   OUT←(TIX∧IN)∨(~TIX)∧OUT
       ∇
         ⍝ POLARITY-HOLD REGISTER

       ∇ ARCHSR
   [1]   OUT←SET∨(~RESET)∧OUT
       ∇
           ⍝ SET-RESET REGISTER

       ∇ ARCHJK
   [1]   OUT←(OUT,0,1,~OUT)[TIX×2⊥JK]
       ∇
           ⍝ JK REGISTER
```

Program 8-2   Register architecture.

becomes 1; therefore the component is also called a D (for data) register.
ARCHREG is particularly suited to a datapath organization in which information
is transferred between sets of registers.

Set–Reset Register.   For the two remaining register types of Program 8-2, the
transitions between register states 0 and 1 are controlled individually. *ARCHSR*
has the set and reset transitions. This *set–reset register* is used in *CTLDIVENC*,
Program 6-13.

JK Register.   *ARCHJK*, the *JK register*, permits the invert transition as well
as the set and reset, such that all three conceivable transitions are available.
ARCHJK is described in true architectural fashion by listing the four possible
actions and indexing them by the value of *JK*. The description is valid only for a
single flip-flop; the descriptions of *ARCHREG* and *ARCHSR* are true for both
registers and single flip-flops.
   ARCHSR and *ARCHJK* are less suitable for the transfer of information and
are therefore more likely to be found in a machine implementation than in its
architecture.

Description of Registers.   The register functions use no explicit operands and
results. An explicit result would also have to appear as an operand, since *OUT*
appears as such in the expression for the register. This is a consequence of the
passing by value of the APL functions. Since these functions moreover allow a
maximum of two explicit operands, no elegant description is obtained. Hence, the
registers are described in the datapath with an expression similar to line 1 of
ARCHREG, and not by a function.

Local Store

   A number of registers treated as a group form a *local store*. The local store may
appear in the architecture. As such, it is sometimes called *scratch-pad* or referred
to as a set of *working registers*. In System/360 the *general-purpose registers* and the
floating-point registers are of this type.

Program 8-3 describes the reading and writing in the registers of a local store. In contrast to the preceding storage types, the concept of addressing is now required. The most prominent addressing methods are the direct addressing, illustrated in Program 8-3, and the LIFO addressing, using the algorithm of Program 7-31. In the latter case the register set is often called a *stack*, or *push-down store*.

```
   ∇ DATA←READLS ADDRESS                    ∇ DATA WRITELS ADDRESS
[1]    DATA←LOCALSTORE[2⊥ADDRESS;]      [1]    LOCALSTORE[2⊥ADDRESS;]←DATA
   ∇                                        ∇
```

Program 8-3   Reading and writing in a local store.

Since these first storage types all have a relatively small capacity, they can be built with more costly components having a short cycle time, such as one or more tens of nanoseconds. This makes them particularly suited for storing, quickly and briefly, data, instructions, or derived information.

Main Store

Main storage contains the part of a program that is in execution. The capacity and cycle time of the main storage therefore determine to a major degree the processing speed of a digital system. Capacities of thousands to millions of words with a cycle time of a few microseconds to a few hundred nanoseconds are normal.

Main storage and local storage have a simple architectural appearance. Both can be considered as a matrix in which each storage location forms a row, while the bits of the words constitute the elements of the rows. The functions *READMS* and *WRITEMS*, Program 8-4, describe the transfer from and to the main store. They are entirely analogous to the functions for the local store, because both storage types differ only in size and speed.

```
   ∇ DATA←READMS ADDRESS                    ∇ DATA WRITEMS ADDRESS
[1]    DATA←STORE[2⊥ADDRESS;]          [1]    STORE[2⊥ADDRESS;]←DATA
   ∇                                        ∇
```

Program 8-4   Reading and writing in a main store.

Auxiliary Store

Main storage is usually supplemented with auxiliary storage. Auxiliary stores are required because most programs cannot be stored permanently in the main store in an economical or reliable manner. Programs are not executed directly from *auxiliary stores*. The operating system sees to it that the necessary information is transferred from the auxiliary store to the main store and, if necessary, returned from the main store to the auxiliary store.

The adjectives 'auxiliary' and 'main' are influenced by computer operation rather than system use. Often auxiliary storage is just called 'storage' and the main store, in contrast, is called 'memory'.

Characteristics of Auxiliary Stores.   The rate at which successive groups of parallel bits are transported to or from storage is called the *transmission rate*. This rate describes quantitatively the series character of storage. Often, it is indicated in *characters per second* (CPS). The term character refers here to the group of bits that are treated in parallel.

The time required for the transmission of a word is the *transfer*, or *cycle, time*. When N words are read successively from storage, N times the transfer time will be required. Some storages are contructed from parts that each require an extra time period, the *waiting time*. The first word that is addressed in such a section requires the waiting time as well as the transfer time. Subsequent words from this section can each be transferred during one transfer time. The sum of transfer time and waiting time is the *access time*.

Auxiliary stores may have a capacity of 100,000 words to 100 million words. Such a capacity becomes economically feasible by allowing a large access time. This large access time is mainly caused by a waiting time of some milliseconds up to a fraction of a minute.

The word length of an auxiliary store is usually a multiple of the word length of main storage, to share the long waiting time. The term *block* is often used instead of 'word,' to avoid confusion with the word length of main storage.

Auxiliary stores need not be mechanically available. They may require a hand operation, such as the mounting of a tape or the entry of a pack of cards. Even though this manual operation involves a relatively very long waiting time, there is no essential difference with the automatically available stores. Provided the storage media remain under control of the system, they can be considered auxiliary storage.

One-Level Store

The combination of main store and auxiliary store forms a *storage hierarchy*. This hierarchy can be presented as one homogeneous main store, which has the capacity of the auxiliary store and which approaches the speed of the main store. Such a composite store is called a *one-level* store. The one-level store was used first in 1962 in the Ferranti Atlas computer (Kilburn et al., 1962).

When the difference in transmission speed of the main and auxiliary stores is several orders of magnitude, as is the case with core storage and disc storage, the two storage components usually remain recognizable in the architecture (Parmelee et al., 1972). The operating system now presents the two components as one store to the user. For this purpose the architecture may provide address translation.

Address Translation.   Address translation permits a program to be interrupted, removed from main storage, reentered at a different location, and resumed without change to any program values. This sequence of actions is typical in a multiprocessing environment. As a result of this action, the data and instructions are *relocated*.

Normally, the addresses of a relocated program no longer match the data locations. With *address translation*, however, the effective storage address, or *logical address*, is changed into a *physical address* by means of a set of tables. Whereas the effective address points at the logical location, the tables refer to the physical location. When a program is relocated, its table entries are changed accordingly. Hence, the program can be resumed without further address manipulation.

Address translation separates the logical address from the physical address. The range of the logical address is now limited only by the number of address bits. When this full address capacity is presented to the user, by the operating system, while actually the physical main store capacity is smaller, the system is said to have *virtual storage*.

Figure 8-5 and *TRANSADR*, Program 8-6, show an address translation architecture similar to one of the options of System/370. The translation uses two sets

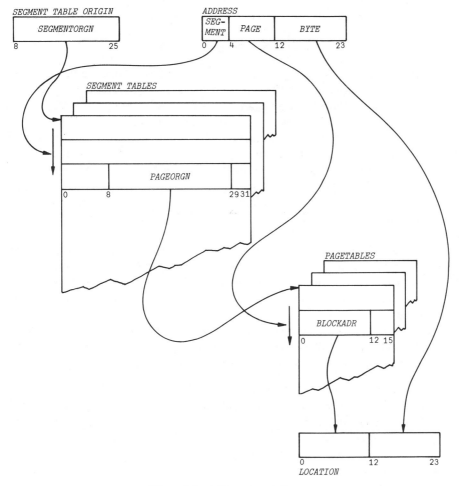

Figure 8-5 Address translation.

```
      ∇ LOCATION←TRANSADR ADDRESS;PAGEORGN;BLOCKADR
 [1]    ⍝ FIND PAGE TABLE ORIGIN IN SEGMENT TABLE
 [2]    PAGEORGN←,STORE[((2⊥SEGMENTORGN,6ρ0)+2⊥ADDRESS[SEGMENT],2ρ0)+⍳4;8+⍳21]
 [3]    ⍝ FIND BLOCK ADDRESS IN PAGE TABLE
 [4]    BLOCKADR←STORE[((2⊥PAGEORGN,3ρ0)+2⊥ADDRESS[PAGE],0);⍳12]
 [5]    ⍝ MAKE PHYSICAL ADDRESS
 [6]    LOCATION←BLOCKADR,ADDRESS[BYTE]
      ∇


      ∇ DECLTRANSADR
 [1]    ⍝ MAIN STORE
 [2]    STORE←N,8ρ0
 [3]    ⍝ SEGMENT ORIGIN IN CONTROL REGISTER 1
 [4]    SEGMENTORGN←18ρ0
      ∇


      ∇ TRANSADRFIELD
 [1]    ⍝ ONE OF FOUR MODES
 [2]    ⍝ 16 SEGMENTS OF 256 PAGES OF 4096 BYTES
 [3]    SEGMENT←⍳4
 [4]    PAGE←4+⍳8
 [5]    BYTE←12+⍳12
      ∇
```

Program 8-6   Address translation.

of tables: *segment* tables and *page* tables. The use of two tables rather than one simplifies the management of the tables by the systems program. Lengthy page tables are thus avoided, and programs may refer to common procedures with different segment names, yet using the same page tables.

The four high-order address bits identify the program segment to which the address refers. These bits are used in *TRANSADR* to select an entry of the segment table. This entry points to the page table that belongs to the program segment. Bits 4 through 11 of the address identify a page within a segment. These bits select an entry in the page table, which points to the block of storage where the page is located. Finally, the byte within the page is identified by the rightmost 12 address bits.

The segment and page tables are located in storage. An effective address therefore requires two storage references before the physical address is known. As such, the delays implied by the extra references would be quite unacceptable. In the implementation, however, the extra references to storage are eliminated a large percentage of the time.

Address translation is complicated by the exception cases that may occur when the table and block address have not been assigned. These exceptions are not treated here, but similar cases will be discussed in Section 8-5.

Cache Store.   When the difference in speed between two types of storage is one order of magnitude, they may be combined into an architecturally single store. Together, they now form the main store. This type of storage hierarchy is called a *cache store* and is discussed as part of storage implementation in Section 8-5.

Input and Output

When, after writing, the information is no longer available to the system, the information is considered *output* and the system component that performs the writing is called a *sink*, not storage. Correspondingly, information that is entered from outside the system is considered *input*. The system component that produces the input is called a *source*. Some equipment may be used either as auxiliary store or as source or sink, depending upon the nature of the operating system.

8-2   STORAGE REALIZATION

A storage medium must have more than one stable state in space or in time. Stable states in time can be obtained when the storage medium causes a delay. Since almost all physical phenomena meet this requirement, many storage media have been investigated. The competition between the various media on the basis of reliability and efficiency, however, is so strong that remarkably few physical phenomena have been applied on a large scale. In this section, the most frequently used types will be briefly considered. Special attention will be given to those realization aspects that affect system behavior. Table 8-7 gives a summary of these storage types.

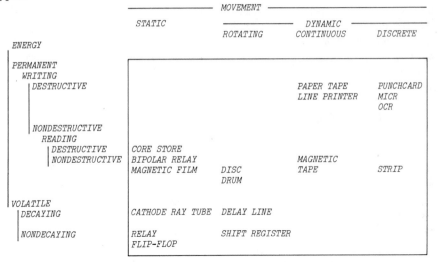

ENERGY	STATIC	MOVEMENT — DYNAMIC		
		ROTATING	CONTINUOUS	DISCRETE
PERMANENT WRITING				
DESTRUCTIVE			PAPER TAPE LINE PRINTER	PUNCHCARD MICR OCR
NONDESTRUCTIVE READING				
DESTRUCTIVE	CORE STORE			
NONDESTRUCTIVE	BIPOLAR RELAY MAGNETIC FILM	DISC DRUM	MAGNETIC TAPE	STRIP
VOLATILE DECAYING	CATHODE RAY TUBE	DELAY LINE		
NONDECAYING	RELAY FLIP-FLOP	SHIFT REGISTER		

Table 8-7   Storage realization forms.

Permanent Stores

The exchange of information, such as reading or writing, always requires energy. For the storing of information, in principle, however, no energy is required. When, indeed, no energy is used to preserve the stored information, the storage type is called *permanent*.

Destructive Writing.   Writing into a permanent store can be either destructive or nondestructive. In *destructive* writing, the storage medium is consumed. Therefore, it should be inexpensive and easily handled. The most suitable medium is paper, in the form of a tape or roll. More complex equipment is required for a card. The discrete nature of the card, however, gives considerable functional advantages, such as its use as a returnable document or in sorting and collating.

Destructive writing usually occurs mechanically by punching or printing. Reading can be done with either a stationary or a moving medium. The punched information is sensed mechanically or electrically. The printed information may be recognized by *optical character recognition*, or *OCR*; or *magnetic-ink character recognition*, or *MICR*.

Destructive writing is used mainly for input and output. It can also be used for auxiliary storage, however. The mechanical nature of this equipment results in a relatively large waiting time.

Nondestructive Writing.   In all subsequent storage types, the writing is not destructive. When a storage medium permits *nondestructive writing*, the medium can be used repeatedly. When the storage medium is permanent, a distinction can be made between static and dynamic stores. In the *static store*, the information does not move with respect to the access mechanism. In the *dynamic store*, the information does move with respect to the access mechanism. In both cases, magnetic methods are almost always used.

For nondestructive writing in a permanent storage medium, the information may be read destructively or nondestructively. The term 'destructive' refers here to the content of the store, not to the storage medium itself as with destructive writing.

Destructive Reading.   In *destructive reading*, the storage medium loses the information that is read. Reading occurs by testing the state of the storage medium statically or dynamically. In the first case, the state of the storage medium, as a rule, is changed. Therefore, the content of the store must be *regenerated* after the reading. As a consequence, it is impossible to ascertain whether the information was written properly without having to write it anew.

Since the storage medium does not move with respect to the access mechanism, there is no waiting time, resulting from mechanical motion. Furthermore, an intense coupling of the medium and the access equipment is possible, which reduces the access time. The most prominent example of a permanent, nondestructive-writing, destructive-reading, static store is the *core store*.

Nondestructive Reading.   The extra time required for regeneration has led to a number of proposals for nondestructive reading. For the *nondestructive read-out*, or *NDRO*, the information remains undisturbed when read. For a permanent, static store, the alternative nondestructive methods have never succeeded in replacing the core store. For the dynamic stores, however, nondestructive reading is universal.

Permanent Dynamic Store.   The permanent dynamic stores can be subdivided into the rotating and streaming types, according to the motion of the storage medium. The streaming type can be subdivided into the continuous tape type and the discrete strip type.

Rotating Store.   The *drum store*, one of the oldest storage types, and the *disc store*, which is currently more prominent, are both examples of a rotating store. Each of these devices contains a large number of circular *tracks*. With a *head*, the information in a track can be read or written.

Since in the dynamic store the information moves with respect to the access mechanism, the desired information is normally not directly available, but hidden, or *latent*. The latency introduces a waiting time into the access of this information. The drum store was originally used as a main store, as, for instance, in the IBM 650. The rotating stores are now normally used as auxiliary stores.

Tape Store.   The major example of a *tape* store is magnetic tape equipment. Here, the tracks run along the length of the tape. Since there are usually few tracks, one head per track is used. The latency is very large for this type of store. Magnetic tape is much used for archival storage. A magnetic tape can be mailed, thereby transmitting large volumes of data at low cost.

Strip Store.   In magnetic *strip stores*, the storage medium is divided into a large number of strips or cards. Each strip is first selected and subsequently treated as a rotating or tape type of store. Very large storage capacities can be obtained with this method, at relatively low cost. The mechanical selection introduces a considerable wait time, however.

Volatile Stores

Storages that require energy to preserve the information are *nonpermanent* or *volatile*. A borderline case is the cryogenic store. Superconducting currents in themselves require no energy to be maintained. A store using this phenomenon is, therefore, permanent. To maintain the extremely low working temperature, however, very definitely requires energy.

Decaying and Nondecaying Stores.   When in the volatile store, the energy preserves the information unchanged, the store is considered *nondecaying*. In other types of volatile stores, however, the information gradually disappears and therefore must be regenerated. These are called *decaying* storage types. In destructive reading, regeneration was required by the reading. In the decaying storage type, regeneration is required as long as the information remains in storage. Therefore, the information must be *refreshed* periodically.

Static Volatile Store.   The volatile stores can also be divided into static and dynamic types. In the static types, the information is stationary with respect to the storage medium or the access mechanism.

A prominent example of the nondecaying store is the electronic flip-flop circuit. Many variation of these flip-flops are used in large integrated storage units.

An example of a decaying store is the cathode-ray store, which was used in the earliest computers and was known as the Williams tube. Some integrated stores are also of the decaying type and require extra refreshing cycles.

Dynamic Volatile Store.   In the dynamic volatile stores, the information moves with respect to the storage medium. The medium is stationary to allow proper coupling with the access equipment. An example of a nondecaying rotating store is the *shift register*. The information streams through the register upon reading and writing. The most common decaying form is the *delay line*. The information is rotated as long as it must be stored.

8-3 IMPLEMENTATION OF A SINGLE STORAGE UNIT

The implementation of storage bridges the gap between the architecture and the realization. What appears as one unit architecturally may, in actuality, be built from several system components. It is the task of the implementation to make the physical reality conform to the architectural ideal.

The internal organization of storage will be discussed in three sections. The present section deals with the implementation of a single storage unit. Section 8-4 concerns the construction of storage from several modules of equal size and speed, the modular construction. Section 8-5 discusses the construction of storage from components that differ in size and speed, the hierarchical construction.

Register Implementation

The implementation of the registers of Program 8-2 is shown in Figure 8-8 and described in Program 8-9. Because of the sequential nature of the circuits a simple implementation description, as illustrated for *IMPREG* and *IMPSR*, cannot be simulated. The description can be made simulatable, however, by enclosing it in a loop that tests for quiescence of the outputs, as shown for *IMPJK*. This procedure is similar to that for *RIPASYNC*, Program 2-45, and aids in testing the logical correctness of the implementation.

In the preceding system implementations, such as *PATHPAR*, the architectural description of the registers is always used, and there is no point in replacing those expressions by the implementation description as long as the registers are available as a unit.

IMPSR shows that for a simultaneous occurrence of the *SET* and *RESET* signals, the true output *OUT* is 1. Thus, the *SET* wins from the *RESET*, which explains the name *set-dominant* flip-flop used for this circuit. Note, however, that for the opposite output, *NOUT*, the signal *RESET* is dominant.

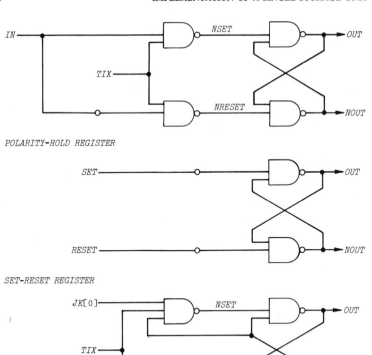

POLARITY-HOLD REGISTER

SET-RESET REGISTER

JK REGISTER

Figure 8-8   Register implementation.

```
      ∇ IMPREG
[1]     NRESET←TIX⋆~IN
[2]     NSET←TIX⋆IN
[3]     NOUT←OUT⋆NRESET
[4]     OUT←NOUT⋆NSET
      ∇
        ⍝ POLARITY-HOLD REGISTER

      ∇ IMPSR
[1]     NOUT←OUT⋆~RESET
[2]     OUT←NOUT⋆~SET
      ∇
        ⍝ SET-RESET REGISTER

      ∇ IMPJK
[1]     NRESET←~∧/JK[1],OUT,TIX
[2]     NSET←~∧/JK[0],NOUT,TIX
[3]   CONT:NOUT←OUT⋆NRESET
[4]     OUT←NOUT⋆NSET
[5]     →(OUT=NOUT)/CONT
      ∇
        ⍝ JK REGISTER
```

Program 8-9   Register implementation.

Type of Operation. Sequential circuits can operate in two modes. In the *fundamental mode*, the duration of a signal is considered to be long with respect to the speed of the circuit. Hence, all changes that are possible in the circuit will take place. In the *pulse mode*, the signal is considered to be short, a pulse, such that only one change in the status of the circuit is effected.

The usual application of *ARCHREG* assumes that the read-in signal *TIX* momentarily transfers the input *IN* to the output *OUT*. The implementation *IMPREG* satisfies this requirement when *TIX* is treated by the circuit as a pulse. Sometimes a more complex circuit, employing two flip-flops, the doubly latched, or master-slave circuit, is used to ensure the momentary operation.

ARCHREG can also be operated in the fundamental mode. In that case, the output *OUT* will follow the input *IN*, as long as the read-in signal *TIX* is 1. *IMPREG* is also a proper implementation for that case.

The set-reset register similarly can operate both in the fundamental mode and in the pulse mode. The *JK* register, however, operates only in the pulse mode, since the invert transition for *JK* equal to 1 1 cannot be made in the fundamental mode.

The various register types are widely available as components. The number of individual flip-flops packaged in one circuit module is usually restricted to two or four, owing to the limited number of pins available on the package.

Local and Main Storage Implementation

Mode of Operation. For a typical local store, only one word can be read or written at a time. As stated, more than one simultaneous operation would be possible, in particular when integrated circuits are used. This, however, increases the number of connections of the storage unit.

In an integrated circuit, the number of connections is limited through the relatively large amount of physical space, also called *real estate*, which each pin requires. Also, the module on which the circuit is mounted can accommodate only a limited number of pins. Hence, the number of connections is limited by the space available for the pins, the *pin limitation*.

For a main store, the cost per bit is decisive, indicating a minimum of complexity. Hence, simultaneous reading and writing is ruled out.

Since only one action takes place at a time, an encoded address can be used to identify the desired location. Thus, relatively large stores can be built as a single unit with a moderate number of pins. For instance, a local store of 8K words of 9 bits each requires 13 address, 9 data, and 2 read-write connections, or a total of some 24 logical connections.

Overlap. The action of a store consists of data selection—the addressing—and data transmission—the reading or writing. When the selection is more complex, it will require more time and lengthen the storage cycle. In some cases, however, it is possible to perform this selection simultaneously with the preceding transmission. These two actions, then, are *overlapped*. Thus, the time between two successive transmissions can be shorter than the time required for a complete storage cycle.

Overlapping is a special case of parallel operation. Therefore, the term 'overlapping' is also used for the simultaneous operation of various system components, such as the processing unit, the instruction unit, storage, input, and output.

Split Cycle. Transmission to or from core storage consists of two parts. During the first part, the storage content is read destructively; hence, the bits in the location become 0. During the second part, new information is placed in the storage location. In reading, the old information is reintroduced into the storage location; that is, the storage content is regenerated. In writing, the old storage content is ignored and the information to be written is introduced in the second part of the cycle.

In this type of storage, it is possible to use one cycle for both reading and writing. The cycle is then split into two parts. The data that are read in the first part can be processed and their results can be written into storage during the second part. This is called a *split cycle*. The split cycle is usually longer than a single cycle but shorter than two successive complete cycles.

8-4 MODULAR CONSTRUCTION

A large main store is often built from a number of elementary storage units. These storage units each have the character of a single store and are called *storage modules*. The storage modules of a main store are usually identical in structure. The ways in which modules may be combined can be described as parallel, juxtaposed, and interleaved. These three modular organizations are shown in Program 8-10.

```
      ∇ DATA←READPAR ADDRESS
[1]    DATA←,STORE[;2⊥ADDRESS;]
      ∇
       ⍝ PARALLEL MODULES

      ∇ DATA←READJXP ADDRESS
[1]    DATA←STORE[2⊥2↑ADDRESS;2⊥2↓ADDRESS;]
      ∇
       ⍝ JUXTAPOSED MODULES

      ∇ DATA←READILV ADDRESS
[1]    DATA←STORE[2⊥‾2↑ADDRESS;2⊥‾2↓ADDRESS;]
      ∇
       ⍝ INTERLEAVED MODULES

      ∇ DECLMODULE
[1]    ⍝ 4 MODULES WITH N[0] LOCATIONS OF N[1] BITS
[2]    ⍝ MAIN STORE
[3]    STORE←(4,N)ρ0
      ∇
```

Program 8-10   Reading from modular store.

Parallel Modules

When, for instance, a store is constructed of four modules, each module can contain one fourth of all words. All modules, then, are active in the transmission of a word. Hence, they are called *parallel modules*. The behavior of such a store does not differ in principle from that of a single store.

Juxtaposed Modules

The modules can also be so combined that, in the transmission of a word, only one module is active. The addressing may now be arranged such that each quadrant of the addressing range pertains to one module. This storage construction is said to use *juxtaposed modules*. It is used by the Univac 1110.

Interleaved Modules

Another approach assigns successive word addresses in turn to the available modules. This method is called the *interleaving* of storage. It is used by many computers, such as the CDC 6600, which uses 32-way interleaving, the System/360 Model 91, using 16-way interleaving, and the System/370 Model 168, using 4-way interleaving.

Performance of Modular Store. When the modules can be active simultaneously, the last two methods may result in a speed improvement. In the juxtaposed method, the programmer can achieve this speed increase, for instance, by placing instructions in one module and data in another. Or, in multiprocessing the processors may have their information in separate modules. Also, in the case of failure within a module, the system is still usable. The organization of storage consequently becomes a part of the architecture.

In the case of interleaving, a user strategy is neither required nor practical. The method counts on the probability of the references being equally divided among the modules.

Table 8-11 demonstrates the working of a four-times interleaved store. The address stream consists of successive instruction addresses alternated with more-or-less random data addresses. In the optimum case, all modules would be constantly busy and the address stream could be four times as fast as the storage

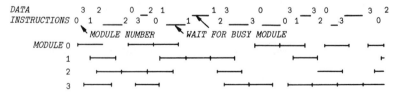

Table 8-11   Example of access to an interleaved store.

module speed. Table 8-11 illustrates that in practice the speed is reduced because modules are addressed that are still occupied by a preceding action. Hellerman (1972) has shown that for N-way interleaving and random addresses, an approximate speed improvement of $N * 0.56$ can be expected (Knuth and Rao, 1975).

The address stream of Table 8-11 cannot be derived from a simple instruction unit. In that case, the addresses of the data are known only after the instructions have been read; hence extra delays occur in the address stream. Section 8-7 discusses the creation of such an address stream with the aid of pipelines.

Addressing of Modular Stores. Program 8-10 shows that the addressing of the modules poses no implementation problems: each module is fed the proper address bits, and either all modules participate or the high- or low-order address bits select the desired module. The gating of data to and from several modules working simultaneously is more involved, however. It is discussed under storage access, Section 8-6.

8-5 HIERARCHICAL CONSTRUCTION

An architecturally single store may be implemented by a storage hierarchy. The simplest and most prominent hierarchy consists of a relatively small, fast store and a large, slower store. The information that is expected to be used currently is kept in the fast store. During the addressing, the system *looks aside* in this secret supply, or cache, to see if the information is available. This concept of cache storage was proposed in 1965 by Wilkes and was used for the first time in the IBM System/360 Model 85 (Conti et al., 1968; Liptay, 1968).

In this section, first the organization of a cache store is described. Next, the alternate look-aside mechanisms as used in System/370 are discussed. Finally the application of the look-aside principle to address translation and instruction buffering is considered.

Cache with Associative Search

Figure 8-12 shows that in the standard Model 85, the fast store, the cache, consists of 16K bytes of 8 bits each. It has a cycle of 80 nanoseconds. The slower large store has a capacity of 512K to 4096K bytes and a cycle of 1 microsecond. Both stores are divided in sectors of 1K bytes. The information in large store is always complete. The cache sectors duplicate some large storage sectors entirely or in part.

Reading from the Cache. *READCACHE*, Program 8-13, illustrates the reading from a cache store and Figure 8-14 shows the corresponding interpretation of the address bits. There are three possibilities:

(a) The cache has no sector that corresponds to the desired address.

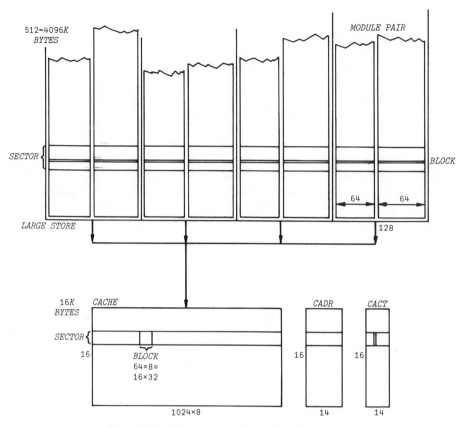

Figure 8-12 Schematic representation of cache store.

This case is recognized in *READCACHE* by the failure of the branches in lines 4 and 10. The information is read from the large store in line 12 and sent both to the cache and the requestor. Since the cache has no corresponding sector space assigned, it must do so at this time by eliminating another sector from the cache. To this end, in line 6, the least recently used (LRU) sector of the cache is assigned to the new sector. In line 7 the sector address is recorded in the set of cache address registers *CADR* at a location corresponding to the assigned cache sector.

ARCHLRU, Program 7-35, obtains the least recently used element from the usage list *LIST*. *LIST* is updated by the algorithm *ARCHRU* each time a sector is used, as indicated in *READCACHE*, line 17.

The data transmission from large storage to the cache occurs 64 bytes at a time. Large storage has a word length of 16 bytes and is constructed from pairs of parallel modules with a word length of 8 bytes each, which always work simultaneously. Furthermore, large storage is interleaved four times. Therefore, the transmission of the 64 bytes requires a cycle of 1 microsecond. Hence, the presence of the cache in this case results in neither a timing advantage nor a disadvantage.

```
     ∇ DATA←READCACHE ADDRESS
[1]    ⍝ TEST FOR SECTOR PRESENT
[2]    MATCH←CADR∧.=ADDRESS[SECTOR]
[3]    WHO←ARCHENC MATCH
[4]    →(∨/MATCH)/SCT
[5]    ⍝ ASSIGN CACHE LOCATION TO SECTOR
[6]    WHO←ARCHLRU
[7]    CADR[2⊥WHO;]←ADDRESS[SECTOR]
[8]    CACT[2⊥WHO;]←0
[9]    ⍝ TEST FOR BLOCK PRESENT
[10] SCT:→CACT[2⊥WHO;2⊥ADDRESS[BLOCK]]]/BLK
[11]   ⍝ FETCH BLOCK
[12]   CACHE[2⊥WHO;2⊥ADDRESS[BLOCK];;]← 16 32 ρSTORE[;2⊥ADDRESS[SECTOR,BLOCK];]
[13]   CACT[2⊥WHO;2⊥ADDRESS[BLOCK]]←1
[14]   ⍝ READ FROM CACHE
[15] BLK:DATA←CACHE[2⊥WHO;2⊥ADDRESS[BLOCK];2⊥ADDRESS[WORD];]
[16]   ⍝ UPDATE USEAGE LIST
[17]   ARCHRU WHO
     ∇


     ∇ DECLCACHE
[1]    ⍝ MAIN STORE WITH 8 MODULES OF N WORDS OF 64 BITS
[2]    STORE←(8,N,64)ρ0
[3]    ⍝ CACHE WITH 16 SECTORS OF 16 BLOCKS OF 16 WORDS OF 32 BITS
[4]    CACHE← 16 16 16 32 ρ0
[5]    ⍝ CACHE ADDRESS REGISTERS
[6]    CADR← 16 14 ρ0
[7]    ⍝ CACHE ACTIVITY BITS
[8]    CACT← 16 16 ρ0
[9]    ⍝ CACHE USEAGE LIST
[10]   LIST←ι16
     ∇


     ∇ CACHEFIELD
[1]    ⍝ ADDRESS SECTIONS
[2]    SECTOR←ι14
[3]    BLOCK←14+ι4
[4]    WORD←18+ι4
[5]    BYTE←22+ι2
     ∇

       ⍝ REFERENCE:                                       PROGRAM:
       ⍝ ARCHENC      ENCODER ARCHITECTURE                   7-19
       ⍝ ARCHLRU      LEAST-RECENTLY-USED ARCHITECTURE       7-35
       ⍝ ARCHRU       LRU UPDATE ARCHITECTURE                7-35
```

Program 8-13 Reading from cache store.

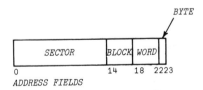

Figure 8-14 Address format used in cache organization.

The sector of the cache is subdivided in 16 blocks of 64 bytes. The 64 bytes of a block are considered as 16 words of 4 bytes, or 32 bits. One of these blocks is now filled in line 12 of *READCACHE*. The fact that this block is filled is noted in line 13 by recording a 1 in the corresponding element of the *validity*, or *activity matrix CACT*.

(b) The cache has a sector corresponding to the address, but the block concerned is not filled.

The branch in line 4 succeeds in this case but not the branch in line 10. Again the information is read from the large store and sent to both the requestor and the cache. A new sector need not be assigned in the cache, but the validity bit of the corresponding block must be set to 1, as occurs in line 13.

(c) The cache has the desired information.

The branches in lines 4 and 10 both succeed and the program continues at line 15. The information can now be read directly from the cache.

Because of the necessary address comparisons, two cycles of 80 nanoseconds each are required for the reading operation. The store is involved in only one of these cycles. Hence, the comparison cycle overlaps the read cycle, and in each cycle, information can be obtained from the cache.

In case (c), the desired speed advantage is obtained. This case occurs for 97% of the addresses.

Writing in the Cache.   In writing, the information is always placed in the large store. The information is also placed in the cache if a corresponding block is available. The usage list *LIST* is not updated, however.

The principle of writing both in storage and in the cache is called *storing through*. This procedure assures that the information in the cache always matches the information in the large store. Therefore, the content of the cache never needs to be transported to the large store when a sector of the cache is reassigned. Only the corresponding validity bits need to be made 0, as is shown in line 8 of *READ-CACHE*.

Writing always requires a cycle of 1 microsecond. The write action may, however, be overlapped with the reading from the cache and with writing in other storage modules. Since writing is associated with about 1 out of 8 addresses, the writing action, on the average, will not introduce a delay. Here it is of particular importance that the speed difference between the two storage components be not more than one order of magnitude.

System Implications of the Cache

The system composed of a cache and a large store is architecturally a homogeneous single store. Model 85 makes no distinction between storage requests for instructions, data, or transmission to and from peripheral units.

Local Cache.   A good part of the speed advantage of the cache is its nearness to the processing unit. This advantage is lost when the cache is shared by several processors. Also the storage areas addressed by the various processors are usually distinct, which would result in a larger cache size. Therefore, in a large computer system, with distinct processors for storage management and for the traffic to peripheral units as well as one or more processors for instruction streams, it is desirable to give each processor its own cache, called a *local cache*.

The use of local caches, however, introduces a problem. When information is stored, the data and corresponding address should be sent to all caches to make sure that copies of the storage area, which may be in the caches, remain up to date. This elaborate procedure is called the *broadcasting* of the address.

Cache Performance. Simulation shows that the average speed of the cache system is 81% of the speed of a homogeneous large store with an 80-nanosecond cycle. Since the size of the cache store is typically 1% of the large store, this gain in speed is remarkable. The cache system is only possible because the addresses of programs are not arbitrary. When the address values are entirely random, the chance of finding the data in the cache is not 97%, but less than 1% (Liptay, 1968).

Look Aside

The look-aside implementation used in the cache organization is a universal implementation tool. When for a large number of potential results a small selection is likely to be obtained repeatedly, it may be worthwhile to store these results and their associated arguments for future reference. This situation is particularly likely in addressing, where references to a sector may recur for a certain time period. This explains why the look-aside implementation is not only used in the cache organization but also in address translation and instruction fetch implementations.

The look-aside implementation requires a search for a given argument. The two most prominent algorithms for this search are the associative search and the set-associative search.

Associative Search. Both in reading and writing, the set of cache registers, *CADR*, is searched for the desired sector address. This is an example of the use of associative addressing within a machine implementation.

In *associative addressing* the addresses of the items in storage are placed in storage locations that are associated with the locations of these items. The address of an item is found by searching through the address locations. Once the address is found, the location of the corresponding item is also known. Thus, the address of a sector of the cache is stored in *CADR*. In line 2 of *READCACHE* this array is searched and the location of the matching address is noted. This address, when encoded in line 3, is now used to address the associated cache sector.

The matrix *CADR* contains 16 addresses of 14 bits each. The expression of *READCACHE* line 2 implies 16 sets of 14 equality circuits combined by 16 'and' circuits with a fan-in of 14. Since 'equal' followed by 'and' is the inverse of exclusive-or followed by 'or,' these components may also be used. In any event, the total number of components is appreciable. Figure 8-15 shows the equipment involved.

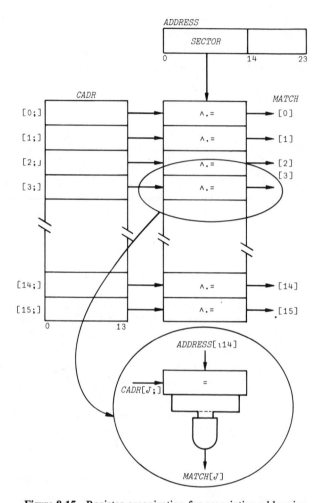

Figure 8-15 Register organization for associative addressing.

Set-associative Search. The associative look-aside implementation for the cache becomes quite expensive when a large number of sectors, hence addresses, is used. As an alternative, set-associative addressing can be used.

The *set-associative addressing* maps the given address into a shorter direct address. This short address now points to a small number of address registers whose contents are compared to the original address.

Cache with Set-associative Search

Figure 8-16 shows the equipment involved in a set-associative search and Program 8-17, the initial implementation algorithm of a cache organization using

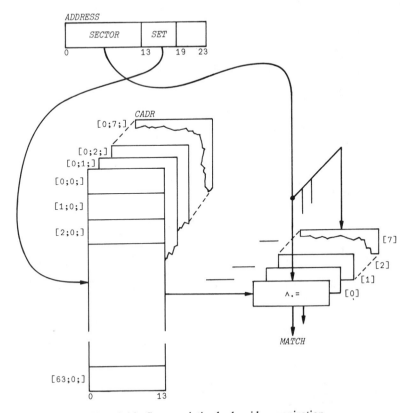

Figure 8-16　Set-associative look-aside organization.

such a search. The organization reflects the method used in the System/370 Models 158 and 168.

The cache for the Model 168 consists of 16K bytes organized as 64 sets of 8 sectors of 32 bytes, or 4 words of 64 bits. The directory for this cache *CADR* contains one entry for each sector. Each set of 8 entries is addressed directly. In the Model 168, bits 13 through 18 of the 24-bit effective address are used for this purpose. The content of the entries is compared with the high-order address bits, bits 0 through 13. The entry that gives a match indicates in which array of the cache the corresponding sector is found.

When the address does not match, or if the corresponding validity bit in *CACT* is 0, one of the eight sectors corresponding to the effective address is assigned by the least recently used algorithm. For this purpose the usage list of that set is updated in *READCACHESET*, line 19. The usage lists of all sets are combined in a matrix *CLRU* of 64 by 8 numbers. *IMPLRU*, Program 7-36, shows that the implementation would require at least 28 bits for each of the 64 sets. Actually,

```
       ∇ DATA←READCACHESET ADDRESS
[1]      ⍝ TEST FOR SECTOR PRESENT
[2]      MATCH←CADR[2⊥ADDRESS[SET];;]∧.=ADDRESS[SECTOR]
[3]      WHO←ARCHENC MATCH
[4]      →(∨/MATCH)/SCT
[5]      ⍝ ASSIGN CACHE LOCATION TO SECTOR
[6]      LIST←CLRU[2⊥ADDRESS[SET];]
[7]      WHO←ARCHLRU
[8]      CADR[2⊥ADDRESS[SET];2⊥WHO;]←ADDRESS[SECTOR]
[9]      CACT[2⊥ADDRESS[SET];2⊥WHO;]←0
[10]     ⍝ TEST FOR BLOCK PRESENT
[11]     SCT:→CACT[2⊥ADDRESS[SET];2⊥WHO;2⊥ADDRESS[BLOCK]]/BLK
[12]     ⍝ FETCH BLOCK
[13]     DATABLOCK←(¯2↑⍴CACHE)⍴READMS ADDRESS[SECTOR,SET,BLOCK]
[14]     CACHE[2⊥ADDRESS[SET];2⊥WHO;2⊥ADDRESS[BLOCK];;]←DATABLOCK
[15]     CACT[2⊥ADDRESS[SET];2⊥WHO;2⊥ADDRESS[BLOCK]]←1
[16]     ⍝ READ FROM CACHE
[17]     BLK:DATA←CACHE[2⊥ADDRESS[SET];2⊥WHO;2⊥ADDRESS[BLOCK];2⊥ADDRESS[WORD];]
[18]     ⍝ UPDATE USEAGE LIST
[19]     LIST←CLRU[2⊥ADDRESS[SET];]
[20]     ARCHRU WHO
[21]     CLRU[2⊥ADDRESS[SET];]←LIST
       ∇


       ∇ DECLCACHE158
[1]      ⍝ MAIN STORE WITH N WORDS OF 128 BITS
[2]      STORE←(N,128)⍴0
[3]      ⍝ CACHE WITH 256 SETS OF 2 SECTORS OF 1 BLOCK OF 4 WORDS OF 32 BITS
[4]      CACHE← 256 2 1 4 32 ⍴0           ∇ CACHEFIELD158
[5]      ⍝ CACHE ADDRESS REGISTERS        [1]    ⍝ ADDRESS SECTIONS
[6]      CADR← 256 2 12 ⍴0                [2]    SECTOR←⍳12
[7]      ⍝ CACHE ACTIVITY BITS            [3]    SET←12+⍳8
[8]      CACT← 256 2 1 ⍴0                 [4]    BLOCK←⍳0
[9]      ⍝ CACHE USEAGE MATRIX            [5]    WORD←20+⍳2
[10]     CLRU← 256 2 ⍴⍳2                  [6]    BYTE←22+⍳2
       ∇                                ∇


       ∇ DECLCACHE168
[1]      ⍝ MAIN STORE WITH N WORDS OF 256 BITS
[2]      STORE←(N,256)⍴0
[3]      ⍝ CACHE WITH 64 SETS OF 8 SECTORS OF 1 BLOCK OF 4 WORDS OF 64 BITS
[4]      CACHE← 64 8 1 4 64 ⍴0           ∇ CACHEFIELD168
[5]      ⍝ CACHE ADDRESS REGISTERS        [1]    ⍝ ADDRESS SECTIONS
[6]      CADR← 64 8 13 ⍴0                 [2]    SECTOR←⍳13
[7]      ⍝ CACHE ACTIVITY BITS            [3]    SET←13+⍳6
[8]      CACT← 64 8 1 ⍴0                  [4]    BLOCK←⍳0
[9]      ⍝ CACHE USEAGE MATRIX            [5]    WORD←19+⍳2
[10]     CLRU← 64 8 ⍴⍳8                   [6]    BYTE←21+⍳3
       ∇                                ∇

       ⍝ REFERENCE:                                 PROGRAM:
       ⍝ ARCHENC     ENCODER ARCHITECTURE              7-19
       ⍝ ARCHLRU     LEAST-RECENTLY-USED ARCHITECTURE  7-35
       ⍝ ARCHRU      LRU UPDATE ARCHITECTURE           7-35
       ⍝ READMS      READ FROM MAIN STORE              8-4
```

Program 8-17   Reading from set-associative cache.

the implementation uses only 64 by 10 bits, by treating sectors in pairs, thus obtaining a two-level *LRU* algorithm.

READCACHESET uses symbolic names for the address sections. The declarations of Program 8-17 show the dimensions for Models 158 and 168. Both machines use only one block per sector. By allowing several blocks per sector the associative addressing for the Model 85 becomes a subset of the set-associative addressing.

```
      ∇ LOCATION←TRANSASIDE ADDRESS
[1]     ⍝ HASH ADDRESS
[2]     HASHADR←ADDRESS[7 8 9 10 11 12]≠ADDRESS[1 6 5 4 3 2]≠ADDRESS[0],IDENT, 0 0
[3]     ⍝ TEST FOR ADDRESS PRESENT
[4]     MATCH←DLAT[2⊥HASHADR;;⍳11]∧.=IDENT,ADDRESS[⍳8]
[5]     WHO←ARCHENC MATCH
[6]     →(∨/MATCH)/CNT
[7]     ⍝ ASSIGN DIRECTORY LOCATION TO ADDRESS
[8]     WHO←CLRU[2⊥HASHADR]
[9]     ⍝ INSERT TRANSLATED ADDRESS
[10]    DLAT[2⊥HASHADR;WHO;]←IDENT,ADDRESS[⍳8],12↑TRANSADR ADDRESS
[11]  CNT:LOCATION←DLAT[2⊥HASHADR;WHO;11+⍳12]
[12]    ⍝ UPDATE USEAGE LIST
[13]    CLRU[2⊥HASHADR]←~WHO
      ∇

      ∇ DECLTRANSASIDE
[1]     ⍝ DIRECTORY LOOK ASIDE TABLE WITH 64 SETS OF 2 ENTRIES OF 23 BITS
[2]     DLAT← 64 2 23 ρ0
[3]     ⍝ PROGRAM IDENTITY BITS
[4]     IDENT←3ρ0
[5]     ⍝ LOOK ASIDE USEAGE LIST
[6]     CLRU←64ρ0
      ∇

        ⍝ REFERENCE:                              PROGRAM:
        ⍝ ARCHENC      ENCODER ARCHITECTURE          7-19
```

Program 8-18   Look-aside for address translation.

The cache of the Models 158 and 168 is updated when data are stored, as for the Model 85. Transmission to input and output does not use the cache. During the reading of input information the cache addresses are searched and the validity bit of a sector is set to 0 upon a match.

Look Aside for Address Translation

The look-aside mechanisms described for the cache storage organization are also applicable for address translation. *TRANSASIDE*, Program 8-18, shows the principle of the look aside for address translation as used on the System/370 Model 168. The look aside uses set-associative addressing. The look-aside table uses 64 sets of 2 entries, which contain the physical addresses corresponding to the effective addresses.

Hash Addressing.   The mapping of the effective address upon the directory address uses the hashing algorithm shown in line 2 of *TRANSASIDE*. The hashing has the advantage over the straight use of the low-order address bits, as for the cache, that the segment bits are incorporated in the addresses, as well as the three bits *IDENT*, which identify the program whose addresses are translated. Thus, the look-aside arrays are used more evenly. Entries remain valid until their tables are switched. The bits of the array entries that are used in the associative search contain the *IDENT* bits and 8 bits of the effective address, thus identifying the address to be translated.

The physical address contained in the entry is sent to the cache, where it is compared with the content of the cache directory. The cache of Model 168 uses address bits 13 through 18 for its array addressing. Since these bits are not translated, both look-aside actions can occur simultaneously.

Address translation is an example of an architecture that is feasible only because the implementation deviates markedly from the straightforward implementation suggested by the architecture.

Instruction Buffer

The behavior of the instruction stream is to some degree predictable. Between branches and interrupts, storage accesses are sequential. Also, certain program sections, such as loops, are executed with high frequency. The look-aside principle therefore may be used again, either through a general mechanism, such as a cache, or with specialized equipment, such as an instruction buffer.

A very simple buffer was shown in *PATHIBOX*, Program 7-16. A more elaborate example is the instruction buffer of the System/370 Model 158, which uses 16 sections of 16 bytes each. The sections are identified by an address in an associative directory. The buffer is loaded via the cache.

The CDC 6600 uses an instruction buffer that can contain eight 60-bit words, equivalent to 32 instructions. The buffer is so controlled that a loop will be preserved in the buffer and therefore can be executed without further storage reference.

The instruction buffer is particularly geared to the repeated execution of the same code. When its capacity is sufficiently large it is more effective than the pipeline, described in Section 8-7, which exploits the sequential character of the instruction stream.

8-6 STORAGE ACCESS

In a digital system, instructions, program status words, operands, results, input, output, and references to auxiliary store all require access to storage. The requests for reading or writing of data or instructions are called *storage requests*.

Since the storage requests may occur simultaneously, a conflict, known as *storage contention*, may arise. In some machine organizations, storage contention is resolved within the processing units. For instance, a processing unit such as that of Figure 7-1 is shared for instructions, operands, input, and output. Since it processes these types of information in sequence, only one request can arise at a time. In a more-parallel machine organization, simultaneous requests cannot be avoided. When, furthermore, storage is constructed out of several independent modules, the traffic to and from these modules also requires control.

The system requirements for multiple storage access will be discussed below. They will be preceded by discussion of a storage unit with single access only.

Single Access

The simplest form of storage access, the *single access*, consists of a set of address lines and a set of data read and write lines. Reading and writing may use the same lines without much loss in speed. Some microprocessors share the address and data lines because of the pin limitation, but with a noticeable loss in speed.

Besides the address and data lines, lines are also required which indicate whether reading or writing should take place. Further lines may be added for storage protection and the signaling of errors. These will not be discussed here. *READMS* and *WRITEMS*, Program 8-4, describe in principle the single access to storage.

Word-Length Adjustment. Both for instructions and operands, the length of the information must be accommodated to the word length of main storage. Figure 8-19 and Program 8-20 illustrate this by describing the actions required for the reading and writing of variable-length information. The writing in storage is particularly complicated because of the need to preserve the environment of the locations where the data are stored.

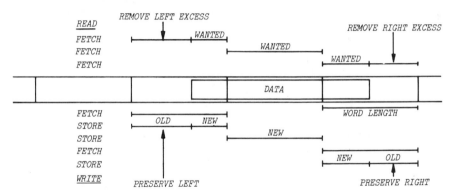

Figure 8-19   Fitting of information to storage words.

The fetching and storing of variable-length information is considerably simplified when the information length is a multiple of the word length. The removal and attaching of the left and right excess is eliminated in that case. Therefore, variable-length information is processed most easily in a serial-by-byte machine organization.

Machines whose store has a word length of several bytes nevertheless sometimes process their variable-length information on a serial-by-byte basis. The transformation to the larger word size is accomplished either by fetching and storing individual bytes, or by disassembling and assembling the words in the processing unit. The first solution has the disadvantage of increased storage traffic and slower operation. It also requires storage to do a *partial store*, that is, to store part of a word without disturbing the environment. The second solution requires equipment

```
     ∇ DATA←LENGTH READVFL ADDRESS
[1]    ⍝ REMOVE LEFT EXCESS
[2]    DATA←READMS ¯3↓ADDRESS
[3]    DATA←(8×2⊥¯3↑ADDRESS)↓DATA
[4]    CONT:→((8×2⊥LENGTH)≤ρDATA)/END
[5]    ADDRESS←((ρADDRESS)ρ2)⊤8+2⊥ADDRESS
[6]    DATA←DATA,READMS ¯3↓ADDRESS
[7]    →CONT
[8]    ⍝ REMOVE RIGHT EXCESS
[9]    END:DATA←(8×2⊥LENGTH)↑DATA
     ∇


     ∇ DATA WRITEVFL ADDRESS
[1]    ⍝ ATTACH LEFT EXCESS
[2]    →(0=2⊥¯3↑ADDRESS)/CONT
[3]    OLD←READMS ¯3↓ADDRESS
[4]    DATA←((8×2⊥¯3↑ADDRESS)↑OLD),DATA
[5]    CONT:→(64>ρDATA)/END
[6]    (64↑DATA) WRITEMS ¯3↓ADDRESS
[7]    DATA←64↓DATA
[8]    ADDRESS←((ρADDRESS)ρ2)⊤8+2⊥ADDRESS
[9]    →CONT
[10]   ⍝ ATTACH RIGHT EXCESS
[11]   END:→(0=ρDATA)/0
[12]   OLD←READMS ¯3↓ADDRESS
[13]   DATA←DATA,(ρDATA)↓OLD
[14]   →CONT
     ∇


     ∇ DECLVFL
[1]    ⍝ MAIN STORE WITH N WORDS OF 8 BYTES OF 8 BITS
[2]    STORE←(N,64)ρ0
     ∇

     ⍝ REFERENCE:                                          PROGRAM:
     ⍝ READMS          READ FROM MAIN STORE                8-4
     ⍝ WRITEMS         WRITE IN MAIN STORE                 8-4
```

Program 8-20   Reading and writing across word boundaries.

in the processing unit which performs a function similar to *READVFL* and *WRITEVFL*, Program 8-20.

Multiple Access

When the various components of a digital system can request storage simultaneously, storage must have a *multiple access*.

The connection of the storage modules with the various units requiring access, the processors, is performed by the *bus unit*. This unit usually is built as part of storage to improve the speed of operation.

Figure 8-21 shows schematically the implementation of a bus unit connecting six processors to a fourfold interleaved storage system. *ACCESS*, Program 8-22, describes the control for one storage module within this bus unit. The address lines of the six processors are combined in the matrix *PROCADR*. Similarly, the data lines to and from storage are combined as the matrices *DATAIN* and *DATAOUT*. The storage requests from the processors are combined in the 6-bit vector *PROCREQ* and the direction of transmission in the vector *DATADIR*.

When a storage module is ready for transmission, it follows the steps of

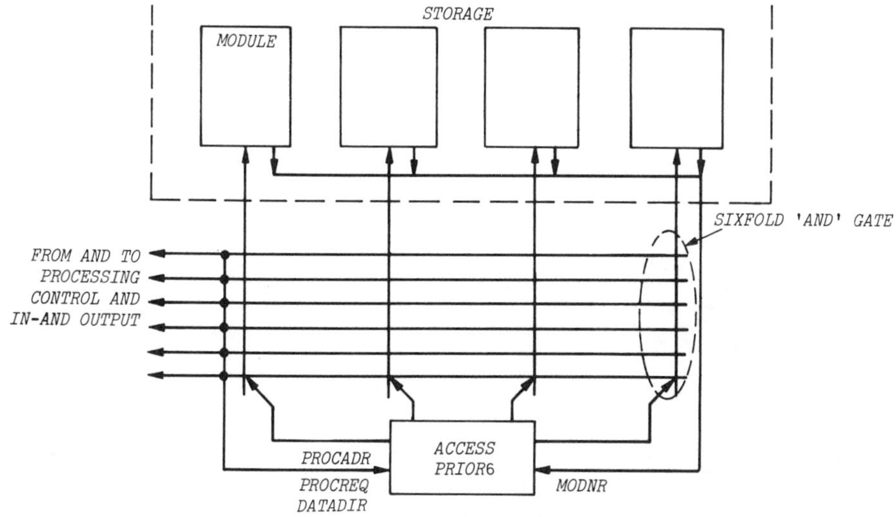

Figure 8-21   Schematic representation of storage access.

ACCESS. In line 2 a processor is selected by the storage module. The selection verifies that the processor address refers to the storage module, that the processor requests service, and that it has priority over other processors. The appropriate addresses are selected in lines 6 and 8 as interleaved reading or writing takes place in the storage module.

The algorithm is described in terms of the processor address *WHO*. As the implementation is further detailed, this scalar would be replaced by a vector of decoded selection signals.

Priority.   The various requests for storage are not equally urgent. The central unit can wait, whereas many peripheral units cannot. Some peripheral units allow much slack in the response. Other peripheral units cannot wait for a long period. A fixed, or leftmost-one, priority therefore seems attractive for the bus unit. Each requester can be given the priority suitable to its requirements.

Monopolization.   Fixed priority has the disadvantage that a unit which enters requests with a high frequency can exclude units with lower priority. This situation is called *monopolization.* Thus, the instruction fetches could block off the operand fetches, whereas a sharing of the storage access between these two processes might be more desirable.

Monopolization can be avoided by combining the fixed order priority with other algorithms. As an example, *PRIOR*6, Program 8-22, combines a leftmost-one algorithm for the first four requesters with a round-robin algorithm for the last two.

Cycle Steal.   The multiple access to storage allows direct communication of peripheral units with storage. The central unit no longer participates in the trans-

```
      ∇ ACCESS;WHO
[1]    ⍝ SELECT PROCESSOR
[2]    WHO←(PRIOR6 PROCREQ∧MODNR∧.=⍉ 6 ‾2 ↑PROCADR)⍳1
[3]    →(6=WHO)/0
[4]    ⍝ TRANSMIT DATA
[5]    →DATADIR[WHO]/WRITE
[6]  READ:DATAIN[WHO;]←READILV PROCADR[WHO;]
[7]    →0
[8]  WRITE:DATAOUT[WHO;] WRITEILV PROCADR[WHO;]
      ∇


      ∇ OUT←PRIOR6 IN
[1]    ⍝ LEFTMOST-ONE PRIORITY
[2]    OUT←LEFTONE IN
[3]    ⍝ TEST FOR ROUND ROBIN
[4]    →(~∨/OUT[4 5])/0
[5]    ⍝ ROUND-ROBIN PRIORITY
[6]    OUT[4 5]←RROBIN IN[4 5]
      ∇


      ∇ DECLACCESS
[1]    ⍝ PROCESSOR ADDRESSES
[2]    PROCADR← 6 24 ⍴0
[3]    ⍝ PROCESSOR SERVICE REQUESTS
[4]    PROCREQ←6⍴0
[5]    ⍝ TRANSMISSION DIRECTION
[6]    DATADIR←6⍴0
[7]    ⍝ DATA TO STORAGE
[8]    DATAIN← 6 8 ⍴0
[9]    ⍝ DATA FROM STORAGE
[10]   DATAOUT← 6 8 ⍴0
[11]   ⍝ MODULE NUMBER
[12]   MODNR←2⍴0
[13]   ⍝ ROUND-ROBIN POINTER
[14]   RBNPTR←0
      ∇
```

```
      ⍝ REFERENCE:                                        PROGRAM:
      ⍝ LEFTONE    LEFTMOST-ONE ARCHITECTURE              7-30
      ⍝ READILV    READ FROM INTERLEAVED STORE            8-10
      ⍝ RROBIN     ROUND-ROBIN ARCHITECTURE               7-30
      ⍝ WRITEILV   WRITE FROM INTERLEAVED STORE           8-10
```

Program 8-22   Access control of storage module.

port to and from these units. Now and then a storage cycle is taken away by the peripheral equipment, which is known as *cycle steal*. Since the peripheral unit has direct access to storage, this procedure is also called *direct memory access* or *DMA*.

Interference.   The stealing of the storage cycles by the peripheral equipment may cause the central unit to wait. The percentage of time that the central unit must wait because of this action is called *storage interference*.

Transmission Rate.   For an instruction or execution unit, the interference results in loss of time. The concept of interference does not apply to peripheral units that transmit information to or from a moving storage medium. The occasional delay in transmitting a single word to or from storage does not affect the outcome of the total transmission operation.

When access to storage is denied, however, for such a period that the buffer space is exhausted and therefore a word is lost, the entire transmission becomes a failure. This case is known as *overrun*. Therefore, the maximum transmission rate that a storage system can guarantee to a peripheral device is determined by the maximum period that storage access can be denied to that peripheral unit. This period depends upon the location of the particular unit in the priority assignment, the nature of the priority assignment, and the moment at which storage access is decided. Thus, a tape unit may have to wait because storage access has just been granted to a low-priority processor such as the instruction unit, followed by access to storage granted to a higher-priority unit, such as a disc unit.

Interlock. Multiple access to storage implies the sharing of storage among several processors. The processes in which these processors are engaged may or may not be related. The access to storage is shared by these processes and thus becomes what is known as a *shared resource*.

The use of a shared resource requires special attention from the designer. Precautions should be taken that a shared resource is not updated simultaneously by different users.

When each storage reference is complete in itself, no special interlocks are required. From an implementation point of view, however, a storage reference may not be completed in a single action. Thus, incrementing a counter may require fetching the word containing the counter, adding 1 to it in a processing unit, and storing the results again. Between the fetch and the store, the same word may be fetched by another processing unit, which also may want to increment the count by 1. As the two stores now follow each other, one of the counts is lost. This problem may be solved in the architecture by admitting its possibility and stating that simultaneous updating of data in storage may not give proper results. The problem is thus handed to the programmer.

To aid in the building of software interlocks, the instructions Test And Set and Compare And Swap have been included in System/370. These instructions guarantee that storage is read and changed as one operation. Since these instructions are infrequent, they can be implemented by blocking all storage actions until completed. Note, however, that such a blocking action reduces the transmission rate to and from peripheral units, as explained above.

8-7 PIPELINE

As instructions are executed more and more in parallel, the storage requests will increase in frequency. These requests are not equally spaced, since some operations, such as multiply and divide, require more time than others, such as add, load, and store. When the increase in request frequency approaches the transmission rate of storage, it becomes desirable to present the addresses in an even flow. Figure 8-23 shows the difference in speed that results from an even and uneven address stream.

An even address stream can be obtained by requesting the instructions and data

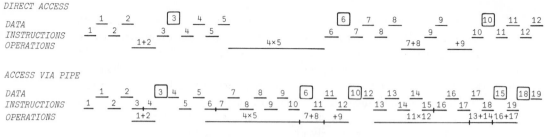

SIMPLEX STORE,   IFETCH PIPE 6 DEEP,   ODFETCH PIPE 4 DEEP, ☐ STORE INSTRUCTION

Figure 8-23   Effect of address supply upon storage speed.

early and buffering these requests in registers. Such a set of registers is called a *pipeline*. Figure 8-24 shows how the organization of Figure 7-1 can be extended with pipelines for instructions, operands and results.

The use of pipelines can also reduce the effect of storage interference. Thus, pipelines even out not only irregularities in demand but also irregularities in supply.

Pipeline Algorithms.   Program 8-26 shows the algorithms for an operand pipeline and Figure 8-25 a schematic representation of the process for a pipe length of 4. The processing unit supplies the storage addresses. These addresses are recorded in pipeline registers. The corresponding operands are subsequently fetched from storage and delivered to the processing unit when it is ready to use them.

ASKPIPE shows the recording of the address. When the pipe is fully occupied, the signal *YES* is made 0 and the processing unit must wait with its request. When space is available in the pipe, the address is recorded in the address section *ADRPIPE* and the corresponding address activity bit in *ADRACT* is set to 1.

The function *INPIPE* requests storage access. When a request is honored storage is addressed and the operand is placed in the register set *DATAPIPE* in a location that corresponds to its address. The data activity bit in *DATAACT* is now set to 1, indicating that the data are available to the processing unit.

OUTPIPE shows the fetching of the data from the registers by the processing unit. As the data are obtained, both the address- and data-activity bits are set to 0.

Pipeline Implementation.   The initial algorithms illustrate that the operands are fetched and used in the same sequence, thus corresponding to first in–first out priority. The main means of implementing this priority consists in a set of counters which represent the pointers *ASKPTR*, *INPTR*, and *OUTPTR*. These counters may be either encoded or decoded depending upon the addressing of the pipe registers.

The organization of a pipeline is in itself simple. It is complicated, however, by store and branch instructions and by interrupts.

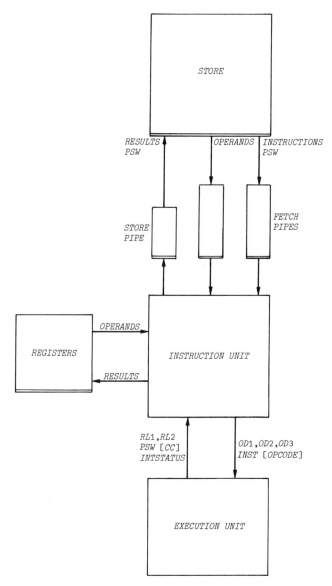

Figure 8-24 Machine organization using pipelines.

Store. Store operations can be processed by a separate, usually somewhat shorter, result pipe. A complication arises when the address of a result matches the address of an instruction or operand that has been placed in one of the fetch pipes. To assure correct operation, the result should be placed both in storage and in the pipe register concerned. Consequently, the addresses must be preserved in the pipe and compared with logically preceding result addresses. Also, the storing of results in registers must be monitored to prevent erroneous address calculations.

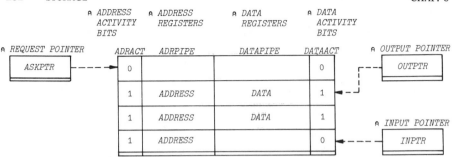

Figure 8-25 Schematic representation of a pipeline.

Branch.   A branch disrupts the normal instruction sequence. When, further-more, the branch is dependent upon the result of a preceding instruction, as is usual in the case of a conditional branch, then the continuation of the instruction sequence is only known at the last moment. As a result, the instruction and operand pipelines become empty, are *drained*, and must be filled anew as soon as the deci-sion is known. This process is time-consuming.

The branch problem can be solved in two ways, both involving added com-plexity. First, a guess can be made about the success of the branch. The subsequent instructions and data are fetched based upon this guess. The implementation should be prepared to correct all anticipatory actions when the guess proves to be wrong, a procedure known as *guess and correct*. A second method fetches information from both sides of the branch (Anderson et al., 1967) and chooses between these sets when the branch decision is known. This procedure is called *late branch*. It uses on a larger scale the method of the carry-select adder.

Interrupt.   The interrupt causes a departure from the normal instruction se-quence similar to that of the branch, except that the interrupt cannot be recognized in advance. Therefore, no remedy like guess and correct or late branch is possible. Upon the occurrence of an interrupt, the content of the fetch pipes no longer is useful and therefore is invalidated. Subsequently, starting with the interrupt ad-dress, the content of the pipes must be filled anew. Thus, an interrupt causes con-siderable delay in a pipeline organization.

Evaluation of Pipeline.   The complications due to storing, branching, and interruption add considerably to the cost of a pipeline organization. Consequently, it is only found in large computers, such as the IBM System/360 Model 91. The advent of high-speed storage at relatively low cost makes it less necessary. An im-plementation with overlapped instruction fetch, address computation, operand fetch, arithmetic, and result store, however, must use a pipeline approach.

Cause of Complication.   The complication of the pipeline operation outlined above illuminates a general implementation problem. As stated, the pipeline operation as such is basically straightforward. So is the operation of interruption,

```
      ∇ YES←ASKPIPE ADDRESS
[1]     ⍝ TEST FOR PIPE SPACE
[2]     YES←~ADRACT[ASKPTR]
[3]     →(~YES)/0
[4]     ⍝ PLACE ADDRESS IN PIPE
[5]     ADRACT[ASKPTR]←1
[6]     ADRPIPE[ASKPTR;]←ADDRESS
[7]     ⍝ INCREMENT REQUEST POINTER
[8]     ASKPTR←(ρADRACT)|ASKPTR+1
      ∇
      ⍝ REQUEST RECORDING

      ∇ YES←INPIPE
[1]     ⍝ TEST FOR ADDRESS WAITING
[2]     YES←ADRACT[INPTR]∧~DATAACT[INPTR]
[3]     →(~YES)/0
[4]     ⍝ PLACE DATA IN PIPE
[5]     DATAACT[INPTR]←1
[6]     DATAPIPE[INPTR;]←READMS,ADRPIPE[INPTR;]
[7]     ⍝ INCREMENT INPUT POINTER
[8]     INPTR←(ρADRACT)|INPTR+1
      ∇
      ⍝ DATA ACQUISITION

      ∇ YES←OUTPIPE
[1]     ⍝ TEST FOR DATA WAITING
[2]     YES←DATAACT[OUTPTR]
[3]     →(~YES)/0
[4]     ⍝ SUPPLY DATA
[5]     DATAACT[OUTPTR]←0
[6]     ADRACT[OUTPTR]←0
[7]     DATA←DATAPIPE[OUTPTR;]
[8]     ⍝ INCREMENT OUTPUT POINTER
[9]     OUTPTR←(ρADRACT)|OUTPTR+1
      ∇
      ⍝ DATA DELIVERY

      ∇ DECLPIPE
[1]     ⍝ FOUR STAGE PIPELINE
[2]     ⍝ DATA REGISTERS
[3]     DATAPIPE← 32 4 ρ0
[4]     ⍝ ADDRESS REGISTERS
[5]     ADRPIPE← 24 4 ρ0
[6]     ⍝ DATA ACTIVITY BITS
[7]     DATAACT←4ρ0
[8]     ⍝ ADDRESS ACTIVITY BITS
[9]     ADRACT←4ρ0
[10]    ⍝ REQUEST POINTER
[11]    ASKPTR←0
[12]    ⍝ INPUT POINTER
[13]    INPTR←0
[14]    ⍝ OUTPUT POINTER
[15]    OUTPTR←0
      ∇

      ⍝ REFERENCE:                          PROGRAM:
      ⍝ READMS        READ FROM MAIN STORE      8-4
```

Program 8-26 Pipeline implementation.

branching, and storing. The combination of these actions, however, leads to complications.

In the IBM 7030 computer, interruption and pipelining, called *look ahead* in that machine, were for the first time incorporated in one major machine design

(Ballance, 1962). The effort required by this design proved to be considerably more than the sum of the efforts of two designs, each involving one of these features only.

Similarly, the cache concept is complicated by multiprocessing, resulting in the broadcasting problem; and the use of multiples in division is complicated by the requirement to terminate the division with a proper quotient and remainder. The implementer should recognize these interactions early in the design. Fixing their consequences after the fact can only increase the complexity.

REFERENCES

ANDERSON, D. W., F. J. SPARACIO, and R. M. TOMASULO: "The IBM System/360 Model 91: Machine Philosophy and Instruction-Handling." *IBM Journal of Research and Development*, vol. 11, no. 1, pp. 8–24 (January, 1967).

BALLANCE, R. S., J. COCKE, and H. G. KOLSKY: "The Look-ahead Unit." In W. BUCH-HOLZ: *Planning a Computer System, Project Stretch*, pp. 228–247. McGraw-Hill, New York, 1962.

CONTI, C. J., D. H. GIBSON, and S. H. PITKOWSKY: "Structural Aspects of the System/360 Model 85, Part I, General Organization." *IBM Systems Journal*, vol. 7, no. 1, pp. 2–14 (1968).

HELLERMAN, H.: *Digital Computer System Principles*. McGraw-Hill, New York, 1972.

KILBURN, T., D. G. B. EDWARDS, M. L. LANIGAN, and F. H. SUMNER: "One-Level Storage System." *IRE Transactions on Electronic Computers*, vol. EC-11, no. 2, pp. 223–235 (1962). Reprinted in C. G. Bell and A. Newell: *Computer Structures: Readings and Examples*, pp. 276–290. McGraw-Hill, New York, 1971.

KNUTH, D. E., and G. S. RAO: "Activity in an Interleaved Memory." *IEEE Transactions on Computers*, vol. C-24, no. 9, pp. 943–944 (September, 1975).

LIPTAY, J. S.: "Structural Aspects of the System/360 Model 85, Part II, The Cache." *IBM Systems Journal*, vol. 7., no. 1, pp. 15–21 (1968).

PARMELEE, R. P., T. I. PETERSON, C. C. TILLMAN, and D. T. HATFIELD: "Virtual Storage and Virtual Machine Concepts." *IBM Systems Journal*, vol. 11, no. 2, pp. 99–130 (1972).

WILKES, M. V.: "Slave Memories and Dynamic Storage Allocation." *IEEE Transactions on Electronic Computers*, vol. EC-14, no. 2, pp. 270–271 (April, 1965).

EXERCISES

8-1   Determine the architecture and implementation description of the set–reset–invert (*SRT*) storage element, which uses a separate signal for the set, the reset, and the invert transition.

8-2   Give the architectural description of the polarity-hold and the set–reset flip-flop in the same manner as *ARCHJK*, Program 8-2.

8-3   Give the architectural description of a *JK* flip-flop in the manner of *ARCH-REG*, Program 8-2.

8-4   Give the programs for writing in a modular store constructed from:
      (a)   Four parallel modules.
      (b)   Four juxtaposed modules.
      (c)   Four interleaved modules.

8-5   Determine the function *WRITECACHE*, which specifies the writing into a storage consisting of a large store and a cache store, as organized in *READ-CACHE*, Program 8-13. Assume that words of 32 bits are written and that the large store can accept such words without disturbing the environment of these words.

8-6   Determine the function *WRITECACHESET* for a storage consisting of a large store and a cache store, as organized in *READCACHESET*, Program 8-17. Assume that words of 32 bits are written and that the large store can accept such words without disturbing the environment of these words.

8-7   Simplify *READCACHESET*, Program 8-17, by taking only the requirements for the System/370 Model 158 into account, that is, one block per sector and only two alternatives per set.

8-8   Give the functions for reading and writing words of 4 bytes positioned on a byte boundary in a store that accesses only full words on word boundaries.

8-9   Give an implementation for the priority assignment specified by *PRIOR6*, Program 8-22.

8-10 Change *ACCESS*, Program 8-22, such that *WHO* is a vector, as in *READ-CACHE*, Program 8-13, and not a scalar.

8-11 Determine a datapath and specialized control for a pipeline; use the functions of Program 8-26 as initial algorithm.

8-12 Develop a set of programs for a pipeline that buffers the data to be written in storage.

8-13 Design the interaction between a fetch pipeline, as described in Program 8-26, and a store pipeline, as mentioned in Exercise 8-12, such that data to be stored are also placed in the fetch pipeline when the addresses match.

8-14 Give the implementation of a 4-level stack, i.e., a set of 4 registers with LIFO addressing.

8-15 Determine *DECLCACHE*85, the declaration of the cache store of the System/360 Model 85 as a subset of the set-associative addressing of *READ-CACHESET*, Program 8-17.

8-16 Give an implementation of an instruction buffer similar to that of the System/370 Model 158, which uses 16 sections of 16 bytes each and identifies the sections with an associative address directory.

9 COMMUNICATION

In previous chapters, the emphasis has been on the processing, control, and storage of information. The implementation of these system functions involves the transmission of information between the system components that perform these functions. Besides this local transmission, one encounters a transmission between distant system components, such as the peripheral units and the central processing unit. The even more distant telecommunication is outside the scope of this text.

The communication problems of configuration, multiplicity, selection, synchronization, and transmission appear both in the local and distant communication. There is, however, a difference in complexity, which is caused by separate housing, interchangeability, distance, time base, and size. As a result, the communication problems are represented more clearly by the communication between distant components. Therefore, the distant communication will be discussed in this chapter. It will be illustrated by the communication between a central unit and several peripheral units.

Horizontal and Vertical Stratification

In each of the preceding chapters, an architecture and its corresponding implementation were given. In most cases, the architecture corresponds to the machine language of a computer. In some cases, the architecture represents a general implementation component, such as a microprogramming control or a decoder. The recognition of such an architecture within an implementation is called the *vertical stratification* of architecture.

It is also possible to divide a system into components and subsequently treat each system component separately. Such an approach is followed by treating the instruction unit, or storage, as a separate system component. This subdivision is called the *horizontal stratification* of an architecture. For each system component, the architecture can now be determined. This architecture is in part derived from the architecture of the overall system and in part from the communication of this system component with the adjoining components.

The subdivision of a system in a proper set of system components and the definition of their mutual relations is an essential design activity of the systems implementer. In a positive sense, he thus can divide and conquer his design. In so doing, he creates a set of interrelated architectures that each allow a separate, even though not isolated, design effort.

Organization of the Chapter

This chapter describes the design of the interconnection of a channel and several peripheral units. This design yields the architecture of the interconnection. Also, part of the architecture of each of these system components as separate entities is obtained. Once this horizontal stratification is accomplished, the implementation of each unit can be determined separately

In Section 9-1, the architecture of the communication of storage with a peripheral unit is described from the point of view of overall machine architecture. The various system components, such as channel, adapter, and device, are identified, but their detailed interconnection does not enter at this point.

In subsequent sections, the interconnection between channel and adapter is considered, thus defining the channel and adapter architecture at that point. Section 9-2 reviews the overall configuration of channel and adapters. Section 9-3 discusses the means of communicating across an interconnection. These general tools for the conversation between system components will be used in Sections 9-4 through 9-7. Thus, Section 9-4 describes the establishment of the conversation, Section 9-5 the discussion about the task to be performed, Section 9-6 the transmission of the data, and Section 9-7 the termination of the conversation. The chapter comes to a close in Section 9-8 by observing that once the architecture of the channel is established, its implementation can again be obtained with the methods described in the preceding chapters.

9-1 COMMUNICATION ARCHITECTURE

The architecture of the communication of storage with a peripheral unit should specify which storage location and which peripheral unit is involved in the communication, and which functions, such as reading or writing, the peripheral unit must perform (Padegs, 1964).

Successive or Concurrent Communication. The transmission of information can be specified by an input or output instruction in a manner analogous to the arithmetic operations. Thus, the beginning of the transmission is determined by the moment at which the instruction is decoded by the control, and after the transmission is completed, the next instruction is executed. This procedure of *successive* transmission was adopted by the very first computers. It has the disadvantage that all peripheral units and the central processing unit must wait for each other, since only one unit works at a given moment.

The relative slowness of the peripheral units and their ability to work independently of other system components makes a *concurrent* transmission to and from the peripheral units possible and desirable. This type of transmission assumes that the central processing unit and a number of peripheral units exchange data with storage at the same time. It is used by all modern computers.

Communication Components

The equipment that takes care of the communication between the peripheral unit and the store is called a *channel*. Figure 9-1 shows the location of the channel in the system organization of a computer, as mentioned in Chapter 1.

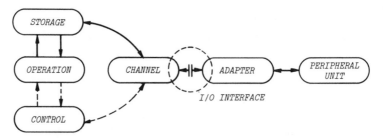

Figure 9-1   Location of the channel within a computer system.

Channel.   The user need not be aware of the channel. He may just specify the transmission to be performed and the peripheral unit that is involved. The concept of channel can therefore be omitted from the architecture. For the sake of an economical transmission, however, several peripheral units may use the same channel. Therefore, at a given moment, the transmission to a peripheral unit may be impossible because the channel is already occupied by another transmission, even though the peripheral unit is available for the purpose. This type of system design makes the configuration of channels and peripheral units a part of the architecture.

I/O Interface.   Channels can have a common architecture even though they may differ in the speed with which they can transmit information. The relation of the channel with the peripheral unit is an example of an interface. This interface can be generalized to make the system more modular. The general relation between channel and peripheral unit has been called *standard interface*, or just *I/O interface*.

The peripheral units of computer installations vary widely. These differences are more substantial than the differences in speed of the central processing unit. They are caused by the different requirements of the installation as well as the availability of equipment. Because of this variability in the use of peripheral units, it is desirable to allow many different combinations of system components, called *system configurations*. A general I/O interface makes these different configurations possible.

Adapter.   Since each type of peripheral unit has its own form of reading, writing, and control, the signals of the I/O interface should be adapted to these requirements. The system component that performs this task is called the *adapter*, or *control unit*.

When the adapter is simple in nature, or closely interwoven with the peripheral unit, each peripheral unit can have its own adapter. When, on the other hand, the adapter is more complex and a part of it is easily shared, one adapter can be used for a number of peripheral units. This is the *common adapter*. The user again will be aware of a common adapter when transmission to the devise is limited by the common function. An example of such a system configuration is given in Figure 9-2.

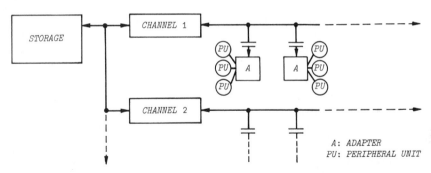

Figure 9-2   System configuration with common channels and adapters.

Channel Program

Since the channel and the central processing unit work simultaneously, the channel must have its own control. The control of the channel is analogous to the control of the central processing unit, using a series of intructions, the *channel instructions*, or *channel control words*. The instructions relating to a channel are collectively called the *channel program*. The set of operations for the channel may be different from that of the central processing unit, but this makes no fundamental difference.

Initiation.   In System/360 a channel program is initiated by giving its starting point and the number of the peripheral unit. The central processing unit specifies this information with the instruction Start I/O (SIO), which is illustrated in Figure 9-3.

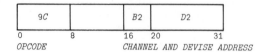

Figure 9-3   System/360 Start I/O instruction.

Return Message.   Since the duration of a channel program is difficult to predict, the termination of the program is normally signaled with an interruption. Following the interruption, the central processing unit can determine if the channel program has finished normally or if errors or exceptions have occurred.

Channel Instruction.   The channel instruction contains an operation code and an operand address, as shown in Figure 9-4 for System/360.

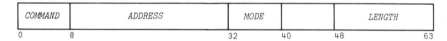

Figure 9-4   Channel instruction for System/360.

The operation code consists of a coded part, the *command*, and several modifier bits.

Channel Operations.   The four most prominent channel operations are Read, Write, Sense, and Control. These operations are sufficiently universal to control all peripheral units. Read and Write transmit data to and from main storage. Sense and Control transmit control information to and from main storage.

The operation Control sends controlling information to the peripheral unit. Thus, the peripheral unit can be set in a certain mode. For example, the density of a magnetic tape unit can be changed in this manner. Control can also be used for addressing data structures within a peripheral unit, which is especially important for auxiliary storages, such as discs. By specifying these specialized instructions indirectly, the universal character of the channel is maintained.

Sense reads status information from a peripheral unit. This information can again be different for each type of peripheral unit without affecting the design of the channel. The status information may indicate an empty hopper or full stacker for a card reader, no paper on the printer, or the end of a magnetic tape.

Since the channel need not know the meaning of the control or status information, it is called *transparent* with respect to that information.

Operand Specification.   The operand address part of the channel instruction gives the beginning address and the length of a storage area in bytes.

9-2 CONFIGURATION

This chapter will limit itself to the architecture of the interface between the channel and the adapters. An *interface* can be defined as the relation between the pertinent system components. Therefore, the architecture of an interface can be obtained by presenting the architecture of the related system components. Thus, the architecture of the I/O interface is known when the architecture of the channel and of the various adapters that it services is presented. It is, however, not necessary to present the architecture of these system components completely. Only those parts of the architecture that bear upon the relation expressed in the interface need be presented in detail; the other parts may omitted or abbreviated (Vissers, 1975).

The I/O interface is not a part of the architecture of a computer system as a whole, since the user is not concerned with the signals that connect the channel with the adapters. When the channel is considered as an entity, however, it is delimited by the interfaces with storage, the processors, and the adapters. Of these interfaces, the I/O interface is considered in particular. Since the I/O interface is an internal specification, the implementation considerations are more prominent in its definition.

Logical Channel.   The channel, as defined by the architecture, is also called the *logical channel*, since it does not need to have an individual implementation. Again, time and space can be traded. These trade-offs will be examined first because they influence the definition of the I/O interface.

Channel Types.   A single logical channel that connects to a single peripheral unit is called a *simplex channel*. A channel that can select a number of peripheral units, but communicates with only one at a time, is called in System/360 a *selector channel*. A channel that allows simultaneous communication with a number of peripheral units is called a *multiplex channel*.

Channel-to-Adapter Connection.   The selector and multiplex channels connect to a number of adapters. This connection can be achieved by giving each adapter its own attachment on the channel, the *star configuration*, or by providing only one attachment on the channel and making the connection from adapter to adapter, the *chain configuration*. Figures 9-5 and 9-6 illustrate these alternatives.

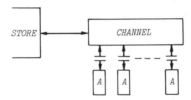

Figure 9-5   Star configuration.

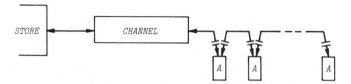

Figure 9-6   Chain configuration.

Star Connection.   In the star connection, the selection circuits are concentrated in the channel. This is attractive from a logical point of view but requires much physical space when the connections are extensive.

A parallel implementation of the connection can contain 20 to 50 wires, which must enter the frame of the channel via connectors. These wires and connectors are voluminous because' they must be able to withstand all sorts of working circumstances. A selector channel must be able to connect tens of adapters, a multiplex channel hundreds. When all these cables come together, there may be a decided lack of space. For a serial implementation of the connection, the space problem is less critical.

Chain Connection.   In the chain connection, the circuits are distributed over the adapters. There is only one connector necessary per channel and two connectors per adapter. Thus, in principle, the space problem is solved. In general, the total length of cable will be noticeably reduced, although the electrical distance to the most distant adapter is increased by the adapters that are placed in between.

When the incoming wires of an adapter are directly connected to the outgoing wires, the chain is said to form a *bus*. When adapter circuits are placed between the incoming and outgoing wires, a *string* connection is obtained. These circuits introduce a delay, which however is in part compensated for by the speed advantage of the one-to-one connection.

When the end of the chain returns to the channel, the connection is called a *loop*. The loop has the advantage that the electrical termination of the connection is kept within the channel. The loop is particularly attractive for high-speed serial transmission.

Matrix Connection.   The previous discussion assumed that a peripheral unit is connected to storage by means of only one channel. There are, however, situations in which it is desirable for a unit to communicate with storage through more than one channel, called *overrouting*. A primary reason for overrouting is reliability. Thus, the failure of one channel makes the equipment connected to it still available via the other channel. Another reason for connecting a unit to more than one channel is data access. For example, in sorting with magnetic tapes, it is sometimes desirable to have all tapes available on two channels.

More generally, one might desire each peripheral unit to be available through each channel. For the chain configuration, this means that each adapter now has as many connectors as there are channels. To avoid the space problems that were found in the star connection, the configuration may be generalized to a matrix configuration, as shown in Figure 9-7.

In the *matrix* configuration, each channel and adapter has a single connection to a central switching unit. The number of connectors that enter this unit is substantial, and it forms an extensive element of a computer installation.

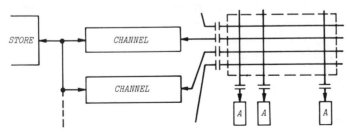

Figure 9-7   Matrix configuration.

The matrix switch should be carefully designed organizationally and electrically. The organization should be modular so that a variable number of channels and adapters can be connected economically. For the sake of reliability, the electrical powering should not be central. Rather, the various circuits of the switch should be electrically dependent on the associated channels and adapters in such a way that a failure does not hinder the units that are still operational.

9-3 COMMUNICATION USING THE INTERFACE

In this section, the communication within an interface will be considered in preparation of the specification of the I/O interface. First, the consequences of *multiplicity*, that is, the fact that one channel may communicate with several adapters, are considered. Since the independence of the system components expresses itself in particular in a difference of time base, the synchronization problem will be discussed next. Finally, the establishment of a conversation, that is, the assurance that the signals which are sent are indeed received, will be described.

Multiplicity

In the multiplex channel, a number of adapters can be active simultaneously. The channel, therefore, must divide its attention between these adapters. The fundamental problem here is to give the necessary attention to each.

This problem is comparable to the seating on airplanes, which can be determined by advance reservation or by the order of arrival of the customers. Since not everyone shows up for his reserved seat, the advance reservation may yield empty seats; whereas in the first-come-first-served procedure, a customer may find a full plane.

Similarly, for each peripheral unit, a time period can be reserved in which it is serviced by the multiplex channel. Such a time period is called a *slot*, or slice. The time-reservation pattern need not be uniform but can give preference to fast equipment. This method solves the conflicts of simultaneous entrance ahead of time. The solution is attractive if traffic is predictable and sufficient time is available. The CDC 6600 makes use of time slots between the central processing unit and the peripheral processors.

When peripheral units have very irregular transmission requirements, the request principle is usually used. The simultaneous service requests must now be resolved by a priority rule. The priority algorithms mentioned in Chapter 7 may be used for this purpose.

Synchronization

The time base, or clock, of a peripheral unit is normally determined by the nature of that unit. Thus, the packing of the bits on the surface of a moving magnetic storage medium and the speed of the surface will determine the transmission speed of these bits. Since these parameters are critical to the design of the peripheral unit, it is undesirable to make them dependent on a central clock signal. As a consequence, most peripheral units have their own clock.

Unlike the peripheral unit, the channel has no constraining time requirements. Therefore, the transmission rate of the channel can adapt itself to either main storage or peripheral unit. Since the channel and the central processing unit often share equipment, the channel usually uses the clock of the central unit, which depends, in turn, upon the storage cycle.

When the cycle time of the channel is derived from the clock of a central processing unit, the channel must fit the signals received from the peripheral unit into its own cycles. Figure 9-8 shows that this may be achieved by delaying the signals for part of a cycle in a local buffer. Program 9-9 gives the program for a simple control of this buffer. Such a buffer need not contain an entire message but only the amount transmitted in parallel, which in System/360 is 9 bits, including parity. This buffering can also take place in the adapter. Here, it will be considered the job of the channel.

Figure 9-8 Synchronization of transmission.

```
     ∇ SYNC
[1]    OUT←(SAMPLE∧IN)∨(~SAMPLE)∧OUT
     ∇
```

Program 9-9 Synchronization buffer control.

Uncertainty in Synchronization. The delay of an incoming signal in a buffer intends to assure that each signal is received once and only once. Although such a control may be logically correct, it still is possible to miss signals in an actual realization. Such a malfunction may occur when the incoming signal arrives almost simultaneously with the sample signal. As a result, the controlling flip-flop may not set correctly. In logic, simultaneous signals are considered impossible. Physically, however, there is a time period, be it very short, in which the proper action of a flip-flop cannot be guaranteed.

Conversation

The channel does not know when a signal that it sends is received by an adapter. This uncertainty arises from the differences in clock, in the delay caused by the distance between channel and adapter, and in the type of circuits used by the adapters. This problem can be solved logically or physically.

Physical Solution. As a physical solution, a delay can be introduced in the channel or the adapter which makes the time for transmission the same for each signal and each adapter. This method has the disadvantage that all units must conform to the slowest unit. Also, the adjustment of these critical delay times creates a maintenance problem.

Handshaking. In the logical solution, a transmitted signal *CALL* is answered upon receipt by a return signal *HEAR*. This now shifts the receiving problem from *CALL* to *HEAR*. Therefore, on the receipt of *HEAR*, the signal *CALL* is removed; and when this removal is recognized, *HEAR* is removed in turn. *CALL* may not be made 1 again before the return of *HEAR* to 0 is recognized. This succession of signals is called *interlocking*, or *handshaking*.

Figure 9-10 shows the elementary handshaking sequence. *PETER* and *PAUL*, Program 9-11, are two functions that are interlocked in this manner. Through this procedure, it is logically impossible to recognize a succesion of signals *CALL* as either too many or too few signals.

The time between the signal changes is required for the transmission and recognition of the signals. This time can be lengthened to allow for some processing. Thus, delaying the change of *HEAR* from 0 to 1 can ensure that there is sufficient time for decoding and reading into a register, whereas a delay in the return of *HEAR* to 0 prevents a new signal *CALL* from being sent too soon.

A pair of signals *CALL* and *HEAR* can accompany a group of signals and assure their proper receipt. This assumes that the transmission speed of the parallel signals is approximately the same for all signals. Small speed differences, the *skew*, are taken care of by sending *CALL* somewhat later than the group that is accompanied by *CALL*. Since the circuit speed of the sending equipment is known, the size of this delay can be determined. Although this is again a physical method, it

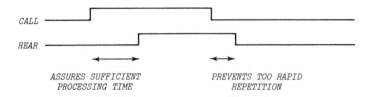

Figure 9-10 Two-way handshake signals.

```
    ∇ PETER                        ∇ PAUL
[1]  HEARYES:→HEAR/HEARYES     [1]  CALLNO:→(~CALL)/CALLNO
[2]   ∧ PAUL HEARS NOT         [2]   ∧ PETER CALLS
[3]   CALL←1                   [3]   HEAR←1
[4]  HEARNO:→(~HEAR)/HEARNO    [4]  CALLYES:→CALL/CALLYES
[5]   ∧ PAUL HEARS             [5]   ∧ PETER CALLS NOT
[6]   CALL←0                   [6]   HEAR←0
[7]   →HEARYES                 [7]   →CALLNO
    ∇                              ∇
      ∧ TALKER                       ∧ LISTENER
```

Program 9-11 Two-way handshake functions.

is much better controlled than the method mentioned above. The group of signals is said to be *enclosed* by *CALL*.

Multiway Handshake. The handshake procedure of *PETER* and *PAUL* assumes one system component, *PETER*, which sends information and one component, *PAUL*, which receives information. This procedure can also be used when one out of several system components must receive the information, provided the desired system component is selected first. This method is described in Section 9-4. When it is desirable, however, that all receiving components respond to a message, a multiway handshake may be used. Figure 9-12 shows the signal sequence for such a conversation. Figure 9-12 also shows the state diagram for the sending system *TOM*, the talker, and the receiving systems *DICK* and *HARRY*, the listeners.

Signal Sequence. Figure 9-12 shows that the multiway handshake responds to the outgoing signal *CALL* with the two signals *HEAR* and *HEARNOT*. Each receiving system component produces a pair of these response signals. The corresponding signals from all receiving system components are connected, thus producing the two signals *HEAR* and *HEARNOT*.

Logic of the Interconnection. It is assumed that the driving circuits of each system component are designed such that a logical 'or' is obtained by simply connecting the corresponding lines, the *dot-or*. Because of the duality of switching algebra, the same connection can be used as an 'and' by interpreting a low signal as 1 and a high signal as 0. Or, using De Morgan's theorem, an 'and' can be obtained by inverting the inputs and outputs of the connection (Appendix D). This procedure is used to ascertain that all system components have heard.

Because of the dot-or, the signal *HEAR* is 1 when at least one component hears and the signal *HEARNOT* is only 0 when all components hear. Thus, *CALL* can be

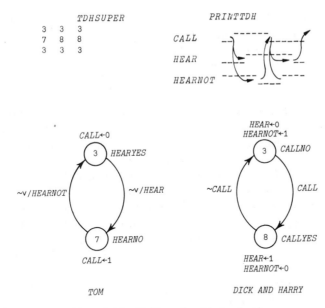

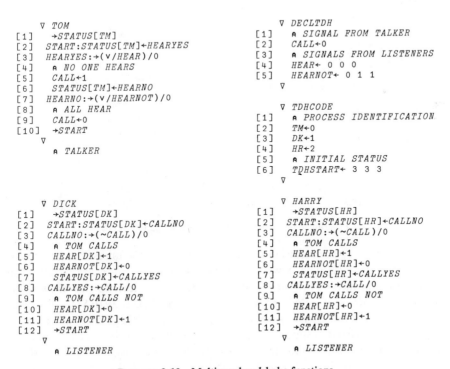

Figure 9-12   Multiway handshake signals.

```
     ∇ TOM
[1]      →STATUS[TM]
[2]   START:STATUS[TM]←HEARYES
[3]   HEARYES:→(∨/HEAR)/0
[4]   ⍝ NO ONE HEARS
[5]   CALL←1
[6]   STATUS[TM]←HEARNO
[7]   HEARNO:→(∨/HEARNOT)/0
[8]   ⍝ ALL HEAR
[9]   CALL←0
[10]  →START
     ∇
     ⍝ TALKER
```

```
     ∇ DECLTDH
[1]   ⍝ SIGNAL FROM TALKER
[2]   CALL←0
[3]   ⍝ SIGNALS FROM LISTENERS
[4]   HEAR← 0 0 0
[5]   HEARNOT← 0 1 1
     ∇
```

```
     ∇ TDHCODE
[1]   ⍝ PROCESS IDENTIFICATION
[2]   TM←0
[3]   DK←1
[4]   HR←2
[5]   ⍝ INITIAL STATUS
[6]   TDHSTART← 3 3 3
     ∇
```

```
     ∇ DICK
[1]      →STATUS[DK]
[2]   START:STATUS[DK]←CALLNO
[3]   CALLNO:→(~CALL)/0
[4]   ⍝ TOM CALLS
[5]   HEAR[DK]←1
[6]   HEARNOT[DK]←0
[7]   STATUS[DK]←CALLYES
[8]   CALLYES:→CALL/0
[9]   ⍝ TOM CALLS NOT
[10]  HEAR[DK]←0
[11]  HEARNOT[DK]←1
[12]  →START
     ∇
     ⍝ LISTENER
```

```
     ∇ HARRY
[1]      →STATUS[HR]
[2]   START:STATUS[HR]←CALLNO
[3]   CALLNO:→(~CALL)/0
[4]   ⍝ TOM CALLS
[5]   HEAR[HR]←1
[6]   HEARNOT[HR]←0
[7]   STATUS[HR]←CALLYES
[8]   CALLYES:→CALL/0
[9]   ⍝ TOM CALLS NOT
[10]  HEAR[HR]←0
[11]  HEARNOT[HR]←1
[12]  →START
     ∇
     ⍝ LISTENER
```

Program 9-13   Multiway handshake functions.

removed when *HEARNOT* is 0, and a new *CALL* signal can only be sent when subsequently *HEAR* has become 0.

The functions *TOM*, *DICK*, and *HARRY*, Program 9-13, describe the multiway handshaking procedure. The number of listeners is two in this example, but is easily extendable.

Simulating Simultaneous Processes.   The functions *TOM*, *DICK*, and *HARRY* are simultaneously active, as was the case with *PETER* and *PAUL*. The descriptions of the two-way handshake by *PETER* and *PAUL* can be simulated by treating *PETER* and *PAUL* as independent processes with their own workspace and by defining *CALL* and *HEAR* as shared variables, using APLSV.

The two-way handshake cannot be simulated in the same workspace, as is evident from the branches in *PETER* and *PAUL*, lines 1 and 4. *TOM*, *DICK*, and *HARRY*, in contrast, can be simulated in one workspace with the aid of the supervisory function *TDHSUPER*, described in Program 9-14.

```
        ∇ TDHSUPER
[1]       ⍝ INITIATION
[2]       TDHCODE
[3]       STATUS←TDHSTART
[4]       PRINTTDH← 6 8 ↑PRINTTDH
[5]       ⍝ EXECUTION
[6]       TDHTRACE
[7]       STATUS
[8]     CONT:TOM
[9]       TDHTRACE
[10]      DICK
[11]      TDHTRACE
[12]      HARRY
[13]      TDHTRACE
[14]      ⍝ END CONDITION
[15]      STATUS
[16]      →(STATUS∨.≠TDHSTART)/CONT
        ∇


        ∇ TDHTRACE
[1]       TERM←'‾ '[2,CALL,2,(∨/HEAR),2,(∨/HEARNOT)]
[2]       PRINTTDH←(PRINTTDH,TERM),TERM
        ∇


        ⍝ REFERENCE:                                     PROGRAM:
        ⍝ DICK           MULTIWAY INTERLOCKING FUNCTION     9-13
        ⍝ HARRY          MULTIWAY INTERLOCKING FUNCTION     9-13
        ⍝ TOM            MULTIWAY INTERLOCKING FUNCTION     9-13
```

Program 9-14 Supervisor for multiway handshake.

Wait Status.   The branches in *PETER* indicate that this function must wait for a signal from *PAUL*. Such a wait condition is indicated in *TOM*, *DICK*, and *HARRY* by a branch to 0, that is, out of the function. Prior to this branch, the status of the function is noted in the status vector *STATUS*. *TDHSUPER* is used to call the various functions, as occurs in lines 8, 10, and 12. These calls are preceded by setting the initial status and are terminated by testing for an end condition. As a function is called, it branches on line 1 to the line corresponding to its status and tests the wait condition. When this condition is satisfied, the function proceeds;

otherwise, it returns to the supervisor. Thus, the proper functioning of the hand-shake procedure can be demonstrated.

The wait condition requires two actions: the recording of the status and the conditional return to the supervisor. In Section 9-4, an auxiliary function will be introduced for this purpose.

TDHSUPER incorporates some auxiliary functions which aid in displaying the process that is simulated. Thus, the vector *STATUS* is printed on lines 7 and 15, giving a record of the internal states as the simulation progresses, as shown in Figure 9-12. Also, a trace of the critical signals is produced by *TDHTRACE*.

Circuit Trace.   The timing diagram of Figure 9-12 has been obtained with the function *TDHTRACE*, shown in Program 9-14. As *TDHTRACE* is called, a matrix *PRINTTDH* is built up which records the signal values. *TDHTRACE* is another example of an auxiliary tool which the designer can introduce quite easily to see what he is doing. Obviously, many alternatives and refinements can be introduced in the behavior of the supervisor as well as in the tracing function.

Handshake Application.   The multiway handshake, which uses one outgoing and two incoming signals, is used in the interface for programmable instrumentation as originally proposed by Hewlett-Packard and after modification recommended by the International Electrotechnical Commission (Nelson and Ricci, 1972).

Contents of the Conversation.   The interlocking of signals is an implementation mechanism which ensures that the speaking partners hear each other and that no part of the conversation is lost. This mechanism may now be used for the messages that the channel and the adapter exchange. These messages concern the selection of the desired peripheral unit, the nature of the operation to be performed, the data transport itself, and the termination of the operation. These four subjects are discussed in the following sections.

The full set of messages that can be sent across an interface and their responses are called the communication *protocol*.

9-4   SELECTION

The interface between channel and adapter is illustrated here with a simple interface design, which contains most of the elements which appear in an interface such as that of System/360 (IBM). The lines of this interface are declared by *DECLINTERFACE* and the messages transmitted within the interface by *INTER-FACECODE*, both shown in Program 9-17.

The initiative for transmission between channel and peripheral unit usually originates in the central processing unit. The central unit instructs the channel to select a peripheral unit with the instruction Start I/O (SIO). The channel program associated with SIO determines the type of transmission.

Initiation of Channel Action

CHANNEL, Program 9-17, describes the behavior of the channel architecturally. The channel may be in one of the 14 states that are shown in the state diagram of Figure 9-16. The states are identified in this diagram by the corresponding line numbers of *CHANNEL*. Only the key signals responsible for a transition are shown next to the transition arrows; the complete expressions are found in *CHANNEL*. The initial state is identified by the label *START* of *CHANNEL*, line 3. The instruction SIO is represented by a signal with the same name. The program proceeds to the label *WORK* when the signal *SIO* is 1.

Source and Sink Functions. The instruction Start I/O is presented to the channel over the interface between channel and central processor. From the point of view of the I/O interface, however, the signals resulting from this instruction suddenly appear in the channel. Since it is necessary to delineate completely the part of the channel architecture that concerns the interface, the signals that enter or leave this part of the architecture, other than through the interface, should be noted. This is done by identifying these signals as the result of *source* functions or as the operands of *sink* functions (Vissers, 1975). Thus, *SIO*, the adapter address, and the data to be written are derived from the channel source; whereas the data that are read and the messages to the central processor disappear in the channel sink. Similarly, adapter source and sink functions can be defined.

The source and sink functions are combined in the supervisory function *SETSOURCESINK*, Program 9-15. Apart from setting *SIO* to 1, *SETSOURCESINK* identifies the adapter to be used, the command to be executed, and the data to be transmitted. These actions are based upon the parameter *IN* which is set prior to the simulation.

Communication Supervisor. The functions that describe the channel and the various adapter types are intended to be simulated by the communication supervisor *COMSUPER*, Program 9-15. This supervisory program is entirely analogous to *TDHSUPER*, discussed above. The wait conditions, which appear in the various functions, are, however, described with the function *WAITFOR*, shown in Program 9-17.

Wait Condition. *WAITFOR* sets in line 6 its output *LABEL*, which is the branch target of the calling function. When the wait condition is satisfied, this target is empty; hence the calling function continues without branch. When the wait condition is not satisfied, *LABEL* is made 0 and the calling function executes a branch to 0, hence terminates.

The status of the calling function is recorded in line 4 in the status vector *STATUS*. Line 2 identifies the calling function, and line 4 determines the calling line within this function. Both lines use the I-beam function 27. This function yields a vector of the current line number of the function that is in execution and

```
      ∇ COMSUPER
[1]     ⍝ PROLOGUE
[2]     DECLINTERFACE
[3]     COMCODE
[4]     INTERFACECODE
[5]     PRINTCOM← 24 8 ↑PRINTCOM
[6]     SETSOURCESINK
[7]     ⍝ INITIAL STATUS
[8]     STATUS←COMSTART
[9]     ⍝ EXECUTION
[10]    COMTRACE
[11]    STATUS
[12] CHAN:CHANNEL
[13]    COMTRACE
[14] ADP1:ADAPTER1
[15]    COMTRACE
[16] ADP2:ADAPTER2
[17]    COMTRACE
[18] ADP3:ADAPTER3
[19]    COMTRACE
[20]    ⍝ END TEST
[21]    STATUS
[22]    →(STATUS∨.≠COMSTART)/CHAN
      ∇
```

```
      ∇ SETSOURCESINK
[1]     ⍝ START I/O
[2]     SIO←1
[3]     ⍝ ADAPTER ADDRESS
[4]     ADADR←(8ρ2)⊤IN[0]
[5]     ⍝ CHANNEL COMMAND
[6]     COMMAND←(8ρ2)⊤IN[1]
[7]     →(IN[1]∊INWARD)/READ
[8]     ⍝ DATA AREAS FOR SENDING
[9]     DATAIN←(16ρ2)⊤IN[2]
[10]    DATAOUT←⍳0
[11]    →0
[12]    ⍝ DATA AREAS FOR RECEIVING
[13] READ:DATAIN←⍳0
[14]    DATAOUT←(16ρ2)⊤IN[2]
      ∇
```

```
      ∇ COMCODE
[1]     ⍝ PROCESS IDENTIFICATION
[2]     CH←0
[3]     AD1←1
[4]     AD2←2
[5]     AD3←3
[6]     ⍝ INITIAL STATUS
[7]     COMSTART← 3 3 3 3
      ∇
```

```
      ∇ COMTRACE;TERM
[1]   TERM←'_ '[2,OPOUT,2,TRANSOUT,2,(∨/MPXOUT),2,(∨/INFOUT),2,SELOUT[CH],2,2]
[2]   TERM←TERM,'_ '[2,SELIN[CH],2,REQUEST,2,OPIN,2,TRANSIN,2,(∨/MPXIN),2,∨/INFIN]
[3]   PRINTCOM←(PRINTCOM,TERM),TERM
      ∇
```

```
      ⍝ REFERENCE:                                        PROGRAM:
      ⍝ ADAPTER1       BYTE ADAPTER ARCHITECTURE           9-22
      ⍝ ADAPTER2       DISCONNECTED ADAPTER                9-23
      ⍝ ADAPTER3       BURST ADAPTER ARCHITECTURE          9-26
      ⍝ CHANNEL        CHANNEL ARCHITECTURE                9-17
      ⍝ DECLINTERFACE  LINE DECLARATION INTERFACE          9-17
      ⍝ INTERFACECODE  INTERFACE MESSAGE ASSIGNMENT        9-17
```

Program 9-15 Supervisor for channel and adapters.

of all functions that preceded it and have been suspended. Element 2 of this sector therefore identifies the line in *COMSUPER* which called a channel or adapter; whereas element 1 identifies the line in the channel or adapter program that called *WAITFOR*.

I-Beam Function. The I-beam functions are listed in Appendix A. They form a class of system functions, which indicate the status of a program or of the APL system as a whole.

Addressing of Peripheral Unit

As a first step in the selection process, the peripheral unit must be addressed. Because of the nature of the chain connection, a binary encoding of the address is desirable. For a given logical channel, addressing never occurs simultaneously with transmission. Therefore, it is attractive to use the signals that are available for transmission also for addressing. Since 8 bits and a parity bit are used in trans-

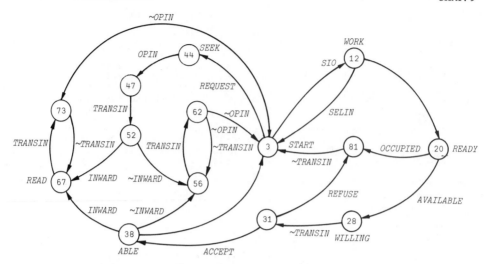

Figure 9-16   State diagram of channel.

mission, a maximum of 256 adapters can be addressed, with the address verified against an error.

Information Signals.   The transmission signals have a general function and are therefore called information signals. Since the signals of the channel go out from the central system to the edge of the system, the name *INFOUT*, derived from information-out, is used. These signals are part of the message path, as listed in *DECLINTERFACE*, Program 9-17.

```
     ∇ DECLINTERFACE                        ∇ INTERFACECODE
[1]     ⍝ SIGNALS FROM CHANNEL        [1]      ⍝ MESSAGE ENCODING
[2]     ⍝ OPERATIONAL-OUT             [2]      ⍝ COMMAND ACCEPTED
[3]     OPOUT←0                       [3]      ACCEPT←(8ρ2)⊤15
[4]     ⍝ TRANSMIT-OUT                [4]      ⍝ ADAPTER AVAILABLE
[5]     TRANSOUT←0                    [5]      AVAILABLE←(8ρ2)⊤14
[6]     ⍝ MULTIPLEX-OUT               [6]      ⍝ ADAPTER OCCUPIED
[7]     MPXOUT← 0  0                  [7]      OCCUPIED←(8ρ2)⊤3
[8]     ⍝ INFORMATION-OUT             [8]      ⍝ SEND INFORMATION
[9]     INFOUT←8ρ0                    [9]      PROCEED←(8ρ2)⊤51
[10]    ⍝ SELECT-OUT                  [10]     ⍝ COMMAND REFUSED
[11]    SELOUT←4ρ0                    [11]     REFUSE←(8ρ2)⊤1
[12]    ⍝ SIGNALS FROM ADAPTERS       [12]     ⍝ TERMINATE OPERATION
[13]    ⍝ OPERATIONAL-IN              [13]     THROUGH←(8ρ2)⊤60
[14]    OPIN←0                        [14]     ⍝ COMMANDS FOR TRANSMISSION TO CHANNEL
[15]    ⍝ TRANSMIT-IN                 [15]     INWARD←ι128
[16]    TRANSIN←0                               ∇
[17]    ⍝ MULTIPLEX-IN
[18]    MPXIN← 0  0
[19]    ⍝ INFORMATION-IN                       ∇ LABEL←WAITFOR CONDITION;WHO
[20]    INFIN←8ρ0                     [1]      ⍝ PROCESS IDENTIFICATION
[21]    ⍝ SELECT-IN                   [2]      WHO←(CHAN,ADP1,ADP2,ADP3)ι(I27)[2]
[22]    SELIN←4ρ0                     [3]      ⍝ STATUS OF PROCESS
[23]    ⍝ SERVICE REQUEST             [4]      STATUS[WHO]←(I27)[1]
[24]    REQUEST←0                     [5]      ⍝ BRANCH TARGET
         ∇                           [6]      LABEL←(~CONDITION)/0
                                               ∇
```

Program 9-17   Channel architecture.

```
        ∇ CHANNEL
[1]     →STATUS[CH]
[2]     ⍝ INITIAL STATE
[3]     START:→WAITFOR SIO∨REQUEST
[4]     →REQUEST/SEEK
[5]     WORK:OPOUT←1
[6]     MPXOUT← 0 1
[7]     INFOUT←ADADR
[8]     TRANSOUT←1
[9]     SELOUT[CH]←1
[10]    SIO←0
[11]    ⍝ ADAPTER SEARCH
[12]    →WAITFOR SELIN[CH]∨OPIN
[13]    →OPIN/READY
[14]    'ADAPTER NOT ATTACHED'
[15]    →END
[16]    ⍝ ADAPTER SELECTED
[17]    READY:SELOUT[CH]←0
[18]    TRANSOUT←0
[19]    ⍝ ADAPTER STATUS
[20]    →WAITFOR TRANSIN
[21]    →(INFIN∧.=AVAILABLE)/WILLING
[22]    'ADAPTER OCCUPIED'
[23]    →FINISH
[24]    ⍝ INSTRUCT ADAPTER
[25]    WILLING:MPXOUT← 1 0
[26]    INFOUT←COMMAND
[27]    TRANSOUT←1
[28]    →WAITFOR~TRANSIN
[29]    TRANSOUT←0
[30]    ⍝ ADAPTER ABILITY
[31]    →WAITFOR TRANSIN
[32]    →(INFIN∧.=ACCEPT)/ABLE
[33]    'ADAPTER NOT ABLE'
[34]    →FINISH
[35]    ABLE:TRANSOUT←1
[36]    MPXOUT← 1 0
[37]    INFOUT←PROCEED
[38]    →WAITFOR~TRANSIN
[39]    →OPIN/WRITE-3
[40]    →END
[41]    ⍝ FIND ADAPTER REQUESTING SERVICE
[42]    SEEK:OPOUT←1
[43]    SELOUT[CH]←1
[44]    →WAITFOR OPIN
[45]    SELOUT[CH]←0
[46]    ⍝ ADAPTER SELECTED
[47]    →WAITFOR TRANSIN
[48]    ADADR←INFIN
[49]    MPXOUT← 1 0
[50]    INFOUT←PROCEED
[51]    TRANSOUT←1
[52]    →WAITFOR~TRANSIN
[53]    TRANSOUT←0
[54]    →((2⊥COMMAND)∈INWARD)/READ
[55]

[55]    ⍝ SEND DATA TO ADAPTER
[56]    WRITE:→WAITFOR TRANSIN
[57]    →(0=ρDATAIN)/FINISH
[58]    MPXOUT← 1 1
[59]    INFOUT←8↑DATAIN
[60]    DATAIN←8↓DATAIN
[61]    TRANSOUT←1
[62]    →WAITFOR~TRANSIN
[63]    TRANSOUT←0
[64]    →OPIN/WRITE
[65]    →END
[66]    ⍝ RECEIVE DATA FROM ADAPTER
[67]    READ:→WAITFOR TRANSIN
[68]    →((MPXIN,INFIN)∧.= 1 0 ,THROUGH)/FINISH
[69]    DATAIN←DATAIN,INFIN
[70]    MPXOUT← 1 0
[71]    INFOUT←PROCEED
[72]    TRANSOUT←1
[73]    →WAITFOR~TRANSIN
[74]    TRANSOUT←0
[75]    →OPIN/READ
[76]    →END
[77]    ⍝ TERMINATE CONTACT
[78]    FINISH:MPXOUT← 1 0
[79]    INFOUT←THROUGH
[80]    TRANSOUT←1
[81]    →WAITFOR~TRANSIN
[82]    END:MPXOUT← 0 0
[83]    INFOUT←8ρ0
[84]    TRANSOUT←0
[85]    SELOUT[CH]←0
[86]    OPOUT←0
[87]    →START
        ∇
```

Program 9-17—Cont.

Line 7 of *CHANNEL* indicates that *INFOUT* receives the value of *ADADR*. *ADADR* is an 8-bit vector derived from the channel source and represents the address of the adapter to be selected. The parity is not shown in *INFOUT*.

Type-Indication Signals. Since *INFOUT* can be used for different purposes, the nature of the information must be indicated along with these signals. This type

indication again can appear either coded or decoded. Where the number of purposes is limited, a decoded signal is often used. Such a decoded signal can also
serve to enclose the given signals. In the given example, the type indication, however, will be coded with the two signals *MPXOUT*. The code used is shown in
Table 9-18. The signals *MPXOUT* obtain their value simultaneously with *INFOUT*
as indicated by line 6 of *CHANNEL*.

```
                    MPXOUT              MPXIN
    CODE            MULTIPLEX-OUT       MULTIPLEX-IN

    00              NOT USED            NOT USED

    01              ADDRESS             ADDRESS

    10              COMMAND             REPORT

    11              DATA                DATA
```

Table 9-18   Coding of *MPXOUT* and *MPXIN*.

Handshaking Signals.   The handshaking signals *TRANSOUT* and *TRANSIN*
enclose the information and the type-indication signals. From the channel side, the
outgoing signal *TRANSOUT* is used. *TRANSOUT* always accompanies the information signals *INFOUT* and the type indication *MPXOUT*. Thus, *TRANSOUT*
is set to 1 in line 8 of *CHANNEL*. *TRANSOUT* becomes 0 when the information
and type-indication signals are no longer valid. In answer to the message of the
channel, the adapter will normally send a message via the signals *INFIN* and
MPXIN to the channel and enclose these with *TRANSIN*.

Selection Signals.   The conversation between channel and adapter may not
necessarily get going. The addressed adapter may be switched off or may not be
present at all. In that case, no answer is given. While the channel keeps waiting for
a response, other actions within the interface are blocked. To avoid this situation,
the selection signals *SELOUT* and *SELIN* are introduced.

Normally, the outward signals of the channel are connected as a bus, logically
in parallel, to all adapters. Electrically, this is effected through the chain connection
mentioned earlier. Except for transmission delays, a signal is received simultaneously by all adapters, since there is no circuit in the bus connection. Correspondingly, the inward signals of the adapters are logically connected by an 'or'
and enter the channel as a single signal. This bus connection cannot apply a priority
to signals that arise simultaneously. In the star connection, a priority circuit can
be built within the channel. For the chain connection, a priority can be obtained
by introducing logical components in the chain, thus making it a string connection.

Priority Determination.   In the given system, the priority determination occurs
with the selection signals *SELIN* and *SELOUT*. The wires of these signals run,
again, from adapter to adapter; but, in contrast to the other wires, either *SELIN*
or *SELOUT* is logically interrupted, as illustrated in Figure 9-19. The adapter
placed at the end of the cable returns the *SELOUT* wire as *SELIN*. Thus, the

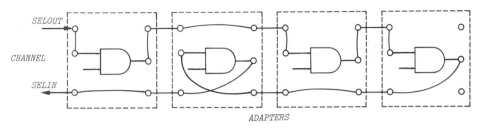

Figure 9-19 Priority determination by means of *SELOUT* and *SELIN*.

signal that leaves the channel as *SELOUT* ultimately returns to the channel as *SELIN*.

The sequence in which the signal *SELOUT* can be interrupted determines the priority of the adapters. Since the outgoing as well as the incoming wire can be interrupted by an adapter, there can be a limited change in the priority at each point of the chain.

Collapse Feature.   The circuits that are a part of the string connection should be so designed that in case the power of a unit is turned off the connection is still valid. A relay may for instance be used to bypass the circuit in that situation. Such a provision is called a *collapse feature*.

Adapter Response

During the selection procedure, *SELOUT* is made 1 in line 9 of *CHANNEL*. When an adapter receives *SELOUT*, it passes this signal on when the address on *INFOUT* is not its own address. When no adapter recognizes the address on *INFOUT*, the selection signal *SELOUT* is passed on unchanged and returns to the channel as *SELIN*. *SELIN* tells the channel that there is no answer. The channel lets all outgoing signals return to 0 and reports the negative result to the central processing unit. This sequence of signals is shown in Figure 9-20.

Figure 9-20 has been obtained with *COMTRACE*, Program 9-15, in a similar way as Figure 9-12. Figures of this kind are very popular in describing interface actions. They serve a useful purpose as illustration and verification. They are, however, not well suited to specification, since they represent the incidental behavior rather than the rules that dictate this behavior. A complete specification of an interface can be given in terms of state diagrams such as Figure 9-16 and the architectural functions such as *CHANNEL* (Knoblock et al., 1975).

The trace of Figure 9-20 has been expanded by showing the channel and adapter states and the semantics of the interface signals. These comments are not part of the normal trace.

Adapter Program.   Programs 9-22, 9-23, and 9-26 show three adapters. *ADAPTER*1 and *ADAPTER*3 illustrate two different transmission methods.

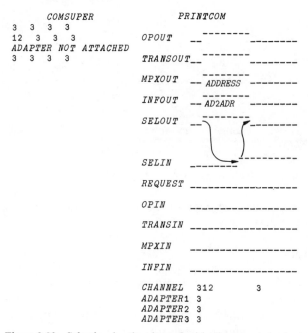

Figure 9-20   Selection by the channel with disconnected adapter.

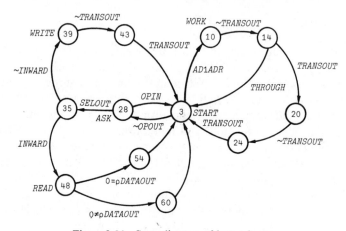

Figure 9-21   State diagram of byte adapter.

ADAPTER2 shows what happens if an adapter is not attached or is not turned on. The state diagram of *ADAPTER1* is shown in Figure 9-21.

Selection Fails. The channel signal *SELOUT* is passed on in line 6 of *ADAPTER1* and in line 2 of *ADAPTER2*, and changed to *SELIN* in line 5 of *ADAPTER3*, after which it returns to the channel. When the addressed adapter does not respond, *SELIN* becomes 1 and *CHANNEL* reports in line 14 that the

```
      ∇ ADAPTER1
[1]     →STATUS[AD1]                          [47]   ⍝ SEND DATA TO CHANNEL
[2]     ⍝ INITIAL STATE                       [48] READ:→WAITFOR~TRANSOUT
[3]   START:→WAITFOR OPOUT∨AD1ACT             [49]   →(0=⍴DATAOUT)/FINISH
[4]     →(~OPOUT)/ASK                         [50]   MPXIN← 1 1
[5]     →((TRANSOUT,MPXOUT,INFOUT)∧.= 1 0 1 ,AD1ADR)/WORK  [51]   INFIN←8↑DATAOUT
[6]     SELOUT[AD1]←SELOUT[CH]                [52]   DATAOUT←8↓DATAOUT
[7]     →0                                    [53]   TRANSIN←1
[8]     ⍝ SEND ACTIVITY STATUS               [54]   →WAITFOR TRANSOUT
[9]   WORK:OPIN←1                             [55]   →END
[10]    →WAITFOR~TRANSOUT                     [56]   ⍝ TERMINATE CONTACT
[11]    MPXIN← 1 0                            [57] FINISH:MPXIN← 1 0
[12]    INFIN←(AD1ACT∧OCCUPIED)∨(~AD1ACT)∧AVAILABLE  [58]   INFIN←THROUGH
[13]    TRANSIN←1                             [59]   TRANSIN←1
[14]    →WAITFOR TRANSOUT                     [60]   →WAITFOR TRANSOUT
[15]    →(INFOUT∧.=THROUGH)/END               [61]   AD1ACT←0
[16]    TASK1←2⊥INFOUT                        [62] END:MPXIN← 0 0
[17]    AD1ACT←TASK1∈CANDO1                   [63]   INFIN←8⍴0
[18]    TRANSIN←0                             [64]   TRANSIN←0
[19]    ⍝ SEND COMMAND RESPONSE              [65]   REQUEST←0
[20]    →WAITFOR~TRANSOUT                     [66]   OPIN←0
[21]    MPXIN← 1 0                            [67]   →START
[22]    INFIN←(AD1ACT∧ACCEPT)∨(~AD1ACT)∧REFUSE        ∇
[23]    TRANSIN←1
[24]    →WAITFOR TRANSOUT
[25]    →END                                        ∇ DECLAD1
[26]    ⍝ REQUEST SERVICE                    [1]    ⍝ ADAPTER ADDRESS
[27] ASK:REQUEST←1                            [2]    AD1ADR←(8⍴2)⊤1
[28]    →WAITFOR SELOUT[CH]∨OPIN              [3]    ⍝ ADAPTER ABILITY
[29]    →OPIN/END                             [4]    CANDO1← 4 12 132 140
[30]    OPIN←1                                [5]    ⍝ ADAPTER TASK
[31]    MPXIN← 0 1                            [6]    TASK1←0
[32]    INFIN←AD1ADR                          [7]    ⍝ ADAPTER ACTIVITY
[33]    TRANSIN←1                             [8]    AD1ACT←0
[34]    REQUEST←0                                    ∇
[35]    →WAITFOR TRANSOUT
[36]    TRANSIN←0
[37]    →(TASK1∈INWARD)/READ
[38]    ⍝ RECEIVE DATA FROM CHANNEL
[39] WRITE:→WAITFOR~TRANSOUT
[40]    MPXIN← 1 0
[41]    INFIN←PROCEED
[42]    TRANSIN←1
[43]    →WAITFOR TRANSOUT
[44]    →((MPXOUT,INFOUT)∧.= 1 0 ,THROUGH)/END-1
[45]    DATAOUT←DATAOUT,INFOUT
[46]    →END
[47]
```

```
      ⍝ REFERENCE:                                     PROGRAM:
      ⍝ WAITFOR      SUPERVISOR CALL FUNCTION            9-17
```

Program 9-22 Adapter for byte transmission.

```
      ∇ ADAPTER2
[1]     ⍝ NOT ATTACHED
[2]     SELOUT[AD2]←SELOUT[AD1]
      ∇
```

Program 9-23 Disconnected adapter.

addressed adapter is not connected. This report should be passed as a sink operand to the part of the channel that communicates with the central processor. For the moment this type of message is printed directly as part of the channel program.

It must be replaced later with the proper channel-processor interface functions. In lines 82 through 86 of *CHANNEL* all interface signals are made 0, and the channel returns to its start status.

Selection Succeeds. When the desired adapter is connected, the selection succeeds. The addressed adapter leaves the corresponding output signal of *SELOUT* 0 and makes the operational-in signal *OPIN* 1, as shown in *ADAPTER*1, line 9, and illustrated in Figure 9-24. The channel knows from *OPIN* that the selection has succeeded and moves to the label *READY*. It now makes both *SELOUT* and *TRANSOUT* 0 in lines 17 and 18.

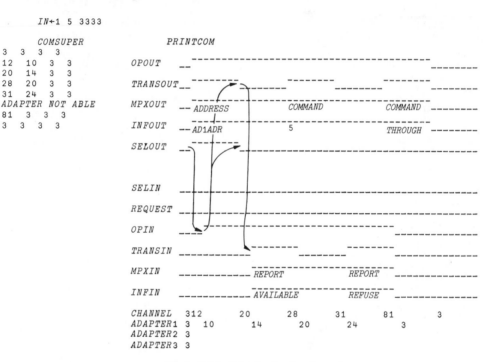

Figure 9-24   Selection by the channel.

OPIN, as well as all other incoming signals except *SELIN*, logically are the 'or' of the corresponding signals produced by the adapters. Such an 'or' was described in lines 3 and 7 of *TOM* by treating the incoming signals as a vector. Since normally only one signal appears on the incoming lines, these signals are treated here as a scalar rather than a vector.

Adapter Occupied. The channel does not know if an adapter is already engaged in an operation, since the status of the adapter is not stored in the channel. The adapter therefore takes the initiative and reports either that it is available for action or still occupied by a preceding action. The adapter remembers its activity status by means of the signal *AD1ACT*.

The adapter signifies that it is already executing a command by sending the message *OCCUPIED* over *INFIN*, in line 12 of *ADAPTER*1, and indicates that *INFIN* carries a report by the code 1 0 of *MPXIN*. *OCCUPIED* is an 8-bit code whose representation is indicated in line 7 of *INTERFACECODE*, Program 9-17. Upon receipt of this message, the channel reports in line 22 'adapter occupied' and terminates its contact with the adapter by sending the message *THROUGH* in lines 78 and 79.

9-5 INSTRUCTION

The channel knows that the adapter can respond when it receives the message *AVAILABLE* and moves to the label *WILLING*. The channel now tells the adapter what function to perform. The channel obtains from the channel source the operation code of the channel instruction, the command, and sends it as control information. For this action, *INFOUT* and *MPXOUT* are again used. *MPXOUT* now has the value 1 0. This action is shown in *CHANNEL*, lines 25 and 26.

Adapter Not Able.   The adapter gives *TASK*1 the value of the channel command as received over *INFOUT*, as shown in *ADAPTER*1, line 16. The adapter determines in line 17 whether it can execute the new task by comparing *TASK*1 with *CANDO*1, the list of tasks it is able to perform. When the command from the channel cannot be executed, the adapter sends the message *REFUSE*. The channel now reports 'adapter not able' and again terminates the contact.

Adapter Able.   When the adapter finds that it can execute the channel command, it sends the message *ACCEPT* over *INFIN*. The channel does not report the acceptance of the command by the adapter. Instead, it tells the adapter to proceed and internally records this fact by moving to the status corresponding to the label *ABLE*.

Termination by the Adapter.   When the peripheral unit needs considerable time to perform the actual transport, the initial contact between channel and adapter is terminated by the adapter. This frees the interface for communication between the channel and the other adapters. The device attached to adapter 1 is assumed to be of this nature. Adapter 3, which will be described in Section 9-6, presents the case where transmission immediately follows the selection.

In each of the cases that the adapter is occupied, not able, or able, the adapter takes the initiative in terminating the contact with the channel. It does so by making *OPIN* 0 as *TRANSIN* returns to 0. This occurs in line 66 of *ADAPTER*1, which is part of the end sequence of the adapter. The adapter remembers its appointed task by means of the signal *AD1ACT* and the scalar *TASK*1. The channel returns to its start status via line 40 and the end sequence and waits until adapter 1 reports for further action. In the meantime, the channel can communicate with other adapters.

9-6 DATA TRANSMISSION

Now that the adapter is selected and instructed, the actual data transmission can take place. The contact between the channel and adapter may be broken after the adapter is instructed and after each character that is transmitted, as is typical for multiplexed operation. This method will be described first. The transmission may also follow immediately after the adapter is instructed and preserve the connection between characters, as is typical for a selector channel, and will be described next. A third method, the *burst*, or *block, multiplex transmission*, disconnects after the channel is instructed but not between characters (Brown et al., 1972). Its operation is left as an exercise for the reader.

Byte Transmission

When the adapter is ready for the transmission of a character, or byte, it asks the channel for service. To do so, the adapter waits until the interface is not used, requests selection, transmits or receives the byte, and terminates the connection. Thus, the transmission proceeds 1 byte at a time. Adapter 1, which operates in this mode, is therefore called a *byte transmission* adapter.

Interface Free. An adapter can only make a request if the operational-out signal *OPOUT* is low, indicating that the channel is not using the interface. *OPOUT* is used to indicate whether the signals that proceed from the channel may be interpreted. Therefore, as shown in the time diagrams, *OPOUT* is always high when other signals are sent out by the channel.

*ADAPTER*1 tests in lines 3 and 4 for the presence of a task to be performed, as indicated by *AD1ACT*, and for the absence of *OPOUT*. When these tests succeed, it proceeds to the label *ASK*.

Selection by Adapter. An adapter asks for selection by making *REQUEST* high. Since the channel does not know which adapter puts in the request, the channel answers *REQUEST* by making *SELOUT* high. *CHANNEL* does so via the labels *START* and *SEEK*. Lines 3 and 4 indicate that in this channel design, servicing a current channel operation has higher priority than starting a new channel operation.

The requesting adapter reacts to *SELOUT* in lines 30 through 34 by making *OPIN* high and dropping *REQUEST*. When several adapters make *REQUEST* high, the route of the selection signals again determines the priority. As soon as *OPIN* is high, all nonselected adapters should drop *REQUEST*, as shown in lines 28, 29, and 65 of *ADAPTER*1.

The selected adapter identifies itself by giving its address to *INFIN* in lines 31 and 32. The channel reacts to the address with a message that determines the termination or continuance of the contact.

In this example, only the satisfactory conversation between channel and adapter is shown. Hence, the channel gives the message *PROCEED* in lines 49 and 50. In reality, the adapter address might not be acceptable, which would result in a termination. The selection initiated by the adapter is illustrated in Figure 9-25.

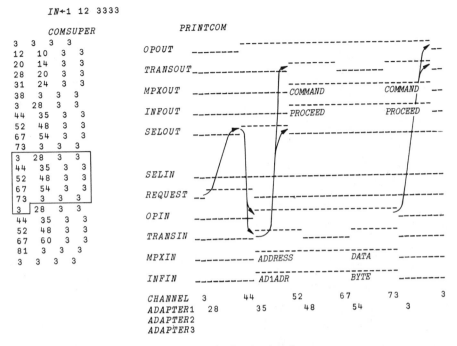

Figure 9-25 Selection by the adapter.

Byte Transfer. The transmission of the data occurs by a succession of 8-bit characters. One such character is now transmitted on the *INFOUT* or *INFIN* lines, identified by *MPXOUT* or *MPXIN* and enclosed by *TRANSOUT* or *TRANSIN*. The response to these signals can indicate the correct reception. The test for proper receipt and the action in case of errors again are not shown.

Figure 9-25 shows the signal succession. The figure shows that the initiative is taken by the adapter. This is desirable because the peripheral unit is asynchronous with respect to the channel. This signal succession is used in reading as well as in writing.

The byte transmission adapter stops the transmission after each byte. The adapter and channel both return to their start state. The adapter, however, keeps remembering its task by means of *AD1ACT* and will start another request when it is ready to resume transmission.

Burst Transmission

*ADAPTER*3, Program 9-26, is an example of a peripheral unit that starts the transport directly following the command and need not stop after each character. Whereas adapter 1 works in the byte mode, adapter 3 works in the *burst mode*.

As soon as *ADAPTER*3 has determined its task in line 15 and has reported its acceptance in line 20, it chooses the required transport status in line 25. For writing, this is implied by the wait on line 27, for reading by the wait on line 37. The state transitions for writing are illustrated in Figure 9-27.

```
     ∇ ADAPTER3
[1]    →STATUS[AD3]
[2]    ⍝ INITIAL STATE
[3]    START:→WAITFOR OPOUT
[4]    →((TRANSOUT,MPXOUT,INFOUT)∧.= 1 0 1 ,AD3ADR)/WORK
[5]    SELIN[CH]←SELOUT[AD2]
[6]    →0
[7]    ⍝ SEND ACTIVITY STATUS
[8]    WORK:OPIN←1
[9]    →WAITFOR~TRANSOUT
[10]   MPXIN← 1 0
[11]   INFIN←AVAILABLE
[12]   TRANSIN←1
[13]   →WAITFOR TRANSOUT
[14]   TASK3←2⊥INFOUT
[15]   AD3ACT←TASK3∈CANDO3
[16]   TRANSIN←0
[17]   ⍝ SEND COMMAND RESPONSE
[18]   →WAITFOR~TRANSOUT
[19]   MPXIN← 1 0
[20]   INFIN←(AD3ACT∧ACCEPT)∨(~AD3ACT)∧REFUSE
[21]   TRANSIN←1
[22]   →WAITFOR TRANSOUT
[23]   →(~AD3ACT)/END
[24]   TRANSIN←0
[25]   →(TASK3∈INWARD)/READ
[26]   ⍝ RECEIVE DATA FROM CHANNEL
[27] WRITE:→WAITFOR~TRANSOUT
[28]   MPXIN← 1 0
[29]   INFIN←PROCEED
[30]   TRANSIN←1
[31]   →WAITFOR TRANSOUT
[32]   →((MPXOUT,INFOUT)∧.= 1 0 ,THROUGH)/END-1
[33]   DATAOUT←DATAOUT,INFOUT
[34]   TRANSIN←0
[35]   →WRITE
[36]   ⍝ SEND DATA TO CHANNEL
[37] READ:→WAITFOR~TRANSOUT
[38]   →(0=ρDATAOUT)/FINISH
[39]   MPXIN← 1 1
[40]   INFIN←8↑DATAOUT
[41]   DATAOUT←8↓DATAOUT
[42]   TRANSIN←1
[43]   →WAITFOR TRANSOUT
[44]   TRANSIN←0
[45]   →READ
[46]   ⍝ TERMINATE CONTACT
[47] FINISH:MPXIN← 1 0
[48]   INFIN←THROUGH
[49]   TRANSIN←1
[50]   →WAITFOR TRANSOUT
[51]   AD3ACT←0
[52] END:MPXIN← 0 0
[53]   INFIN←8ρ0
[54]   TRANSIN←0
[55]   OPIN←0
[56]   →START
     ∇
```

```
     ∇ DECLAD3
[1]    ⍝ ADAPTER ADDRESS
[2]    AD3ADR←(8ρ2)⊤3
[3]    ⍝ ADAPTER ABILITY
[4]    CANDO3← 4 20 132 148
[5]    ⍝ ADAPTER TASK
[6]    TASK3←0
[7]    ⍝ ADAPTER ACTIVITY
[8]    AD3ACT←0
     ∇
```

```
⍝ REFERENCE:                                    PROGRAM:
⍝ WAITFOR        SUPERVISOR CALL FUNCTION          9-17
```

Program 9-26 Adapter for burst transmission.

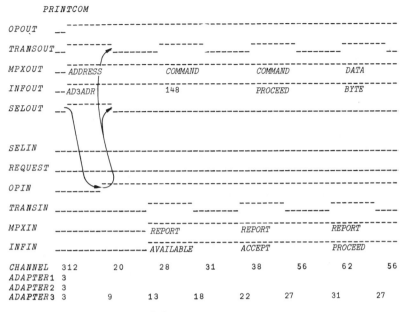

Figure 9-27   Burst transmission.

9-7 TERMINATION

The channel can terminate the communication between channel and adapter by returning both *OPOUT* and *TRANSOUT* to 0. Normally, a number of control messages will be exchanged preceding the termination. The termination may, however, also be abrupt as a consequence of errors in the communication.

    End of Transmission.   The adapter terminates when all data are transmitted. For *ADAPTER*1, this is determined in line 49; for *ADAPTER*3, in line 38, as illustrated in Figure 9-28. When the channel sends data to the adapter, it determines the end of the data in line 57. Both in reading and writing, the message *THROUGH* is sent by the channel to the adapter. This message is recognized by the recipient, and both channel and adapter come to rest.

    This description of the conversation between channel and adapter again gives the ideal procedure. In reality, the channel and adapter can exchange diverse error messages, which add greatly to the complexity of the protocol.

9-8 CHANNEL IMPLEMENTATION

Once the architecture of the channel is completely defined and verified as working correctly, an implementation can be designed. The design methods mentioned in the previous chapters can be applied. When this implementation in turn

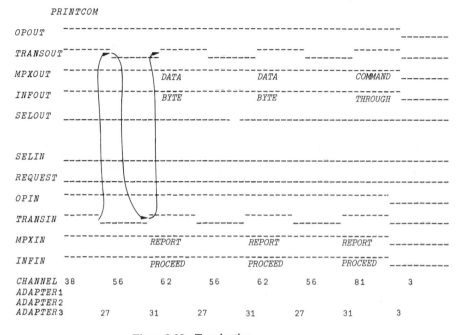

Figure 9-28   Termination.

is described in APL, it can be verified against the channel architecture. The simulation of the channel-adapter interaction is, in principle, no longer necessary.

REFERENCES

BROWN, D. T., R. L. EIBSEN, and C. A. THORN: "Channel and Direct Access Device Architecture." *IBM Systems Journal*, vol. 11, no. 3, pp. 186–199 (1972).

IBM System/360 I/O interface—Channel to Control Unit. IBM Publication A22–6843.

KNOBLOCK, D. E., D. C. LOUGHRY, and C. A. VISSERS: "Insight into Interfacing." *IEEE Spectrum*, vol. 12, no. 5, pp. 50–57 (May, 1975).

NELSON, G. E., and D. W. RICCI: "A Practical Interface System for Electronic Instruments." *Hewlett-Packard Journal*, vol. 24, no. 2, pp. 2–7 (October, 1972).

PADEGS, A.: "Channel Design Considerations." *IBM Systems Journal*, vol. 3, no. 2, pp. 165–180 (1964).

VISSERS, C. A.: *Lecture Notes on Interface Design*. Technische Hogeschool Twente, Enschede, Netherlands, 1975.

EXERCISES

9-1 Design *ADAPTER*4, a burst multiplex adapter, which terminates its contact with the channel after the command is received and later requests service to transmit data in the burst mode.

9-2 Design an implementation for the channel functions specified by *CHANNEL*, Program 9-17, using microprogrammed internal control.

9-3 Design an implementation for the adapter functions specified by *ADAPTER*1, Program 9-19, using hard-wired internal control.

9-4 Give the state diagram for *ADAPTER*3, Program 9-22.

9-5 Give the program *STATETRACE* that constructs the character matrix *PRINTSTATE* which preserves the states of channel and adapters as a simulation proceeds. *PRINTSTATE* should match *PRINTCOM*, as shown in Figure 9-27 and others. Indicate how *STATETRACE* should be introduced in the supervisor *COMSUPER*, Program 9-15.

9-6 *Review exercise.* To the operation repertoire of a computer, the operation square root is added. Indicate the successive algorithms that would be required, how they are derived from each other, the way they are verified, and the considerations that lead to a choice between various alternatives at each level. It is not necessary to generate any specific algorithm or to make a study of square-root implementations. It may be assumed that the design of the implementation for the remainder of the subject machine still permits modification.

9-7 *Review exercise.* Design a datapath and internal control that can perform the arithmetic and logical operations of the Intel 8080, as shown in Appendix B. First give the initial algorithms, then the datapath and gateprograms, finally a horizontal microprogram control. Assume that the instruction and operand fetch are provided. Ignore the implementation constraints peculiar to the need to place datapath and internal control on a single chip, as for the actual Intel design.

9-8 *Review exercise.* Design a datapath and internal control to perform normalized floating-point addition and multiplication according to the architecture of Program 9-29. Use separate datapaths for the arithmetic upon the exponents and upon the coefficients. Use, where appropriate, the initial algorithms, datapaths, and internal controls treated in this text. Use a selection that gives a reasonable balance between speed and cost, assuming addition to be three times as frequent as multiplication.

```
       ∇   N←FPI R;EXPONENT;COEFFICIENT                    ∇   FPFIELD
 [1]       EXPONENT←TWOC R[EXP]                       [1]      EXP←ι8
 [2]       COEFFICIENT←TWOC R[COEF]                   [2]      COEF←8+ι24
 [3]       N←COEFFICIENT×2*EXPONENT-POINT             [3]      POINT←23
       ∇                                                  ∇


       ∇   R←FPR N;EXPONENT;COEFFICIENT
 [1]       EXPONENT←(N≠-2*⌊2⊛|N+N=0)+⌊2⊛|N+0.5×N=0
 [2]       COEFFICIENT←(¯1*N<0)×⌊|N÷2*EXPONENT-POINT
 [3]       R←((8ρ2)⊤EXPONENT),(24ρ2)⊤COEFFICIENT
 [4]       OFFP←EXPONENT>TWOC R[EXP]
 [5]       UFFP←EXPONENT<TWOC R[EXP]
       ∇


       ∇   FPADD;SUM                                       ∇   FPMPY;PRODUCT
 [1]       SUM←(FPI A)+FPI B                          [1]      PRODUCT←(FPI MR)×FPI MD
 [2]       S←FPR SUM                                  [2]      PD←FPR PRODUCT
       ∇                                                  ∇


           ⍝ REFERENCE:                                        PROGRAM:
           ⍝ TWOC        2-COMPLEMENT INTERPRETATION            3-1
```

Program 9-29   Floating-point architecture.

9-9   *Review exercise.* Design a floating point division architecture, which uses the formats of Program 9-29, for the divisor, dividend, and quotient. No remainder is required. Design an initial algorithm, specialized datapath and hard-wired control, that implements this architecture.

9-10   *Review exercise.* Two elevators serve N floors. Each floor has an Up and a Down button, except that the top and bottom floors each have only one button. The elevator cages each have N buttons to request one or more destination floors. When no service is requested, at least one cage rests at the ground floor, floor 0. Design the architecture and implementation for a simple control of this system. Ignore the controls for the opening and closing of doors. Give a datapath and internal control.

SUMMARY OF APL

This section summarizes the subset of APL that is used in this book. The summary is given in the tables and examples. The text is intended to be a brief introduction to APL for those who prefer to get a feel for the language before they are introduced to it in the various chapters of the book.

For a discussion of the full language and of the terminal operation of APL\360 and APLSV, the introduction by Polivka and Pakin (1975) and the reference manual by Pakin (1972) are recommended. The differences between APL\360 and APLSV are described by Falkoff and Iverson (1973). These differences, however, do not affect the subset used in this text.

Introduction

$DOG \leftarrow CAT + 5$ is a simple APL expression. The expression is sufficiently close to common algebraic notation that the reader will guess that 5 is added to the value of CAT and that DOG is given this new value. If the value of CAT is 7, then the value of DOG becomes 12.

The concepts that an interpretation of $DOG \leftarrow CAT + 5$ presupposes are:

(a) Evaluation of an expression, such as adding 5 to CAT and assigning this value to DOG.
(b) Data, such as 5.
(c) Variables, such as CAT and DOG, and the use of identifiers, such as the term 'CAT,' for such a variable.
(d) Operators, such as the + operator.
(e) Functions, such as the repeated use of this expression with different values of CAT.

These concepts will be treated in turn.

A-1 EVALUATION OF AN EXPRESSION

Expressions are evaluated in APL from right to left. Thus, $5 + 7 \times 2 - 1$ is evaluated as $5 + 7 \times 1$, next as $5 + 7$, and finally as 12. In contrast, the algebraic evaluation would give $5 + 14 - 1$, or $19 - 1$, or 18, and the left-to-right evaluation $12 \times 2 - 1$, or $24 - 1$, or 23.

The order of evaluation may be changed with *parentheses*. The expression between parentheses is evaluated first. Thus, $5 + (7 \times 2) - 1$ is evaluated as $5 + 14 - 1$, or $5 + 13$, or 18.

A-2 DATA

Data may be numbers or characters. They are normally treated as arrays.

Numbers.   *Numbers* are represented in our subset as decimal integers, or fractions, or both. The *minus sign* is attached to the left and is raised to distinguish it from the negation operator. Thus, the result of $7 - 12$ is $^-5$.

Characters.   Each of the *characters* of Table A-1 may be used as a data element. These characters are the characters of the APL keyboard that are used in this text, including the overstruck characters. The *overstruck characters* are made by striking a key, backspacing, and striking another key. Table A-1 shows the elements from which the overstruck characters are obtained. Their order is arbitrary.

```
A  B  C  D  E  F  G  H  I  J  K  L  M  N  O  P  Q  R  S  T  U  V  W  X  Y  Z

0  1  2  3  4  5  6  7  8  9

,  .  ;  :  '  ‾  _  [  ]  (  )  ⍺

+  -  ×  ÷  *  ●  ⌊  ⌈  |  ?  <  ≤  =  ≥  >  ≠  ~  ∧  ∨  ⍲  ⍱

ρ  ⍳  /  ⍉  ⊥  ⊤  ↑  ↓  ∊  ∇  ⌶
```

```
            ⍺ APL CHARACTERS USED IN THIS TEXT

OVERSTRIKE       ⍺    ⊛    ⍟    ⍣    ⍉    ⌶
OBTAINED FROM    ∩    ○    ∧    ∨    ○    ⊤
         AND     ○    *    ~    ~    \    ⊥
```

Table A-1   Subset of APL characters.

Arrays

A number or a character normally is treated as an element of an array. In APL, *arrays* have a regular structure that is obtained by ordering the elements in groups of equal size. Subsequently, these groups may be ordered in the same fashion again. The size of a group is called a *dimension* of the array. The number of times the grouping is repeated is the *rank* of the array. Each grouping is called a *coordinate* of the array.

Vector, Matrix, Scalar. A single group of elements is called a *vector*. The dimension of the vector is the number of elements in the vector. The rank is 1. Thus, the vector 2 5 4 7 2 1 has one coordinate and dimension 6.

When groups of groups are taken, the array is called a *matrix*. Table A-2 shows an example of a 2 by 5 matrix. The dimension of this matrix is the vector 2 5. The rightmost element of the *dimension vector* gives the lowest-order grouping; the elements to the left each time represent the next coordinate.

VECTOR	MATRIX	ARRAY
3 8 0 9 ¯5 11	5 2 ¯3 9 1 ¯4 0 8 12 2	4 7 3 ¯1 ¯2 11 0 ¯5 4 8 9 ¯6
		¯8 3 9 4 2 ¯13 10 1 0 ¯3 ¯7 6

Table A-2 Arrays.

When the data comprise only a single element, that element is called a *scalar*. Since no grouping takes place, the dimension is empty and the rank is 0.

Table A-2 also shows an array of rank 3 with dimension vector 2 3 4. In general, the dimension of the dimension vector is the rank. This is also true for a vector; its dimension vector is a one-element vector, not a scalar.

The low-order groupings of an array are called *rows*.

Representation of Arrays. A numeric array is displayed by placing the numbers, separated by spaces, in the pertinent groupings, as shown in Figure A-2. A numeric vector may appear in an expression. Thus, $DOG \leftarrow CAT + 2\ 5\ 8$ indicates the addition of the vector 2 5 8 to *CAT*.

A character array is represented without space between the elements of a row. Thus, a character vector with the three characters *C*, *A*, and *T* as elements is displayed as *CAT*.

Specification of Characters. The three symbols *CAT* may either represent a three-element character vector or the name of a variable. When such a group of characters appears in an expression, they are always interpreted as a name, as was the case in $DOG \leftarrow CAT + 5$. When a character vector appears in an expression, it is enclosed with *quotes*. Thus, '*CAT*' represents a three-element character vector.

When the quote itself is an element of a character vector, it is specified by two quotes in succession: '*DON''T CARE*' specifies the 10-character vector *DON'T CARE*.

Indexing

Elements of an array can be identified by an index. An *index* is placed between two square brackets, and the values for each coordinate are separated by a semicolon. The higher coordinates are placed to the left of the lower. The numbering of the elements is from low to high, that is, from left to right and from top to bottom. The numbering starts with 0, the *zero origin*, or with 1, the *one origin*. In this text, only the zero origin is used. Thus, 2 5 7 8[1] is 5. The element in the third row and the fifth column of a matrix, counting from the top left corner, is specified by [2; 4]. Table A-3 gives further examples using the arrays of Table A-2. In each of these examples, the first line, which is indented 6 spaces, gives a specification; and the following lines, without indentation, give the result.

```
      VECTOR[5 4 4 1]              MATRIX[1;3]              ARRAY[1;0;3]
 11  ¯5  ¯5  8                 12                      4

      VECTOR[]                     MATRIX[;3]               ARRAY[;0;]
 3  8  0  9  ¯5  11            9  12                         4  7  3  ¯1
                                                           ¯8  3  9   4

                                   MATRIX[1;]
                               ¯4  0  8  12  2
```

Table A-3   Indexing examples.

For each coordinate, as many values may be specified as desired in any order, including repetitions. Thus, 'CAT'[1 0 2] gives *ACT*, and 'DOG'[2 1 1 0] gives *GOOD*. An index may also be specified by an expression: 2 5 7 8[3 − 1] is the same as 2 5 7 8[2], which gives 7. When the index value for a coordinate is empty, all elements along that coordinate participate. Thus, 2 5 7 8[ ] is the same as 2 5 7 8, and *MATRIX*[; 3] gives all elements of column 3 of *MATRIX*.

A-3 VARIABLES AND IDENTIFIERS

An array may be identified by a name. Both the structure of the array and the value of its elements may change as the array is assigned a value in an expression.

Identifiers.   *Identifiers*, or *names*, for variables and for the functions to be mentioned in Section A-5 may be composed of the alphabetic characters and the numeric characters. A numeric may not be the first character. No spaces are allowed in a name. *CAT5* is interpreted as one name, *CAT 5* as a name and the number 5, and *5CAT*, or 5 *CAT*, as the number 5 to the left of the name *CAT*.

A-4 OPERATORS

Operators are also called *primitive functions* in APL. They can be classified according to the number of operands as *monadic*, applying to one operand, or *dyadic*, applying to two operands. The same symbol may be used both monadically and dyadically.

The operators can also be classified according to the type of operand. The *scalar* operators apply to scalars and have a scalar result. They may, however, also be used with arrays. The *composite* operators apply only to arrays but use scalar operators. All other operators are called *mixed* operators.

Scalar Operators

Table A-4 lists the monadic and dyadic operators used in the subset of this text. The operators apply primarily to numbers rather than characters.

The logical operators apply only to numbers with the value 0 or 1. Hence, it is useful to recognize the class of *logical values*, even though the logical values are represented by numbers and participate in many operations as numbers.

Monadic Scalar Operators. The monadic scalar operators of the subset used in this book are the negation, the absolute value, the floor, the ceiling, the random, and the not. These operators are explained by the examples of Table A-4.

The *negation* gives the opposite of the operand; the *absolute value* gives the magnitude of the operand. The *floor* is the greatest integer less than the operand. The *ceiling* is the smallest integer greater than the operand. The *random*, or roll, selects randomly one of the integers smaller than the operand. The *not* gives the inverse of the operand, which must be a logical value.

Dyadic Scalar Operators. The subset of this book comprises as dyadic scalar operators:

(a) The *arithmetic* operators: *addition, subtraction, multiplication, division, exponentiation, logarithm, minimum, maximum,* and *residue.*
(b) The *relations*: *less than, greater than or equal, less than or equal, greater than, equal,* and *unequal.*
(c) The *logical* operators: *and, or, nand,* and *nor.*

These operators follow closely the established meaning as illustrated in Table A-4. The symbol for exponentiation is *, for logarithm ⊛, for nand ∧, and for nor ∨. When a relation is true, it has the value 1; when false, it has the value 0. The logical operators again apply only to logical values.

Extension to Arrays. The scalar operators can also be used for arrays. The monadic operators are simply applied to each element of an array. Thus, $|5\ ^{-}2\ 3$ gives 5 2 3.

For the dyadic operators, both operands must have the same dimension. The operator is applied to corresponding elements of both arrays. Thus, 5 8 3 × 2 8 1 gives 10 64 3, a result that differs from classical vector multiplication.

The dyadic operators also allow one operand to be an array and the other a scalar. In that case, the scalar participates as operand with all elements of the array. Thus, 9 2 5 + 2 or 2 + 9 2 5 gives 11 4 7.

Composite Operators

The three composite operators are the reduction, the inner product, and the outer product.

```
      -3.14 ¯2.17                        |3.14 ¯2.17
¯3.14  2.17                        3.14   2.17
      ⍝ NEGATION                         ⍝ ABSOLUTE VALUE

      ⌊3.14 ¯2.17                        ⌈3.14 ¯2.17
3  ¯3                              4  ¯2
      ⍝ FLOOR                            ⍝ CEILING

      ?1 2 5 5 17                        ~0 1
0  1  2  1  1  6                   1  0
      ?1 2 5 5 17                        ⍝ NOT
0  0  4  4  0  15
      ?1 2 5 5 17
0  1  1  4  2  4
      ⍝ RANDOM

      ⍝ MONADIC SCALAR OPERATORS


      3 ¯2+5 4                           3 ¯2-5 4
8  2                              ¯2  ¯6
      ⍝ ADDITION                         ⍝ SUBTRACTION

      3 ¯2×5 4                           3 ¯2÷5 4
15  ¯8                            0.6  ¯0.5
      ⍝ MULTIPLICATION                   ⍝ DIVISION

      3 ¯2*5 4                           3 2⍟5 4
243 16                           1.464973521  2
      ⍝ EXPONENTIATION                   ⍝ LOGARITHM

      3 ¯2⌊5 ¯4                          3 ¯2⌈5 ¯4
3  ¯4                             5  ¯2
      ⍝ MINIMUM                          ⍝ MAXIMUM

      3 2|5 ¯2.17
2  1.83
      ⍝ RESIDUE


      1 2 3<3 2 1                        1 2 3≥3 2 1
1  0  0                           0  1  1
      ⍝ LESS THAN                        ⍝ GREATER THAN OR EQUAL

      1 2 3≤3 2 1                        1 2 3>3 2 1
1  1  0                           0  0  1
      ⍝ LESS THAN OR EQUAL               ⍝ GREATER THAN

      1 2 3=3 2 1                        1 2 3≠3 2 1
0  1  0                           1  0  1
      ⍝ EQUAL                            ⍝ UNEQUAL

      0 0 1 1∧0 1 0 1                    0 0 1 1∨0 1 0 1
0  0  0  1                        0  1  1  1
      ⍝ AND                              ⍝ OR

      0 0 1 1⍲0 1 0 1                    0 0 1 1⍱0 1 0 1
1  1  1  0                        1  0  0  0
      ⍝ NAND                             ⍝ NOR

      ⍝ DYADIC SCALAR OPERATORS
```

Table A-4 Scalar operators.

Reduction. The *reduction* operator is composed of a scalar dyadic operator placed to the left of the slash, /. The reduction is applied monadically to an array. The effect of the operator is the same as if the dyadic operator were placed between the row elements of the array. Thus, all rows are reduced to one element, and the rank of the array is reduced by 1.

The add reduction, +/, is equivalent to the algebraic summation, Σ. Thus, +/5 ⁻2 3 gives 6. Similarly, the multiply reduction is equivalent to algebraic repeated multiplication, Π; ×/5 ⁻2 3 gives ⁻30. Table A-5 gives further examples.

```
        +/2 ⁻5 12        3 ⁻2+.×5 4              0 1 2∘.+0 1 2
9                   7                       0  1  2
        ×/2 ⁻5 12        3 ⁻2×.+5 4          1  2  3
⁻120                16                      2  3  4
        ⌊/2 ⁻5 12        0 1 4 7⌊.⌈5 3 2 1      0 1 2∘.×4 5 6
⁻5                  3                   0  0  0
        ⌈/2 ⁻5 12        0 1 4 7⌈.⌊5 3 2 1   4  5  6
12                  2                   8 10 12
        ∨/0 1 1 0        0 1∨.≠0 1              0 1∘.∨0 1
1                   0                   0 1
        ∧/0 1 1 0        0 1∧.=0 1           1 1
0                   1                   0 1∘.∧0 1
                                        0 0
                                        0 1
        ⍝ REDUCTION      ⍝ INNER PRODUCT        ⍝ OUTER PRODUCT
```

Table A-5 Composite operators.

Inner Product. The *inner product* is specified by two dyadic scalar operators separated by a period, such as ∧.=. The right operator, here =, is applied first to the elements of the two operands. Each row of the left operand is combined as a vector with the elements selected along the highest dimension of the right operand. Thus, for two matrices, the rows of the left operand are combined with the columns of the right operand. Each vector result is subsequently reduced by the second operator, here ∧, to a single element.

When the two operators are + and ×, the classical matrix product is obtained.

Outer Product. The *outer product* is specified by one dyadic scalar operator placed to the right of the symbol ∘ and period, such as ∘.+. Each element of the right operand is combined with all elements of the left operand using the scalar operator, here +. The result therefore has a rank that is the sum of the ranks of the two operands.

Mixed Operators

Monadic Mixed Operators. The monadic mixed operators used in the subset of this book are the dimension, the ravel, the index generator, and the transposition. They are illustrated in Table A-6.

```
         VECTOR                      MATRIX                    ARRAY
3   8   0   9  ⁻5  11        5   2  ⁻3   9   1        4    7   3  ⁻1
                          ⁻4   0   8  12   2       ⁻2   11   0   5
                                                    4    8   9  ⁻6
         ρVECTOR                   ρMATRIX
6                                 2   5                  ⁻8   3   9   4
                                                    2  ⁻13  10   1
         ρρVECTOR                 ρρMATRIX            0   ⁻3  ⁻7   6
1                                2
                                                         ρARRAY
                                                    2   3   4

                                                         ρρARRAY
                                                    3
```

A DIMENSION

```
    ,MATRIX
5   2  ⁻3   9   1  ⁻4   0   8  12   2
```

```
    ,ARRAY
4   7   3  ⁻1  ⁻2  11   0   5   4   8   9  ⁻6  ⁻8   3   9   4   2  ⁻13  10   1   0  ⁻3  ⁻7   6
A RAVEL
```

```
    ι24
0   1   2   3   4   5   6   7   8   9   10   11   12   13   14   15   16   17   18   19   20   21   22   23
A INDEX GENERATOR
```

```
    ⍉MATRIX
5  ⁻4
2   0
⁻3   8
9  12
1   2
A TRANSPOSITION
```

Table A-6 Monadic mixed operators.

Dimension. The *dimension*, or size, operator, represented by the Greek letter rho, ρ, yields the dimension of an array. The dimension of the dimension is the rank of the array. Thus, ρ 9 5 2 gives 3 and $\rho\rho$ 9 5 2 gives 1.

Ravel. The *ravel* is represented by a comma. When applied to an array, the ravel yields the vector comprising the elements of the array. Table A-6 shows that the elements are taken left to right and low to high order.

Index Generator. The *index generator* is represented by the Greek letter iota, ι. The index generator of the integer N yields a vector composed of the N integers 0 through $N - 1$, assuming zero-origin indexing. Thus, ι5 gives 0 1 2 3 4.

Transpose. The *transpose* is represented by the overstruck symbol, $\otimes$. In this text, transposition is applied only to matrices. The rows of a matrix become columns, and the columns become rows.

Dyadic Mixed Operators. The dyadic mixed operators that are used in this book are reshape, catenation, index of, decode, encode, compression, take, drop, and membership. These are illustrated in Table A-7 and will be discussed briefly below.

`      7ρ2`
`2  2  2  2  2  2  2`
	`      MATRIX`
	` 5   2  ‾3   9   1`
	`‾4   0   8  12   2`

`      2 4ρ0 1 2`
`  0  1  2  0`
`  1  2  0  1`
`   ⍝ RESHAPE`
	`      3 4ρMATRIX`
	` 5   2  ‾3   9`
	` 1  ‾4   0   8`
	`12   2   5   2`

`      VECTOR`
`3  8  0  9  ‾5  11`
	`      MATRIX,7 2`
	` 5   2  ‾3   9   1   7`
	`‾4   0   8  12   2   2`

`      VECTOR,12 13 14`
`3  8  0  9  ‾5  11  12  13  14`
`   ⍝ CATENATION`
	`      MATRIX,[0]10 11 12 13 14`
	` 5   2  ‾3   9   1`
	`‾4   0   8  12   2`
	`10  11  12  13  14`

`      3 5 0 2 3ι3 2 0 1 2 3 4`
`0  3  2  5  3  0  5`
`   ⍝ INDEX OF`
	`      3 8 12 0 1ιMATRIX`
	`5  5  5  5  4`
	`5  3  1  2  5`

`      3⊥2 2 0`
`24`
`   ⍝ DECODE`
	`      10⊥2 2 0`
	`220`

`      2 2 2 2⊤12`
`0  1  1  0  0`
`   ⍝ ENCODE`
	`      10 10 10 10⊤1984`
	`1  9  8  4`

`      0 1 1 0 0 1/0 1 2 3 4 5`
`1  2  5`
`   ⍝ COMPRESSION`	

`      2 3↑MATRIX`
` ‾5  2  ‾3`
` ‾4  0  8`
`   ⍝ TAKE`
	`      3 ‾4↑MATRIX`
	`2  ‾3   9   1`
	`0   8  12   2`
	`0   0   0   0`

`      1 2↓MATRIX`
`  8  12   2`
`   ⍝ DROP`
	`      0 ‾3↓MATRIX`
	`‾5  2`
	`‾4  0`

`      3∊0 1 2 3 4`
`1`
`   ⍝ MEMBERSHIP`
	`      0 1 2 3 4∊3`
	`0  0  0  1  0`

Table A-7   Dyadic mixed operators.

Reshape. The *reshape*, or restructure, is represented by the dyadically used rho. The reshape gives to the elements of an array—the right operand—the dimension specified by the left operand. When the number of elements in the array is insufficient, they are used repeatedly.

Catenation. The comma, used dyadically, represents catenation. The *catenation* of two vectors results in a vector comprised of the elements of the left operand placed next to the elements of the right operand. The catenation of two arrays catenates the rows of these arrays, assuming that the other dimensions are compatible. When it is desired to catenate along other coordinates, the number of the coordinate can be placed to the right of the comma. Thus, $MATRIX1,[0]MATRIX2$ gives the column catenation of the two matrices.

Index of.   The *index of* is represented by the dyadically used iota. The result has the same dimension as the right operand. The left operand must be a vector.

When the right element is a scalar, the leftmost element of the left operand that equals the scalar is found. The index of this element is the result. When no equality is found, the dimension of the left argument is recorded.

When the right operand is an array, the above process is repeated for each element of the array. Thus, $'ACT'\iota'CAT'$ results in 1 0 2, and 8 5 4 5 ι 5 7 results in 1 4.

Decode.   The *decode*, or base value, represented by $\bot$, determines the value of the right operand as interpreted in the number system, specified by the left operand. The left operand may be a scalar or vector; the right operand may be an array. The operation will be explained for the case that the left operand is a scalar and the right operand a vector. In that case, the right operand is interpreted as the digits in the number system of the left operand and evaluated accordingly. Thus, $2 \bot 1$ 1 0 is 6, $3 \bot 1$ 1 0 is 12, and $10 \bot 1$ 1 0 is 110.

Encode.   The *encode*, or representation, is represented by the symbol $\top$ and is the opposite of the decode. The left argument of the encode represents the number system in which the elements of the right argument are to be encoded. When the right operand is a scalar, the result is the vector of the digits of this scalar in the number system specified by the left operand. Thus, 2 2 2 2 $\top$ 37 gives the four low-order digits of the binary representation of 37, that is, 0 1 0 1.

Compression.   The *compression* is represented by the dyadically used slash, /. The left operand should be a logical vector, that is, a vector comprising only 0s and 1s. The right operand should be an array of which the rows have the same dimension as the left operand. For each 0 in the left operand, the corresponding element in the rows of the right operand is deleted. For a 1 in the left operand, the corresponding element in the rows of the right array is maintained. Thus, 1 0 1 0 1 / $'CRAFT'$ gives CAT, and 0 0 1 0 / 0 1 2 3 gives 2.

Take.   The *take* is represented by the upward arrow, $\uparrow$. The left operand should be a vector whose dimension equals the rank of the right operand. The right operand may be an array. Each element of the left operand determines how many elements along the corresponding coordinate of the right operand are taken. When the element is positive, the first elements are taken; when the element is negative, the last elements are taken. Thus, $^-3 \uparrow 'FACT'$ gives ACT, and $2 \uparrow 0$ 1 2 3 4 gives 0 1.

When the take specifies more elements than are contained in the right operand, a numeric operand is thought to be extended with 0s and a character operand with blanks. Thus, $^-6 \uparrow 1$ 2 3 gives 0 0 0 1 2 3, and $6 \uparrow 1$ 2 3 gives 1 2 3 0 0 0.

Drop. The *drop* operator is the opposite of the take. It is represented by a downward arrow and indicates the number of elements along each coordinate that must be eliminated. Thus, 1 ↓ *'FACT'* gives *ACT*, and ⁻2 ↓ 0 1 2 3 4 gives 0 1 2.

Membership. The *membership* operator is represented by the Greek letter epsilon, ϵ. The operator determines for each element of the left operand if it also occurs in the right operand and indicates a positive result with 1 and a negative result with 0. Thus, *'FACTUAL'* ϵ *'CAT'* gives 0 1 1 1 0 1 0, and 2 5 ϵ 0 1 2 3 2 1 gives 1 0.

Specification. A variable, identified by a name, such as *DOG*, is given a value by the *specification*, or assignment, operator, the left-pointing arrow, ←. The value of the expression to the right of the arrow, including its dimensions, becomes the new value of the variable. Thus, if in *DOG* ← *CAT* + 5, *CAT* is a 3 by 5 matrix, *DOG* will be a 3 by 5 matrix whose elements are 5 greater than the corresponding elements of *CAT*.

A-5 FUNCTIONS

One or more expressions may be combined into a function. A function has a name and may specify two, one, or no explicit operand and one or no explicit result. The names of the function, the operands, and the result are given in the function header.

The functions have the same appearance as the primitive functions or operators of APL. Since they are specified by the user and not by the system, they are called *defined functions*. Here, we shall call them *functions* for short.

Function Header. The function *header* gives the form of the function when it is used in an expression. Because of the variations in the number of operands and results, there are six forms of functions, as shown in Table A-8.

Table A-8 shows an example of each of these forms as they appear in an expression. Below the expression, the corresponding function definition is given.

The names used for the operands and the result are valid only within the function; that is, they are *local* names. As the function is used in an expression, the value of an operand in that expression is passed on to the operand of the function. Conversely, the value of the result of the function is made available to the calling expression.

Local Variables. Any variable that is used in a function may be declared to be *local*, that is, valid only within the function and the functions called by it. A variable is made local by placing the variable name after the main part of the header, separated by a semicolon. A local variable is distinct from a variable of the same name, as used outside the function. Program A-9 illustrates the use of a local variable *CAT* in the function *DOGGETCAT*. A variable that is accessible both

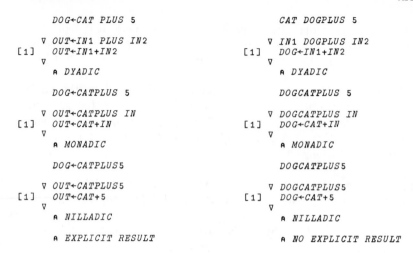

```
        DOG←CAT PLUS 5                          CAT DOGPLUS 5

     ∇ OUT←IN1 PLUS IN2                      ∇ IN1 DOGPLUS IN2
[1]    OUT←IN1+IN2                      [1]    DOG←IN1+IN2
     ∇                                      ∇
     ⍝ DYADIC                                ⍝ DYADIC

        DOG←CATPLUS 5                          DOGCATPLUS 5

     ∇ OUT←CATPLUS IN                       ∇ DOGCATPLUS IN
[1]    OUT←CAT+IN                       [1]    DOG←CAT+IN
     ∇                                      ∇
     ⍝ MONADIC                               ⍝ MONADIC

        DOG←CATPLUS5                           DOGCATPLUS5

     ∇ OUT←CATPLUS5                         ∇ DOGCATPLUS5
[1]    OUT←CAT+5                        [1]    DOG←CAT+5
     ∇                                      ∇
     ⍝ NILLADIC                              ⍝ NILLADIC

     ⍝ EXPLICIT RESULT                       ⍝ NO EXPLICIT RESULT
```

Table A-8   Forms of functions.

```
        ∇ DOGGETCAT;CAT
[1]       ⍝ START
[2]       DOG←0
[3]       ⍝ LOOP
[4]     CONT:CAT←?5
[5]       DOG←5|DOG+1
[6]       →(DOG≠CAT)/CONT
        ∇
```

Program A-9   Example of local variable, label, and comment.

within and outside a function is called *global*. An example is *DOG* in *DOGGET-CAT*.

Function Declaration.   A function is declared by giving the header and preceding it by a downward-pointing delta, the *del*, ∇. Under the header are listed the expressions that form the body of the function. The end of the function declaration is again given by a del.

Branch.   The expressions of a function are evaluated in their numeric order. This order may be changed by a branch. The *branch* is represented by the right-pointing arrow, →. The arrow should always be leftmost in an expression. The value to the right of the arrow indicates the number of the expression to be executed next, the *branch target*. Thus, →5 specifies a branch to line 5. An expression to the right of the arrow is evaluated first, and its result is used as the branch target. Thus, →5 − 3 specifies a branch to line 2.

When there is no line number corresponding to the branch target, the execution of the function terminates. This also includes a branch to 0, which is a standard way of terminating a function.

Conditional Branch.   When the branch target is empty, the branch is not taken and the function execution continues with the next expression. Thus, *TEST*/5 appearing on line 12 results in a branch to line 5 when *TEST* equals 1 and results in no branch, hence continuation with line 13, when *TEST* equals 0.

Label.   An expression of a function may be identified by a label. The label is a name which is placed to the left of an expression and separated from the expression by a colon. Thus, line 4 of *DOGGETCAT* is identified by the label *CONT*, indicating the continuation of the loop. The value of a label equals the number of the line on which it appears. Thus, *CONT* has the value 4. A label is a local variable and may be used in an expression such as *CONT* + 1. The use of a label in a branch statement has the advantage that the target remains correct when lines are deleted or inserted in the function.

Comment.   Text, which is not to be executed, may be introduced in a function by preceding it with the *comment* symbol ⍝. The comment always occupies a full line. *DOGGETCAT* lines 1 and 3 illustrate the use of comments.

The terminal implementations give several aids for the entering, editing, and debugging of functions. These will not be discussed in this text.

System Functions.   Table A-10 lists a number of system functions that may be used in an expression. These are the I-beam functions, identified by the symbol I. Of these, the I27 is of particular interest. This function gives the *state indicator* vector, which lists the line number of the current expression and the line numbers of all expressions that are calling functions whose execution is suspended. Thus, if function *ONE* calls function *TWO* on line 12 and if line 3 of *TWO* contains I27, the value of this expression is 3 12.

```
TIME OF DAY IN 60TH OF A SECOND           I20
CURRENT DAY REPRESENTED AS MMDDYY         I25
VALUE OF CURRENT LINE NUMBER              I26
VALUE OF LINE NUMBERS IN STATE INDICATOR  I27

    ⍝ SUBSET OF I-BEAM FUNCTIONS
```

Table A-10   Some system functions.

REFERENCES

FALKOFF, A. D., and K. E. IVERSON: *APLSV User's Manual, APL Shared Variable System*. IBM Publication SH20–1460. IBM Philadelphia Scientific Center, 1973.

PAKIN, S.: *APL/360 Reference Manual*. Science Research Associates, Chicago, 2nd ed., 1972.

POLIVKA, R. P., and S. PAKIN: *APL: The Language and Its Usage*. Prentice-Hall, Englewood Cliffs, N.J., 1975.

B IBM SYSTEM/360 AND INTEL 8080 INSTRUCTIONS

RR FORMAT

xxxx	Branching and Status Switching 0000xxxx	Fixed-Point Fullword and Logical 0001xxxx	Floating-Point Long 0010xxxx	Floating-Point Short 0011xxxx
0000		LOAD POSITIVE	LOAD POSITIVE	LOAD POSITIVE
0001		LOAD NEGATIVE	LOAD NEGATIVE	LOAD NEGATIVE
0010		LOAD AND TEST	LOAD AND TEST	LOAD AND TEST
0011		LOAD COMPLEMENT	LOAD COMPLEMENT	LOAD COMPLEMENT
0100	SET PROGRAM MASK	AND	HALVE	HALVE
0101	BRANCH AND LINK	COMPARE LOGICAL		
0110	BRANCH ON COUNT	OR		
0111	BRANCH/CONDITION	EXCLUSIVE OR		
1000	SET KEY	LOAD	LOAD	LOAD
1001	INSERT KEY	COMPARE	COMPARE	COMPARE
1010	SUPERVISOR CALL	ADD	ADD N	ADD N
1011		SUBTRACT	SUBTRACT N	SUBTRACT N
1100		MULTIPLY	MULTIPLY	MULTIPLY
1101		DIVIDE	DIVIDE	DIVIDE
1110		ADD LOGICAL	ADD U	ADD U
1111		SUBTRACT LOGICAL	SUBTRACT U	SUBTRACT U

RX FORMAT

xxxx	Fixed-Point Halfword and Branching 0100xxxx	Fixed-Point Fullword and Logical 0101xxxx	Floating-Point Long 0110xxxx	Floating-Point Short 0111xxxx
0000	STORE	STORE	STORE	STORE
0001	LOAD ADDRESS			
0010	STORE CHARACTER			
0011	INSERT CHARACTER			
0100	EXECUTE	AND		
0101	BRANCH AND LINK	COMPARE LOGICAL		
0110	BRANCH ON COUNT	OR		
0111	BRANCH/CONDITION	EXCLUSIVE OR		
1000	LOAD	LOAD	LOAD	LOAD
1001	COMPARE	COMPARE	COMPARE	COMPARE
1010	ADD	ADD	ADD N	ADD N
1011	SUBTRACT	SUBTRACT	SUBTRACT N	SUBTRACT N
1100	MULTIPLY	MULTIPLY	MULTIPLY	MULTIPLY
1101		DIVIDE	DIVIDE	DIVIDE
1110	CONVERT-DECIMAL	ADD LOGICAL	ADD U	ADD U
1111	CONVERT-BINARY	SUBTRACT LOGICAL	SUBTRACT U	SUBTRACT U

RS, SI Format

xxxx	*Branching Status Switching and Shifting* 1000xxxx	*Fixed-Point Logical and Input/Output* 1001xxxx	1010xxxx	1011xxxx
0000	SET SYSTEM MASK	STORE MULTIPLE		
0001		TEST UNDER MASK		
0010	LOAD PSW	MOVE		
0011	DIAGNOSE	TEST AND SET		
0100	WRITE DIRECT	AND		
0101	READ DIRECT	COMPARE LOGICAL		
0110	BRANCH/HIGH	OR		
0111	BRANCH/LOW-EQUAL	EXCLUSIVE OR		
1000	SHIFT RIGHT SL	LOAD MULTIPLE		
1001	SHIFT LEFT SL			
1010	SHIFT RIGHT S			
1011	SHIFT LEFT S			
1100	SHIFT RIGHT DL	START I/O		
1101	SHIFT LEFT DL	TEST I/O		
1110	SHIFT RIGHT D	HALT I/O		
1111	SHIFT LEFT D	TEST CHANNEL		

SS Format

xxxx	1100xxxx	*Logical* 1101xxxx	1110xxxx	*Decimal* 1111xxxx
0000				
0001		MOVE NUMERIC		MOVE WITH OFFSET
0010		MOVE		PACK
0011		MOVE ZONE		UNPACK
0100		AND		
0101		COMPARE LOGICAL		
0110		OR		
0111		EXCLUSIVE OR		
1000				ZERO AND ADD
1001				COMPARE
1010				ADD
1011				SUBTRACT
1100		TRANSLATE		MULTIPLY
1101		TRANSLATE AND TEST		DIVIDE
1110		EDIT		
1111		EDIT AND MARK		

NOTE: N = NORMALIZED   DL = DOUBLE LOGICAL   S = SINGLE
      SL = SINGLE LOGICAL   U = UNNORMALIZED   D = DOUBLE

System/360 instructions.

```
⍝ DATA TRANSFER                                      ∇ CODE8080
MOV:RL1←OD2                                          ⍝ WORKING REGISTERS
LXI:REGLRP;]←INST[ADR]                           [1] B←0
LDA:STORE[ADRDIR;]←REGLA;]                        [2] C←1
STA:STORE[ADRDIR;]←REGLA;]                        [3] D←2
LHLD:REGLH,L;]←STORE[ADRDIR+REVERT;]              [4] E←3
SHLD:STORE[ADRDIR+REVERT;]←REGLH,L;]              [5] ⍝ STORAGE ADDRESS
LDAX:REGLA;]←STORE[2↓,REGLRP;];]                  [6] H←4
STAX:STORE[2↓,REGLRP;];]←REGLA;]                  [7] L←5
XCHG:REGLH,L,D,E;]←REGLD,E,H,L;]                  [8] ⍝ PROGRAM STATUS WORD
⍝ ARITHMETIC                                      [9] PSW← 6  7
ADD:REGLA;]←REGLA;]PLUS OD2                      [10] ⍝ STACK POINTER
ADC:REGLA;]←REGLA;]PLUS OD2 PLUS REGLF;CY]       [11] SP← 8  9
SUB:REGLA;]←REGLA;]MINUS OD2                     [12] ⍝ ACCUMULATOR
SBB:REGLA;]←REGLA;]MINUS OD2 PLUS REGLF;CY]      [13] A←7
INR:RL1←OD1 PLUS 1                               [14] ⍝ FLAGS
DCR:RL1←OD1 MINUS 1                              [15] F←6
INX:REGLRP;]←REGLRP;]PLUS 1                      [16] SIGN:S←0
DCX:REGLRP;]←REGLRP;]MINUS 1                     [17] ZERO:Z←1
DAD:REGLH,L;]←REGLH,L;]PLUS REGLRP;]             [18] CARRY:CY←7
DAA:REGLA;]←REGLF;CY,AC]DECADJUST REGLA;]        [19] AUXCARR:AC←3
⍝ LOGIC                                          [20] PARITY:P←5
ANA:REGLA;]←REGLA;]↑OD2                          [21] ⍝ STORAGE SPECIFICATION
XRA:REGLA;]←REGLA;]≠OD2                          [22] M←6
ORA:REGLA;]←REGLA;]∨OD2                          [23] ⍝ CONSTANTS
CMP:REGLA;]MINUS OD2                             [24] ALWAYS←1
RLC:1 ROTATE REGLA;]                             [25] REVERT← 1  0
RRC:⁻1 ROTATE REGLA;]                            [26]
RAL:1 ROTATE REGLA;,REGLF;CY]
RAR:⁻1 ROTATE REGLA;,REGLF;CY]
CMA:REGLA;]←~REGLA;]                                 ∇ INSTFIELD8080
CMC:REGLF;CY]←~REGLF;CY]                          [1] OPCODE←↓2
STC:REGLF;CY]←1                                   [2] R1←2+↓3
⍝ BRANCH                                          [3] R2←5+↓3
JMP:BRANCH ALWAYS                                 [4] I2←8+↓8
JXX:BRANCH CONDITIONAL                            [5] ADR← 2  8  ρ(16+↓8),8+↓8
CALL:LINK ALWAYS
CXX:LINK CONDITIONAL                                  ∇ INSTDECODE;REGPAIR
RET:RETURN ALWAYS                                 [1] ADR1←2↓INST[R1]
RXX:RETURN CONDITIONAL                            [2] ADR2←2↓INST[R2]
RST:RESTART                                       [3] ADRDIR←2↓,INST[ADR]
PCHL:INSTADR←REGLH,L;]                            [4] REGPAIR←(2↓INST[2 3],0)↓↓2
⍝ STACK, I/O, MACHINE CONTROL                     [5] RP←(B,C,D,E,H,L,SP)[REGPAIR]
PUSH:DOWN REGLRS;]                                [6] RS←(B,C,D,E,H,L,PSW)[REGPAIR]
POP:REGLRS;]←UP
XTHL:SWAPTOP                                          ∇ S←A PLUS B;SUM
SPHL:REGLSP;]←REGLH,L;]                           [1] SUM←(2↓,A)+2↓,B
IN:REGLA;]←READDEVICE INST[I2]                    [2] S←(ρA)ρ((ρ,A)ρ2)⊤SUM
OUT:REGLA;]WRITEDEVICE INST[I2]
EI:'ENABLE AFTER NEXT INSTRUCTION'                   ∇ S←A MINUS B;DIF
DI:'DISABLE INTERRUPT'                            [1] DIF←(2↓,A)-2↓,B
HLT:'STOP'                                        [2] S←(ρA)ρ((ρ,A)ρ2)⊤DIF
NOP:'NO OPERATION'
⍝ FLAG SETTING NOT SHOWN                              ∇ RL←COC4 DECADJUST OD;SUM
⍝ REFERENCE: INTEL8080 MANUAL,                    [1] SUM←10⊥(6×COC4)+2↓Q 4  ρOD
⍝           SEPTEMBER 1975                        [2] RL←,Q(4ρ2)⊤(2ρ10)⊤SUM

                                                     ∇ DIR ROTATE OD;N
                                                  [1] N←(ρOD)|DIR
                                                  [2] REGLF;CY]←DIR↑REGLA;]
                                                  [3] REGLA;]←8↑N↓OD,N↑OD
```

```
∇ DECL8080                                           ∇ SWAPTOP;DATA
STORE←(K64,8)ρ0                               [1]     DATA←UP                              [1]
REG← 10  8  ρ0                                [2]     DOWN REGLH,L;]                        [2]
INSTADR← 2  8  ρ0                             [3]     REGLH,L;]←DATA                        [3]
REGLF;6]←1                                    [4]
                                                     ⍝ BRANCH CONDITION
⍝ ODFETCH                                             →(~CONDITION)/0                       [1]
OPERAND1:→(M=ADR1)/STORAGE1                   [1]     INSTADR←INST[ADR]                     [2]
OD1←REGLADR1;]                                [2]
→OPERAND2                                     [3]     ⍝ LINK CONDITION
STORAGE1:OD1←STORE[2↓,REGLH,L;];]             [4]     →(~CONDITION)/0                       [1]
OPERAND2:→(M=ADR2)/STORAGE2                   [5]     DOWN INSTADR                          [2]
→(=INSTLOPCODE])/IMMEDIATE                    [6]     INSTADR←INST[ADR]                     [3]
OD2←REGLADR2;]                                [7]
→0                                            [8]     ⍝ RETURN CONDITION
STORAGE2:OD2←STORE[2↓,REGLH,L;];]             [9]     →(~CONDITION)/0                       [1]
→0                                           [10]     INSTADR←UP,                           [2]
IMMEDIATE:OD2←INST[I2]                        [11]
                                                     ⍝ RESTART
⍝ RLSTORE                                             DOWN INSTADR                          [1]
→(M=ADR1)/STORAGE                             [1]     INSTADR← 2  8  ρ⁻16+INSTLR1],3ρ0      [2]
REGLADR1;]←RL1                                [2]
→0                                            [3]     ⍝ YES←CONDITIONAL;FLAG
STORAGE:STORE[2↓,REGLH,L;];]←RL1              [4]     FLAG←(Z,CY,S,P)[2↓INST[2 3]]          [1]
                                                     YES←REGLF;FLAG]=INST[4]               [2]
⍝ DOWN DATA
REGLSP;]←REGLSP;]MINUS 2                      [1]
STORE[2↓,REGLSP;])+REVERT;]←DATA              [2]

⍝ DATA←UP
DATA←STORE[2↓,REGLSP;],1)+REVERT;]            [1]
REGLSP;]←REGLSP;]PLUS 2                       [2]
```

Intel 8080 instructions.

APPENDIX

C   MACHINE ARITHMETIC

Machine arithmetic frequently uses positional representation with radix 2. Since the number of positions is fixed, as a rule, machine arithmetic is modular in nature. This modular nature can be used to represent negative numbers by their complement. Each of these subjects—positional representation, binary arithmetic, modular arithmetic, and representation of negative numbers—will be discussed briefly in this appendix.

C-1 POSITIONAL REPRESENTATION

The representation of a number by a sequence of symbols called *digits*, such as the number 1,359.708, assumes that the value of the digit as well as the location of the digit determines the contribution of this digit to the number. This convention characterizes the *positional representation*.

Power Series.   The usual application of the positional representation assumes that the digits are the coefficients of a power series. Thus, a number *NBR* is represented by the coefficients *A* of the powers of *B* according to the formula (in APL notation):

$$NBR \leftarrow (A[0] \times B * P) + (A[1] \times B * P \doteq 1) + \cdots + (A[P] \times B * 0) +$$
$$+ (A[P + 1] \times B * -1) + \cdots + A[P + Q] \times B * -Q)$$

When *A* is positive or zero and smaller than *B*, the representation is unique. *A*, however, need not be so restricted, as illustrated by the encoding of multiplier and quotient in Chapters 3 and 4, respectively.

Radix.   The number B, which is raised to the exponent, is called the base or the *radix*. For each radix, the radix itself is represented as 10. Thus, 37 is represented as 10 in the base 37 system.

Expandability.   The written positional representation can denote unbounded large and small numbers with unlimited precision by extending the numbers of digits to the left and to the right of the radix point. This expandability contrasts to the fixed number of digit positions that is normally available within a machine.

C-2 BINARY NUMBER SYSTEM

The binary number system may be unfamiliar, but it is not essentially different from the decimal system. The arithmetic rules for the decimal system also apply to the binary system. Since the binary system uses only the two digits 0 and 1, these rules, in fact, are even simpler in the binary system than in the decimal system. Table C-1 summarizes the rules for binary addition, subtraction, and multiplication.

+	0 1		−	0 1		×	0 1
0	0 1		0	0 −1		0	0 0
1	1 10		1	1 0		1	0 1

Table C-1   Binary addition, subtraction, and multiplication.

Human Considerations.   Binary arithmetic is easier to learn than decimal arithmetic. The binary system, however, is more difficult for people to use. Numbers that are made up exclusively of 0s and 1s are difficult to recognize and remember. Thus, 1914 is remembered much more easily than 11101111010.

Physical Considerations.   The two values of a binary digit can be represented in a machine by the two limits of a continuously variable physical phenomenon. Thus, a transistor may pass a saturation current on one end of its operation range, whereas at the other end of its range, hardly any current is passed at all. Similarly, the armature of a relay may be pushed by a spring to one extreme of its range of motion, whereas the coil, when energized, will pull it to the other extreme. In both examples, the limits of the operation range are clearly defined. Hence, it is easy to associate two values such as 0 and 1 with these areas of operation.

By defining two more areas of operation, a total of four values can be recognized. Since these new areas have no natural boundaries, they are more difficult to recognize and maintain. In practice, it is invariably less expensive to use two binary devices instead of representing four values by one device.

Logical Considerations.   The physical considerations suggest a binary representation of symbols. Thus, the decimal digits can be represented within a machine by a group of binary signals, a *binary code*. These decimal digits are then processed according to the rules of decimal arithmetic.

The binary number system is, however, often chosen over the decimal system for machine arithmetic because of the simplicity of the arithmetic rules and the efficiency of the binary system in representing numbers. Thus, four binary signals are used to represent the 10 decimal digits. In binary, the same number of signals can represent the numbers 0 through 15.

C-3 MODULAR ARITHMETIC

The use of a fixed number of digit positions is a less striking, but actually more essential, point of difference between machine arithmetic and manual arithmetic (Garner, 1965). The fixed number of digit positions makes machine arithmetic modular.

Residue. For each two integers NBR and MOD with MOD larger that 0, two integers, QNT and RES, can be found such that $NBR \leftarrow RES + QNT \times MOD$, while $0 \leq RES$ and $RES < MOD$. Here RES is called the *residue* modulo MOD of NBR. MOD is called the modulus.

The definition of the residue resembles that of the remainder in division. A key difference, however, is that in division the remainder has the sign of the dividend, whereas the residue is always positive. In division, also, the attention is usually focused on the quotient; while for modular arithmetic, the interest is focused on the residue.

Modular Operations. In modular arithmetic, the sum, difference, product, or quotient of two residues is defined as the residue of their sum, difference, product, or quotient, respectively. As in regular arithmetic, division by 0 is not allowed. Table C-2 shows the operations of modular arithmetic with modulus 3.

+	0	1	2		−	0	1	2		×	0	1	2		÷	0	1	2
0	0	1	2		0	0	2	1		0	0	0	0		0	−	0	0
1	1	2	0		1	1	0	2		1	0	1	2		1	−	1	2
2	2	0	1		2	2	1	0		2	0	2	1		2	−	2	1

Table C-2   Modular arithmetic with modulus 3.

The hours of the day are determined by modular arithmetic. Seven hours after 10 o'clock is 5 o'clock. The modulus here is 12. Another example of modular arithmetic is the odometer, which gives 00,000.0 as the result of 99,999.9+.1. The modulus here is 100,000.0.

Visual Representation. The clock suggests a visual representation of modular numbers as points on a circle. Figure C-3 illustrates this representation for modulus 1000. Addition corresponds to a clockwise displacement along the circumference; subtraction corresponds to a counterclockwise displacement. The transition from 999 to 000 has no significance in a purely modular system.

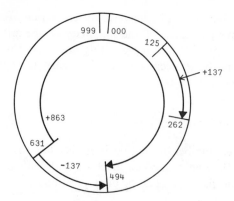

Figure C-3   Visual representation of modulo 1000 arithmetic.

C-4 COMPLEMENTING

Figure C-3 shows that a counterclockwise displacement along a sector of the circle, representing a subtraction, can be replaced by a clockwise displacement along the remainder of the circle circumference, representing an addition. Thus, 631 − 137 is 494. But also, 631 + (1000 − 137) is 631 + 863, or 494 for modulus 1000.

The difference between a number and the modulus is called the *complement* of this number. In the given example, 863 is the complement of 137. Therefore, in modular arithmetic, the subtraction of a number is equivalent to the addition of its complement.

Subtraction Algorithm.   The complement of a number represented by N digits for radix B is the complement of this number upon $B * N$. This complement can be determined in two steps:

(a) Determine the complement upon $(B * N) − 1$.
(b) Add 1 to this complement.

The number $(B * N) − 1$ has for each digit position the digit $B − 1$. For the three decimal places of the above example, $(B * N) − 1$ is the number 999; for five binary places, it is the number 11111. When NBR is subtracted from this number, there will be no borrows between the digit positions. Therefore, the complement of a number can be obtained by complementing each digit individually upon $B − 1$. Thus, the complement of 137 upon 999 is 862.

The result of step (a) above is called the *9's-complement* in decimal and the *1's-complement* in binary. In contrast, the complement on $B * N$ is called the *10's-complement* and *2's-complement*, respectively. These names are most satisfactory when the radix point is to the right of the highest digit position.

In binary, complementing of the digits is equivalent to replacing 0 by 1 and 1 by 0, which is called *inverting*.

The addition of 1, which is required in step (b) to obtain the $B * N$ complement, is called the *complement correction*. For the given example, the complement correction gives $862 + 1$, or 863. The complement correction can often be combined with a subsequent addition by making the carry-in for that addition equal to 1.

A complementer is simpler than a subtract unit, since there is no borrow between digits. By using a complementer in conjunction with an adder, both addition and subtraction can be performed.

C-5 REPRESENTATION OF POSITIVE AND NEGATIVE NUMBERS

A number system with radix B and N digit positions can represent $B * N$ numbers. Each of these numbers can be considered as the residue modulo $B * N$ of an unlimited class of numbers. From these classes, the numbers should be chosen that are the normal interpretation of the representation.

Figure C-4 illustrates the nature of representation and interpretation. Representation is modular and therefore can be pictured as a circle. The interpretation, however, may involve any number and therefore is represented as a line. When this line is placed along the circle, the area of direct interpretation is identified with the representation.

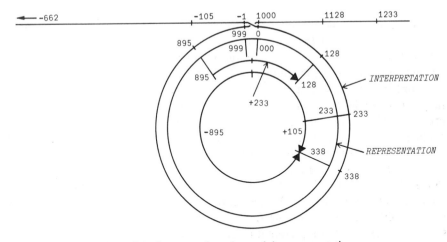

Figure C-4 Interpretation of a modular representation.

When a number outside the range of direct representation is represented, such as the number 1128 in Figure C-4, extra information is required besides the normal set of digits. This is similar to using a calendar along with a clock.

Two favorite interpretations are:

(a) 0 and the adjacent positive integers.
(b) 0 and the adjacent positive and negative integers.

In the first case, the interpretation always equals the representation. Only positive numbers are represented. This interpretation is used in the signed-magnitude notation.

In the second case, the interpretation equals the representation for the positive numbers. Negative numbers are represented by their complement.

The addition and subtraction for each of these notations will be discussed below.

Signed-Magnitude Notation.   In the *signed-magnitude notation*, only the positive numbers 0 up to $B * N$ are represented. A separate sign is used for the representation of negative numbers.

When the signs of the numbers are taken into account, addition and subtraction of the numbers can be replaced by the addition or subtraction of the magnitudes of the numbers and a separate sign determination.

Addition of the Magnitudes of the Numbers.   This case occurs for the addition of numbers with equal signs, or for the subtraction of numbers with unequal signs. In either case, the sign is determined by the left operand.

The sum exceeds the representation range when a carry out of the highest-digit position is obtained during the addition. Thus, 895 + 233 will result in 128. The carry-out, however, indicates that the proper interpretation should be 1128.

Subtraction of the Magnitude of the Numbers.   This case occurs when the operation is equivalent to adding numbers with opposite signs. The number with the smallest absolute value should be subtracted from the number with the largest magnitude to obtain the magnitude of the sum. The sign of the sum is the sign of the number with the largest magnitude. To find out which of two numbers has the largest magnitude, however, requires a subtraction in itself. Therefore, the usual procedure is to select one of the two numbers more or less arbitrarily and to assume that its sign will coincide with the sign of the sum. The other number is now complemented and added to the first.

When the addition results in a carry-out, the sum exceeds the representation range. The equivalent subtraction, however, would not have exceeded the representation range for this case. Therefore, the result is represented correctly. When, on the other hand, no carry-out appears during the addition, the equivalent subtraction has passed the representation range, and the result is the complement of the representation. The original assumption apparently was wrong and an extra complementation must now take place. This extra step is called *recomplementing*. Since the original assumption for the sign was wrong, the sign must be inverted also.

Thus, 233 − 895 might be calculated by assuming that the sign of the result is the sign of 233, hence positive. Therefore, 895 is complemented and, as such, added to 233: 233 + 105 is 338. This addition does not give a carry-out, which indicates that the sign is not positive, as assumed, but negative. Therefore, the magnitude of the result is the complement of 338. Recomplementation yields 662. Inverting the sign gives as the result −662.

Exceeding the representation range is not possible when numbers with unequal signs are added.

10's- and 2's-Complement Notation. For *complement notation*, the modular representation is interpreted in part as positive and in part as negative. Usually, the positive and negative ranges are made about equal. Thus, in Figure C-5, the break in interpretation is between 499 and 500.

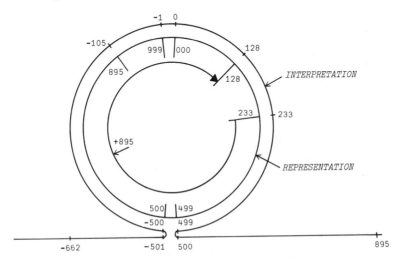

Figure C-5   10's-complement notation.

The numbers 500 up to and including 999 are interpreted now as −500 up to and including −1. The representation is the complement of the magnitude of the interpretation, hence the name complement notation.

Positive and negative numbers can be treated alike in complement notation. A number that should be subtracted is first complemented and subsequently added, independently of its sign or the sign of the other operand. It never is necessary to recomplement.

The representation range is exceeded when two positive numbers result in a negative sum, or two negative numbers in a positive sum. The representation range cannot be exceeded when the two operands have unequal signs. The sign of a number can be determined from its high-order digit.

9's- and 1's-Complement Notation. During complementing, the complement upon $(B * N) - 1$ is formed first, as stated above. Therefore, some equipment uses this complement as the representation of negative numbers rather than the complement upon $B * N$.

Since the modulus of the arithmetic should match the complement, module

$(B * N) - 1$ arithmetic should be used. Hence, for three decimal digits, the modulus is 999 instead of 1000.

The change in modulus has two consequences. First, one of the $B * N$ numbers that can be represented by N digits should be eliminated. This is done by interpreting the representations 0 and $(B * N) - 1$ both as 0. The two 0s are distinguished as +0 and −0. For three-decimal digits, 000 is interpreted as +0 and 999 as −0, as illustrated in Figure C-6.

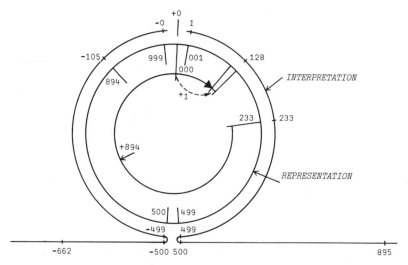

Figure C-6   9's-complement notation.

A second consequence of the modulus $(B * N) - 1$ is that a sum will be 1 too small when 0 is passed during an addition. Hence, 1 must be added to the sum to obtain the correct result. The passing of the all-zero representation can be recognized from the carry-out of the highest digit position. Therefore, the correction of 1 can be made by entering this carry-out of the highest position into the lowest digit position, hence the name *end-around carry*.

Comparison of Notations.   In Table C-7, the various interpretations of three binary digits are shown. The left column gives the eight possible representations. The next column gives the interpretation as a positive integer, and the other columns give the three interpretations for positive and negative numbers discussed above. In the case of signed-magnitude representation, the leftmost bit is used as the sign bit, assuming 0 for positive and 1 for negative.

A comparison of the three notations shows:

(a) The positive and negative ranges are equal for the $(B * N) - 1$ complement and for signed-magnitude notation. The opposite of a number can always be represented in these notations. In contrast, for the $B * N$ complement,

REPRESENTATION	ABSOLUTE	SIGNED MAGNITUDE	1-COMPLEMENT	2-COMPLEMENT
000	0	0	0	0
001	1	1	1	1
010	2	2	2	2
011	3	3	3	3
100	4	-0	-3	-4
101	5	-1	-2	-3
110	6	-2	-1	-2
111	7	-3	-0	-1

Table C-7   Binary representation and interpretation.

the maximum negative number cannot be represented. Thus, in Table C-7, the opposite of -4 is not representable in 2's-complement.

(b) There are two representations for zero in the $(B * N) - 1$ complement and signed-magnitude notation. Attributing a sign to 0 is mathematically meaningless and therefore undesirable. Often, extra care must be taken that -0 is not considered unequal to $+0$.

```
MANUAL        SIGNED-MAGNITUDE    9-COMPLEMENT       10-COMPLEMENT


  125            +0125              0125               0125
   37            +0037              0037               0037
  ─── +          ─── +             ─── +              ─── +
  162            +0162              0162               0162


  125            +0125              0125               0125
   37    +0037 → 9962     +0037 → 9962      +0037 → 9962
  ───                1                1                  1
   88            ─── +          ┌ 10087            ─── +
                 +0088          └─→ 1              0088
                                   ─── +
                                   0088


 -125            -0125              9874               9875
   37    +0037 → 9962              0037               0037
  ─── +              1             ─── +              ─── +
  -88            ─── +             9911               9912
                 -0088


 -125            -0125              9874               9875
  -37            -0037              9962               9963
  ─── +          ─── +             ─── +              ─── +
 -162            -0162          ┌ 19836               9838
                                └─→ 1
                                   ─── +
                                   9837


   37            +0037              0037               0037
 -125    -0125 → 9874              9874               9875
  ─── +              1             ─── +              ─── +
  -88            ─── +             9911               9912
                 -0087 ← +9912
                     1
                 ───
                 -0088
```

Table C-8   Examples of machine arithmetic.

(c) The $(B * N) - 1$ complement has simple complementing, while the $B * N$ complement has simple addition. The correction by 1 occurs at the end of the addition for the $(B * N) - 1$ complement, while it occurs in advance for the $B * N$ complement. The latter tends to be faster than the former.

(d) The $B * N$ complement matches the modulus of the equipment. As a result, the algorithms for multiplication and division are simpler.

(e) Signed-magnitude notation matches the traditional representation of positive and negative numbers. The recomplementation, however, makes it slower and less simple than complement notation.

Table C-8 shows a few operations in the three notations that have been discussed.

REFERENCE

GARNER, H. L.: "Number Systems and Arithmetic." In F. L. ALT and M. RUBINOFF: *Advances in Computers*, vol. 6, pp. 131–194. Academic Press, New York, 1965.

D   SWITCHING ALGEBRA

Switching algebra uses a limited number of postulates and a set of theorems derived from these postulates. Switching algebra applies to combinational circuits. In *combinational circuits*, the value of the outputs at a given moment is determined by the value of the inputs at that moment. In contrast, the outputs of *sequential circuits* are determined not only by the inputs of the given moment but also by the value of the inputs at earlier moments. Combinational circuits can be divided into circuits with one output and circuits with multiple outputs. Only the combinational circuits with a single output will be discussed in this summary.

D-1   POSTULATES

The postulates of switching algebra are shown in Table D-1.

Duality. The variables of switching algebra are either 0 or 1, as expressed by the postulates P1. The postulates do not say which signal of a physical realization is considered 1 and which is considered 0. Thus, for a relay, the electric conduction through the contacts, the *transmission*, can be considered 1, while an open contact may be considered 0. For a transmission of 1, a relay coil will be energized. For such a definition, in Figure D-2, the relation $Z \leftarrow X$ holds.

The lack of conduction, the *hindrance*, can also be defined as 1 for a relay. A signal 1 will now leave a relay coil de-energized. Again in Figure D-2, the formula $Z \leftarrow X$ holds. This, of course, must be so, since the closed working contact is the result of an energized coil independent of conventions about 0 or 1.

The fact that the physical reality is independent of the assignment of 0 or 1 implies that for each postulate concerning 0 there is a corresponding postulate

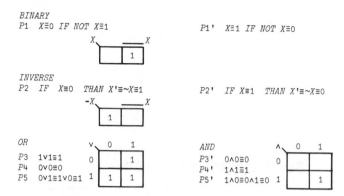

BINARY
P1   *X≡0 IF NOT X≡1*   P1'   *X≡1 IF NOT X≡0*

INVERSE
P2   *IF   X≡0   THAN X'≡~X≡1*   P2'   *IF X≡1   THAN X'≡~X≡0*

OR		$\lor$	0	1
P3	1∨1≡1	0		1
P4	0∨0≡0			
P5	0∨1≡1∨0≡1	1	1	1

AND		$\land$	0	1
P3'	0∧0≡0	0		
P4'	1∧1≡1			
P5'	1∧0≡0∧1≡0	1		1

Table D-1   Postulates of switching algebra.

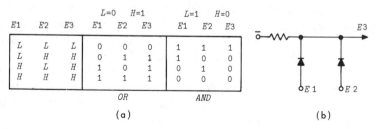

	TRANSMISSION	HINDRANCE	
X←1	COIL ENERGIZED Z←1 Y←0	COIL NOT ENERGIZED Z←1 Y←0	
X←0	COIL NOT ENERGIZED Z←0 Y←1	COIL ENERGIZED Z←0 Y←1	

Figure D-2   Duality of a relay contact.

concerning 1. This correspondence is called *duality*. The postulates and theorems of this section express this duality.

Inverse.   Postulate P2 defines the operator *not*, represented by the symbol ~, which makes the inverse of a signal. The inverse of signal X is indicated as X'.

'Or' and 'And.'   Postulates P3, P4, and P5 define the operators '*or*' and '*and*' represented by the symbols $\lor$ and $\land$. Figure D-3 shows an elementary diode circuit that can be used for the 'or' and 'and' operations. The table in this figure shows that the nature of the operation depends upon the definition of a low and a high voltage as either 0 and 1 or vice versa. Therefore, the 'or' and the 'and' operators are each other's dual.

			L=0	H=1		L=1	H=0				
E1	E2	E3	E1	E2	E3	E1	E2	E3			E3
L	L	L	0	0	0	1	1	1			
L	H	H	0	1	1	1	0	0			
H	L	H	1	0	1	0	1	0			
H	H	H	1	1	1	0	0	0			
				OR			AND				

(a)   (b)

Figure D-3   Interpretation of a diode circuit.

D-2 THEOREMS

The theorems that can be derived from the postulates are shown in Table D-4. They have been grouped according to the number of variables involved.

Theorem of De Morgan. Theorem T13 is the *theorem of De Morgan*, which dates from 1847. For two variables, this theorem is the well-known logical rule: 'Not John or Mary' is equivalent to 'Neither John nor Mary.' The dual of this theorem is that 'Not John and Mary' is equivalent to 'Not John or not Mary.' The theorem is expressed in the figure by means of APL notation.

Duality Theorem. The principle of duality is expressed by Theorem T14. Exchanging 0 and 1 for the variables of a function implies that the inverse of these variables must be taken. The exchange of 0 and 1 also means that the function value itself must be inverted. Furthermore, the operators 'and' and 'or' must be replaced by their duals. The operator 'not' remains unchanged, since it is its own dual, as expressed by Postulate P2.

Canonical Form. Theorem T15 shows that a variable can be taken out of an expression by putting this variable as well as its inverse in front of the expression. When Theorem T15 is applied successively to all variables, the function becomes

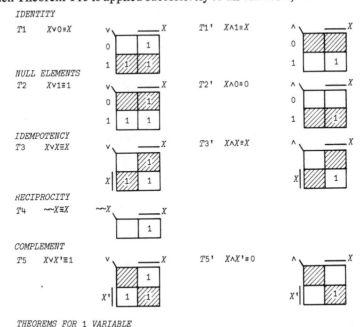

Table D-4   Theorems of switching algebra (Part 1).

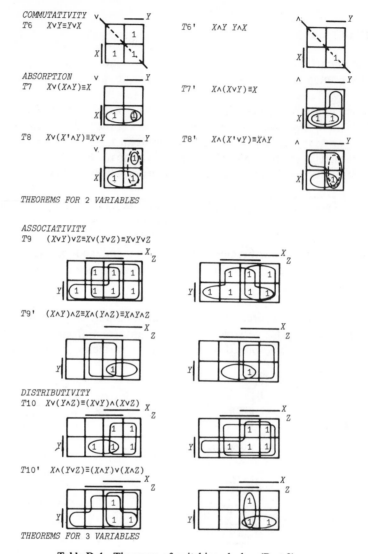

COMMUTATIVITY
T6 $X \vee Y \equiv Y \vee X$ T6' $X \wedge Y \; Y \wedge X$

ABSORPTION
T7 $X \vee (X \wedge Y) \equiv X$ T7' $X \wedge (X \vee Y) \equiv X$

T8 $X \vee (X' \wedge Y) \equiv X \vee Y$ T8' $X \wedge (X' \vee Y) \equiv X \wedge Y$

THEOREMS FOR 2 VARIABLES

ASSOCIATIVITY
T9 $(X \vee Y) \vee Z \equiv X \vee (Y \vee Z) \equiv X \vee Y \vee Z$

T9' $(X \wedge Y) \wedge Z \equiv X \wedge (Y \wedge Z) \equiv X \wedge Y \wedge Z$

DISTRIBUTIVITY
T10 $X \vee (Y \wedge Z) \equiv (X \vee Y) \wedge (X \vee Z)$

T10' $X \wedge (Y \vee Z) \equiv (X \wedge Y) \vee (X \wedge Z)$

THEOREMS FOR 3 VARIABLES

Table D-4   Theorems of switching algebra (Part 2).

written as the 'or' of a number of 'and's; while for Theorem T15', the 'and' of a number of 'or's is attained. The first expression is called the *disjunctive canonical form*, or the sum of *minterms*, the latter expression the *conjunctive canonical form*, or the product of *maxterms*. Thus, for the expressions of Theorem T12, the disjunctive canonical form is

$$(X \wedge Y \wedge Z) \vee (X \wedge Y \wedge Z') \vee (X' \wedge Y \wedge Z) \vee (X' \wedge Y' \wedge Z)$$

and the conjunctive canonical form is

$$(X \vee Y \vee Z) \wedge (X \vee Y' \vee Z) \wedge (X' \vee Y \vee Z) \wedge (X' \vee Y \vee Z')$$

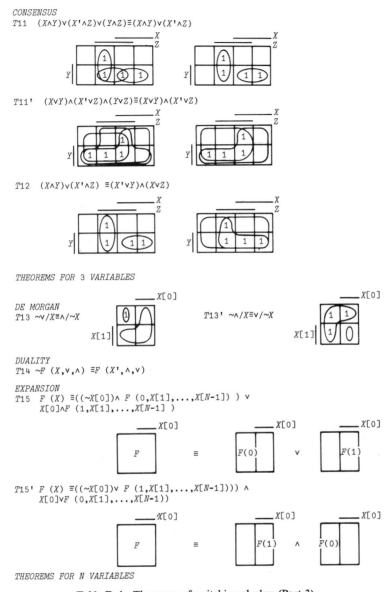

CONSENSUS
T11 $(X{\wedge}Y){\vee}(X'{\wedge}Z){\vee}(Y{\wedge}Z)\equiv(X{\wedge}Y){\vee}(X'{\wedge}Z)$

T11' $(X{\vee}Y){\wedge}(X'{\vee}Z){\wedge}(Y{\vee}Z)\equiv(X{\vee}Y){\wedge}(X'{\vee}Z)$

T12 $(X{\wedge}Y){\vee}(X'{\wedge}Z)\equiv(X'{\vee}Y){\wedge}(X{\vee}Z)$

THEOREMS FOR 3 VARIABLES

DE MORGAN
T13 $\sim{\vee}/X\equiv{\wedge}/\sim X$

T13' $\sim{\wedge}/X\equiv{\vee}/\sim X$

DUALITY
T14 $\sim F\ (X,{\vee},{\wedge})\equiv F\ (X',{\wedge},{\vee})$

EXPANSION
T15 $F\ (X)\equiv((\sim X[0]){\wedge}\ F\ (0,X[1],\ldots,X[N-1])\ )\ {\vee}$
      $X[0]{\wedge}F\ (1,X[1],\ldots,X[N-1]\ )$

T15' $F\ (X)\equiv((\sim X[0]){\vee}\ F\ (1,X[1],\ldots,X[N-1]))){\wedge}$
      $X[0]{\vee}F\ (0,X[1],\ldots,X[N-1))$

THEOREMS FOR N VARIABLES

Table D-4 Theorems of switching algebra (Part 3).

D-3 VISUAL REPRESENTATION

The relation between switching variables can be illustrated by three- and two-dimensional representations. Figure D-5 shows the spatial representation of one, two, and three variables. A single variable is represented by the ends of a line, two variables jointly can be represented by the corners of a square, and three

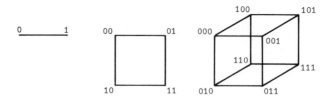

Figure D-5 Spatial representation of binary variables.

variables are represented by the corners of a cube. The spatial representation becomes more cumbersome for larger numbers of variables.

Figure D-6 shows how a two-dimensional representation can be derived from the spatial representation. The cube that represents three variables is cut open and folded into a flat surface.

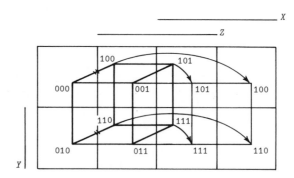

Figure D-6 Karnaugh diagram obtained from cube.

Distance. The various corners of the cubes and squares, as well as the cells within the flat representation, each correspond to one set of values of the subject variables. In the spatial representation, adjacent sets of values differ only in the value of one variable. This fact is expressed by saying that the sets of values have a *distance* of 1. By folding the cube into the flat surface, this distance relationship is preserved except for the side that was cut. The leftmost and rightmost cells of the diagram, therefore, should be considered adjacent.

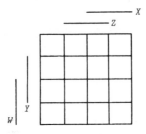

Figure D-7 Karnaugh diagram for 4 variables.

Karnaugh Diagram.   The flat diagram was proposed by Veitch (1952) and, in the given form, by Karnaugh (1953). It is called a *Karnaugh diagram.*

The Karnaugh diagram is not limited to three variables. For each variable that is added, the diagram is reflected along either its horizontal or vertical axis and thus doubles. Figure D-7 shows the Karnaugh for four variables. The diagram shows the traditional way of indicating the names of the variables and the cells for which those variables are 1. The postulates and theorems of Tables D-1 and D-4 are also illustrated by the applicable Karnaugh diagrams.

D-4 BINARY FUNCTIONS

As a result of the binary character of the variables of switching algebra, only a limited number of functions is possible for a given number of variables. In classical algebra, the number of functions of one variable, such as the trigonometric and logarithmic functions, is unlimited. In switching algebra, only four functions of one variable are possible. The function is the constant 0, the constant 1, the argument, or the inverse of the argument.

Number of Functions of N Variables. N variables can assume $2*N$ different values. Their Karnaugh diagrams have a corresponding number of cells. The value of a function can be either 0 or 1 for each of these values. Therefore, the number of possible functions is $2*2*N$. Table D-8 shows the number of functions for up to five variables.

Variables N	States $2*N$	Functions $2*2*N$	Unsymmetric functions
0	1	2	2
1	2	4	3
2	4	16	6
3	8	256	22
4	16	65,536	402
5	32	4,294,967,296	1,228,158

Table D-8   Number of functions for a limited number of variables.

A function that is invariant upon the interchange of two variables, or upon replacing a variable by its inverse, is called *symmetric.* When only one representative of a set of symmetric functions is counted, the number of functions is reduced noticeably, as shown in Table D-8. Nevertheless, the number of these unsymmetric functions increases rapidly with the number of variables.

The fact that the binary functions can be enumerated allows an exhaustive treatment of these functions. Such an approach is only possible for a limited number of variables, however.

Specification of Functions. A switching function can be specified by an algebraic expression. To avoid confusion between seemingly different expressions which actually are equivalent, the algebraic expression can be transformed to one of its canonical forms.

The disjunctive canonical form of a function can be presented by listing the inputs for which the function is 1. These input values can be listed in binary form, or their decimal equivalent can be given. Thus, Figure D-9 shows the decimal equivalents for the input values corresponding to the cells of a 4-bit Karnaugh diagram.

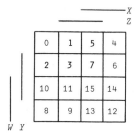

Figure D-9 Karnaugh diagram with decimal function values.

Functions of Two Variables

Figure D-10 shows all functions of two variables, their Karnaugh diagram, and a realization of the functions with relays and with nand circuit elements. The functions of two variables include the functions of one or zero variables. The nand itself is one of the functions of two variables and is listed as number 14 in this table.

Necessary and Sufficient Functions. All 16 functions of two variables can be made with the 'and,' 'or,' and 'inverse' operators because these are the only operators occurring in the postulates. Figure D-10 shows that all 16 functions can also be made by just the 'nand' operator. Since the 'nor' is the dual of the 'nand,' it can also make all 16 functions.

Passive and Active Circuit Elements. The realization of a switching circuit uses passive and active circuit elements. *Passive* elements do not contribute any energy to the switching circuits. Rather, the passive elements always dissipate some of the energy of the signals. The outgoing signal, therefore, is physically degenerated with respect to the incoming signals.

Active circuit elements supply power to the output signals. The input signal is physically regenerated by the circuit. This regeneration makes the output signal more suitable as input to other circuits. Also, the shape of the signal is restored to the full amplitude.

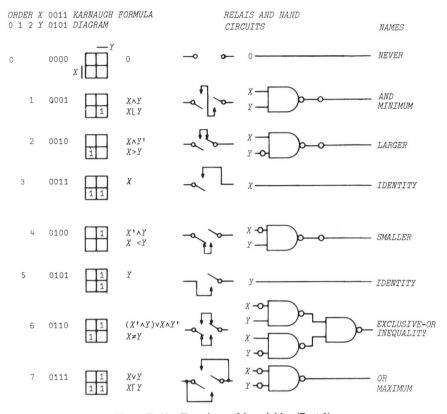

ORDER X 0011 *KARNAUGH FORMULA*   *RELAIS AND NAND*
0 1 2 Y 0101 *DIAGRAM*   *CIRCUITS*   *NAMES*

Figure D-10   Functions of 2 variables (Part 1).

The simplest logical conditions to be realized in a circuit are the 'and' and 'or.' In these circuits, the output is a discrete monotone-increasing function of the algebraic sum of the inputs. Thus, the output of the 'and' is 1 as soon as both inputs are 1, while the output of the 'or' becomes 1 as soon as at least one input is 1. A monotone-increasing function can be built with passive circuit elements. For instance, a resistor network can be used. The linear current/voltage characteristic of the resistor, however, does not match the discrete characteristic of the output function very well. A nonlinear characteristic, such as that of a diode or relay contact, is much more desirable.

The inverse function cannot be obtained with passive circuit elements. The minimal electronic regeneration circuit, the amplifier, is logically equivalent to an inverter. Therefore, the use of active circuit elements is not only required for physical considerations, it is also necessary for logical reasons.

Nand and Nor.   In the nand and nor, an 'and' or 'or' circuit is followed by an inverter. Therefore, a circuit element is obtained which is not only logically uni-

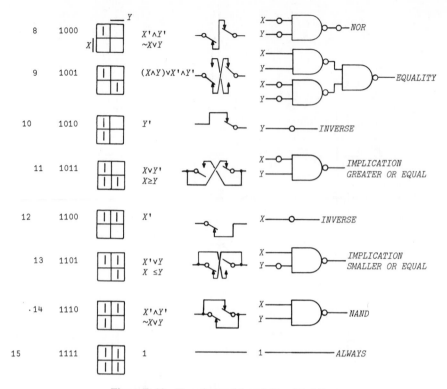

Figure D-10   Functions of 2 variables (Part 2).

versal, in that all functions can be made exclusively with this element, but also the circuit is physically universal, in that the signals are regenerated to the proper power and amplitude values.

D-5   SYNTHESIS OF COMBINATIONAL CIRCUITS

Specification.   The specification of a combinational circuit can be given by stating the requirements for the circuit in words. As an alternative, a table of the input values for which the output should be 1 can be derived; or in the Karnaugh diagram, the cells for which the function should be 1 can be marked. Figure D-11 shows a table and Karnaugh diagram specification for a simple function. The decimal equivalent of the input values for which the function should be 1 is placed in the corresponding cells of the Karnaugh diagram.

Constraints.   A combinational circuit can be characterized by certain parameters. Thus, the maximum number of inputs of a circuit element is called the *fan-in*; the maximum number of circuit elements that may be connected to the output of a circuit element is called the *fan-out*; and the maximum number of

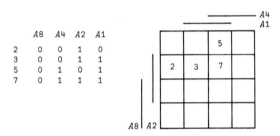

	A8	A4	A2	A1
2	0	0	1	0
3	0	0	1	1
5	0	1	0	1
7	0	1	1	1

Figure D-11 Specification of a function by a table and a Karnaugh diagram.

circuit elements that must be passed to reflect a change of the input signals fully in the output signals is called the *number of levels* of the circuit. When these parameters are restricted, they become a constraint of the design. For the initial phase of the design, no such constraints will be assumed.

Initial Solution

From the function specification, the disjunctive or conjunctive canonical form of the function can be obtained. For the given function, the first is:

$$(A8' \wedge A4' \wedge A2 \wedge A1') \vee (A8' \wedge A4' \wedge A2 \wedge A1) \vee (A8' \wedge A4 \wedge A2' \wedge A1) \vee$$
$$\vee (A8' \wedge A4 \wedge A2 \wedge A1)$$

The disjunctive canonical expression can be translated in an 'and-or' circuit, as shown in Figure D-12. By applying the theorem of De Morgan to the 'or' circuit, it can be replaced by an 'and' with inverters on its inputs and output. From this, the nand circuit, also shown in Figure D-12, is obtained.

Quine–McCluskey Minimization

The initial solution of a switching function is unique and readily obtained. The circuit, however, is usually more expensive than necessary. Each input value requires an 'and' circuit; furthermore, all input variables enter into the 'and' circuit either directly or in inverted form.

There are many methods which obtain a less expensive circuit. The most prominent of these is the *Quine–McCluskey* method. This method assumes that both polarities of the input signals are available and that a circuit of two levels is desired. For these assumptions, the number of circuits and the number of inputs to all circuits combined are minimized. The principle of this method was given by Quine (1952). A tabular form suitable for automation was developed by McCluskey in 1956.

Prime Implicants.   By applying the complement Theorem T5, the terms of two adjacent input values, that is, two input values differing only in one variable, can

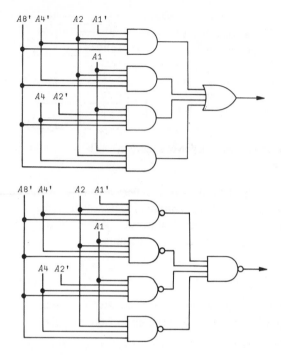

Figure D-12 And-or and nand circuit for function of Figure D-11.

be combined to a single term. Thus, in Figure D-11, the terms for the decimal equivalents 2 and 3 can be combined to the term $A8' \wedge A4' \wedge A2$. This process can be applied to all input values which are adjacent and continued for pairs of input values which, in turn, are adjacent. Thus, the prime implicants are found. An *implicant* is a function that is only 1 when the given function is also 1. A *prime implicant* is an implicant from which no input variable can be removed while still remaining an implicant.

The prime implicants are easily recognized in the Karnaugh diagram by noting input values that form a regular substructure of $2*N$ adjacent cells. The prime implicant is marked by drawing an oval through the cells.

Complete Solution. As a first step in the Quine–McCluskey method, all prime implicants are found. The 'or' of all these terms is called the *complete solution*. The complete solution for the example of Figure D-11 is

$$(A8' \wedge A4 \wedge A1) \vee (A8' \wedge A2 \wedge A1) \vee (A8' \wedge A4' \wedge A2)$$

The complete solution is unique, as was the initial solution. For the initial solution, however, no term could be missed. For the complete solution, this is not necessarily the case. Thus, the term $A8' \wedge A2 \wedge A1$ can be eliminated from the solution for Figure D-11. The complete solution therefore may be redundant and is not necessarily minimal.

Minimal Solution. The *minimal solution* is obtained from the complete solution by eliminating the redundant terms. For the example of Figure D-11, the minimal solution is represented by the expression $(A8' \wedge A4 \wedge A1) \vee (A8' \wedge A4' \wedge A2)$. The corresponding circuit is shown in Figure D-13.

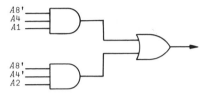

Figure D-13 Minimal circuit for function of Figure D-11.

A minimal solution need not be unique. There may be a choice in the redundant terms to be removed, as illustrated from Figure D-14.

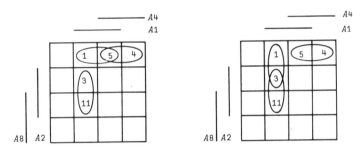

Figure D-14 Non-unique minimal solutions.

Tabular Determination of Prime Implicants

Function Table. McCluskey has indicated how the prime implicants can be found systematically using a *function table*. The input values that make a function 1 are listed with their binary value in the function table. The entries in the table are grouped according to the number of bits that are 1. The groups are separated by a horizontal line, as shown in Table D-15. Next to the binary entry, the decimal equivalent may be entered for identification purposes.

The function table is searched for pairs of entries that have a distance 1. When such a pair is found, it is entered as an extension to the table. The bit that is differ-

```
        A8421                              2   3   5   7
                            2-3  A8'∧A4'∧A2  2   3
   2    0010 ✓
   3    0011 ✓              3-7  A8'∧A2 ∧A1      3       7
   5    0101 ✓
   7    0111 ✓              5-7  A8'∧A4 ∧A1              5   7

  2-3   001X
  3-7   0X11                               *       *
  5-7   01X1
```

Table D-15 Tabular solution.

ent within the pair is replaced by an x. The pairs that form the new entry are checked off. The search continues until all pairs have been found. An entry is checked off only once but continues to participate in the search. Since pairs of distance 1 must be located in adjacent groups, it is only necessary to compare each element of a group with all elements of the next-higher group.

The comparison process is continued with the newly found pairs. Again, these can be grouped according to the number of 1 bits, and new pairs can be found from these. In this case, it is required that the entries which differ in 1 bit have an x in the same position. In the given example, no further combinations are possible, however. The table entries that are not checked off are the prime implicants.

Table D-16 shows an example where a table can be continued. The example illustrates that a higher-order term is found in two ways, by the combination 1 3 and 5 7, as well as the combination of 1 5 and 3 7. The corresponding Karnaugh diagram illustrates how these combinations arise. Since the two table entries are equivalent, the second one is crossed off, as indicated by the x, next to the entry.

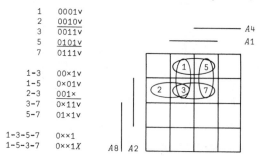

1	0001v
2	0010v
3	0011v
5	0101v
7	0111v
1-3	00×1v
1-5	0×01v
2-3	001×
3-7	0×11v
5-7	01×1v
1-3-5-7	0××1
1-5-3-7	0××1X

Table D-16 Tabular recognition of a square.

Prime-Implicant Table.   Having found the prime implicants from the function table, McCluskey now uses a prime-implicant table to find the minimal solution. The *prime-implicant table* is a matrix that has a column for each input value for which the output of the function should be 1 and a row for each prime implicant. The elements of the row that correspond to the function values which are made 1 by the prime implicant are marked by an x or by the decimal equivalent of the input value. The remaining elements of the matrix are left blank.

Closed Cover.   A row that has a mark in a given column is said to *cover* that column. A group of rows that together cover all columns is called a *closed cover*. The purpose of the prime-implicant table is to find a closed cover with a minimal number of rows. The concepts of essential rows, row dominance, and column implication are used to find such a solution.

Essential Row.   A row is called *essential* when it contains an element that is the only cover for its column. Thus, in Table D-15, column 2 is only covered by the first row and column 5 by the last row. Therefore, these two rows are essential.

The prime implicant corresponding to an essential row is always part of the solution and is recorded as such. The essential row is now eliminated from the matrix as well as all columns which are covered by that row. Thus, a reduced prime-implicant table is found. In the example of Table D-15, the minimal solution is formed by the two essential rows, corresponding again to the circuit of Figure D-13.

Row Dominance. When a row covers all elements which also are covered by another row, this row is said to *dominate* that other row. When we assume that both rows represent a circuit of equal cost, the dominated row may be removed. When two rows are equal, they dominate each other. Only one of these two rows may be removed.

In the example of Table D-17, row A dominates row B. Hence, B may be removed.

Table D-17   Row dominance and column implication.

Column Implication. In Table D-17, column P is dominated by column Q. Conversely, column Q is implied by column P. When a column is covered by a row, the columns that are *implied* by this column are also covered. Hence, an implied column, in this case column Q, may be removed.

In general, the removal of a column implication may lead to a row dominance, which, in turn, may result in essential rows and column implications.

Branch and Bound. When a prime-implicant table can no longer be reduced, a solution may be found with a *branch-and-bound method*. A column of the prime-implicant table is selected, and within that column, a row which covers this column. This row now is assumed to be essential and therefore allows the table to be reduced further. This procedure is repeated for all rows that cover the selected column. A solution is abandoned as soon as it is clear that it will be at least as expensive as an earlier solution. When, during this process, a prime-implicant table arises which again cannot be reduced further, the branch-and-bound procedure is repeated.

Incomplete Specification. The specification of a function may include input values for which the output may be either 1 or 0. Such an input value is called a *don't-care value*. In the Karnaugh diagram, the don't-care values are indicated by a D. In finding a minimal solution, the values assigned to the don't cares are chosen as advantageously as possible.

The don't-care values participate as 1s in finding the prime implicants of the function. Thus, the largest-possible prime implicants are found. In determining the minimal solution, however, only the required function values are taken into account. Prime implicants which cover only don't-care values are eliminated from the table by inspection or by applying row dominance.

Extensions. The Quine–McCluskey method assumes that both polarities are available as input signals. The circuits, however, produce only one polarity as output. When, therefore, several circuits are placed behind each other, an extra level of inverters must occasionally be introduced. When the circuits are built as two-level nands, the third level also might be constructed from nands. Thus, a circuit is obtained which uses only the true input and is built from three levels of nand circuits. Such a circuit is called a TANT circuit, for "three-and-not-true." The synthesis of TANT circuits has been given by Gimpel (1967) as an extension of the Quine–McCluskey method.

Another extension of the method of Quine–McCluskey is its use for multiple-output circuits. The reader is referred to the literature for these subjects.

REFERENCES

GIMPEL, J. F.: "The Minimization of TANT Networks." *IEEE Transactions on Electronic Computers*, vol. EC-16, no. 1, pp. 18–38 (February, 1967).

KARNAUGH, M.: "The Map Method for Synthesis of Combinational Logic Circuits." *Transactions of the AIEE*, vol. 72, pt. I, pp. 593–598 (November, 1953).

McCLUSKEY, E. J.: "Minimization of Boolean Functions." *Bell System Technical Journal*, vol. 35, pp. 1417–1444 (November, 1956).

McCLUSKEY, E. J.: *Introduction to the Theory of Switching Circuits*, pp. 114–179. McGraw-Hill, New York, 1965.

QUINE, W. V.: "The Problem of Simplifying Truth Functions." *American Mathematical Monthly*, vol. 59, pp. 521–531 (October, 1952).

VEITCH, E. W.: "A Chart Method for Simplifying Truth Functions." *Proceedings of the ACM*, pp. 127–133 (1952).

AUTHOR INDEX

SUBJECT INDEX

PROGRAM TERM INDEX

NAME	USAGE	TYPE	PROGRAM	SECTION	PAGE
A	AUGEND	V	2-5	2-2	22
AAD	ADDRESS GATE	S	5-30	5-7	174
ABLE	ADAPTER IS ABLE	L	9-17	9-4	302
ABS	ABSOLUTE VALUE CONTROL GATE	S	5-5	5-2	142
ACCEPT	ADAPTER ACCEPT CODE	V	9-17	9-4	302
ACCESS	STORAGE ACCESS	F	8-22	8-6	278
ACT	MICROADDRESS CONTROL FIELD	V	6-17	6-3	203
ADADR	ADAPTER ADDRESS	V	9-15	9-4	301
ADAPTER1	BYTE ADAPTER ARCHITECTURE	F	9-22	9-4	307
ADAPTER2	DISCONNECTED ADAPTER	F	9-23	9-4	307
ADAPTER3	BURST ADAPTER ARCHITECTURE	F	9-26	9-6	312
ADD	ADD	L	5-1	5-1	138
ADDRESS	STORAGE ADDRESS	V	8-3	8-1	253
ADDTAB	LOCATION OF ADD TABLE	V	2-23	2-7	40
ADP1	ADAPTER 1 IDENTIFICATION	S	9-15	9-4	301
ADP2	ADAPTER 2 IDENTIFICATION	S	9-15	9-4	301
ADP3	ADAPTER 3 IDENTIFICATION	S	9-15	9-4	301
ADR	ADDRESS FIELD IN MICROINSTRUCTION	V	6-4	6-1	189
ADRA	MICROADDRESS BIT A	V	6-17	6-3	203
ADRACT	ADDRESS ACTIVITY VECTOR	V	8-26	8-7	283
ADRB	MICROADDRESS BIT B	V	6-17	6-3	203
ADRPIPE	ADDRESS REGISTERS OF PIPELINE	M	8-26	8-7	283
AD1	IDENTIFIER OF ADAPTER 1	S	9-15	9-4	301
AD1ACT	ADAPTER 1 BUSY	S	9-22	9-4	307
AD1ADR	ADDRESS OF ADAPTER 1	V	9-22	9-4	307
AD2	IDENTIFIER OF ADAPTER 2	S	9-15	9-4	301
AD3	IDENTIFIER OF ADAPTER 3	S	9-15	9-4	301
AD3ACT	ADAPTER 3 BUSY	V	9-26	9-6	312
AD3ADR	ADDRESS OF ADAPTER 3	V	9-26	9-6	312
AFLD	A-INPUT CONTROL FIELD	V	6-17	6-3	203
ALU	ALU CONTROL FIELD	V	6-17	6-3	203
AND	AND	L	5-1	5-1	138
ARCHADD	ADDER ARCHITECTURE	F	2-5	2-2	22
ARCHBCDTO7	BCD TO 7-SEGMENT CODE ARCHITECTURE	F	7-39	7-E	248
ARCHBITADD	BIT ADDER ARCHITECTURE	F	2-7	2-3	25
ARCHDEC	DECODER ARCHITECTURE	F	7-23	7-4	235
ARCHDIV	DIVIDER ARCHITECTURE	F	4-1	4-1	105
ARCHDOWN	DECREMENTING COUNTER ARCHITECTURE	F	2-52	2-E	69
ARCHENC	ENCODER ARCHITECTURE	F	7-19	7-3	234
ARCHFIRSTIN	FIFO INPUT ARCHITECTURE	F	7-31	7-5	243
ARCHFIRSTOUT	LIFO AND FIFO OUTPUT ARCHITECTURE	F	7-31	7-5	243

LEGEND: E←EXERCISE; F←FUNCTION; L←LABEL; M←MATRIX; S←SCALAR; V←VECTOR

LEGEND: E←EXERCISE; F←FUNCTION; L←LABEL; M←MATRIX; S←SCALAR; V←VECTOR

LEGEND: E←EXERCISE; F←FUNCTION; L←LABEL; M←MATRIX; S←SCALAR; V←VECTOR

LEGEND: E←EXERCISE; F←FUNCTION; L←LABEL; M←MATRIX; S←SCALAR; V←VECTOR

LEGEND: E←EXERCISE; F←FUNCTION; L←LABEL; M←MATRIX; S←SCALAR; V←VECTOR

LEGEND: E←EXERCISE;   F←FUNCTION;   L←LABEL;   M←MATRIX;   S←SCALAR;   V←VECTOR

LEGEND: E←EXERCISE;   F←FUNCTION;   L←LABEL;   M←MATRIX;   S←SCALAR;   V←VECTOR

LEGEND: E←EXERCISE; F←FUNCTION; L←LABEL; M←MATRIX; S←SCALAR; V←VECTOR

LEGEND: E←EXERCISE; F←FUNCTION; L←LABEL; M←MATRIX; S←SCALAR; V←VECTOR

LEGEND: E←EXERCISE; F←FUNCTION; L←LABEL; M←MATRIX; S←SCALAR; V←VECTOR

LEGEND: E←EXERCISE; F←FUNCTION; L←LABEL; M←MATRIX; S←SCALAR; V←VECTOR

LEGEND: E←EXERCISE; F←FUNCTION; L←LABEL; M←MATRIX; S←SCALAR; V←VECTOR

LEGEND: E←EXERCISE; F←FUNCTION; L←LABEL; M←MATRIX; S←SCALAR; V←VECTOR

NAME	USAGE	TYPE	PROGRAM	SECTION	PAGE
WORD	WORD FIELD OF ADDRESS	V	8-13	8-5	267
WORK	WORK TO BE DONE	L	9-17	9-4	302
WRITE	WRITE ACTION	L	5-29	5-7	173
WRITELS	WRITE IN LOCAL STORE	F	8-3	8-1	253
WRITEMS	WRITE IN MAIN STORE	F	8-4	8-1	253
WUS	ADDER INPUT GATE	S	7-16	7-2	229
WX	NEW BALANCE	V	3-16	3-4	88
X	RUNNING VARIABLE	V	2-49	2-15	64
X	INPUT VARIABLE	S	2-50	2-15	66
XOR	EXCLUSIVE OR	L	5-1	5-1	138
XZRO	ZERO INDEX TEST	V	7-16	7-2	229
X2	INDEX ADDRESS IN INSTRUCTION	V	7-7	7-1	220
Y	GATEVECTOR	V	5-6	5-2	145
YES	AFFIRMATIVE RESULT	V	4-2	4-1	106
ZB	ZERO TEST BUFFER	V	5-25	5-6	169

LEGEND: E←EXERCISE; F←FUNCTION; L←LABEL; M←MATRIX; S←SCALAR; V←VECTOR